Jack in the Forecastle; or, Incidents in the Early Life of Hawser Martingale

John Sherburne Sleeper

JACK IN THE FORECASTLE

OR

INCIDENTS IN THE EARLY LIFE OF HAWSER MARTINGALE

by John Sherburne Sleeper

Chapter I Farewell to New England

I was born towards the close of the last century, in a village pleasantly situated on the banks of the Merrimack, in Massachusetts. For the satisfaction of the curious, and the edification of the genealogist, I will state that my ancestors came to this country from England in the middle of the seventeenth century. Why they left their native land to seek an asylum on this distant shore whether prompted by a spirit of adventure, or with a view to avoid persecution for religion's sake is now unknown. Even if they "left their country for their country's good, " they were undoubtedly as respectable, honest, and noble, as the major part of those needy ruffians who accompanied William the Conqueror from Normandy in his successful attempt to seize the British crown, and whose descendants now boast of their noble ancestry, and proudly claim a seat in the British House of Peers.

From my earliest years I manifested a strong attachment to reading; and as matters relating to ships and sailors captivated my boyish fancy, and exerted a magic influence on my mind, the "Adventures of Robinson Crusoe, " "Peter Wilkins, " "Philip Quarle, " and vagabonds of a similar character, were my favorite books. An indulgence in this taste, and perhaps an innate dispostion to lead a wandering, adventurous life, kindled in my bosom a strong desire, which soon became a fixed resolution, TO GO TO SEA. Indeed, this wish to go abroad, to encounter dangers on the mighty deep, to visit foreign countries and climes, to face shipwrecks and disasters, became a passion. It was my favorite theme of talk by day, and the subject of my dreams by night. As I increased in years my longing for a sailor's life also increased; and whenever my schoolfellows and myself were conversing about the occupations we should select as the means of gaining a livelihood hereafter, I invariably said, "I will be a sailor. "

Had my parents lived, it is possible that this deep-seated inclination might have been thwarted; that my destiny might have taken another shape. But my father died while I was quite young, and my mother survived him but a few years. She lived long enough, however, to convince me that there is nothing more pure, disinterested, and enduring than a mother's love, and that those who are deprived of this blessing meet at the outset of their pilgrimage a misfortune which can never be remedied. Thus, before I had numbered fifteen years, I found myself thrown a waif on the waters of life, free to follow the bent of my inclination to become a sailor.

Fortune favored my wishes. Soon after the death of my parents, a relation of my mother was fitting out a vessel in Portsmouth, N.H., for a voyage to Demarara; and those who felt an interest in my welfare, conceiving this a good opportunity for me to commence my salt-water career, acceded to my wishes, and prevailed on my relative, against his inclination, to take me with him as a cabin boy.

With emotions of delight I turned my back on the home of my childhood, and gayly started off to seek my fortune in the world, with no other foundation to build upon than a slender frame, an imperfect education, a vivid imagination, ever picturing charming castles in the air, and a goodly share of quiet energy and perseverance, modified by an excess of diffidence, which to this day I have never been able to overcome.

I had already found in a taste for reading a valuable and never-failing source of information and amusement. This attachment to books has attended me through life, and been a comfort and solace in difficulties, perplexities, and perils. My parents, also, early ingrafted on my mind strict moral principles; taught me to distinguish between right and wrong; to cherish a love of truth, and even a chivalric sense of honor and honesty. To this, perhaps, more than to any other circumstance, may be attributed whatever success and respectability has attended my career through life. It has enabled me to resist temptations to evil with which I was often surrounded, and to grapple with and triumph over obstacles that might otherwise have overwhelmed me.

When I reached Portsmouth, my kinsman, Captain Tilton, gave me an ungracious reception. He rebuked me severely for expressing a determination to go to sea.

"Go to sea! " he exclaimed in a tone of the most sovereign contempt. "Ridiculous! You are a noodle for thinking of such a thing. A sailor's life is a dog's life at best! Besides, you are not fit for a sailor, either by habits, taste, or constitution. With such a pale face, and slight figure, and sheepish look, how can you expect to fight the battle of life on the ocean, and endure all the crosses, the perils, and the rough- and-tumble of a sailor's life? Hawser, you are not fit for a sailor. You had much better go home and try something else. "

Finding me unconvinced by his arguments, and unshaken in my determination, he concluded his remarks by asking me abruptly the startling question, "Are you ready to die? "

I replied, that I had not bestowed much thought on the subject; but frankly admitted I was not altogether prepared for such a solemn event.

"Then, Hawser, " said he with marked emphasis, "if you are not prepared to die to die of YELLOW FEVER don't go to Demarara at this season of the year! " And he left the room abruptly, apparently disgusted at my obstinacy.

On the following day, Captain Tilton took me on board the brig Dolphin. I did not mark her imperfections, which were many. She was a vessel, bound on a voyage to a foreign port, and, therefore, I was charmed with her appearance. In my eyes she was a model of excellence; as beautiful and graceful as the celebrated barge in which Cleopatra descended the Cyndnus to meet Mark Antony.

The captain led me to the mate, who was busily engaged about the decks. "Mr. Thompson, " said he, "here is a lad who wants to go to sea, and I have foolishly engaged to take him as a cabin boy. Keep him on board the brig; look sharp after him; don't let him have an idle moment; and, if possible, make him useful in some way until the vessel is ready for sea. "

Mr. William Thompson was a worthy man, who subsequently became a shipmaster and merchant of great respectability in Portsmouth. He treated me with consideration and kindness, and took pleasure in teaching me the details of the business I was about to undertake.

During the few days in which the Dolphin lay at the wharf I gained much nautical information. I learned the names of the different parts of a vessel; of the different masts, and some portions of the rigging. But the great number of ropes excited my admiration. I thought a lifetime would hardly suffice to learn their different names and purposes. I accomplished successfully the feat of going aloft; and one memorable day, assisted the riggers in "bending sails, " and received an ill- natured rebuke from a crusty old tar, for my stupidity in failing to understand him when he told me to "pass the gasket: while furling the fore-topsail. Instead of passing the gasket around the yard, I gravely handed him a marlinspike!

In the course of my desultory reading, I had learned that vessels at sea were liable to "spring a leak, " which was one of the most dreaded perils of navigation; and I had a vague notion that the hold of a ship was always so arranged that a leak could be discovered and stopped. I was, therefore, not a little puzzled when I found the hold of the Dolphin was crammed with lumber; not a space having been left large enough to stow away the ghost of a belaying pin. Finding the captain in a pleasant mood one day, I ventured to ask him what would be the consequence if the brig should spring a leak in her bottom.

"Spring a leak in her bottom! " he replied, in his gruff manner; "why, we should go to the bottom, of course"

The brig was now ready for sea. The sailors were shipped, and I watched them closely as they came on board, expecting to find the noble-looking, generous spirited tars I had become so familiar with in books. It happened, however, that three out of the five seamen who composed the crew were "old English men-of-war's-men, " and had long since lost any refinement of character or rectitude of principle they originally possessed. They were brought on board drunk by the landlord with whom they boarded; for the "old tars" of those days fifty years ago had no homes; when on shore all they cared for was a roof to shelter them, and plenty of grog, in which they would indulge until their money was gone, when they would go to sea and get more.

Now ensued the bustle incident to such occasions. Captain William Boyd, who had volunteered to pilot the brig down the harbor, came on board; the sails were hoisted; the deck was crowded with persons to take leave of their friends, or gratify a morbid curiosity; and what with the numerous questions asked, the running to and fro, the peremptory commands of the mate, the unmusical singing and shouting of the crew as they executed the various orders, together with the bawling of the handcartmen and truckmen as they brought down the last of the trunks, chests, stores, and provisions, my brain was in a whirl of excitement; I hardly knew whether I stood on my head or my heels.

At last the captain came down the wharf, accompanied by Joshua Haven, one of the owners, and some friends, who had made arrangements to proceed in the brig so far as the mouth of the harbor. The single rope which connected the Dolphin with the shore was cast loose; the pilot gave some orders; that were Greek to me, in a loud and energetic tone; the men on the wharf gave three cheers, which were heartily responded to by the temporary passengers and crew; and with a pleasant breeze from the westward, we sailed merrily down the river.

Some few persons lingered on the wharf, and continued for a time to wave their handkerchiefs in token of an affectionate farewell to their friends. I seemed to stand alone while these interesting scenes were enacted. I took no part in the warm greetings or the tender adieus. I had bidden farewell to my friends and relatives in another town some days before; and no one took sufficient interest in my welfare to travel a few miles, look after my comforts, and wish me a pleasant voyage as I left my native land.

Although from the reception I had met with I had little reason to expect present indulgences or future favors from my kinsman who commanded the brig, I did not regret the step I had taken. On the contrary, my bosom bounded with joy when the last rope was severed, and the vessel on whose decks I proudly stood was actually leaving the harbor of Portsmouth, under full sail, bound to a foreign port. This was no longer "the baseless fabric of a vision. " The dream of my early years had come to pass; and I looked forward with all the confidence of youth to a bold and manly career, checkered it might be with toil and suffering, but replete with stirring adventure, whose wild and romantic charms would be cheaply won by wading through a sea of troubles. I now realized the feeling which has since been so well described by the poet:

"A life on the ocean wave,
A home on the rolling deep,
Where the scattered waters rave,
And the winds their revels keep.

"Like an eagle caged, I pine
On this dull, unchanging shore;
O, give me the flashing brine,
The spray, and the tempest's roar."

Chapter II INCIDENTS AT SEA

The Dolphin was what is termed, in nautical parlance, an "hermaphrodite brig, " of about one hundred and fifty tons burden; and had been engaged, for some twelve or fifteen years, in the West India trade. This vessel could not with propriety be regarded as a model of grace and beauty, but gloried in bluff bows, a flat bottom, and a high quarter-deck; carried a large cargo for her tonnage, and moved heavily and reluctantly through the water.

On this particular voyage, the hold of the brig, as I have already stated, was filled with lumber; and thirty-five thousand feet of the same article were carried on deck, together with an indefinite quantity of staves, shooks, hoop poles, and other articles of commerce too numerous to mention. On this enormous deck-load were constructed, on each side, a row of sheep-pens, sufficiently spacious to furnish with comfortable quarters some sixty or seventy sheep; and on the pens, ranged along in beautiful confusion, was an imposing display of hen-coops and turkey-coops, the interstices being ingeniously filled with bundles of hay and chunks of firewood. The quarter-deck was "lumbered up" with hogsheads of water, and casks of oats and barley, and hen-coops without number.

With such a deck-load, not an unusually large one in those days, the leading trucks attached to the fore-rigging were about half way between the main deck and the foretop. It was a work of difficulty and danger to descend from the deck-load to the forecastle; but to reach the foretop required only a hop, skip, and a jump. The locomotive qualities of this craft, misnamed the Dolphin, were little superior to those of a well constructed raft; and with a fresh breeze on the quarter, in spite of the skill of the best helmsman, her wake was as crooked as that of the "wounded snake, " referred to by the poet, which "dragged its slow length along. "

It was in the early part of July, in the year 1809, that the brig Dolphin left Portsmouth, bound on a voyage to Dutch Guiana, which at that time, in consequence of the malignant fevers that prevailed on the coast, was not inaptly termed "the grave of American seamen. " The crew consisted of the captain and mate, five sailors, a green hand to act as cook, and a cabin boy. There was also a passenger on board, a young man named Chadwick, who had been residing in Portsmouth, and was going to Demarara, in the hope which fortunately for him was not realized of establishing himself in a mercantile house.

The forecastle being, for obvious reasons, untenable during the outward passage, these ten individuals, when below deck, were stowed away in the cabin and steerage, amid boxes, bales, chests, barrels, and water casks, in a manner somewhat miscellaneous, and not the most commodious or comfortable. Indeed, for several days after we left port, the usual and almost only access to the cabin was by the skylight; and those who made the cabin their home, were obliged to crawl on all fours over the heterogeneous mass of materials with which it was crowded, in order to reach their berths!

The owners of the brig must have calculated largely on favorable weather during the passage; for had we experienced a gale on the coast, or fallen in with the tail-end of a hurricane in the tropics, the whole deck-load would have been swept away, and the lives of the ship's company placed in imminent peril. The weather, however, proved remarkably mild, and the many inconveniences to which the crew were subjected were borne with exemplary patience, and sometimes even regarded as a capital joke.

We passed the Whale's Back at the mouth of the Piscataqua, and the Isles of Shoals loomed up through the hazy atmosphere; and although the wind was light, and the sea apparently smooth, the brig began to have a motion an awkward, uneasy motion for which I could not account, and which, to my great annoyance, continued to increase as we left the land. I staggered as I crossed the quarter-deck, and soon after we cleared the harbor, came near pitching overboard from the platform covering the sheep-pens. My head was strangely confused, and a dizziness seized me, which I in vain struggled to shake off. My spirits, so gay and buoyant as we sailed down the harbor, sunk to zero.

At length I could not resist the conviction that I was assailed with symptoms of seasickness, a malady which I had always held in contempt, believing it to exist more in imagination than in fact, and which I was determined to resist, as unsailor-like and unmanly. Other symptoms of a less equivocal description, soon placed the character of my illness beyond a doubt. My woe-begone looks must have betrayed my feelings, for one of the men told me, with a quizzical leer, that old Neptune always exacted toll in advance from a green hand for his passage over the waters.

Mr. Thompson, who seemed to pity my miserable condition, gravely assured me that exercise was a capital thing as a preventive or cure for seasickness, and advised me to try the pump. I followed his advice: a few strokes brought up the bilge water, than which nothing at that time could have been more insufferably nauseous! I left the pump in disgust, and retiring to the after part of the quarter-deck, threw myself down on a coil of rope, unable longer to struggle with my fate. There I remained unnoticed and uncared for for several hours, when, the wind having changed, the rope which formed my bed, and proved to be the "main sheet, " was wanted, and I was unceremoniously ejected from my quarters, and roughly admonished to "go below and keep out of the way! " I crawled into the cabin, and, stretched on some boxes, endeavored to get a little sleep; but the conglomeration of smells of a most inodorous character, which, as it seemed to my distempered fancy, pervaded every part of the vessel, prevented my losing a sense of suffering in sleep.

As I lay musing on the changes which a few days had wrought in my condition, and, borne down by the pangs of seasickness, was almost ready to admit that there was prose as well as poetry in a sailor's life, I was startled by a terrific noise, the announcement, I supposed, of some appalling danger. I heard distinctly three loud knocks on the deck at the entrance of the steerage, and then a sailor put his head down the companion-way, and in a voice loud, cracked, and discordant, screamed in a tone which I thought must have split his jaws asunder, "LA-AR-BO-A-RD W-A-T-CH A-H-O-O-Y. "

In spite of my sickness I started from my uncomfortable resting place, scrambled into the steerage, and by a roll of the brig was tumbled under the steps, and suffered additional pains and apprehensions before I ascertained that the unearthly sounds which had so alarmed me were nothing more than the usual mode of "calling the watch, " or in other words, the man with the unmusical voice had gently hinted to the sleepers below that "turn-about was fair play, " and they were wanted on deck.

To add to my troubles, the wind in the morning shifted to the south-east, and thus became a head wind, and the old brig became more restless than ever, and pitched and rolled to leeward occasionally with a lurch, performing clumsy antics in the water which my imagination never pictured, and which I could neither admire nor applaud.

For several days we were beating about Massachusetts Bay and St. George's Bank, making slow progress on our voyage. During that time I was really seasick, and took little note of passing events, being stretched on the deck, a coil of rope, or a chest, musing on the past or indulging in gloomy reflections in regard to the future. Seasickness never paints ideal objects of a roseate hue. Although I was not called upon for much actual work, I received no sympathy for my miserable condition; for seasickness, like the toothache, is seldom fatal, notwithstanding it is as distressing a malady as is found in the catalogue of diseases, and one for which no preventive or cure, excepting time, has yet been discovered. Time is a panacea for every ill; and after the lapse of ten or twelve days, as the brig was drawing towards the latitude of Bermuda, my sickness disappeared as suddenly as it commenced; and one pleasant morning I threw aside my shore dress, and with it my landsman's habits and feelings. I donned my short jacket and trousers, and felt every inch a sailor!

The Bermudas are a cluster of small islands and rocks lying in the track of vessels bound from New England to the West Indies. The climate is mild, and the atmosphere remarkably salubrious, while the trace of ocean in the vicinity has long been noted for severe squalls at every season of the year. A squall at sea no unusual occurrence is often the cause of anxiety, being attended with danger. Sometimes the rush of wind is so violent that nothing will resist its fury, and before the alarm is given and the canvas reduced, the masts are blown over the side or the vessel capsized. Therefore, on the approach of a squall, a vigilant officer will be prepared for the worst, by shortening sail and making other arrangements for averting the threatened danger.

I hardly knew how it happened, but one afternoon when we were a little to the northward of Bermuda, and should have kept a lookout for squalls, we were favored with a visit from one of a most energetic character. Its sudden approach from under the lee was either unnoticed or unheeded until the captain accidentally came on deck. He was instantly aware of the perilous condition of the brig, for the "white caps" of the waves could be distinctly seen, and even the roar of the wind could be heard as it rushed towards us over the water. Before any orders could be executed before the sails could be taken in, the yards braced round, or even the helm shifted, the tempest broke over us. The rain fell in torrents, the wind blew with tremendous violence, and a scene of indescribable confusion ensued.

The captain stood near the companion-way, much excited, giving directions with energy and rapidity. "Hard up your helm! " said he; "Hard up! Lower away the mainsail! Let go the peak halliards! Why DON'T you put the helm hard up? Let go all the halliards fore and aft! Clew down the fore-topsail! Haul in the starboard braces! There steady with the helm! "

The mate and sailors were running about the decks, looking frightened and bewildered, eagerly casting loose some ropes, and pulling desperately upon others; the sails were fluttering and shaking, as if anxious to quit the spars and fly away to unknown regions; the brig felt the force of the wind, and for a few moments was pressed over on her side until her beam ends were in the water; and what with the shouting of the captain, the answering shouts of the mate, the unearthly cries of the sailors, as they strove to execute the orders so energetically given; the struggling of the canvas, the roaring of the winds and the waves, the creaking of the cordage, the beating of the rain against the decks, and the careening of the vessel, it is not remarkable that I felt somewhat alarmed and excited, as well as deeply interested in witnessing for the first time in my life A SQUALL AT SEA.

The squall was of short duration; although the rain continued for a time, the wind, after a few minutes, gave but little inconvenience. In the course of an hour the murky clouds had disappeared, the sun shone out brightly as it was sinking towards the horizon, and the brig was again pursuing her way towards her destined port, urged slowly along by a light but favorable breeze.

Having got my sea legs on, I could proudly strut about among the lumber and sheep-pens without fear of rolling overboard. I found the sailors a rough but good-natured set of fellows, with but little refinement in ideas or language. Although they amused themselves with my awkwardness, and annoyed me with practical jokes, they took a pride and pleasure in inducting me into the mysteries of their craft. They taught me the difference between a granny knot and a square knot; how to whip a rope's end; form splices; braid sinnett; make a running bowline, and do a variety of things peculiar to the web-footed gentry. Some of them also tried hard, by precept and example, but in vain, to induce me to chew tobacco and drink grog! Indeed, they regarded the ability to swallow a stiff glass of New England rum, without making a wry face, as one of the most important qualifications of a sailor!

The "old men-of-war's-men" had passed through strange and eventful scenes; they were the type of a class of men which have long since passed away; they could spin many a long and interesting yarn, to which I listened with untiring eagerness. But no trait in their character astonished me more than their uncontrollable passion for intoxicating drinks. As cabin boy, it was my duty to serve out to the crew a half pint of rum a day. These old Tritons eagerly looked forward to the hour when this interesting ceremony came off; their eyes sparkled as they received their allotted portion of this enemy to the human race; and they practised every art to procure, by fair means or foul, an increased allowance. If by accident or shrewd management one of them succeeded in obtaining half a glass more than he was fairly entitled to, his triumph was complete. But if he imagined he had not received the full quantity which was his due, ill humor and sulky looks for the next twenty-four hours bore testimony to his anger and disappointment. These men ignored the good old proverb that "bread is the staff of life, " and at any time, or at all times, would prefer grog to bread.

In those days it was believed that ardent spirit would strengthen the constitution, and enable a man to endure hardship and perform labor to a greater extent that would be the case if he drank nothing stronger than water. Rum was, therefore, included among the ship's stores as an important means of keeping the ship's company in good humor, reviving their spirits and energies when overcome with fatigue or exposure, and strengthening them for a hard day's work.

Those days have passed away. It is now known that those doctrines were false; that spiritous liquors, as a drink, never benefit mankind, but have proved one of the greatest scourges with which the human race has been afflicted. It is no longer believed that grog will insure the faithful performance of a seaman's duty, and it is excluded from our ships, so far as the forecastle is concerned; and if it were never allowed to visit the cabin, the crews, in some cases, would lead happier lives, there would be fewer instances of assault and battery, revolts and shipwrecks, and the owners and underwriters would find the balance at the end of the voyage more decidedly in their favor.

Among the customs on shipboard which attracted my particular attention, was the manner in which the sailors partook of their meals. There was no tedious ceremony or fastidious refinement witnessed on these occasions. At twelve o'clock the orders were promptly given, "Call the watch! Hold the reel! Pump ship! Get your dinners! " With never-failing alacrity the watch was called, the log thrown, and the ship pumped. When these duties were performed, a bustle was seen about the camboose, or large cooking stove, in which the meals were prepared. In pleasant weather it was usual for the sailors to take their meals on deck; but no table was arranged, no table-cloth was spread, no knives and forks or spoons were provided, no plates of any description were furnished, or glass tumblers or earthen mugs. The preliminary arrangements were of the simplest description.

The signal being given, the cook hastily transferred from his boilers whatever food he had prepared, into a wooden vessel, called a kid, resembling in size and appearance a peck measure. The kid with its contents was deposited on the spot selected; a bag or box, containing ship's biscuits was then produced, dinner was ready, and all hands, nothing loth, gathered around the kid and commenced operations.

The usual fare was salt beef and bread, varied at stated times or according to circumstances; and this has probably for centuries been the standing dish for the forecastle in English and American ships. On this passage, the Sunday dinner varied from the usual routine by the addition of fresh meat. Every Sabbath morning a sheep, the finest and fattest of the flock, was missing from the pens. Portions of the animal, however, would appear a few hours afterwards in the shape of a luscious sea-pie for the sailors, and in various inviting shapes during the following week to the inmates of the cabin. This loss of property was recorded by Mr. Thompson in the ship's log-book, with his accustomed accuracy, and with Spartan brevity. The language he invariably used was, "A sheep died this day. "

Among the crew of the Dolphin were two weather-beaten tars, who were as careless of their costumes as of their characters. They recked little how ridiculously they looked, excepting in one respect. They could each boast of a magnificent head of hair, which they allowed to grow to a great length on the back of the head, where it was collected and fashioned into enormous queues, which, when permitted to hang down, reached to the small of their backs, and gave them the appearance of Chinese mandarins, or Turkish pachas of a single tail. These tails were their pets the only ornaments about their persons for which they manifested any interest. This pride in their queues was the weak point in their characters. Every Sunday they performed on each other the operation of manipulating the pendulous ornaments, straightening them out like magnified marlinspikes, and binding them with ribbons or rope-yarns, tastily fastened at the extremity by a double bow knot.

Queues, in those days, were worn on the land as well as on the sea, and were as highly prized by the owners. On the land, they were harmless enough, perhaps, and seldom ungratefully interfered with the comfort of their benefactors or lured them into scrapes. On shipboard the case was different, and they sometimes proved not only superfluous but troublesome.

On our homeward passage a case occurred which illustrated the absurdity of wearing a queue at sea a fashion which has been obsolete for many years. A gale of wind occurred on the coast, and the crew were ordered aloft to reef the fore-topsail. Jim Bilton, with his queue snugly clubbed and tucked away beneath his pea-jacket, was first on the yard, and passed the weather ear- ring; but, unfortunately, the standing rigging had recently been tarred, and his queue, escaping from bondage, was blown about, the sport of the wind, and after flapping against the yard, took a "round turn" over the lift, and stuck fast. Jim was in an awkward position. He could not immediately disengage his queue, and he could not willingly or conveniently leave it aloft. All hands but himself were promptly on deck, and ready to sway up the yard. The mate shouted to him in the full strength of his lungs to "Bear a hand and lay in off the yard, " and unjustly berated him as a "lubber, " while the poor fellow was tugging away, and working with might and main, to disengage his tail from the lift, in which he at length succeeded, but not without the aid of his jackknife.

I was greatly troubled during this passage by the impure character of the water. I had been taught to place a high value on water as a beverage; but when we had been three weeks at sea, and had entered the warm latitudes, on knocking a bung from one of the water casks on the quarter-deck, there issued an odor of "an ancient and fish-like" nature, which gave offence to my olfactories. On tasting the water, I found to my disgust that it was impregnated with a flavor of a like character, and after it was swallowed this flavor would cling to the palate with provoking tenacity for several minutes. The sailors smacked their lips over it once or twice, and pronounced it "from fair to middling. " When boiled, and drank under the name of tea or coffee, it might have deserved that character; but when taken directly from the cask, and quaffed in hot weather, as a pleasant and refreshing beverage it was a signal failure.

To the inmates of the cabin, myself excepted, the peculiar flavor of the water served as an excuse, if any were required, for drawing liberally on the brandy kegs and liquor cases. A little "dash of spirit" removed the unpleasant taste by adding another, which, to my unsophisticated palate, was equally offensive. The water in every cask proved of a similar character; and I could hardly imagine how use, or even necessity, could reconcile a person to such water as that. The problem was solved, but not entirely to my satisfaction, on my next voyage.

The duties of cabin boy were of a nature different from my occupations in previous years. They engrossed a considerable portion of my time; and though they were not the kind of duties I most loved to perform, I endeavored to accommodate my feelings to my situation, comforting myself with the belief that the voyage would not be of long duration, and that I was now taking the first step in the rugged path which led to fame and fortune.

I devoted the hours which I could spare from my appropriate duties to the acquisition of a knowledge of seamanship, and developing its mysteries. I was fond of going aloft when the vessel was rolling or pitching in a strong breeze. I loved to mount upon the top-gallant yard, and from that proud eminence, while rocking to and fro, look down upon the sails and spars of the brig, take a bird's eye view of the deck, and scan the various operations; look at the foam beneath the bows, or at the smooth, eddying, serpentine track left far behind. I also loved to gaze from this elevated position upon the broad ocean, bounded on every side by the clear and distant horizon a grand and sublime sight. And then I indulged in daydreams of the most pleasing description, and built gay and fantastic castles in the air, which my reason told me the next moment would never be realized.

Chapter III MANNING THE WOODEN WALLS OF OLD ENGLAND

One morning, soon after daybreak, as I was lying asleep in my berth, I was awakened by a trampling on deck and loud shouts. Aware that something unusual had occurred, I lost no time in hastening to the scene of action. Ere I reached the deck, I heard the word "porpoises" uttered in a loud key by one of the sailors, which explained the cause of the excitement.

The mate, with sparkling eye and rigid features, in which determination was strongly stamped, as if resolved "to do or die, " was busily engaged in fitting a line to the harpoon, which had been sharpened and prepared for use some days before. I cast my eye to windward, and saw the ocean alive with fish. Hundreds of porpoises were swimming around the brig, crossing the bows, or following in the wake, or leaping out of water and snuffing the air, and racing with each other as if for a wager; passing so rapidly through the liquid element that it wearied the eye to follow them.

The mate was soon ready with the harpoon, and took his station on the bowsprit, within six feet of the water. The line, one end of which was fastened to the harpoon, was rove through a block attached to the main-topmast stay; and the cook, one of the sailors, and myself firmly grasped the rope, and stood ready, whenever the word might be given, to bowse the unsuspecting and deluded victim out of his native element and introduce him to the ship's company.

Mr. Thompson stood on the bowsprit, poising the death-dealing instrument, and with a keen eye watched the gambols of the fish. He looked as formidable and fierce as a Paladin intent on some daring and desperate enterprise. As I eyed him with admiration and envy I wondered if the time would ever arrive when, clad with authority, I should exercise the privilege of wielding the harpoon and striking a porpoise! Several of these interesting fish, not aware of the inhospitable reception awaiting them, and seemingly prompted by curiosity, rapidly approached the brig. "Stand by, my lads! " exclaimed the mate, his face lighted by a gleam of anticipated triumph. One huge fellow passed directly beneath the bowsprit, and Mr. Thompson let drive the harpoon with all the strength and energy he possessed. We hauled upon the line with vigor alas! It required but little exertion to haul it in; the mate had missed his mark.

In a few minutes another of these portly inhabitants of the deep came rolling along with a rowdy, swaggering gait, close to the surface of the water. The mate, cool and collected, took a careful aim, and again threw the iron, which entered his victim, and then shouted with the voice of a Stentor, "Haul in! Haul in! " And we did haul in; but the fish was strong and muscular, and struggled hard for liberty and life. In spite of our prompt and vigorous exertions, he was dragged under the brig's bottom; and if he had not been struck in a workmanlike manner, the harpoon would have drawn out, and the porpoise would have escaped, to be torn to pieces by his unsympathizing companions. As it was, after a severe struggle on both sides, we roused him out of the water, when the mate called for the jib down-haul, with which he made a running bowline, which was clapped over his tail and drawn tight; and in this inglorious manner he was hauled in on the deck.

The porpoise is a fish five or six feet in length, weighing from one hundred and fifty to three hundred pounds. The name is derived from the Italian word PORCO-PERCE, or hog-fish; and indeed this animal resembles a hog in many respects. It has a long head, terminated by a projection of its jaws, which are well filled with sharp teeth, white as polished ivory. The body is covered with a coat of fat, or blubber, from one to three inches in thickness, which yields abundance of excellent oil; and the flesh beneath is not very unlike that of a hog, but more oily, coarser, and of a darker color. The flesh, excepting the harslet, is not much prized, though some sailors are fond of it, and rejoice at the capture of a porpoise, which gives them an agreeable change of diet.

A few days after this event, being to the southward of Bermuda, I climbed to the fore-top-gallant yard, and casting my eyes around, saw on the verge of the horizon a white speck, which made a singular appearance, contrasting, as it did, with the dark hue of the ocean and the clear azure of a cloudless sky, I called to a sailor who was at work in the cross-trees, and pointed it out to him. As soon as he saw it he exclaimed, "Sail, ho! "

The captain was on the quarter-deck, and responded to the announcement by the inquiry of "Where away? "

"About three points on the larboard bow, " was the rejoinder.

We had not spoken a vessel since we left Portsmouth. Indeed, we had seen none, excepting a few fishing smacks on St. George's Bank. The sight of a vessel on the broad ocean ordinarily produces considerable excitement; and this excitement is of a pleasing character when there is no reason to believe the stranger an enemy. It varies the incidents of a tedious passage, and shows that you are not alone on the face of the waters; that others are traversing the ocean and tempting its dangers, urged by a love of adventure or thirst of gain.

The captain looked at the strange vessel through his spy-glass, and said it was standing towards us. We approached each other rapidly, for the stranger carried a cloud of sail, and was evidently a fast sailer. By the peculiar color and cut of the canvas, the captain was led to believe we were about to be overhauled by a British man-of-war. This announcement gave me pleasure. I longed for an opportunity to behold one of that class of vessels, of which I had heard so much. But all the crew did not participate in my feelings. Two of the sailors, whom I had good reason to believe were not "native Americans, " although provided with American protections, looked unusually grave when the captain expressed his opinion, manifested no little anxiety, and muttered bitter curses against the English men-of-war!

I then learned that the British navy "the wooden walls of Old England" whose vaunted prowess was in every mouth, was manned almost exclusively by men who did not voluntarily enter the service, prompted by a feeling of patriotism, a sense of honor, or the expectation of emolument, but were victims to the unjust and arbitrary system of impressment.

It is singular that in the early part of the present century, when Clarkson, Wilberforce, and other philanthropists, with a zeal and perseverance which reflects immortal honor on their names, labored unceasingly and successfully to abolish an important branch of the African slave trade, no voice was raised in the British parliament to abolish the impressment of seamen a system of slavery as odious, unjust and degrading, as was ever established by a despotic government!

At that time Great Britain was engaged in sanguinary wars, and her flag was borne by her ships on every sea. It was difficult to man her navy, the pay being small, and the penalties for misconduct or venial errors terribly severe. Therefore, when on the ocean, British ships of war in want of men were in the habit of impressing sailors from merchant vessels, and often without regard to national character. American ships were fired at, brought to, and strictly searched by these tyrants of the ocean; and when foreigners were found on board, whether British, Swedes, Dutch, Russians, Norwegians, or Spaniards, they were liable to be claimed as fit persons to serve "His Majesty. " In spite of remonstrances and menaces, they were conveyed on board the British men-of-war, doomed to submit to insult and injustice, and to risk their lives while fighting in quarrels in which they felt no interest.

British seamen were seized wherever met, whether pursuing their lawful business on the high seas, or while on shore walking quietly through the streets of a city or town; even in the bosom of their families, or when quietly reposing on their pillows! Press-gangs, composed of desperate men, headed by resolute and unscrupulous officers, were constantly on the lookout for men, and took them, sometimes after hard fighting, and dragged them away to undergo the horrors of slavery on board a man-of-war!

It is not remarkable that a sailor in those days should have dreaded a "man-of-war" as the most fearful of evils, and would resort to desperate means to avoid impressment or escape from bondage. Those few fortunate men, who, by resolution or cunning, had succeeded in escaping from their sea-girt prisons, detailed the treatment they had received with minute and hideous accuracy to others; and that they could not have exaggerated the statements is proved by the risks they voluntarily encountered to gain their freedom. The bullets of the marines on duty, the fear of the voracious shark in waters where they abounded, the dangers of a pestilential climate, or the certainty, if retaken, of being subjected to a more revolting and excruciating punishment than was every devised by the Spanish Inquisition FLOGGING THROUGH THE FLEET could not deter British seamen from attempting to flee from their detested prison-house.

American seamen were sometimes forcibly taken from American ships, and their protestations against the outrage, and their repeated declarations, "I am an American citizen! " served only as amusement to the kidnappers. Letters which they subsequently wrote to their friends, soliciting their aid, or the intercession of the government, seldom reached their destination. It was rarely that the poor fellows were heard of after they were pressed on board a man-of-war. They died of disease in pestilential climates, or fell in battle while warring in behalf of a government they hated, and principles with which they had no sympathy.

This gross violation of the laws of nations and the principles of justice furnished one of the strongest motives for the war which was declared in 1812.

Nor were these insults on the part of British cruisers confined to American merchant ships. Our government vessels were, in more than one instance, boarded with a view to examine the crews and take the men, if any, who happened to be born under the British flag. A successful attempt was made in the case of the Chesapeake, which frigate, under the command of Commodore Barron, made a feeble show of resistance, and was fired into in a time of peace, several of her crew killed and wounded, and compelled to strike her colors! The Chesapeake was then boarded, and the Englishmen found on board were seized upon and transferred to the British ship!

An attempt of a similar kind was made some years before, but with a different result. When the heroic Tingey commanded the Ganges, in 1799, being off Cape Nicola Mole, he was boarded by a boat from the English frigate Surprise, and a demand was very coolly made that all the Englishmen on board the Ganges should be given up, as they were wanted for the service of His Majesty, George III!

Captain Tingey returned the following noble reply: "Give my respects to your commander; the respects of Captain Tingey, of the American navy; and tell him from me, that A PUBLIC SHIP CARRIES NO PROTECTION FOR HER MEN BUT HER FLAG! I may not succeed in a contest with you, but I will die at my quarters before a man shall be taken from my ship! "

The crew gave three cheers, hastened with alacrity to their guns, and called for "Yankee Doodle. " The captain of the Surprise, although one of the bravest officers in the British service, on hearing the determination of the Yankee, chose rather to continue on his cruise than do battle for dead men.

In less than an hour after the strange sail was seen from the decks of the Dolphin the surmises of the captain were proved to be correct.

The stranger was undoubtedly an English brig-of-war of the largest class. We could see the port-holes, through which the cannon protruded, and distinguish the gleam of muskets and cutlasses, and other instruments of destruction. The sails were so large and so neatly fitted, and the hull was so symmetrical in its model, and the brig glided along so gracefully over the waves, that I was charmed with her appearance, and could hardly express my satisfaction.

We continued on our course, with the American ensign flying, our captain hoping that this emissary of John Bull, seeing the character of our vessel, which no one could mistake, would suffer us to pass on our way unmolested, when a volume of flame and smoke issued from the bow of the sloop-of-war, and a messenger, in the shape of a cannon ball, came whistling over the waves, and, after crossing our bows in a diagonal direction, and striking the surface of the water several times, buried itself in a huge billow at no great distance. This was language that required no interpreter. It was a mandate that must be obeyed. The helm was ordered "hard-a-lee, " the foresail hauled up, and the topsail laid to the mast.

The armed brig hoisted British colors, and her boat was soon alongside the Dolphin. An officer sprang on board, followed by several sailors. With an off-hand, swaggering air, the officer addressed Captain Tilton, demanding where we were from, whither we were bound, and the character of our cargo. He then expressed an intention to examine the ship's papers, and went with the captain into the cabin for that purpose. When they returned on deck, Captain Tilton ordered the mate to summon aft the crew. This was not a work of difficulty, for they were standing in the waist, deeply interested spectators of the proceedings. At least three of them were trembling with fear, and speculating on the chances of being again impressed on board an English man-of-war.

"Where are these men's protections? " demanded the lieutenant.

By "protection, " was meant a printed certificate, under the signature and seal of the collector of one of the revenue districts in the United States, stating that the person, whose age, height, and complexion were particularly described, had adduced satisfactory proof of being an American citizen. An American seaman found without this document, whether in a foreign port or on the high seas, was looked upon as an Englishman, notwithstanding the most conclusive proof to the contrary, and regardless of his rights or the engagements by which he might be bound, was dragged on board a man-of-war as a lawful prize.

"Here are the protections, " said Captain Tilton, handing the papers to the Englishman.

The men were, one by one, examined, to see if the descriptions corresponded with their persons. They were found to correspond exactly.

The officer was not to be easily balked of his prey. Turning suddenly to one of them, a weather-beaten, case-hardened old tar, who wore a queue, and whose name was borne on the shipping paper as Harry Johnson, he sternly asked, "How long is it since you left His Majesty's service? "

The poor fellow turned pale as death. He lifted his hand to his hat, in a most anti-republican style, and stammered out something indistinctly.

"'Tis of no use, Johnson, " exclaimed the officer. "I see how it is; and we must be better acquainted. Your protection was obtained by perjury. Get ready to go in the boat. "

In vain Captain Tilton represented that Johnson was sailing under the American flag; that he had the usual certificate of being an American citizen; that his vessel was already short manned, considering the peculiar character of the cargo, and if his crew should be reduced, he might find himself unable to manage the brig in heavy weather, which there was reason to expect at that season in the latitude of the West Indies.

To these representations the lieutenant replied in a brief and dry manner. He said the man was an Englishman, and was wanted. He repeated his orders to Johnson, in a more peremptory tone, to "go in the boat. "

To the threats of the captain that he would lay the matter before Congress, and make it a national affair, the officer seemed altogether indifferent. He merely bade his trembling victim "bear a hand, " as he wished to return to the brig without delay.

When Johnson saw there was no alternative, that his fate was fixed, he prepared to meet it like a man. He looked at the American ensign, which was waving over his head, and said it was a pity the American flag could not protect those who sailed under it from insult and outrage. He shook each of us by the hand, gave us his best wishes, and followed his baggage into the boat, which immediately shoved off.

The officer told Captain Tilton that when the British ensign was hauled down, he might fill away, and proceed on his voyage. In about fifteen minutes the ensign was hauled down. Orders were given to fill away the foretopsail. The helm was put up, and we resumed our course for Demarara.

Steering to the southward, we reached that narrow belt of the Atlantic, called "the doldrums, " which lies between the variable and the trade winds. This tract is from two to three degrees in width, and is usually fallen in with soon after crossing the thirtieth degree of latitude. Here the wind is apt to be light and baffling at all seasons; and sometimes calms prevail for several days. This tract of ocean was once known as the "horse latitudes, " because many years ago vessels from Connecticut were in the habit of taking deck-loads of horses to the West India islands, and it not unfrequently happened that these vessels, being for the most part dull sailers, were so long detained in those latitudes that their hay, provender, and water were expended, and the animals died of hunger and thirst.

The Dolphin was a week in crossing three degrees of latitude. Indeed it was a calm during a considerable portion of that time. This drew largely on the patience of the captain, mate, and all hands. There are few things so annoying to a sailor at sea as a calm. A gale of wind, even a hurricane, with its life, its energy, its fury, though it may bring the conviction of danger, is preferred by an old sailor to the dull, listless monotony of a calm.

These slow movements in the "horse latitudes" were not distasteful to me. A calm furnished abundant food for curiosity. The immense fields of gulf-weed, with their parasitical inhabitants, that we now began to fall in with; the stately species of nautilus, known as he Portuguese man-of-war, floating so gracefully, with its transparent body and delicate tints; and the varieties of fish occasionally seen, including the flying- fish, dolphin, boneta, and shark, all furnish to an inquiring mind subjects of deep and abiding interest. My wonder was also excited by the singularly glassy smoothness of the surface of the water in a dead calm, while at the same time the long, rolling waves, or "seas, " kept the brig in perpetual motion, and swept past as if despatched by some mysterious power on a mission to the ends of the earth.

Several kinds of fish that are met with on the ocean are really palatable, and find a hearty welcome in the cabin and the forecastle. To capture these denizens of the deep, a line, to which is attached a large hook baited with a small fish, or a piece of the rind of pork, shaped to resemble a fish, is sometimes kept towing astern in pleasant weather. This was the custom on board the Dolphin; and one afternoon, when the brig, fanned by gentle zephyrs, hardly had "steerage way, " my attention was aroused by an exulting shout from the man at the helm, followed by a solemn asserveration, that "a fish was hooked at last. "

All was bustle and excitement. Discipline was suddenly relaxed, and the captain, mate, and crew mounted the taffrail forthwith to satisfy their curiosity in regard to the character of the prowling intruder, which was distinctly seen struggling in the wake. It proved to be a shark. But the fellow disdained to be captured by such ignoble instruments as a cod line and a halibut hook. He remained comparatively passive for a time, and allowed himself to be hauled, by the united efforts of the crew, some three or four fathoms towards the brig, when, annoyed by the restraint imposed upon him, or disliking the wild and motley appearance of the ship's company, he took a broad sheer to starboard, the hook snapped like a pipestem, and the hated monster swam off in another direction, wagging his tail in the happy consciousness that he was "free, untrammelled, and disinthralled. "

"Never mind, " said Mr. Thompson, making an effort to console himself for the disappointment, "we'll have the rascal yet. "

The shark manifested no disposition to leave our neighborhood, or in any other way showed displeasure at the trick we had played him. On the contrary, he drew nearer the vessel, and moved indolently and defiantly about, with his dorsal fin and a portion of his tail above the water. He was undoubtedly hungry as well as proud, and it is well known that sharks are not particular with regard to the quality of their food. Every thing that is edible, and much which is indigestible, is greedily seized and devoured by these voracious fish.

We had no shark hook on board; nevertheless, the mate lost no time in making arrangements to capture this enemy of sailors. He fastened a piece of beef to the end of a rope and threw it overboard, letting it drag astern. This attracted the attention of the shark, who gradually approached the tempting morsel, regarding it with a wistful eye, but with a lurking suspicion that all was not right.

It was now seen that the shark was not alone, but was attended by several fish of small size, beautifully mottled, and measuring from four to eight or ten inches in length. They swam boldly around the shark, above and beneath him, and sometimes passed directly in front of his jaws, while the shark manifested no desire to seize his companions and satisfy his hunger. These were "pilot fish, " and in the neighborhood of the tropics a shark is seldom seen without one or more attendants of this description.

Two of these pilot fish swam towards the beef, examined it carefully with their eyes, and rubbed it with their noses, and then returned to their lord and master. It required but a slight stretch of the imagination to suppose that these well-meaning servants made a favorable report, and whispered in his ear that "all was right, " and thus unwittingly betrayed him to his ruin.

Be that as it will, the shark now swam boldly towards the beef, as if eager to devour it; but Mr. Thompson hauled upon the rope until the precious viand was almost directly beneath the taffrail. In the mean time the mate had caused a running bowline, or noose, to be prepared from a small but strong rope. This was lowered over the stern into the water, and by a little dexterous management, the shark was coaxed to enter it in his eagerness to get at the beef. The mate let fall the running part of the bowline and hauled upon the other, and to the utter bewilderment of the hungry monster, he found himself entrapped in the power of his mortal enemies being firmly and ingloriously fastened by the tail. When he discovered the inhospitable deception of which he was the victim he appeared angry, and made furious efforts to escape; but the rope was strong, and his struggles served only to draw the noose tighter.

The shark was hauled on board, and made a terrible flouncing on the quarter-deck before he could be despatched. It was interesting to witness the eagerness with which he was assailed by the sailors. This animal is regarded as their most inveterate foe, and they seize with avidity any chance to diminish the numbers of these monsters of the deep. It was some time before he would succumb to the murderous attacks of his enemies. He wreaked his vengeance on the ropes around him, and severed them with his sharp teeth as completely and smoothly as if they had been cut with a knife. But when his head was nearly cut off, and his skull beat in by the cook's axe and handspikes, the shark, finding further resistance impossible as well as useless, resigned himself to his fate.

Sharks not unfrequently follow a vessel in moderate weather for several days, and in tropical latitudes sometimes lurk under a ship's bottom, watching a chance to gratify their appetites. For this reason it is dangerous for a person to bathe in the sea during a calm, as they are by no means choice in regard to their food, but will as readily make a meal from the leg of a sailor as from the wing of a chicken.

Mr. Thompson related a case which occurred on board a vessel belonging to Portsmouth, the year before, and to which he was a witness. One Sunday morning, in the warm latitudes, while the sea was calm, a young man, on his first voyage, quietly undressed himself, and without a word to any one, thoughtlessly mounted the cathead and plunged into the water. He swam off some distance from the ship, and laughing and shouting, seemed greatly to admire the refreshing exercise. The captain, on being informed of his imprudent conduct, called to him, rebuked him severely, and ordered him to return immediately to the ship. The young sailor turned about, wondering what impropriety there could be in taking a pleasant bath during such sultry weather. He swam beneath the fore-chain-wales, and took hold of a rope to aid him in getting on board. A couple of his shipmates also seized him by the wrists to assist him in climbing up the side. For a moment he remained motionless, with half his body in the water, when a huge shark, that had been lying in wait under the ship's bottom, seized him by the leg. The unfortunate young man uttered the most piteous screams, and every one was instinctively aware of the cause of his terrible agony. The captain ordered the men who held the arms of the sufferer to "hold on, " and jumped in the chain-wale himself to assist them. By main strength the poor fellow was dragged fainting on board; but his foot was torn off, together with a portion of the integuments of the leg, and the bones were dreadfully crushed. He lived in agony a few days, when he expired. Incidents of this nature will satisfactorily account for the hatred which a sailor bears towards a shark.

Chapter IV LAND, HO!

On the day succeeding the capture of the shark a fine breeze sprung up. Once more the white foam appeared beneath the bows, as the old brig plunged, and rolled, and wriggled along on her way towards Demarara. With a strong breeze on the quarter, it required not only labor, but skill, to steer the interesting craft. One of the "old salts, " having been rebuked by the captain for steering wildly, declared, in a grave but respectful tone, that he could steer as good a trick at the helm as any man who ever handled a marlinspike; but he "verily believed the old critter knew as much as a Christian, and was obstinately determined to turn round and take a look at her starn! "

The regular "trade wind" now commenced, and there was a prospect, although still a distant one, of ultimately reaching the port to which we were bound. The trade winds blow almost constantly from one direction, and prevail in most parts of the Atlantic and Pacific Oceans, between the latitudes of twenty-eight degrees north and twenty-eight degrees south. In northern latitudes the trade wind blows from north-east, or varies but a few points from that direction. South of the equator it blows constantly from the south-east; and the "south-east trade" is more steady than the trade wind north of the line.

It often happens that vessels bound to the United States from India, after passing the Cape of Good Hope, steer a course nearly north-west, carrying studding-sails on both sides, uninterruptedly, through fifteen or twenty degrees of latitude.

The cause of the trade winds is supposed to be the joint influence of the higher temperature of the torrid zone and the rotation of the earth on its axis. On the equator, and extending sometimes a few degrees on either side, is a tract where light easterly winds, calms, and squalls, with thunder, lightning, and inundating rains, prevail.

From what I have said, it will be seen that vessels bound from the American coast to the West Indies or Guiana should steer to the eastward in the early part of their passage, while they have the advantage of variable winds. And this precaution is the more important, as these vessels, being generally dull sailers and deeply laden, will fail to reach their port if they fall to leeward, unless by returning north into the latitude of the variable winds, and making another trial, with the benefit of more experience.

In those days there were no chronometers in use, and but few of our West India captains were in possession of a sextant, or indeed able to work a lunar observation. The latitude was accurately determined every day by measuring the altitude of the sun as it passed the meridian. To ascertain the longitude was a more difficult matter. They were obliged to rely mainly on their dead reckoning; that is, to make a calculation of the course and distance run daily, from the points steered by the compass and the rate as indicated by the log-line and half-glass. A reckoning on such a basis, where unknown currents prevail, where a vessel is steered wildly, or where the rate of sailing may be inaccurately recorded, is liable to many errors; therefore it was customary with all prudent masters, in those days, especially if they distrusted their own skill or judgment in keeping a reckoning to KEEP WELL TO THE EASTWARD. This was a general rule, and looked upon as the key to West India navigation. Sometimes a vessel bound to the Windward Islands, after reaching the latitude of her destined port, found it necessary to "run down, " steering due west, a week or ten days before making the land.

An incident occurred in those waters, a few weeks after we passed over them, which will illustrate this mode of navigation, and the consequences that sometimes attend it. A large brig belonging to an eastern port, and commanded by a worthy and cautious man, was bound to St. Pierre in Martinico. The latitude of that island was reached in due time, but the island could not bee seen, the captain having steered well to the eastward. The brig was put before the wind, and while daylight lasted every stitch of canvas was spread, and every eye was strained to catch a glimpse of the high land which was expected to loom up in the western horizon. This proceeding continued for several days; the brig carrying a press of sail by day, and lying to by night, until patience seemed no longer a virtue. The worthy captain began to fear he had not steered far enough to the eastward, but had been carried by unknown currents to leeward of his port, and that the first land he should make might prove to be the Musquito coast on the continent. He felt anxious, and looked in vain for a vessel from which he could obtain a hint in regard to his true position. Neither land nor vessel could he meet with.

At the close of the fifth day after he had commenced "running down, " no land, at sunset, was in sight from the top-gallant yard; and at eight o'clock the brig was again hove to. The captain declared with emphasis, that unless he should make the island of Martinico on the following day, he would adopt some different measures. The nature of those measures, however, he never was called upon to explain. In the morning, just as the gray light of dawn was visible in the east, while a dark cloud seemed to hang over the western horizon, all sail was again packed on the brig. A fresh breeze which sprung up during the night gave the captain assurance that his passage would soon be terminated; and terminated it was, but in a manner he hardly anticipated, and which he certainly had not desired. The brig had not been fifteen minutes under way when the dreadful sound of breakers was heard a sound which strikes dismay to a sailor's heart. The dark cloud in the west proved to be the mountains of Martinico, and the brig was dashed upon the shore. The vessel and cargo were lost, and it was with difficulty the crew were saved.

Captain Tilton, however, was a good navigator. He had been a European trader, understood and practised "lunar observations, " and always knew with sufficient accuracy the position of the brig.

Few things surprised me more on my first voyage to sea than the sudden and mysterious manner in which the coverings of the head were spirited away from the decks of the Dolphin. Hats, caps, and even the temporary apologies for such articles of costume, were given unwittingly and most unwillingly to the waves. A sudden flaw of wind, the flap of a sail, an involuntary jerk of the head, often elicited an exclamation of anger or a torrent of invectives from some unfortunate being who had been cruelly rendered bareheaded, attended with a burst of laughter from unsympathizing shipmates.

The inimitable Dickens, in his best production, says, with all the shrewdness and point of a practical philosopher, "There are very few moments in a man's existence when he experiences so much ludicrous distress, or meets with so little commiseration, as when he is in pursuit of his own hat. " But, unfortunately, on shipboard, if a man's hat is taken off by the wind, he cannot chase it and recover it; nor is it swept from his sight into the DEPTHS of the sea. On looking astern, he will see it gracefully and sportively riding on the billows, as if unconscious of any impropriety, reckless of the inconvenience which such desertion may cause its rightful proprietor, and an object of wonder, it may be, to the scaly inhabitants of old Neptune's dominions.

Before we reached Demarara every hat and cap belonging to the ship's company, with a single exception, had been involuntarily given, as a propitiatory offering, to the god of Ocean. This exception was a beaver hat belonging to the captain; and this would have followed its leaders, had it not been kept in a case hermetically sealed. After the captain's stock of sea-going hats and caps had disappeared he wore around his head a kerchief, twisted fancifully, like a turban. Others followed his example, while some fashioned for themselves skullcaps of fantastic shapes from pieces of old canvas; so that when we reached Demarara we looked more like a ship's company of Mediterranean pirates than honest Christians.

I became accustomed to a sea life, and each succeeding day brought with it some novelty to wonder at or admire. The sea is truly beautiful, and has many charms, notwithstanding a fresh- water poet, affecting to be disgusted with its monotony, has ill naturedly vented his spleen by describing the vanities of a sea life in two short lines:

"Where sometimes you ship a sea,
And sometimes see a ship."

Yet in spite of its attractions, there are few persons, other than a young enthusiast on his first voyage, who, after passing several weeks on the ocean, are not ready to greet with gladness the sight of land, although it may be a desolate shore or a barren island. Its very aspect fills the heart with joy, and excites feelings of gratitude to Him, whose protecting hand has led you safely through the dangers to which those who frequent the waste of waters are exposed.

The gratification of every man on board the Dolphin may therefore be conceived, when, after a passage of FIFTY-THREE DAYS, in a very uncomfortable and leaky vessel, a man, sent one morning by the captain to the fore-top-gallant yard, after taking a bird's eye view from his elevated position, called out, in a triumphant voice, LAND, HO!

The coast of Guiana was in sight.

Guiana is an extensive tract of country, extending along the sea coast from the Orinoco to the Amazon. When discovered in 1504, it was inhabited by the Caribs. Settlements, however, were soon made on the shore by the Dutch, the French, and the Portuguese; and the country was divided into several provinces. It was called by the discoverers "the wild coast, " and is accessible only by the mouths of its rivers the shores being every where lined with dangerous banks, or covered with impenetrable forests. Its appearance from the sea is singularly wild and uncultivated, and it is so low and flat that, as it is approached, the trees along the beach are the first objects visible. The soil, however, is fertile, and adapted to every variety of tropical production, sugar, rum, molasses, coffee, and cacao being its staple commodities.

To the distance of thirty or forty miles from the sea coast the land continues level, and in the rainy season some districts are covered with water. Indeed, the whole country bordering on the coast is intersected with swamps, marshes, rivers, artificial canals, and extensive intervals. This renders it unhealthy; and many natives of a more genial clime have perished in the provinces of Guiana by pestilential fevers.

These marshes and forests are nurseries of reptiles. Alligators of immense size are found in the rivers, creeks, and pools, and serpents are met with on the swampy banks of the river, as large as the main-topmast of a merchant ship, and much larger! The serpents being amphibious, often take to the water, and being driven unconsciously down the rivers by the currents, have been fallen in with on the coast several miles from the land.

An incident took place on this coast in 1841, on board the bark Jane, of Boston, Captain Nickerson, which created quite a sensation on the decks of that vessel. The bark was ready for sea, and had anchored in the afternoon outside the bar at the mouth of the Surinam River, when the crew turned in and the watch was set that night. The bark was a well-conditioned, orderly vessel, harboring no strangers, interlopers, or vagrants of any description.

The next morning, soon after daybreak, the mate put his hand into an open locker, at a corner of the round-house, for a piece of canvas, when it came in contact with a soft, clammy substance, which, to his consternation and horror, began to move! He drew back, uttering an exclamation, in a voice so loud and startling as to alarm the captain and all hands, who hastened on deck in time to see an enormous serpent crawl sluggishly out of the closet, and stretch himself along the deck, with as much coolness and impudence as if he thought he really belonged to the brig, and with the monkeys and parrots, constituted a portion of the ship's company!

Not so thought Captain Nickerson and the brave men with him. The word was passed along "There is a snake on board, as long as the main-top bowline! Kill him, kill him! "

The sailors seized handspikes, the cook flourished his tormentors, the mate wielded an axe, and the captain grasped a pistol! Thus equipped and armed, they rushed to the encounter.

The reptile found himself among foes instead of friends. Where he looked for hospitality and kind treatment he found cruelty, oppression, and even murder! He saw it was useless to contend against his fate when the odds were so decidedly against him, and wisely made no resistance. He was stabbed by the cook, cudgelled by the crew, brained by the mate, and shot by the captain. And, adding insult to injury, he was stripped of his skin, which was beautifully variegated and measured fourteen feet in length, and brought to Boston, where it was examined and admired by many of the citizens.

This snake was doubtless an aboma, a species of serpent of large size and great beauty, which is not venomous. In attempting to cross the river, it had probably been drifted down with the current, and carried out to sea. It might have been swimming about in the waters for some time without finding a resting- place, and, having fallen in with a vessel at anchor, thought no harm would accrue to itself or others if it should silently glide on board through the rudder-hole, and take up its residence for the night. But Captain Nickerson entertained a different opinion. He looked upon "his snakesnip" as an "ugly customer, " and gave him a reception as such.

In the course of the day on which land was discovered we reached the mouth of Demarara River, and received a pilot on board, and a queer-looking fellow, for a pilot I thought him. He was a negro, with a skin dark as ebony, which shone with an exquisite polish. His costume was simplicity itself consisting of an old straw hat, and a piece of coarse "osnaburg" tied around the waist! But he was active and intelligent, notwithstanding his costume and color, and carried the brig over the bar in safety. Soon after twilight the Dolphin was snugly anchored in smooth water in the river opposite the capital of the province.

The next morning, at an early hour, I went on deck, anxious to scrutinize the surrounding objects. The river was about a mile and a half wide, the tide flowed with great rapidity, and the waters were turbid in the extreme. The shores were lined with trees and shrubs, presenting nothing of an attractive character. A number of vessels, chiefly English and American, were moored in the river, engaged in taking in or discharging cargoes; and sundry small schooners, called "droghers, " manned by blacks, nearly naked, were sailing up or down the river, laden with produce.

The town, half concealed in the low, swampy grounds, appeared insignificant and mean, and the wharves and landing places at the river's side were neither picturesque nor beautiful. The architecture of the houses, however, with porticoes, verandas, and terraces, excited my admiration. I also saw, in the distance, palm and cocoanut trees, and banana and plantain shrubs, with leaves six or eight feet long. These Various objects, with the sultry stagnation of the atmosphere, and the light and airy costume of those of the inhabitants I had seen convinced me that I was not laboring under a dream, but was actually in a foreign port, two thousand miles from home, and in a tropical climate.

The following day being Sunday, I accompanied Mr. Thompson on a visit to the market, in order to obtain a supply of fresh provisions and vegetables. I was surprised to find the public market open on the Sabbath. The very idea of such a custom conflicted with my pre-conceived notions of propriety and religion. But Sunday was a great holiday in Demarara indeed the only day which the slaves on the plantations could call their own. On Sunday they were allowed to visit each other, frolic as they pleased, cultivate their little gardens, make their purchases at the shops which were open on that day, and carry their produce to market.

Hence the spacious market square, in the midst of the town, was covered with articles of traffic. The venders were chiefly negro women, who exposed for sale immense quantities of yams, tomatoes, cassava bread, sugar-cane, plantains, water-cresses, oranges, bananas, avocado pears, etc., with fancy articles of almost every description.

The scene was a novel and interesting one. The market women were habited in garments of a marvelously scanty pattern, better adapted to the sultry character of the climate than to the notions of delicacy which prevail among civilized people in a more northern clime. The head-dress consisted, in almost every instance, of a calico kerchief, of gaudy colors, fantastically wreathed around the head. They were respectful in their deportment, exhibited their wares to the best advantage, and with cheerful countenances and occasional jokes, accompanied with peals of merry laughter, seemed happier than millionaires or kings! Their dialect was a strange jumble of Dutch, English, and African. All were fond of talking, and, like aspiring politicians in happy New England, neglected no chance to display their extraordinary power of language. And such a jabbering, such a confusion of tongues, as I listened to that Sunday morning in the market-place of Demarara, overwhelmed me with wonder, and days elapsed before I could get the buzz out of my head!

In answer to inquiries relative to the health of the place, it was gratifying to learn that the province had not been so free from yellow fever at that season for several years. While the Dolphin remained in port but few fatal cases occurred in the harbor, and the origin of those could be traced to intemperance or other imprudent conduct. There was no serious sickness on board the brig while we remained, and only one "regular drunken scrape. " This occurred a few days after we arrived in port. Two of the crew, on some plausible pretext, one afternoon obtained leave of Mr. Thompson to go on shore. He cautioned them to keep sober, and be early on board, and they solemnly promised to comply with his instructions.

But these "noble old tars" had no sooner set their feet upon the land than they rushed to a grog shop. It is well know that grog shops are found in abundance in all parts of the world where civilization extends its genial influence. Temptations of the most alluring character are every where offered to weak-minded and unprincipled men to abandon the prerogative of reason and become brutes. In exchange for their money, these sailors procured the means of becoming drunk! They quarreled with the shopkeeper, insulted his customers, were severely threshed for their brutality and insolence, and were finally picked up in the street, and brought on board by two of the crew of an American vessel which was moored near the Dolphin.

They looked wretchedly enough. Their clothes, which were neat and trim when they went ashore, were mostly torn from their backs, their faces were bruised and bloody, and their eyes surrounded by livid circles. Their shipmates, seeing their degraded condition, assisted them on board, and persuaded them to go into the forecastle, which was now appropriated to the accommodation of the ship's company. But instead of retiring to their berths, and sleeping off the effects of their liquor, these men determined to have a ROW.

The craziest of them made his way on deck, and began to sing, and dance, and halloo like a madman. One of his shipmates, named Wilkins, remonstrated against such unruly conduct, and received in return a blow on the side of the head, which sent him with great force against the gunwale. The peacemaker, indignant at such unexpected and undeserved treatment, returned the blow with interest. The other inebriate, hearing the disturbance, came to the assistance of his drunken companion. A general fight ensued; some heavy blows were interchanged, and for a few minutes there was a scene of confusion, profanity, and hard fighting on the decks of the Dolphin, which showed me a new, and not very attractive phase in the sailor's character.

Mr. Thompson, armed with authority and a heaver, soon made his appearance among them, and with the assistance of the sober ones, after a severe struggle, succeeded in mastering and pinioning the two men, who, though in full possession of their physical faculties, were actually crazed with alcoholic drinks. When thus rendered harmless, their yells were terrific, until it was found necessary for the peace of the harbor to GAG THEM; which was done by gently placing an iron pump-bolt between the jaws of each of the maniacs, and fastening it by a rope-yarn behind the ear. Thus, unable to give utterance to their feelings, and exhausted by fruitless struggles, they fell asleep.

In the morning cool reflection came. They looked as ruefully as Don Quixote after his battle with the shepherds, and bore as many marks of the prowess of their opponents. But, unlike "the Knight of the Rueful Countenance, " they seemed heartily ashamed of their exploits, and promised better behavior in future.

Nevertheless, a few days after this affair, Jim Bilton, one of the men who had figured so conspicuously in the row, and owed Wilkins a grudge for the black eye he had received in the melee, challenged his shipmate to a "fair stand-up fight! "

The challenge was accepted; but as the main deck of the brig was still "lumbered up, " and the forecastle furnished a field altogether too confined for such recreations, it was agreed that this "stand-up fight" should take place while each of the combatants were sitting astride a chest! Accordingly a large chest was roused up from below, and placed athwart-ships on the forecastle, between the bowsprit bitts and the cathead. The parties took their seats on the ends of the chest, facing each other, and the business was to be settled by hard knocks.

The men faced each other boldly, some weighty compliments were interchanged, when Bilton, to avoid a favor from his antagonist which in all probability would have finished him, slipped off the end of the chest, to the disgust of his shipmates and his own everlasting disgrace.

One of the crew, however, who was ingenious at expedients, and determined to see fair play, by means of a hammer and a tenpenny nail fastened both parties firmly to the chest by the seats of their canvas trousers. There being no longer a possibility of BACKING OUT, the battle was resumed, but did not last long; for Bilton soon received a blow on his left temple, which, in spite of the tenpenny nail, knocked him off the chest, and decided the contest.

Chapter V DEMARARA

A circumstance occurred not long before our arrival at Demarara, which, being somewhat remarkable in its character, furnished a fruitful theme for conversation and comment. This was the arrival of a vessel from Cadiz, with only one person on board.

It seems that a Captain Shackford, of Portsmouth, N.H., was the master and owner of a sloop of some sixty or eighty tons. He proceeded to Cadiz, and there took in a cargo for Guiana. When on the eve of sailing, his crew, dissatisfied with some of his proceedings, left the vessel.

Captain Shackford, a resolute but eccentric man, resolved not to be disappointed in his calculations, or delayed in his voyage by the desertion of his crew, and boldly put to sea on the day appointed for sailing, trusting in his own unaided efforts and energies to manage the vessel on a passage across the ocean of thirty-five hundred miles. He was seventy-four days on his passage; but brought his vessel into port in tolerable order, having experienced no difficulty on his way, and losing only one day of his reckoning.

The arrival of a vessel in Demarara, under such singular circumstances, caused quite a sensation among the authorities, and gave rise to suspicions by no means favorable to the character of the captain as an honest man, and which his long, tangled locks and hirsute countenance for he had not combed his hair or shaved his face during the passage tended to confirm. It was thought by some that a mutiny might have broken out among the crew of the sloop, which resulted in scenes of violence and bloodshed, and that this wild-looking man was the only survivor of a desperate struggle between the officers and crew. Indeed, he looked not unlike a mutineer and murderer.

Captain Shackford was indignant at these suspicions, and would hardly deign to give explanations. It was fortunate for him that some vessels belonging to Portsmouth were in the harbor, the captains of which recognized him as an old acquaintance, and vouched for his character as an honest, well-meaning man, although at times indulging in strange freaks, more akin to madness than method. He was released from arrest, and subsequently disposed of his merchandise at remunerating prices, and with a cargo of assorted articles, and a crew, sailed for a port in the United States.

After the cargo of the Dolphin was discharged, preparations were made for receiving a return cargo, to consist principally of molasses. The process of taking in and stowing a cargo of this description is a peculiar one; and as I shall recur to this subject hereafter, I avail myself of this opportunity to describe, briefly, the mode of operation.

The empty casks are carefully stowed in the hold, with small pieces of board between the quarter-hoops of each cask, so that the bilge of a cask shall touch no other substance whatever. The bungholes must also be uppermost; thus, in the brief but expressive language of commerce, "every cask must be bung up and bilge free. " A "molasses hose" is then procured, consisting of a half barrel with a hole in the bottom, to which is attached a leathern hose an inch and a half in diameter, and long enough to reach to the most distant part of the hold. A hogshead filled with molasses is then hoisted over the hatchway, hung down, and the hose-tub is placed directly beneath; the bung is taken out, and the molasses passes through the hose to any cask in the hold that may be wished. When the cask is filled the hose is shifted to another, and in this way the casks are all filled and the cargo stowed. The process is tedious; and although a sweet, by no means a pleasant one, to those engaged in it.

It may be imagined that the crew, after working all day among molasses in that hot climate, should wish to bathe in the evening; and the river alongside, although the element was neither pure nor transparent, offered, at high or low water, a tempting opportunity. To the very natural and proper inquiry whether the harbor of Demarara was infested with sharks a man- eating shark not being the most desirable "companion of the bath" we were told that a shark had never been seen in the harbor; that the river water, being turbid and fresher than the ocean water, was offensive to that much dreaded animal, which delights in the clear waters of the salt sea. We were further told that up the river, in the creeks and pools which abound in that region, alligators were met with in large numbers; some of them of large size, and had been known to attack a man in the water; but they never ventured down the river among the shipping.

The reports being thus favorable, the crew of the Dolphin, being good swimmers, were indeed, whenever it was "slack water" of an evening, to take a swim in the river; and the crews of other American vessels followed the example. One evening, at twilight, there were swimming about and sporting in the water, deriving the highest enjoyment from this healthy and refreshing exercise, some fifteen or twenty American sailors. On the following day an incident occurred, which operated as an impressive warning against bathing in the waters of the Demarara.

On the afternoon of that day, a sailor at work on the mizzen- topsail yard of an English ship moored within the distance of a cable's length from the Dolphin, accidentally fell from the yard. As he fell he caught hold of the main brace, and was suspended for a minute over the water. There was quite a commotion on the deck of the ship, which attracted the attention of the crews of neighboring vessels. On hearing the distressing cry of the man, and witnessing the tumult on board the ship, the crew of the Dolphin ran to the side of the brig and gazed with interest on the scene.

The poor fellow was unable to retain his hold of the rope until he could receive assistance. He fell into the water alongside, but rose to the surface almost immediately, and being, apparently, a good swimmer, struck out vigorously towards the ship. Some of his shipmates jumped into the boat to pick him up, as, notwithstanding his exertions, he was swept away by the tide; but none of the lookers-on apprehended any danger.

While we were intently watching the result, the unfortunate man gave a shrill and piercing shriek; and we then saw by the commotion in the water, and the appearance of a large fin above the surface, that a shark had seized the unlucky sailor, which caused him to give utterance to that dreadful cry. He immediately sank with his prey, and the muddy state of the water prevented the ruthless monster or his victim from being seen.

We were still gazing on the spot where this fearful tragedy was enacted, transfixed and mute with horror, when the shark again rose to the surface, bearing in his jaws the lifeless body of the English sailor; and for a brief period we beheld the voracious fish devouring his human food.

The cargo of the Dolphin being completed, there ensued the usual bustle and confusion in making preparations for sea. Owing to the lateness of the season, Captain Tilton was unwilling to encounter the storms of the New England coast in a vessel hardly seaworthy, and expressed an intention to proceed to Charleston, in South Carolina.

About a week before we left Demarara a small English brig-of-war arrived in the harbor, causing much consternation among the sailors, and not without reason. The brig was deficient in her complement of men, and this deficiency was supplied by impressment from crews of British vessels in port. The commander was a young man, who in common with most of the British naval officers of that day, had an exalted opinion of his dignity and importance, and held the Yankees in contempt.

The pennant at the main is a distinguishing mark of a man-of-war, and it was considered disrespectful on the part of the master of a merchant vessel to wear a pennant in the presence of a cruiser. But on the Sunday following the arrival of the gun brig the captain of a fine-looking American brig, who did not entertain that respect for John Bull which the representatives of that dignitary were disposed to exact, hoisted his colors, as usual, on the Sabbath. He did not confine his display of bunting to the ensign at the peak, a burgee studded with stars at the fore, and a jack on the bowsprit, but ran up a pennant of most preposterous length at the main, which proudly flaunted in the breeze, as if bidding defiance to the Englishman.

The young naval commander foolishly allowed himself to be annoyed by this proceeding on the part of the Yankee, and resolved to administer an appropriate rebuke. He sent an officer alongside the American brig, who, in a peremptory tone, told the mate to cause that Yankee pennant to be hauled down immediately.

The captain, hearing of the mandate, made his appearance on deck; and on a repetition of the order from the officer, exhibited unequivocal symptoms of a choleric temper. After letting off a little of his exuberant wrath, he declared with emphasis that he had a RIGHT to wear a pennant, and WOULD wear it in spite of all the officers in the British navy.

The midshipman, finding it of no avail to continue the parley, told his cockswain to go aloft and "dowse the pennant and leave it in the cross-trees. " This was done, regardless of the protest of the captain, and his threats to lay the subject before the government and make it a national matter. The boat had hardly reached the man-of-war, when the pennant was again flying on board the American brig, and seemed to wave more proudly than before.

The man-of-war's boat was sent back, and some sharp words were exchanged between the British officer and the Yankee captain; but the former, possessing superior physical force, was triumphant. The pennant was again hauled down, but this time it was not left in the cross-trees. The cockswain took it with him and it was carried on board the English brig, in spite of the denunciation hurled against men-of-war's men, in which the epithets "thieves, " "robbers, " and "pirates, " were distinctly heard.

A few nights after the above-mentioned occurrence we received an unexpected addition to the number of our crew. It was about an hour after midnight, when the man who had the watch on deck was comfortably seated on a coil of rope beneath the main deck awning, and probably dozing, while sheltered from a heavy and protracted shower of rain. The night was dark and gloomy; the ebb tide made a moaning, monotonous noise under the bows, and rushed swiftly by the sides of the vessel, leaving a broad wake astern. The sailor was roused from his comfortable position by a sound resembling the cry of a person in distress. He started to his feet, and stepped out from beneath the awning. He listened, and again distinctly heard the cry, which seemed to come from the water under the bows. Supposing it might proceed from some person who had fallen overboard and wanted help, he went forward to the knight-heads, and called out, "Who's there? "

A voice from below the bowsprit faintly replied, "Shipmate, for God's sake bear a hand, and give me help. I can hold on but a few minutes longer. "

He was now aware that a man, in an exhausted condition, was clinging to the cable, and required immediate assistance. He called up his shipmates, and with little difficulty they succeeded in hauling him safely on board. He proved to be a fine-looking English sailor; and as soon as he recovered strength enough to converse, explained the cause of his perilous situation.

He belonged to the brig-of-war, which was lying at anchor about half a mile above. He had been impressed two years before; and being treated with cruelty and harshness, had been eagerly watching an opportunity to escape from his inhuman bondage. At length he formed a plan with one of his messmates, to slip overboard quietly the first dark night, and relying on skill in swimming, attempt to reach some vessel at anchor in the harbor.

The plan was carried into effect. They succeeded in eluding the vigilance of the sentries, dropped gently into the water, and were soon floating astern. But their situation was one of extreme peril. The current was stronger than they anticipated, and the darkness of the night prevented them from distinguishing any vessel in time to get on board. As soon as they were swept out of hearing of the man-of-war, they shouted loudly for help; but the murmuring of the tide, the pattering of the rain, and the howling of the wind prevented their voices from being heard, as, notwithstanding their exertions to stem the tide, they floated rapidly down the river towards the bar.

What risks will a man encounter to secure his liberty! It was not long before these friends separated, never to meet again. One of them sank beneath the waters. The other had given up all expectation of being rescued, when he beheld an object, darker than the murky atmosphere by which it was surrounded, rising, as it appeared to him, out of the water. His heart beat quicker within his bosom. In a moment more he had seized the cable of the Dolphin, and shouted for help. This man was grateful for the succor he had received, and expressed a wish to work his passage to the United States. To this suggestion Captain Tilton offered no objection, and he subsequently proved to be one of the best men on board.

That very morning the black pilot made his appearance, grinning as he thrust his dark muzzle over the gunwale. He was greeted with answering smiles, for we were "homeward bound, " and all hands cheerfully commenced heaving up the anchor and making sail. With a favorable breeze and an ebb tide we soon passed the bar, and entered upon the broad ocean. The fresh trade wind was welcome after sweltering for weeks in the sultry and unwholesome atmosphere of Demarara; and the clear and pellucid waters of the ocean bore a cheerful aspect, contrasted with the thick and opaque waters of the river in which we had remained several weeks at anchor.

Nothing remarkable occurred during the homeward passage, until we reached the Gulf Stream, that extraordinary current, sixty or seventy miles in width, and many degrees warmer than the ocean water on either side, and which reaches from the Gulf of Florida to the Shoals of Nantucket. There can be no doubt that this current of the Gulf Stream is owing to the trade winds in the tropical seas, which, blowing at all times from the eastward, drive a large body of water towards the American continent. Vessels bound to India invariably meet with a strong westerly current within the tropics, and particularly in the vicinity of the equator. This volume of water is thus forced along the shores of Brazil and Guiana, until it enters the Caribbean Sea, from which it has no outlet excepting through the strait bounded by Cape Catouche in Yucatan, on one side, and Cape St. Antonio, in Cuba, on the other.

Through this strait, after a strong trade wind has been blowing for a time, the current sets into the Gulf of Mexico at the rate of two or three knots an hour. Here the waters of the tropical seas are mingled with the waters of the Mississippi, the Balize, the Rio Grande, the Colorado, the Alabama, and other large streams which empty into the Gulf of Mexico; and turning off to the eastward, this body of water is driven along between the coasts of Cuba and Florida until it strikes the Salt Key Bank and the Bahamas, when it receives another considerable addition from the currents, which, from the same causes, are continually setting west through the Old Bahama and New Providence Channels. It is then forced northward along the coast of Florida and the Middle States. The stream becomes wider as it extends north, diminishes its velocity, and gradually changes its temperature, until it strikes the shoals south of Nantucket and the Bank of St. George, when it branches off to the eastward, washes the southern edge of the Bank of Newfoundland, and a portion of it is lost in the ocean between the Western and Canary Islands; and another portion, sweeping to the southward past the Cape de Verdes, is again impelled to the westward across the Atlantic, and performs its regular round.

The current always moving in the same circuitous track, forms, according to Mr. Maury, to whose scientific labors the commercial world is deeply indebted, an IMMENSE WHIRLPOOL, whose circuit embraces the whole North Atlantic Ocean. In the centre of the whirl is a quiet spot, equal in extent of area to the whole Mississippi valley, unaffected by currents of any kind. And here, as a matter of course, the greater part of the gulf-weed and other floating materials, which are carried round by the current, is eventually deposited. This is the "Sargasso Sea" of the ancients. Columbus crossed this "weedy sea" on his quest after a western passage to India. And the singular appearance of the ocean, thickly matted over with gulf-weed, caused great alarm among his companions, who thought they had reached the limits of navigation.

A current of a character similar to the Gulf Stream only not so strong is experienced along the east coast of Africa, from Mozambique to the Lagullas Bank, off the Cape of Good Hope. This current is undoubtedly caused by the trade wind forcing the water towards the coast of Africa. But in this case it is not driven into a narrow passage, like the Gulf of Florida, which would greatly increase its velocity. The temperature of the water in the current off the Cape of Good Hope is also several degrees higher than the ocean waters in the neighborhood of the current.

On the afternoon on which we entered the Gulf Stream the wind hauled suddenly to the eastward, and the heavens were obscured by clouds. The breeze also increased, and the sea became rough, causing the brig to assume various unseemly attitudes, and perform gymnastic exercises wonderful to behold. As the wind increased and the sea became more turbulent, the Dolphin tumbled about like an elephant dancing a hornpipe, insomuch that it was difficult for a person to keep his perpendicular. Indeed, as I was passing along from the camboose to the cabin, with a plate of toast in one hand and a teapot in the other, the brig took a lee lurch without giving notice of her intention, and sent me with tremendous force across the deck, to leeward, where I brought up against the sail. But the tea and toast were ejected from my hands into the sea, and I never saw them more.

At twilight, Captain Tilton came on deck, and looking around the horizon, said, addressing the mate, "Mr. Thompson, the weather looks GREASY to windward; I fear a gale is brewing. You may find the top-gallant sail and jib, and take a reef in the mainsail. "

This work was soon accomplished. The captain's prediction was verified; for the wind continued to increase, accompanied with fine drizzling rain, until about nine o'clock, when orders were given to take another reef in the mainsail, and double reef the fore-topsail. It was not long before the wind swept across the waves with almost resistless force, when it was found necessary to strip the brig of all canvas, excepting a storm main-staysail and close-reefed fore-topsail;

the yards were braced up, the helm lashed a-lee, and the brig was laid to.

The gale continued unabated all night. Our vessel rolled heavily to leeward, and strained considerably, her bulkheads groaning and her seams opening, making it necessary to keep one of the pumps in constant operation. As soon as it was daylight I went on deck, anxious to witness a spectacle I had often heard described A GALE OF WIND AT SEA and it was a sight to call forth my wonder and admiration. The wind, blowing furiously, whistled wildly among the rigging; the waves of alarming size and threatening appearance, came rushing in swift succession towards us, as if eager to overwhelm our puny bark, which nevertheless floated unharmed, now riding on the crest of a wave, and anon plunging into a deep and angry-looking gulf, taking no water on deck, excepting from an occasional spray.

I asked one of the sailors who had just taken a spell at the pump, if this were not a hurricane.

"Hurricane! " said he, with a good-natured grin. "Nonsense! This is only a stiff breeze. 'Tis as different from a hurricane as a heaver is from a handspike. When you see a hurricane, my lad, you will know it, even if the name is not lettered on the starn. "

"Then I suppose there is no actual danger in a gale like this, although it does not look very inviting. "

"Danger! I don't know about that. In a good seaworthy vessel a man is as SAFE in a gale of wind as if he was cooped up in a grog-selling boarding house on shore; and a thousand times better off in other respects. But this miserable old craft is strained in every timber, and takes in more water through the seams in her bottom than 'the combers' toss on her decks. If her bottom does not drop out some of these odd times, and leave us in the lurch, we may think ourselves lucky. "

After uttering these consolatory remarks, accompanied with a significant shrug, he resumed his labors at the pump.

The wind blew with violence through the day, and the leak kept increasing. There is probably no exercise more fatiguing than "pumping ship, " as practised with the clumsy, awkward contrivances called PUMPS, which were generally in use among the merchant vessels of those days. It being necessary to keep the pumps in constant operation, or in nautical parlance, "pump or sink, " the crew, although a hardy, vigorous set of men, became exhausted and disheartened, and, to my astonishment and disgust, instead of manifesting by their solemn looks and devout demeanor a sense of the danger with which they were threatened, alternately pumped, grumbled, and swore, and swore, grumbled, and pumped.

Change is incident to every thing; and even a gale of wind cannot last forever. Before night the tempest was hushed, the waves diminished, and in a few hours the brig was under full sail, jogging along to the westward at the rate of six or seven knots. The next day we got soundings on the coast of Carolina, and, with a fair wind, rapidly approached the land.

Off the mouth of the bay which forms the harbor of Charleston extends a long line of shoals, on which the breakers are continually dashing. These shoals are intersected by narrow channels, through which vessels of moderate draught may pass at high water with a smooth sea. The principal channel, or main passage, for ships over the bar is narrow, and never attempted without a pilot. About three miles from the bar is the lighthouse, which stands on a low, sandy shore. Indeed, the whole coast is low and sandy, abounding in mosquitoes, sandflies, and oysters. Inside the bar there is good anchorage, but the tide at certain periods ebbs and flows with great velocity.

We crossed the bar, and, without anchoring, proceeded to the city. We passed Sullivan's Island on the right a long, low, sandy island, which is the summer residence of many of the inhabitants of Charleston. On this island Fort Moultrie is situated, which commands the passage to the city, about four miles distant. This fort proved an awkward obstacle to the capture of Charleston, when that feat was rashly attempted by Sir Peter Parker, during the revolutionary war.

On all the surrounding objects I gazed with a deep and intense interest, which was not relaxed until the Dolphin dropped anchor off the wharves of this celebrated city.

Chapter VI SCENES IN CHARLESTON

Soon after the Dolphin arrived in Charleston the crew were discharged, with the exception of one of the seamen and myself. We retained our quarters in the brig. Mr. Thompson, the mate, took passage in a vessel for Boston, and not long afterwards sailed from Portsmouth in command of a ship. Captain Tilton took up his residence at a fashionable boarding house, and I seldom had any communication with him. I supposed, as a matter of course, that he would soon enter on another voyage, and I should go with him. In the meantime, having provided me with a temporary home, he left me to associate with whom I pleased, and struggle single-handed against the many temptations to which a young sailor in a strange maritime city is always exposed.

About a week after our arrival in Charleston, as I was passing through one of the principal streets, clad in strict sailor costume, I met a good-looking gentleman, who, to my surprise, accosted me with great politeness, his pleasant features lighted up with a benevolent smile, and inquired if I had not recently returned from a voyage to sea. Upon being assured that such was the case, he remarked that he liked my appearance, and doubted not I was a smart, capable lad, who would be a valuable acquisition to the crew of a good ship. I was flattered and pleased with the conduct of this genteel looking stranger, convinced that he was a person of good judgment and nice discrimination. He further informed me, with a patronizing air, that he was the captain of a fine fast-sailing vessel, bound on a pleasant voyage, and should be delighted to number among his crew some active and intelligent young men, like myself. He even went so far as to say he was so well satisfied with my appearance, that if I would accompany him to a counting-room on an adjoining wharf, he would ship me without asking further questions, and advance a month's wages on the spot. But the amount he offered as monthly wages was so much greater than I, being but little better than a very green hand, had a right to expect, that a person acquainted with human nature would have suspected this pleasant-spoken gentleman to have some other reason for his conduct than admiration of my appearance and interest in my welfare. I was eager to place myself at once under the protection of my new friend; yet I could not forget that I was still under the care of my kinsman, Captain Tilton, and that it would be neither decorous nor proper to make this new engagement without consulting him.

But I did not for a moment doubt he would give his consent to the proposed arrangement, and be rejoiced to get me fairly off his hands.

I communicated my objections to the stranger, but assured him that I would meet him in the afternoon at the place he designated, and in all probability sign "the articles. " He seemed, nevertheless, disappointed at the result of the interview, and bidding me not fail to come, turned away, and walked slowly towards the wharf.

As I left this kind-hearted stranger, brim full of newborn confidence and hope, and exulting in the fact that I had fallen in with a man of influence and position, who could appreciate my merit, I met a couple of sailors of my acquaintance, who had been standing at a corner of the street witnessing our interview, with which they seemed greatly amused. One of the sailors, with a deficiency of respect for my would-be patron which I could not approve, said, "Hawser, what were you talking with that fellow about? "

I explained, with great glee and at full length, the nature of our conversation to which they greedily listened, winking mysteriously at each other. When I had concluded, they indulged in a hearty laugh.

It was some time before they could sufficiently restrain their merriment to enlighten me on the cause of their mirth. I was then told, to my mortification, that my kind friend, the GENTLEMAN on whose benevolence and protection I had already built hopes of success in life, was neither more nor less than the captain of an armed clipper brig, a SLAVER, anchored in the outer roads, which had been for a fortnight ready for sea, but was detained in consequence of the desertion of three several crews, who had been induced by false representations to ship, and had deserted EN MASSE as soon as they learned the true character of the vessel and the voyage. He was now using all possible means to entrap a crew of men or boys for this abominable traffic, and was by no means particular in his choice.

This was a severe blow to my vanity. I felt not a little indignant at being so easily cajoled, played upon, and almost kidnapped by this unprincipled scoundrel. It was a valuable lesson, however; for experience is a good, although expensive teacher.

A few days passed away, when, one morning about three o'clock, as some members of the city patrol were passing through Church Street, they discovered a man, apparently n a dying state, lying in the street. He was conveyed to the guard house, or patrol station, where he died in the course of half an hour, without being able to articulate a syllable. Several wounds in different parts of his body, made by a small penknife, which was subsequently found, were undoubtedly the cause of his death. The unfortunate man thus murdered was the captain of the slaver, who had sought to entrap me by his honeyed words. A pool of blood was on the spot on which he was first discovered, and his steps could be traced by the blood on the pavements for several rods. The marks of blood were found only in the middle of the street; and none of the persons residing in that part of the city heard any disturbance, brawl, or cries for assistance in the course of the night.

The mysterious tragedy caused a great excitement. The police were unceasing in their efforts to discover the circumstances connected with this assassination, but in vain. The veil which concealed it was not lifted, and no clew was ever given by which even conjecture could develop the mystery.

It was supposed by some that the unfortunate man fell a victim to the rage of a jealous husband whose honor he had outraged, or of a lover whose affections he had supplanted. Others thought the fatal injuries he received were the result of a drunken quarrel, commenced in a gaming house; while many believed that private revenge inflicted the stabs, which, from their number and direction, appeared to have been given under the influence of ungovernable fury. Some thought the wounds were inflicted by a vigorous man, others, that a woman had imbrued her hands in his blood.

The first, and perhaps most natural supposition, was that some negro, knowing the character of the voyage which the murdered man had contemplated, had taken this desperate mode of arresting his proceedings. This theory, however, was soon generally abandoned for another. It was suggested that one of the sailors who had shipped in the slaver and subsequently deserted, knowing the captain was seeking them in every direction, had met him in the street, and fearful of being arrested, or seeking to revenge a personal wrong, had committed the terrible crime. This hypothesis was, doubtless, as false as either of the others, and more absurd. It was, nevertheless, adopted by the city authorities, and promptly acted upon, with a disregard to the rights of individuals which seems strangely at variance with republican institutions. The police force was strengthened, and on the evening succeeding the discovery of the murder received orders to arrest and place in confinement every individual seen in the streets wearing the garb of a sailor. This arbitrary edict was strictly enforced; and Jack, on leaving his home in the forecastle or a boarding house to visit the haunts of dissipation, or perhaps to attend to some pressing and important duty, was pounced upon by the members of the city guard, and, much to his astonishment and anger, and maugre his struggles, expostulations, and threats, was carried off without any assigned reason, and securely placed under lock and key.

Some two or three hundred of these unoffending tars were caught, captured, cribbed, and confined. No respect was paid to age, color or nation. They were huddled together in rooms of very moderate dimensions, which precluded, for one night at least, any idea of rest or comfort; and such a confusion of tongues, such anathemas against the city officials, such threats of vengeance, such rare specimens of swearing, singing, and shouting, varied occasionally by rough greetings and jeers whenever a new squad of blue jackets was thrust in among them, would have commanded the admiration of the evil dwellers in Milton's Pandemonium.

This arbitrary measure failed of success. The kidnapped sailors, on the following day, were separately examined in the presence of the mate of the brig, but no reasons were found for detaining a single individual.

A few days after this occurrence, Captain Tilton told me he had sold the brig Dolphin to a Captain Turner, of New York, a worthy man and his particular friend; that Captain Turner intended proceeding immediately to some neutral port in the West Indies. The non-intercourse act, at that time, prohibited all trade to places belonging to either of the great belligerent powers. He also said he had made no arrangements in regard to himself; that he was undecided what course to pursue, and might remain on shore for months. Anxious, however, to promote my interest by procuring me active employment, he had stipulated with Captain Turner that I should have "a chance" in the Dolphin, on her next voyage, before the mast. I had not a word to say against this arrangement, but gave my cheerful consent, especially as it was represented that Captain

Turner would "treat me with kindness, and help me along in the world. "

I was thus unceremoniously dismissed by Captain Tilton from his charge. Under the plea of promoting my interest, he had procured me a situation before the mast in an old, leaky vessel, which he had got rid of because she was not seaworthy, and commanded by a man of whose character he was entirely ignorant. I expressed gratitude to my kinsman for his goodness, notwithstanding I had secret misgivings in regard to his disinterestedness, and signed with alacrity "the articles" with Captain Turner. A new and interesting scene in the drama of life was about to open, and I looked forward with impatience to the rising of the curtain.

The brig was laden with a cargo of lumber, rice, and provisions, and her destination was Cayenne, on the coast of Guiana. In January, 1810, we left the wharf in Charleston, and proceeded down the harbor. The wind was light, but the tide ebbed with unusual velocity, sweeping us rapidly on our way. We had nearly reached the bar when it suddenly became calm. The brig lost steerage way, and the current was setting towards the shoals. The pilot, aware of the danger, called out, "Let go the anchor! "

The order was promptly obeyed, and the small bower anchor was let go. The tide was so strong that when a sufficient quantity of cable was run out, the attempt to "check her, " and to "bring up, " resulted in capsizing the windlass, and causing, for a few minutes, a sense of indescribable confusion. The windlass, by its violent and spasmodic motion, knocked over two of the sailors who foolishly endeavored to regain control of its actions, and the cable, having commenced running out of the hawse-hold, would not be "snubbed, " but obstinately persisted in continuing its course in spite of the desperate exertions of the captain, mate, pilot, and a portion of the crew, who clung to it as if it was their last hope. But their efforts were vain. Its impetuosity could not in this way be checked; and as the end of the cable by some strange neglect, had not been clinched around the mast, the last coil followed the example of "its illustrious predecessors, " and disappeared through the hawse-hole, after having, by an unexpected whisk, upset the mate, and given the captain a rap across the shins, which lamed him for a week.

The "best bower" anchor was now let go, and the end hastily secured around the foremast, which fortunately "brought up" the brig "all standing, " within half a cable's length of the shoal. No buoy having been attached to the small bower anchor, the anchor and cable were lost forever.

This accident, of course, prevented us from proceeding immediately to sea; and the wind having changed, the anchor was weighed at the flood tide, and the brig removed to a safer anchorage. Night came on, and as the brig was riding in a roadstead, at single anchor, in a tempestuous season, it was necessary to set an anchor watch. It fell to my lot to have the first watch; that is, to keep a look out after the wind, weather, and condition of the vessel, and report any occurrence of importance between the hours of eight and ten in the evening. The crew, fatigued with the labors of the day, took possession of their berths at an early hour, the mate and the captain also disappeared from the deck, after having instructed me in my duties, and cautioned me against falling asleep in my watch.

I was thus intrusted with a responsible charge, and realized the importance of the trust. I walked fore-and-aft the deck, with a step and a swagger that would have become a Port Admiral in the British navy. I felt that I had gained one important step; and, bound on a pleasant voyage, with kind and indulgent officers, had every thing pleasant to expect in the future. As Captain Turner would undoubtedly treat me with indulgence and overlook any shortcomings on my part, for the sake of his intimate friend, Captain Tilton, I determined, by my attention to duty, and my general conduct, to deserve the favors which I was sure I should receive.

Communing thus with myself, and lost in the rosy vagaries of a vivid imagination, I unhappily for the moment forgot the objects for which I was stationed on deck. I seated myself involuntarily on a spar, which was lashed alongside the long boat, and in a few minutes, without any intention or expectation of being otherwise than vigilant in the extreme, WAS TRANSPORTED TO THE LAND OF DREAMS!

A check was suddenly put to my vagabond thoughts and flowery visions, and I was violently dragged back to the realities of life by a strong hand, which, seizing me roughly by the collar, jerked me to my feet! At the same time, the voice of my kind friend and benefactor, Captain Turner, rung in my ears like a trumpet, as he exclaimed in a paroxysm of passion, "You little good-for-nothing rascal! This is the way you keep watch! Hey? Wake up, you lazy ragamuffin! Rouse yourself! And, suiting the action to the word, he gave me two or three severe shakes. "Let me catch you sleeping in your watch again, and I'll send you to the cross-trees for four hours on a stretch. I knew I had got a hard bargain when your uncle shoved you upon me, you sneaking, sanctimonious-looking imp of Satan! But mind how you carry your helm, or you will have cause to curse the day when you shipped on board the Dolphin! "

This was a damper, with a vengeance, to my aspirations and hopes. The ladder on which I was about to ascend to fame and fortune was unfeelingly knocked away, and I was laid prostrate flat on my back almost before I began to mount! I was deceived in Captain Turner; and what was of greater consequence to me, my self- confidence was terribly shaken I was deceived in myself. My shipmates, nevertheless, sympathized with me in my abasement; gave me words of encouragement; bade me be of good cheer; keep a stiff upper lip; look out sharper for squalls in the future, and I should yet "weather the cape. "

An awkward accident happened to me the following day, which tended still further to diminish the self-confidence I had so recently cherished. The small boat had returned about sunset from a mission to the city, and as I formed one of the boat's crew, the mate ordered me to drop the boat astern, and hook on the tackles that it might be hoisted to the davits. But the tide running furiously, the boat when under the quarter took a sudden sheer. I lost my hold on the brig, and found myself adrift.

I shouted lustily for help, but no help could be afforded; the long-boat being snugly stowed amidships, and the tide sweeping me towards the bar at the rate of several knots an hour. Sculling was a manoeuvre of which I had heard, and seen practised, but had never practised myself. I therefore took one of the oars and made a desperate attempt to PADDLE towards the brig. The attempt was unsuccessful; the distance between the brig and the boat was rapidly increasing, darkness was coming on, a strong breeze was springing up, and I was in a fair way to be drifted among the breakers, or swept out to sea over the bar!

It happened, fortunately, for me, that a large brig was riding at anchor within a short distance of the Dolphin. This was the very slaver whose captain was so mysteriously assassinated. The mate of the brig was looking around the harbor at the time; he espied my misfortune, and forthwith despatched a boat, pulled by four men, to my assistance. They took me in tow, and, after an hour of hard work, succeeded in towing the boat and myself safely alongside the brig.

I was soundly rated by the mate for my carelessness in allowing the boat to get adrift, and my shipmates were unsparing in their reproaches for my ignorance of the important art of sculling. I was completely crest-fallen; but during the few remaining days we remained in port I applied myself with zeal to gain a practical knowledge of the art, and could soon propel a boat through the water with a single oar over the stern, with as much dexterity as the most accomplished sailor.

A new cable an anchor were brought on board, the wind became favorable, and the rig Dolphin proceeded to sea, bound NOMINALLY for Cayenne. I carried with me, engraven on my memory in characters which have never been effaced, THE ART OR SCULLING A BOAT, and the admonition "NEVER FALL ASLEEP IN YOUR WATCH! "

Chapter VII DELIBERATE ROGUERY

After we reached the blue water, and the wind began to blow and the sea to rise, the old brig, with corresponding motion, tossed and wallowed about as if for a wager. Although while in port her bottom had been calked and graved, the leak, which gave so much trouble the previous voyage, had not been stopped. In a fresh breeze and a head sea the seams would open, and a good "spell at the pump, " every twenty minutes at least, was required to keep her free.

The captain grumbled and swore like a pirate; but this had no perceptible effect in stopping the leak. On the contrary, the more he raved, denouncing the brig as a humbug, and the man who sold her to him as a knave and a swindler, the more the brig leaked. And what was remarkable, after the first ten days, the brig leaked as much in a light breeze and a smooth sea as in rough weather. It was necessary to keep one pump in action the whole time. But when the men, wearied by their unremitting exertions, talked of abandoning the vessel to her fate, and taking refuge in the first vessel they might fall in with, the leak seemed suddenly to diminish, until the bottom of the old craft was comparatively tight!

All this was inexplicable to me, and the mystery caused much philosophical discussion and sage remark among the ship's company. As we were in a part of the ocean which abounded in flying fish, it was the general opinion that the stoppage of the leak was caused by the involuntary action of a flying fish! The theory was, that an unfortunate fish, swimming beneath the bottom of the vessel, in the neighborhood of the crevice through which the water rushed, unsuspicious of danger, was suddenly "sucked in, " and plugged up the hole until it was drawn through or removed by decomposition!

One day the cook, a negro not remarkable for quickness of apprehension or general intelligence, received such an unmerciful beating from the captain that he was unable to attend to his manifold duties, and a portion of them fell to my share. Among them was the task of drawing off the regular allowance of rum, half a pint to each man, and serving it out to the crew. The rum was in the after part of the vessel, beneath the cabin, a place designated as "the run. " It was approached by a scuttle in the cabin floor, and of course could not be explored by any of the crew without the especial permission of the captain or mate. I entered the dark hole, aided by the glimmering light of a lantern, groped my way to the barrel which contained the liquid so highly prized by the sons of Neptune as the liquor of life, the pure AQUA VITAE, and filled my can with the precious fluid.

When I inserted the spigot I still heard a gurgling sound, as of the rush of water through a narrow passage. I listened, and examined further, and became convinced I had discovered the leak. I hastily emerged from "the run, " and passed up on deck. The captain was taking a meridian observation of the sun, when, with a radiant countenance and glistening eye, my whole frame trembling with joy and anticipated triumph, I communicated the important information that I had discovered the leak; it was in the run, could be easily reached, and with a little ingenuity and labor stopped.

Instead of rewarding me for my intelligence and zeal with a smile of approbation and a word of encouragement, the captain gave me a look which petrified me for a time, and would have killed me on the spot if looks could kill in those degenerate days. Seizing me roughly by the shoulder, he addressed me in a hissing, hoarse voice, yet so low that his words, although terribly intelligible to me, could be distinctly heard by no other person: "Mind your own business, my lad, and let the leaks take care of themselves! Go about your work; and if you whisper a syllable of what you have told me to any other person, I WILL THROW YOU OVERBOARD, you officious, intermeddling little vagabond! " And he indorsed his fearful threat by an oath too impious to be transcribed.

This unexpected rebuke, coupled with the fact that I had seen in "the run" the large screw auger which had been missing from the tool-chest for more than a week, furnished a key to unlock the mysteries connected with the leak. The captain, for some purpose which he did not choose to reveal, with the connivance and aid of the mate, had bored holes through the bottom of the brig, and could let in the water at his pleasure!

A few days after this interesting incident which threw a new light on the character of the man to whose charge I had been intrusted, we reached the latitude of Martinico. As the brig now leaked more than ever, and the men, one and all, were worn out with continued pumping, the captain proclaimed to the crew that in consequence of the leaky condition of the brig, he did not consider it safe to proceed further on the voyage to Cayenne, and had determined to make the first port.

This determination met the approbation of all hands, without a dissenting voice. The yards were squared, the helm was put up, the course was given "due west, " and with a cracking trade wind, away we bowled off before it for the Island of Martinico.

Captain Turner, although not remarkable for the strictness of his principles, was a shrewd and intelligent man. On shore he had the semblance of a gentleman. On shipboard he was a good sailor and a skilful navigator. If to his energy, talents, and intelligence had been added a moderate share of honesty, he would probably have been successful in his struggle for wealth, and might have attained respectability. I have often had occasion to note that "a rogue in grain" finds it more difficult to achieve success in life than an honest man. Shakespeare, the great exponent of human nature, makes the unscrupulous Cardinal Wolsey say, when crushed by the hand of royalty, deserted by his friends, and a prey to disgrace and ignominy,

> "Had I but served my God with half the zeal
> I served my king, he would not in mine age
> Have left me naked to mine enemies."

On the morning after this change in our course, the high land of Martinico was seen in the distance; and in the afternoon, before the sun had reached the horizon, we were snugly anchored in the roadstead of St. Pierre. This port, at the bottom of a wide bay, with good anchorage close to the beach, is open to the sea. But being on the lee of the island, it is protected from the trade winds, which, with rare exceptions, blow throughout the year. From a westerly tempest there is no protection, and a hurricane always carries destruction among the shipping.

The reason why the brig was made to spring a leak was now evident. Captain Turner never intended to go to Cayenne, but wished to be justified in the eye of the law in proceeding to what he considered a better market. The non-intercourse act being in operation, American vessels were prohibited from entering an English or a French port, EXCEPTING IN CASES OF DISTRESS. It was therefore determined that the Dolphin should spring a leak, and SEEM in danger of foundering, in order to furnish a pretext for entering the harbor of St. Pierre!

Captain Turner expected to find no American vessels in port, and of course no American produce. He calculated to realize a high price for his cargo, and was surprised and disappointed to ascertain that other Yankees were as shrewd and unscrupulous as himself. The anchorage was thickly sprinkled with American vessels, and the market was overstocked with American produce. These vessels had been driven into St. Pierre by "stress of weather" or "dangerous leaks, " and their commanders cherished as little respect for the revenue laws, or any other mandates of the United States government, as Captain Turner. A protest, carefully worded, and signed and sworn to by the mate and two seamen, and a survey of the vessel made by persons JUDICIOUSLY selected, acted as a protecting shield against any subsequent troublesome interference on the part of the American authorities.

The wisdom of the "Long Embargo, " and the "Non-intercourse Act" is greatly doubted by the statesmen of the present day. Besides crippling our own resources, and paralyzing the whole commercial interest of the United States, a craven spirit was thus manifested on the part of our rulers, which exposed us to insults and outrages from the belligerent powers. And if the policy of these extraordinary measures can be defended, it must be admitted that they were the direct cause of more roguery than would compensate for an immense amount of good.

Having arrived at Martinico in distress, we were precluded from proceeding to any other port in search of a better market. The cargo was sold at prices that would hardly pay the expenses of the voyage. In delivering the lumber, however, an opportunity offered in making up in QUANTITY the deficiency in price, of which our honest captain, following the example, I regret to say, of many of the West India captains OF THOSE DAYS, eagerly availed himself.

The lumber was taken to the shore on large rafts, and hauled up on the beach by men belonging to the brig. The mark on every separate board or plank was called out in a clear voice by the man who dragged it from the raft to the beach, and was noted down by the mate of the brig and a clerk of the mercantile house that purchased the lumber. Those parties were comfortably seated beneath the shade of a tamarind tree, at some distance, smoking cigars and pleasantly conversing. They compared notes from time to time, and there was no difference in their accounts. Every thing on our part was apparently conducted on the strictest principles of honesty. But each sailor having received a hint from the mate, who had been posted by the captain, and a promise of other indulgences, often added from fifteen to twenty per cent, to the mark which had been actually scored by the surveyor on every board or plank. Thus, if a board was MARKED twelve feet, the amount given was fifteen feet; a board that measured only eighteen or twenty feet, would be represented as twenty- five; and sometimes a large, portly-looking board, measuring thirty or thirty-five feet, not only received an addition of eight or ten feet, but was suddenly transformed into a PLANK, which was counted as containing DOUBLE the measurement of a board of the same superficial dimensions. Thus a board actually measuring only thirty feet was passed off upon the unsophisticated clerk of the purchaser as a piece of lumber measuring seventy feet. In this way Captain Turner managed, in what he contended was the usual and proper manner among the Yankees, to make a cargo of lumber "hold out! " Another attempt which this gentleman made to realize a profit on merchandise greater than could be obtained by a system of fair trading was not attended with so favorable a result.

A portion of the cargo of the Dolphin consisted of barrels of salted provisions. This part of the cargo was not enumerated among the articles in the manifest. Captain Turner intended to dispose of it to the shipping in the harbor, and thus avoid the payment of the regular duties. He accordingly sold some ten or a dozen barrels of beef and pork, at a high price, to the captain of an English ship. The transaction, by some unknown means, was discovered by the government officials, who, in a very grave and imposing manner, visited the brig with a formidable posse. They found in the hold a considerable quantity of the salted provisions on which no duty had been paid; this they conveyed on shore and confiscated to the use of His Majesty the King of Great Britain. The brig also was seized, but was subsequently released on payment of a heavy fine.

The merchant vessels lying in St. Pierre are generally moored head and stern, one of the anchors being carried ashore, and embedded in the ground on the beach. A few days after we were thus moored, a large Spanish schooner from the Main hauled in and moored alongside, at the distance of only a few fathoms. Besides the captain, there were several well-dressed personages on board, who appeared to take an interest in the cargo, and lived in the cabin. But harmony did not characterize their intercourse with each other. At times violent altercations occurred, which, being carried on in the Spanish language, were to us neither edifying nor amusing.

One Sunday morning, after the Spanish schooner had been about a week in port, and was nearly ready for sea, a fierce quarrel took place on the quarter-deck of the vessel, which, being attended with loud language, menacing looks, and frantic gesticulations, attracted the attention of all who were within sight or hearing.

Two of the Spaniards, large, good-looking men, were apparently very bitter in their denunciations of each other. They suddenly threw off their coats, which they wrapped around the left arm, and each grasping a long Spanish knife, the original of the murderous "bowie-knife, " — attacked each other with a ferocity terrible to behold. Every muscle seemed trembling and convulsed with passion, their eyes flashed with desperation, and their muscles seemed endued with superhuman power, as they pushed upon each other.

Many furious passes were made, and dexterously parried by the left arm, which was used as a buckler in which to receive the thrusts. At length one of the combatants received a wound in the chest, and his shirt bosom was instantly stained with blood. This served only to rouse him to more desperate exertions if possible; and, like two enraged tigers, these men no longer thought of defending themselves, but were bent only on assailing each other.

Such a combat could not last long. One of the Spaniards sank to the deck, covered with wounds and exhausted with blood, while the victor, who, from the gory condition of his linen, his pallid cheeks, and staggering steps seemed in little better plight, was assisted into the cabin by his companions.

Duels of a similar character, fought on the spot with knives, the left arm protected with a garment used as a shield, were by no means unfrequent among the Spaniards in the New World, and the barbarous custom is not yet obsolete.

The vessel, on whose decks this horrible scene of butchery was enacted, left the harbor on the following day, to the great gratification of her neighbors; and a rusty, ill-looking schooner, called the John, hauled from another part of the roadstead, and took the berth vacated by the Spaniards. Like other American vessels that had been coquetting with the revenue laws, neither the name of the schooner nor the place to which she belonged was painted on her stern. A close intimacy, intended doubtless for their mutual advantage, existed between Captain Turner and the master of the John. The crews of the two vessels also became acquainted, and when the day's work was ended, often assembled on board one of the vessels, and indulged in singing, conversing, skylarking, or spinning yarns.

Swimming was an agreeable and refreshing exercise, in which we often indulged, notwithstanding the harbor of St. Pierre was an open bay in a tropical climate; the very place which the shark would be likely to frequent. It was said, however, that sharks were seldom seen in the bay, and NEVER among the shipping. This statement was regarded as a sufficient assurance of safety; and although I retained a vivid recollection of the dreadful tragedy I had seen enacted a few months before in Demarara, with all the recklessness or a young sailor I hesitated not to indulge freely in this pleasant and healthy exercise in the harbor of St. Pierre.

I was careful, however, to follow the advice of a veteran tar, to KEEP IN MOTION WHILE IN THE WATER. The shark, unless very ferocious and hungry, will not attack a man while he is swimming, or performing other aquatic evolutions. At such times he will remain quiet, close at hand, eyeing his intended victim with an eager and affectionate look; but the moment the unsuspecting swimmer throws himself on his back, begins to tread water, or discontinues the exercise of swimming preparatory to getting on board, this man-eating rascal will pounce on a leg or an arm, drag his victim beneath the surface, and accomplish the dreadful work.

After the many unfavorable specimens of "old salts" I had met with, I was agreeably surprised to find that two of the crew of the John were educated men. One of these was the son of a wealthy merchant of Boston, who lived in the style of a prince at the "North End. " This young sailor had been wild and dissipated, and had lost for a time the confidence of his relatives, and as a matter of course, WENT TO SEA. He made a good sailor; and while I knew him in St. Pierre, and during the subsequent years of his life, his conduct was in every way correct. His conversation was improving, and his chest was well stored with books, which he cheerfully loaned, and to which I was indebted for many happy hours.

The other was an Irishman by birth, prematurely aged, of diminutive stature, and unprepossessing appearance. He had been many years at sea; had witnessed perilous scenes; had fought for his life with the savages on board the Atahualpa on "the north- west coast"; had served in an English man-of-war, from which he escaped by swimming ashore, a distance of several miles, one night while cruising off the island of Antigua. He reached the land completely exhausted more dead than alive and was concealed for a time among the slave habitations on one of the plantations.

Little Jack, as he was familiarly called, was a type of the old sailor of those days, so far as his habits and general conduct was concerned. He was reckless, bold, dissolute, generous, never desponding, ever ready for a drunken frolic or a fight, to do a good deed, plan a piece of mischief, or head a revolt. He seemed to find enjoyment in every change which his strange destiny presented. And this man, who seemed at home in a ship's forecastle, or when mingling with the lowest dregs of society, had been educated at Trinity College, Dublin. He was well read in the classics, and familiar with the writings of the old British poets. He could quote elaborate passages from the best authors, and converse fluently and learnedly on almost any subject.

Notwithstanding his cultivated mind and intellectual powers, which should have placed him in a high position in society, he appeared satisfied with his condition, and aspired to no loftier sphere than that of a common sailor. We often meet with anomalies in the human character, for which it would puzzle the most learned psychologist to account. What strange and sad event had occurred in the early part of that man's career, to change the current of his fortune, and make him contented in a condition so humble, and a slave to habits so degrading? His story, if faithfully told, might furnish a record of ambitious projects and sanguine expectations, followed by blighted hopes which palsied all succeeding exertions, and plunged him into the depths of dissipation and vice.

Captain Turner and the worthy master of the John, the better to conceal their iniquities from the lynx-eyed satellites of the law, agreed to make an exchange of vessels, both having been officially condemned as unseaworthy. For an equivalent, the schooner was to be laden with a cargo, principally of molasses, and properly furnished with stores, provisions, and water, for a passage to the United States by the way of St. Bartholomew. The crews of the two vessels were then to be interchanged, and Captain Turner his mate and crew, were to take up their quarters in the John.

The arrangement was carried into effect; but two of the Dolphin's crew, dissatisfied with the proceedings on board the brig, and thinking matters would not be improved by a transfer to the schooner, and being under no obligation to follow Captain Turner to another vessel, demanded their discharge. In their stead he shipped a boy, about fourteen years of age, whom he had persuaded to run away from an English merchant ship, in which he was an apprentice, and an old Frenchman, who had served many years in the carpenter's gang in a French man-of-war, and who understood hardly a word of the English language.

We sailed from St. Pierre the day after we had taken possession of the schooner, bound directly for St. Bartholomew.

Chapter VIII THE WINDWARD ISLANDS

It is well known that one of the principal reasons for the declaration of war against Great Britain in 1812, were the insults heaped on the American flag, in every sea, by the navy of Great Britain. The British government claimed and exercised THE RIGHT to board our ships, impress their crews when not natives of the United States, examine their cargoes, and subject our citizens navigating the high seas, to inconvenience, detention, and conduct often of an annoying and insulting character. The British government contended that the flag which waved over the decks of our ships should be no protection to our ships or seamen. For years our merchant vessels were compelled to submit to such degrading insults from the navy of Great Britain.

The mode of exercising this "right of search, " so far as relates to the impressment of seamen, I have already had occasion to illustrate, and the incident which I now relate will explain with tolerable clearness the mode in which the British exercised this right in relation to property.

Previously to the war with Great Britain, a profitable trade was carried on between the United States and the English West India Islands. The exports from the islands were limited chiefly to molasses and rum; sugar and coffee being prohibited in American bottoms. According to the British interpretation of the "right to search, " every American vessel which had taken in a cargo in a British, or any other port, was liable to be searched, from the truck to the keelson, by any British cruiser when met with on the high seas. And this inquisitorial process was submitted to as a matter of course, though not without murmurs loud and deep, from those who were immediately exposed to the inconveniences attending this arbitrary exercise of power.

On the afternoon succeeding the day on which the schooner John left Martinico, as we were quietly sailing along with a light breeze, under the lee of the mountainous Island of Gaudaloupe, we saw a large ship at anchor on a bank about a mile from the land, with the British ensign at her peak, and a pennant streaming from her mast-head, sufficient indications that we had fallen in with one of John Bull's cruisers. But Captain Turner, conscious that his schooner was an American vessel, and had been regularly cleared at St. Pierre, with a cargo of rum and molasses, and there being no suspicious circumstances connected with her appearance, her cargo, or her papers, apprehended no detention or trouble from the British man-of-war.

A boat was soon seen to put off from the frigate, and it was not long before it was alongside the John. An officer stepped on deck, and politely asked the privilege of examining the ship's papers. This was accorded. After having ascertained we were from a British port, the officer coolly remarked it would be necessary to take the schooner nearer the land and bring her to anchor, in order to institute a thorough search into the true character of the cargo. He added that the frigate was stationed there for the express purpose of intercepting and overhauling such Yankee vessels as might pass along.

A signal was made to the frigate, and two additional boats were despatched, which took our small vessel in tow, and in less than an hour we found ourselves at anchor, in thirty fathoms of water, within half musket shot of an English man-of-war. The launch was soon alongside, the hatchways were taken off, tackles were rove, and a gang of the frigate's crew went to work breaking out the cargo and hoisting it into the launch. After the launch and other boats were laden, they hoisted the casks on deck, and continued the operations in no gentle manner until they reached the ground tier. They thus examined every cask, but found nothing but molasses and rum.

They then commenced "stowing the cargo, " as they called it; and the hogsheads of molasses were tossed into the hold, and handled as roughly as hogsheads of tobacco. It was about sunset on the following day when the last cask was stowed. The anchor was then weighed, the sails set, and the lieutenant, having put into the hands of the captain a certificate from the commander of the frigate that the schooner had been searched, for the purpose of preventing a repetition of that agreeable ceremony, told him he was at liberty to go where he thought proper, and politely wished him a pleasant voyage.

Our vessel was thus detained twenty-four hours; and in consequence of this detention, the passage to St. Bartholomew was lengthened several days, as a calm commenced soon after we were liberated, which lasted that time. The cargo also received injury from the rough handling of the British tars, insomuch that before we reached St. Bartholomew, several casks had lost nearly all their contents; and if we had been bound directly to the United States, it is probable that a considerable portion of the cargo would have been pumped out with the bilge water.

This is only one of a thousand cases which might be cited to show the PRINCIPLE on which the British acted towards neutral powers on the broad ocean, as well as in the British waters, at that time. The British government, since the war of 1812, have attempted by negotiations to reestablish this principle. But the attempt has been firmly and successfully resisted; and it may be safely predicted that this "right" will never again be claimed by Great Britain, or conceded by the United States.

Our government, which is a government of the people, and supported mainly by commerce, cannot be too vigilant and firm in its endeavors to protect the persons and property of our citizens on the ocean against the oppression or outrages of any naval power. Let us, as an honorable, high-minded nation, cordially cooperate with any other nation in attempts to check and destroy the traffic in slaves, so revolting in its character, which is carried on between Africa and places on this continent. Let us be a party to any honorable treaty having this for its object; but let us never listen to the idea that the American flag, waving at the peak or masthead of an American vessel, is no protection to the property on board, or the liberties of the passengers and crew.

Captain Turner promptly availed himself of the permission so graciously given by the commander of the British cruiser, and we proceeded on our way to St. Bartholomew. There is probably no sailing in the world more pleasant and interesting than among the group of beautiful islands reaching from Trinidad to St. Bartholomew. With a smooth sea and a gentle, refreshing trade wind, as the vessel glides past these emerald gems of the ocean, a picturesque and ever-varying landscape is produced, as if by the wand of some powerful enchanter. Grenada, the Grenadines, St. Vincent, St. Lucia, Martinico, Dominica, Guadaloupe, Montserrat, Saba, St. Kitts, Nevis, and St. Bartholomew, all seem to pass in swift succession before the eye of the observer.

These islands are all, with the exception of St. Bartholomew, more or less cultivated, but being mountainous and of volcanic origin, the productive lands lie on the base of the mountains, or on the spacious intervals and valleys near the sea shore. Studded with plantations, each of which resembles a little village planned by some skilful landscape gardener; with crystal streams dashing down the mountain sides; with dense forests covering the high lands and mountain summits; with bays and indentations along the coast, each with a thriving village at the extremity, defended by fortifications; with ships at anchor in the roadsteads, and droghers coasting along the shores; with an atmosphere richly laden with sweets, and all the interesting associations connected with a tropical climate; these islands furnish an array of attractions which are hardly surpassed in the Western Hemisphere. The beautiful description in the song of Mignon, in the "Wilhelm Meister" of Goethe, of a land of fruits and flowers, will apply with singular felicity to these Windward Islands:

> "Know'st thou the land where the pale citron grows,
> And the gold orange through dark foliage glows?
> A soft wind flutters from the deep blue sky,
> The myrtle blooms, and towers the laurel high.
> Know'st thou it well?"

I have sometimes wondered why the capitalists of New England, in search of recreation and pleasure for themselves and families instead of crossing the Atlantic to visit the oft-described and stale wonders of the Old World, do not charter a yacht or a packet schooner, and with a goodly company take a trip to the West Indies, sail around and among these islands, visit places of interest, accept the hospitality of the planters, which is always freely bestowed, and thus secure a fund of rational enjoyment, gratify a laudable curiosity in relation to the manners and habits of the people of the torrid zone, and bring away a multitude of agreeable impressions on their minds, which will keep vivid and fresh the remainder of their lives.

After leaving Martinico, we found, on broaching our provisions, that they were of bad quality, of the worst possible description. The bread, deposited in bags, was of a dark color, coarse texture, and French manufacture. It must have been of an inferior kind when new and fresh, and a long tarry in a tropical climate was not calculated to improve its character. Besides being mouldy, it was dotted with insects, of an unsightly appearance and unsavory flavor. The quality of the beef was, if possible, worse than that of the bread, and we had no other kinds of provisions. Before we arrived at St. Bartholomew the water began to give signs of impurity. The casks, stowed in the half- deck, had been filled through a molasses hose. In all likelihood, the hose had not been cleansed, and the saccharine property of the molasses mingling with the water in that hot climate had caused a fermentation, the effect of which was nauseous to the taste and unpleasant to the eye. We consoled ourselves, however, with the idea that the passage would be a short one, only a few days, and that better provisions would be furnished when we reached St. Bartholomew.

The Island of St. Bartholomew is a mountainous rock, three or four miles in diameter, with here and there a few patches of verdure, but destitute of trees or cultivated lands. The inhabitants are dependent on the neighboring islands, and importations from distant countries, for the means of sustaining life. Even water for drinking and culinary purposes is brought from St. Martin, Nevis, or St. Kitts. It has a snug harbor on the western side, easy of access, in which many vessels can lie safely moored, excepting in a hurricane. Indeed, there is hardly a harbor in the Windward Islands, north of Grenada, where a vessel can be secure during the hurricane months. These tempests, when blowing from any quarter, seem to defy all the efforts of man to withstand their violence; twist the ships from their anchors, force them on the reefs or drive them out to sea, sometimes without ballast or the fraction of a crew.

It may appear singular that St. Bartholomew, with no productions whatever, and lying almost in the midst of the most fertile and productive of the Windward Islands, should nevertheless have been a place of great trade, and at certain times the most important depot for merchandise in those islands. St. Bartholomew has belonged to Sweden during the whole of the present century; and Sweden having been occasionally exempted form the wars waged against each other by England and France, this island, of no intrinsic value in itself, became a sort of neutral ground; a port where all nations could meet on friendly terms; where traders belonging to England, France, the United States, or other powers, could deposit or sell their goods, purchase West India produce, and transact business of any description.

At the time to which I refer, in 1810, the "Orders in Council" of England, and the "Berlin and Milan Decrees" of Napoleon, were in force. As a counteracting stroke of policy, the Non-intercourse Act, to which I have already alluded, was passed by our government, and the neutral port of St. Bartholomew suddenly became a place of immense importance. When we entered the harbor in the John, it was with difficulty that a berth could be found; at least two hundred and fifty vessels, a large portion of which were Americans, were in port, discharging or taking in cargo. Captain Turner found no trouble in selling his molasses. He dared not run the risk of taking it to the United States, lest his roguery should be discovered through some flaw in his papers, and his vessel and cargo seized by revenue officers. He retained only a few casks of rum, sufficient to pay port charges, and prepared to sail for a southern port.

Shortly before we arrived at St. Bartholomew, a ship belonging to Connecticut, in consequence of some irregularity in her proceedings, was seized by the authorities and taken possession of by a guard of ten or a dozen soldiers. The ship was about ready for sea when this event took place; and on the following day, according to a preconcerted plan between the captain and Mr. Arnold, the supercargo, the officers and crew rose upon the soldiers, deprived them of their arms, and forced them below. Then they quietly slipped the cables, and let the ship drift gradually out of the harbor, until past the shipping, when every sail was instantly spread, as if by magic, and before the mystified garrison of the fort could understand the curious manoeuver, realize the audacity of the Yankees, and get ready their guns, the ship was beyond the reach of their shot. In the offing the ship fell in with one of the large boats trading between St. Bartholomew and St. Martin, and put the soldiers on board, who were thus promptly returned to their barracks.

The Swedish authorities were justly indignant at such high-handed proceedings. Arnold remained behind to transact some unfinished business, but was arrested and thrown into prison, where he remained several weeks. Seeing no prospect of being released, he feigned insanity, and acted the madman to the life; insomuch that the authorities were glad to discharge him on condition that his friends would send him from the island.

During the year 1809, a French privateer, called the Superior, a large schooner of the "Baltimore pilot boat" model, was the terror of the British in the Caribbean seas. The pilot boats built at Baltimore, to cruise off the mouth of the Chesapeake, have ever been celebrated for their sailing qualities, especially their ability to beat to windward; and vessels of larger size than the pilot boats, reaching to the capacity of three hundred tons, but built according to this peculiar Baltimore model, were for many years acknowledged the swiftest class of sailing vessels in any country at any period. At what particular time this model was introduced, it may be difficult to ascertain; but as early as the period to which I refer, the term "Baltimore clipper" was a familiar term. Numbers of them were sold to individuals residing in ports belonging to the belligerent powers, and commissioned as privateers; others were purchased for slavers; and during the wars carried on by Spain and Portugal with their provinces in South America, the "Baltimore clippers" made a conspicuous figure, being fitted out as privateers and manned in the ports of a nation which held out to them the olive branch of peace.

The privateer Superior was commanded by a brave and energetic Frenchman, who took a singular pleasure in inflicting injuries on British commerce. This privateer, fitted out at Port Royal in Martinico, was said to have been the fastest vessel every known among the islands, and her commander laughed to scorn the attempts made to capture him by the finest vessels in the English navy. Indeed, the Superior seemed to be ubiquitous. One day she would be seen hovering off the island of Antigua, and after pouncing on an unfortunate English ship, would take out the valuables and specie, if there were any on board, transfer the officers and crew to a drogher bound into the harbor, and then scuttle the vessel. On the day following, a ship would be seen on fire off Montserrat or St. Kitts, which would prove to have been an English merchantman captured and destroyed by the Superior; and perhaps, a few days afterwards, this privateer would be pursuing a similar career on the shores of Barbadoes, far to windward, or levying contributions from the planters on the coasts of Grenada or Trinidad.

Indeed, the sailing qualities of this privateer were a marvel to all "old salts"; and many an honest man who had never heard of a "Baltimore pilot boat built" craft, was sorely puzzled to account for the success of the Superior in avoiding the many traps that had been set by the long-headed officers of the British ships on that station. By many it was believed that the French captain had unlawful dealings with the enemy of mankind, and for the pleasure of annoying the English, and the gratification of filling his pockets with the spoils of the enemies of France, had signed away his soul!

The company of men-of-war seemed to be no protection against capture by this privateer. A fleet of merchantmen, convoyed by several armed ships, would be intruded on during the night, and one or more of them captured without alarm, and then rifled, and scuttled or burned. On one occasion, after combined efforts had been made to capture the Superior, and it was believed that vessel had been driven from those seas, a homeward bound fleet of merchantmen, on the first night after leaving Antigua, was approached by this privateer, and in the course of a couple of hours three different ships, in different stations of the squadron, had been captured, plundered, and fired by that indefatigable enemy of the English.

At last, one after another, every French port in the islands was taken by the British, and there was no longer a nook belonging to France to which this privateer could resort for protection, supplies, or repairs, It was furthermore rumored that this vessel was not regularly commissioned; and that, if captured by an enemy, the officers and crew to a man, and the captain more especially, would be hanged at the yard arm, AS PIRATES, without any very formal process of law.

The privateer was by this time well laden with spoils, having on board, in silks, specie, gums, and bullion, property to the amount of nearly a million of dollars. One fine morning, a British sloop-of-war, cruising between Nevis and St. Bartholomew, was astonished at beholding the Superior, that "rascally French Privateer, " as well known in those seas as the Flying Dutchman off the Cape of Good Hope, come down from the windward side of St. Bartholomew under easy sail, pass round the southern point of the island, hoist the tri-colored flag, as if by way of derision, and boldly enter the harbor belonging to the Swedish government, and a neutral port.

It was not many hours before the sloop-of-war, having hauled her wind, was off the harbor, lying off and on; and the captain, in full uniform, his mouth filled with menaces and denunciations of British vengeance, and his cranium well crammed with quotations from Vattel, Grotius, Puffendorf, and other venerable worthies, was on his way to the shore in a state of great excitement. When he reached the landing, he found only the HULL of the privateer, with the spars and rigging. The officers and crew had already disappeared, each carrying off his portion of the spoils. The captain was not visible; but it was said he left the island a few days afterwards for the United States, under an assumed name, whence he subsequently proceeded to France, with an immense amount of property, which the fortune of war had transferred from British subjects to his pockets. The schooner was hauled up to the head of the careenage, and on examination it appeared that every part of the vessel had been so strained by carrying sail, and so much damage had been done to her planks and timbers by worms, that she was good for nothing. The spars, sails, and rigging were sold; but the hull, which soon filled with water, remained for years, admired by every genuine sailor as the most perfect model of a fast-sailing vessel that could be devised by the ingenuity of man.

When the schooner John was nearly ready for sea, my uncle, Captain Tilton, whom I had left in Charleston, arrived in port in a clipper schooner called the Edwin. He was bound for Mobile, where he intended establishing a mercantile house in connection with a gentleman named Waldron, a native of Portsmouth, who had resided several years in Charleston. I had one brief interview with him, but no opportunity offered of entering into the details of my unenviable position on board the John. On a hint from me that I was dissatisfied, and should not object to accompany him in the Edwin, he gravely shook his head, and remarked that such a course would be unusual and improper; that he was about to retire from the sea; that it would be best for me to stick by Captain Turner, in whom I should always find a friend, and perform the whole voyage I had undertaken.

He left the port on the following day, bound for the Gulf of Mexico, and I never saw him again. He encountered a "norther" on the coast of Cuba, and the Edwin struck on the Colorado Reef, and all on board perished!

It was believed that Captain Turner, as a matter of course, would procure a sufficient quantity of good water, and some tolerable provisions for the forecastle hands, before we proceeded on our voyage. But our worthy captain, who was a great worshipper of the "almighty dollar, " in whatever shape it appeared, had no intentions of the kind. Water was scarce, and cost ten dollars a cask. Beef and bread also cost money, and we left St. Bartholomew with only the wretched apology for provisions and water which were put on board in Martinico.

Probably no American vessel ever left a port with such miserable provisions for a voyage. Bread, beef, and water constituted our variety. We had no rice, beans, Indian meal, fish, or any other of the numerous articles usually furnished by merchants for the sustenance of the sailors who navigate their ships; and SUCH beef, bread, and water as we were doomed to live upon for three successive weeks after we left St. Bartholomew, was surely never prescribed by the most rigid anchorite and exacting devotee as a punishment for the sins of a hardened transgressor.

Chapter IX ARRIVAL AT SAVANNAH

Captain Turner, on being urged to provide some palatable food and drink, declared with an oath that he did not select the provisions of fill the water; that this was done by others who knew what they were about; that every thing on board was good enough for us, and if we did not like it we might starve and BE HANGED!

This was a clincher it ended the argument. There was nothing left for us but to put the best face, even if it should be a wry face, on troubles we could not overcome or diminish.

In a choice of food there is a wide difference in taste. One people will regard as a luxury a viand or condiment which is repugnant to another. Locusts have been used from time immemorial for food by different tribes of Arabs. Snail soup was once regarded in Europe as a delicious dish. In the West Indies and South America the guano, a species of lizard, is devoured with gusto. Bird's nests command enormous prices as an edible in China, where also dogs and cats are ordinary food. At Rome camels' heels were a tidbit for an epicure. Whale's tongues ranked among the delicacies feasted on by the Europeans in the middle centuries. The bark of the palm tree is the abiding place of a large worm, which is sought for, roasted, and devoured as a delicacy. In Brazil, a monkey pie is a favorite dish, and the head of the monkey is made to protrude and show its teeth above the crust by way of ornament. Indeed, habit, we are told, will reconcile a person to unsavory diet. But neither habit nor necessity could reconcile me to the food and drink which, to sustain life, I was compelled to swallow on board the John.

The water, owing to causes to which I have already alluded, was exceedingly offensive to the palate and the olfactories. It was also slimy and ropy; and was drank only as a means and a wretched one of prolonging life. For the inmates of the cabin the water was boiled or diluted with brandy, which, in a slight degree, lessened its disgusting flavor. But this was a luxury that was denied the seamen, who had to quaff it in all its richness.

Our beef, in quality, was on a par with the water. It was Irish beef, so called, wretchedly poor when packed; but having been stored in a hot climate, probably for years, it had lost what little excellence it once possessed, and acquired other qualities of which the packer never dreamed. The effluvia arising from a barrel of this beef, when opened, was intolerable. When boiled in clean salt water the strong flavor was somewhat modified, and it was reduced by shrinkage at least one half. The palate could not become reconciled to it; and the longer we lived upon it the less we liked it.

But our bread! What shall I say of our bread? I have already spoken of it as mouldy and ANIMATED. On several occasions, in the course of my adventures, I have seen ship bread which could boast of those abominable attributes, remnants of former voyages put on board ships by unfeeling skinflints, to be "used up" before the new provisions were broached, but I never met with any which possessed those attributes to the extent which was the case on board the schooner John. Although many years have passed since I was supported and invigorated by that "staff of life, " I cannot even now think of it without a shudder of disgust! On placing a biscuit by my side when seated upon deck, it would actually be put in motion by some invisible machinery, and if thrown on the hot coals in order to destroy the living works within, and prevent the biscuit from walking off, it would make an angry sputtering wondrous to hear!

Such was the character of our food and drink on our passage to the United States. It initiated me, even at the beginning of my sea-going career, into the most repulsive mysteries of a seaman's life. And whenever, in subsequent voyages, I have been put upon poor diet, I mentally contrasted it with the wretched fare during my second voyage to sea, smacked my lips, and called it luxury.

Steering to the northward we passed near the Island of Sombrero, glided from the Caribbean Sea into the Atlantic Ocean, and wended our way towards the Carolinas.

Sombrero is an uninhabited island, a few miles only in circumference. It offers to the dashing waves on every side a steep, craggy cliff, from thirty to fifty feet high. Its surface is flat, and entirely destitute of vegetation; and at a distance, a fanciful imagination can trace, in the outline of the island, a faint resemblance to the broad Spanish hat, called a "sombrero, " from which it takes its name.

This island, as well as all the other uninhabited islands in that part of the world, has ever been a favorite resort for birds, as gulls of several varieties, noddies, man-of-war birds, pelicans, and others. It has recently been ascertained that Sombrero is entitled to the proud appellation of "a guano island, " and a company has been organized, consisting of persons belonging to New England, for the purpose of carrying off its rich deposits, which are of a peculiarly valuable character, being found beneath a bed of coral limestone several feet in thickness, and must consequently possess all the advantages which antiquity can confer.

It was on this island, many years ago, that an English brig struck in a dark night, while "running down the trades. " The officers and crew, frightened at the dashing of the breakers and the gloomy aspect of the rocks which frowned upon them from above, made their escape on shore in "double quick time, " some of them marvellously thinly clad, even for a warm climate. As soon as they had safely landed on the cliffs, and congratulated each other on their good fortune, the brig, by a heave of the sea, became disengaged from the rocks, and floating off, drifted to leeward, to the great mortification of the crew, and was fallen in with a day or two afterwards, safe and sound, near Anegada Reef, and carried into St. Thomas. The poor fellows, who manifested such alacrity in quitting "a sinking ship, " suffered greatly from hunger and exposure. They erected a sort of flagstaff, on which they displayed a jacket as a signal of distress, and in the course of a few days were taken off by an American vessel bound to Santa Cruz.

The feeling which prompts a person, in the event of a sudden danger at sea, to quit his own vessel and look abroad for safety, appears to be instinctive. In cases of collision, portions of the crews are sometimes suddenly exchanged; and a man will find himself, unconscious of, an effort, on board a strange vessel, then arouse himself, as if from an unquiet sleep, and return to his ship as rapidly as he left her.

It sometimes happens that vessels, which have run into each other in the night time, separate under circumstances causing awkward results. The ship Pactolus, of Boston, bound from Hamburg through the English channel, while running one night in a thick fog near the Goodwin Sands, fell in with several Dutch galliots, lying to, waiting for daylight, and while attempting to steer clear of one, ran foul of another, giving the Dutchman a terrible shaking and carrying away one of the masts. The captain, a young man, was below, asleep in his berth, dreaming, it may be, of happy scenes in which a young and smiling "jung frow" formed a prominent object. He rushed from his berth, believing his last hour was come, sprang upon deck, and seeing a ship alongside, made one leap into the chainwales of the strange vessel, and another one over the rail to the deck. A moment afterwards the vessels separated; the galliot was lost sight of in the fog, and Mynheer was astonished to find himself, while clad in the airy costume of a shirt and drawers, safely and suddenly transferred from his comfortable little vessel to the deck of an American ship bound across the Atlantic.

The poor fellow jabbered away, in his uncouth native language, until his new shipmates feared his jaws would split asunder. They furnished him with garments, entertained him hospitably, and on the following day landed him on the pier at Dover.

We met with no extraordinary occurrences on our passage to the United States until we reached the Gulf Stream, noted for heavy squalls, thunder storms, and a turbulent sea, owing to the effect on the atmosphere produced by the difference of temperatures between the water in the current and the water on each side.

The night on which we entered the Gulf Stream, off the coast of the Carolinas, the weather was exceedingly suspicious. Dark, double-headed clouds hung around the horizon, and although the wind was light, a hurricane would not have taken us by surprise at any moment; and as the clouds rose slowly with a threatening aspect, no calculation could be made on which side the tempest would come. The lightnings illumined the heavens, serving to render the gloom more conspicuous, and the deep-toned rumblings of the thunder were heard in the distance.

At eight o'clock, when the watch was called, the schooner was put under short canvas, and due preparations were made for any change in the weather. The starboard watch was then told to go below, but to "be ready for a call. " This watch, all told, consisted of the old French carpenter and myself, and we gladly descended into the narrow, leaky, steaming den, called the forecastle, reposing full confidence in the vigilance of our shipmates in the larboard watch, and knowing that if the ship should be dismasted, or even capsized, while we were quietly sleeping below, it would be through no fault of ours, and we could not be held responsible. In five minutes after the forescuttle was closed, we were snugly ensconced in our berths, oblivious of squalls and gales, and all the disagreeable duties of making and taking in sail on a wet and stormy night, enjoying a comfortable nap and dreaming of happy times on shore.

We were soon aroused from our dreams, and brought back to the realities of life, by the rough voice of my old shipmate, Eastman, yelling out in tones which would have carried terror to the soul of an Indian warrior, "ALL HANDS AHOY! Tumble up, lads! Bear a hand on deck! " I jumped out of my berth, caught my jacket in one hand, and my tarpaulin in the other, and hastened on deck, closely followed by the carpenter, and also the cook, whose office being little better than a sinecure, he was called upon whenever help was wanted. The wind was blowing a gale, and the rain was falling in heavy drops, and the schooner was running off to the southward at a tremendous rate, with the wind on the quarter.

"There is a waterspout after us, " exclaimed Captain Turner, as we made our appearance, and we must give it the slip, or be grabbed by Davy Jones. Be alive for once! If that fellow comes over us, he will capsize, perhaps sink us! Stand by! "

I looked astern, and saw, about a point on the larboard quarter, a black, misshapen body, which seemed to reach from the heavens down to the surface of the sea. Although the night was dark as Erebus, this mass could easily be distinguished from the thick clouds which shut out the stars, and covered the whole surface of the sky. It moved towards us with fearful rapidity, being much fleeter in the race than our little schooner.

The captain, who, to do him justice, was not only a good sailor, but cool and resolute in the hour of danger, would fix his eye one moment on the waterspout, and the next on the compass, in order to ascertain the course which this unwelcome visitor was taking. A minute had scarcely elapsed, during which every man breathed harder and quicker than he was wont to do, being in a state of agonizing suspense, when Captain turner decided on his plan of operations; and it was time, for the waterspout was but a few hundred yards off, and came rushing towards us like a ferocious monster intent on mischief.

"Stand by to gibe! " cried the captain. "Hard a-port your helm! Look out for that foresheet. " As the schooner fell off and again came gradually to the wind, she shot across the hawse of the waterspout, which swept closely along under our stern, almost spattering the water in our very faces, and tearing and roaring like the cataract of Niagara!

We watched its progress with thrilling interest, and when it got upon our quarter, and we were convinced it could not come on board, Captain Turner called out in exulting tones, "We have dodged it handsomely boys, and cheated Davy Jones of his prey this time. Hurrah! "

It is hardly necessary to say we all breathed easier as the waterspout sailed majestically away, and in a few minutes was out of sight. This was one of those occurrences which might well shake the nerves of the most firm and courageous tar. Indeed, the whole scene on that memorable night was far more akin to the sublime than the beautiful. There were the heavy black clouds piled upon each other near the horizon, or hanging loosely and dripping overhead, portending a fearful conflict among the elements; there was the wind, which came in fitful gusts, whistling and singing in mournful cadence among the blocks and rigging; there was the agitated and furrowed face of the ocean, which had been lashed to fury by successive storms, and lighted up in every direction by innumerable brilliant phosphorescent particles, in which, it is well known, the waters of the Gulf Stream abound; there were the rolling echoes of the thunder, and the zig zag, chain lightning, which every few seconds enveloped the heavens and the ocean in a frightful livid garment; and, as if to cap the climax, there was the giant column, darker, much darker than the dark clouds around us, reaching from those clouds and resting on the waters, and threatening to sweep our whole ship's company into eternity.

On the day succeeding our adventure with the waterspout, the wind died away, although the heavy clouds still hung about the horizon. The schooner, lying in the trough of the sea, was fearfully uneasy; but towards night a regular gale of wind commenced, and our vessel was hove to under a double-reefed foresail. It was near the close of the first watch when the fore-topsail getting loose on the lee yard arm, I went aloft to secure it. After I had accomplished this work, I lingered a few minutes on the yard to enjoy the beauty of the storm. The waves, urged by the fury of the gale, were breaking around us in majestic style; the schooner was rocking to and fro, and occasionally took a lee lurch, which made every timber in her bottom quiver.

I had finished my survey of the wind and weather, and was about to descend to the deck, when I carelessly cast my eyes aloft, and there beheld a sight which struck terror to my soul. On the very summit of the main-topmast on the truck itself, was A HUGE BALL OF FIRE! It seemed a mass of unearthly light of livid hue, which shed a dismal radiance around. The rain fell at the time, but quenched it not; and the heaviest gusts of wind served neither to extinguish it, nor increase its brilliancy. It kept its station unmoved, shining terribly through the storm, like some dread messenger, sent by a superior power to give warning of impending disaster.

I was appalled with terror at the sight. Although by no means credulous or superstitious, I could hardly resist the belief that this globe of fire, which appeared thus suddenly in the midst of a furious storm, at dead of night, and on a spot where it could not have been placed or kindled by the hand of man, was of supernatural origin. I shuddered with fear; a strange giddiness came over me; and I had hardly strength to cling to the shrouds as I descended to the deck.

I pointed out the object of my terror to my watch-mate, the French carpenter, who gazed at it earnestly, and then, turning to me, nodded his head emphatically two or three times, like a Chinese mandarin, and grinned. This pantomimic display was intended to convey much meaning more than I could interpret. But it convinced me that the carpenter was familiar with such sights, which, perhaps, were not very remarkable, after all.

When the watch was called, I pointed out the fiery ball to Eastman, and to Mr. Adams, the mate, and learned that the object which gave me such a fright was not of very unfrequent occurrence during a gale of wind. It was known among seamen by the name of CORPOSANT, or COMPLAISANT, being a corruption of "cuerpo santo, " the name it received from the Spaniards. It is supposed to be formed of phosphorescent particles of jelly, blown from the surface of the water during a storm, and which, clinging to the rigging, gradually accumulate, and ascend until they reach the truck. The mass remains there for a time, and then disappears. Sometimes it is seen on the topsail yard or at the end of the flying jib-boom.

A few days afterwards, having crossed "the Gulf, " we made the land off the mouth of Savannah River; saw Tybee Lighthouse; took a pilot, and proceeded up to the city. When we left St. Bartholomew, it was given out that we were bound to Wilmington; on the passage we spoke a vessel, and Captain Turner, on being questioned, said we were bound to Charleston. For good and sufficient reasons, known to himself, he did not think proper to gratify idle curiosity.

But while our shrewd captain was dexterously managing to deceive the revenue officers, and obtain all the advantages of the fair trader, a circumstance occurred through his own ignorance or neglect, which brought about the very catastrophe he was taking such pains to avoid.

The cargo, as I have stated, consisted of only a few puncheons of rum. A permit was obtained, and one morning they were landed on the wharf. At that time there was a law of the United States which forbade the importation of rum in casks containing less than ninety gallons. The officer appointed to gauge the casks that were landed from the schooner ascertained that one of them measured only seventy-eight gallons. He proclaimed the fact, and hastened to the Custom House to notify the collector. In the mean time, Mr. Howard, the merchant who transacted business for Captain Turner, heard of the affair, and, accompanied by the captain, came on board.

Instead of acknowledging an involuntary violation of law, and explaining to the collector the cause of the error, these gentlemen very imprudently ordered the objectionable cask to be rolled in on deck, and all hands were set at work to transfer its contents to an empty water cask, which was of greater capacity than ninety gallons. The trick might have succeeded had the revenue officers allowed sufficient time. The work was commenced, and the liquor was running out, making a gurgling noise, when down came the collector with a numerous posse at his heels!

We were caught in the very act. A war of words ensued; but the explanations given under the attendant circumstances were so unsatisfactory, that the vigilant chief of the customs clapped his broad mark on the mainmast, and seized the vessel and the unfortunate cask of rum in the name and behalf of the United States!

Chapter X "HOME! SWEET HOME! "

The afternoon of the day on which we arrived in Savannah, after the vessel was secured to the wharf, and the decks put in proper condition, the four half-starved individuals, composing the crew of the schooner John, gayly stepped ashore, and proceeded in quest of some wholesome and palatable food. Our pockets were not well lined, and we sought not for luxuries; but we yearned for a good, full meal, which would satisfy our appetite a blessing we had not enjoyed for several weeks.

After passing through a couple of streets, we came to a humble but neat-looking dwelling house, with an apology for a garden in front. Tables and seats were arranged beneath some trees; "spruce beer" was advertised for sale, but there were indications that other kinds of refreshments could be obtained. The place wore a comfortable aspect. We nodded smilingly to each other, as much as to say, "This will do! " entered the gateway, which stood invitingly open, and took seats at a table.

Eastman, who was a native of New Hampshire, had resided many years on a farm, and knew what was good living, inquired boldly of the master of the establishment if he could furnish each of us with a capacious bowl of bread and milk. The man replied that he could. On inquiring the price, we found, to our great joy, that it was within our means. He was told to bring it along; and in a few minutes, which seemed an age, the bread and milk were placed before us.

The milk was cool, and of good quality. The bread was in the form of rolls, newly baked, and manufactured of the finest flour. The aspect of these "refreshments" was of the most tempting character! To our excited imaginations, they equalled the nectar and ambrosia which furnished the feasts on Mount Olympus. We did not tarry long to gaze upon their beauties, or contemplate their excellence. Each one broke a roll into his basin of milk, seized a spoon, and without speaking a word, commenced operations with exemplary energy, with cheeks glowing with excitement, and eyes glistening with pleasure; while our good-natured host gazed in wonder on our proceedings, and grinned approbation!

Our gratification was complete. We returned to the schooner in better spirits and in better health, after having partaken of this invigorating meal; and although I have since dined with epicures, and been regaled with delicious food prepared in the most artistic style, I never tasted a dish which seemed so grateful to my palate, which so completely suffused my whole physical system with gratification bordering on ecstasy, as that humble bowl of bread and milk in Savannah.

The schooner having been seized by the government for unlawful transactions, the crew were compelled to wait until the trial took place before they could receive the wages due for their services. If the vessel should not be condemned, they were to look to Captain Turner for their pay. But on the other hand, if the vessel should be confiscated, the United States authorities would be obliged to pay the wages due at the time the seizure took place. In the mean time we were furnished with board, such as it was, and lodging in the schooner, and awaited with impatience the result of the trial.

Captain Turner, being a shrewd business man, was not idle during this intermission. Having reasons to believe his vessel would be condemned, he resolved that the government authorities should obtain possession of nothing more than the bare hull and spars. Under cover of the night he stripped the schooner of the cables and anchors, the running rigging, the spare spars, water casks, boats, sails, cabin furniture, blocks, compasses, and handspikes. The government got "a hard bargain, " when the naked hull of this old worn-out craft came into their hands.

One beautiful morning while lying at the wharf in Savannah, two barges, each having its stern-seats occupied by three well- dressed gentlemen, looking as serious and determined as if bent on some important business, left the landing place astern of the schooner, and proceeded rapidly down the river. A throng of inquisitive observers, who knew the nature of their errand, collected ere they started from the wharf, and gazed intently on the boats until the intervening marshes concealed them from view.

These gentlemen were to act as principals, seconds, and surgeons, in a duel for which all proper arrangements had been made. At a ball the evening before, a dispute had arisen between two high- spirited youths, connected with highly-respectable families, in relation to the right of dancing with a beautiful girl, the belle of the ball-room.

Irritating and insulting language was indulged in by both parties; a challenge was given and promptly accepted. They proceeded in the way I have related to the South Carolina bank of the river, there to settle the controversy by gunpowder logic, and shoot at each other until one or both parties should be fully satisfied.

Having seen the duellists fairly embarked, I felt a deep interest in the result, and eagerly watched for the return of the barges. In the course of little more than an hour, one of the boats was seen ascending the river, and rapidly approached the wharf. One of the principals, followed by his friend, stepped ashore with a triumphant air, as if he had done a noble deed, and walked up the wharf. But no satisfactory information could be obtained respecting the result of the duel.

In about half a hour the other boat made its appearance. It moved slowly along, propelled by only a couple of oars. The reason for this was soon explained by the sight of a man, extended on the thwarts, and writhing with pain. This proved to be one of the duellists, who was shot in the groin at the second fire, and dangerously wounded. The boat reached the landing place, and the surgeon and the second both went up the wharf in search of some means of transporting the unfortunate man to his home. Meanwhile he lay upon his rude couch exposed to the nearly vertical rays of the sun; his only attendant a negro, who brushed away the flies which annoyed him. His features were of a deadly pallor; he breathed with difficulty, and appeared to suffer much from pain.

Some ten or fifteen minutes elapsed ere the friends of the wounded man returned, bringing a litter, mattress, and bearers. He was too ill to be conveyed through the streets in a coach. A mournful procession was formed, and he was thus carried, in a bleeding and dying condition, to his relatives, a mother and sisters, from whom he had parted a few hours before, in all the strength and vigor of early manhood.

As I gazed upon this wounded man, the absurdity of the custom of duelling, as practised among civilized nations, struck me in all its force. One scene like this, taken in connection with the attendant circumstances, is more convincing than volumes of logic, or a thousand homilies. For a few hasty words, exchanged in a moment of anger, two men, instructed in the precepts of the Christian religion, professing to be guided by true principles of honesty and honor, who had ever borne high characters for worth, and perhaps,

IN CONSEQUENCE of the elevated position they hold among respectable men, meet hy appointment in a secluded spot, and proceed in the most deliberate manner to take each other's lives to commit MURDER a crime of the most fearful magnitude known among nations, and denounced as such by the laws of man and the laws of God.

In due time the fate of the schooner John was decided. The vessel was condemned, and the crew received notice to bring in their bills for the amount of wages due. Captain Turner kindly offered to make out my account, and shortly afterwards handed me my bill against the United States government for services on board, the amount of which overwhelmed me with astonishment.

"There is surely a mistake in this bill, sir, " said I; "the amount is far more than I am entitled to. You forget I shipped for only fifteen dollars a month, and including my advanced month's pay, I have already received a considerable portion of my wages. "

"I forget nothing of the kind, Hawser, " replied the captain, with a benevolent smile. "You may just as well receive fifty dollars as five and twenty. The government will be none the poorer for it. "

"But, sir, will it be RIGHT for me to carry in an account so greatly exceeding in amount what is my due? "

"My lad, " replied the captain, a little embarrassed, "You must not be so scrupulous in these trifling matters, or you will never make your way through the world at any rate you will never do for a sailor. The rest of the men make no objections to putting a little money in their pockets, and why should YOU? Even Mr. Adams, the mate, will receive double the amount of money which rightfully belongs to him! "

"But, sir, " I replied, greatly shocked at this intelligence, and my features undoubtedly expressed my abhorrence of this strange system of ethics, "do you expect me to go before a magistrate and take a solemn oath that the account you have jut put into my hands is a just and true one? You surely would not ADVISE me to commit such a crime! "

The captain's face glowed like a firebrand, and his eyes sparkled with wrath, as he loudly exclaimed, "What difference does it make to you, you ungrateful cur, whether the account is true or false, so long as you get your money? Bring none of your squeamish objections here. Either take the account as I have made it out, and swear to it, without flinching, or" — and here he swore an oath too revolting to transcribe "not a cent of money shall you receive. "

He stepped ashore, and walked with rapid strides up the wharf. I went forward, and seating myself on the windlass, burst into tears!

It struck me as hard and unjust that I should be deprived of my well-earned wages, unless on condition of committing an unworthy act, at which my soul revolted. My decision, however, was taken. Although the loss of my money would have subjected me to inconvenience perhaps distress I resolved to submit to any ills which poverty might inflict, rather than comply with the wishes and advice of this unprincipled man, who should have acted towards me as a faithful monitor and guide.

I remained in this disconsolate condition for about an hour, when Captain Turner returned on board. As he stepped leisurely over the gangway, he greeted me with a benignant smile, and beckoned me to the quarter deck.

"Well, Hawser, " said he in his blandest manner, as if he sought to atone for his coarse language and dishonorable conduct a short time before, "so you refuse to do as others do take a false oath? You are too sanctimonious by half, and you will find it out some day. You are an obstinate little fool, but may do as you like. Here is another paper; look over it, and see if it will suit you. "

I opened the paper; it was a true statement of my claim against the government for wages. In the course of the day, the ship's company proceeded in a body to the office of the government agent, swore to our several accounts, and received our money.

The amount which fell to my share was not large. I purchased some clothes, paid a few trifling debts that I had contracted while subjected to the "law's delay, " which Shakespeare, a keen observer of men and manners, classes among the most grievous of human ills, and had a few dollars left.

After my experience of a sailor's life, after the treatment I had received, the miserable fare on which I had barely existed during a portion of the time, and the disgusting specimen of nautical morality I had met with in Captain Turner, it will not be considered surprising if my views of a sailor's life had been a little changed during my last voyage. I entertained some doubts whether "going to sea, " instead of being all poetry and romance, was not rather a PROSY affair, after all; and I more than once asked myself if a young man, of correct deportment and industrious habits, who could find some good and respectable business on shore, would not be a consummate fool to "go to sea. " I deliberated anxiously on the subject, and finally determined to return to my home in New Hampshire, and visit my friends before I undertook another voyage.

The schooner Lydia, of Barnstable, commanded by Captain Burgess, an honest, noble-hearted son of Cape Cod, was the only vessel in Savannah at that time bound for Boston. I explained to him my situation, told him I was anxious to get home, and asked as a favor that he would allow me to work my passage to Boston.

He replied that he had a full crew for his vessel, even more hands than could be properly accommodated below, as the cabin and steerage were both encumbered with bales of cotton. But if I was willing to sleep on deck, and assist in working ship and doing other duty, he would cheerfully give me a passage. I accepted his offer on these conditions, and thanked him into the bargain.

We left Savannah on our way to Boston. My heart beat quicker at the idea of returning home. The wind proved light and baffling on the passage, and as we drew towards the north, the weather was foggy with drizzling rains. My quarters on deck, under the lee of a bale of cotton, were any thing but comfortable. I often awoke when the watch was called, shivering with cold, and found it difficult, without an unusual quantity of exercise, to recover a tolerable degree of warmth.

I uttered no complaints, but bore this continual exposure, night and day, and other inconveniences, with a philosophical spirit, conceiving them to be a part of the compact. If the passage had only been of moderate length, I should, in all likelihood, have reached Boston in good health; but nineteen days had passed away when we sailed through the Vineyard Sound, and anchored in the harbor of Hyannis, on the third of July, 1810.

Some days before we reached Hyannis, I found myself gradually losing strength. I was visited with occasional fits of shivering, succeeded by fever heats. But on the morning of the glorious Fourth, I felt my whole system renovated at the idea of celebrating "Independence Day" on shore. The captain and mate of the Lydia both belonged to Barnstable, where their families resided. They both left the schooner for their homes as soon as the anchor reached the bottom, boldly predicting head winds or calms for at least thirty-six hours, at the end of which time they calculated to rejoin the schooner.

On the morning of the fourth, the crew, to a man, followed the example of our trustworthy officers, and determined to have a jovial time on shore. We left the good schooner Lydia soberly riding at anchor, to take care of herself. There were several other vessels in the harbor, all of which were deserted in the same manner. Not a living animal was to be found in the whole fleet. After passing weeks at sea, the temptation to tread the firm earth, and participate in a Fourth of July frolic, was too strong to be resisted.

Hyannis was then quite a humble village with a profusion of salt works. Farm houses were thinly scattered around, and comfort seemed inscribed on every dwelling. There seemed to be an abundance of people moving about on that day; where they came from was a problem I could not solve. Every one seemed pleased and happy, and, with commendable patriotism, resolved to enjoy Independence Day. The young men were neatly apparelled, and bent on having a joyous time; and the girls Cape Cod girls, ever renowned for beauty and worth gayly decked out with smiles, and dimples, and ribbons, ready for a Fourth of July frolic, dazzled the eyes of the beholders, and threw a magic charm over the scene.

And a frolic they had; fiddling, dancing, fun, and patriotism was the order of the day. In the evening, however, the entertainments were varied by the delivery of a sermon and other religious exercises in the school-house by a young Baptist clergyman, who subsequently became well known for his praiseworthy and successful efforts to reduce the rates on postage in the United States. This good man accomplished the great work of his life and died. A simple monument is erected to his memory at Mount Auburn, with no more than these words of inscription:

"BARNABAS BATES,
FATHER OF CHEAP POSTAGE. "

Hardly a person visits that consecrated ground who has not reaped enjoyment from the labors of that man's life. And as the simple epitaph meets the eye, and is read in an audible tone, the heart- felt invocation, "Blessings on his memory! " is his oft-repeated elegy.

It was about nine o'clock in the evening when the crew returned to the schooner. After we gained the deck I was seized with an unpleasant sensation. A sudden chill seemed to congeal the blood in my veins; my teeth chattered, and my frame shook with alarming violence. After the lapse of about thirty minutes the chills gave place to an attack of fever, which, in an hour or two, also disappeared, leaving me in a weak and wretched condition. This proved to be a case of intermittent fever, or FEVER AND AGUE, a distressing malady, but little known in New England in modern times, although by no means a stranger to the early settlers. It was fastened upon me with a rough and tenacious grasp, by the damp, foggy, chilly atmosphere in which I had constantly lived for the last fortnight.

Next morning, in good season, the captain and mate were on board. The wind was fair, and we got under weigh doubled Cape Cod, and arrived alongside the T Wharf in Boston, after a tedious and uncomfortable passage of twenty-two days from Savannah.

I left my home a healthy-looking boy, with buoyant spirits, a bright eye, and features beaming with hope. A year had passed, and I stood on the wharf in Boston, a slender stripling, with a pale and sallow complexion, a frame attenuated by disease, and a spirit oppressed by disappointment. The same day I deposited my chest in a packet bound to Portsmouth, tied up a few trifling articles in a handkerchief, shook hands with the worthy Captain Burgess, his mate and kind-hearted crew, and with fifteen silver dollars in my pocket, wended my way to the stage tavern in Ann Street, and made arrangements for a speedy journey to my home in Rockingham County, New Hampshire.

Chapter XI EMBARKING FOR BRAZIL

It seemed to be generally conceded that I had got enough of the sea; that after the discomforts I had experienced, and the unpleasant and revolting scenes I had witnessed, I should manifest folly in trying another voyage. My friends took it for granted that in my eyes a ship had lost all her attractions, and that I would henceforth eschew salt water as zealously and devoutly as a thrice-holy monk is wont to eschew the vanities of the world.

Indeed, for a time I reluctantly acknowledged that I had seen enough of a sailor's life; that on trial it did not realize my expectations; that if not a decided humbug, it was amazingly like one. With my health the buoyancy of my spirits departed. Hope and ambition no longer urged me with irresistible power to go forth and visit foreign lands, and traverse unknown seas like a knight errant of old in quest of adventures. While shivering with ague, and thinking of my wretched fare on board the schooner John, and my uncomfortable lodgings during the passage from Savannah, I listened, with patience at least, to the suggestions of my friends about a change of occupation. Arrangements were accordingly made by which I was to bid adieu to the seas forever.

It cost me something to abandon a vocation to which I had looked for years as the stepping-stone to success in life; and as my health and spirits returned, I began to doubt whether I was acting wisely; but having embarked in a new pursuit, I determined to go ahead, and to this determination I unflinchingly adhered, for at least THREE MONTHS, when I fell in with a distant relation, Captain Nathaniel Page, of Salem, who was about proceeding on a voyage to the Brazils. After expressing surprise at my course in abandoning the sea, he more than hinted that if I wished a situation before the mast with him, it was at my service.

This was applying the linstock to the priming with a vengeance. My good resolutions vanished like a wreath of vapor before a westerly gale. Those longings which I had endeavored to stifle, returned with more than their original force. In fancy's eye, I saw a marlinspike where Macbeth saw the dagger, and snuffed the fragrance of a tar-bucket in every breeze.

At the expiration of three days after my interview with Captain Page, I took the stage coach and proceeded to Salem. The brig Clarissa was then preparing to take in cargo for Maranham and Para, ports on the north coast of Brazil, which had just been thrown open to American commerce. The Clarissa was a good- looking, substantial vessel, of about two hundred tons burden, belonging to Jere. L. Page, Abel Peirso, and others, and had recently returned from a successful voyage to Calcutta.

The sight of the brig, and the flurry about the wharves, where several Indiamen were discharging cargoes or making ready for sea, confirmed me in my resolution to try the ocean once more. Indeed I began to be heartily ashamed of having seriously entertained the idea of quietly settling down among "the land- lubbers on shore, " and felt that the sooner I retrieved my error the better.

Filled with this idea, I sought Captain Page, and without further consideration, and without daring to consult my friends in New Hampshire, lest they should overwhelm me with remonstrances, I engaged to go in the Clarissa as one of the crew before the mast.

I returned home with all speed, gathered together my few sea- going garments and nautical instruments, again bade adieu to my relations, who gravely shook their heads in doubt of the wisdom of my conduct, and elated by visions of fairy castles in the distance, hastened to join the brig, which was destined to bear Caesar and his fortunes.

This may have been the wisest step I could have taken. It is not likely I should have been long reconciled to any other occupation than that of a mariner. When a boy's fixed inclinations in the choice of an occupation are thwarted, he is seldom successful in life. His genius, if he has any, will be cramped, stunted, by an attempt to bend it in the wrong direction, and will seldom afterwards expand. But when a person, while attending to the duties of his profession or occupation, whether literary, scientific, or manual, can gratify his inclinations, and thus find pleasure in his business, he will be certain of success.

It was at the close of January, 1811, that the brig Clarissa was cast loose from Derby's Wharf in Salem, and with a gentle south- west breeze, sailed down the harbor, passed Baker's Island, and entered on the broad Atlantic. Our cargo was of a miscellaneous description, consisting of flour and salt provisions, furniture, articles of American manufacture, and large assortment of India cottons, which were at that time in general use throughout the habitable parts of the globe.

The Clarissa was a good vessel, and well found in almost every respect; but like most of the vessels in those days, had wretched accommodations for the crew. The forecastle was small, with no means of ventilation or admission of the light of day, excepting by the fore-scuttle. In this contracted space an equilateral triangle, with sides of some twelve or fifteen feet, which was expected to furnish comfortable accommodations for six individuals, including a very dark-complexioned African, who filled the respectable and responsible office of cook were stowed six large chests and other baggage belonging to the sailors; also two water-hogsheads, and several coils of rigging.

The deck leaked badly, in heavy weather, around the bowsprit- bitts, flooding the forecastle at every plunge; and when it is considered that each inmate of the forecastle, except myself, was an inveterate chewer of Indian weed, it may be imagined that this forecastle was about as uncomfortable a lodging place, in sinter's cold or summer's heat, as a civilized being could well desire. It undoubtedly possessed advantages over the "Black Hole of Calcutta, " but an Esquimaux hut, an Indian wigwam, or a Russian cabin, was a palace in comparison. And this was a type of the forecastles of those days.

After getting clear of the land the wind died away; and soon after came from the eastward, and was the commencement of a snow storm which lasted twelve hours, when it backed into the north-west, and the foresail was set with the view of scudding before the wind. It soon blew a heavy gale; the thermometer fell nearly to zero; ice gathered in large quantities on our bowsprit, bows, and rigging, and the brig labored and plunged fearfully in the irregular cross sea when urged through the water by the blustering gale.

To save the vessel from foundering, it became necessary to lay her to under a close-reefed main-topsail. It was about half past eleven o'clock at night, when all hands were called for that purpose. Unfortunately my feet were not well protected from the inclemency of the weather, and became thoroughly wet before I had been five minutes on deck. We had difficulty in handling the foresail, in consequence of the violence of the wind and the benumbing effect of the weather, and remained a long time on the yard. When I reached the deck, my stockings were frozen to my feet, and I suffered exceedingly from the cold.

It was now my "trick at the helm, ": for notwithstanding we were lying to, it was considered necessary for some one to remain near the tiller, watch the compass, and be in readiness for any emergency. I stamped my feet occasionally, with a view to keep them from freezing, and thought I had succeeded; and when at four o'clock I went below and turned into my berth, they felt comfortable enough, and I fell into a deep sleep, from which I was awakened by burning pains in my feet and fingers. My sufferings were intolerable, and I cried out lustily in my agony, and was answered from another part of the forecastle, where one of my watchmates, a youth but little older than myself, was extended, also suffering from frozen feet and hands.

Our united complaints, which by no means resembled a concert of sweet sounds, aroused from his slumbers our remaining watchmate, Newhall, an experienced tar, who cared little for weather of any description, provided he was not stinted in his regular proportion of sleep. In a surly mood he inquired what was the trouble. On being told, he remarked with a vein of philosophy and a force of logic which precluded all argument, that if our feet were frozen, crying and groaning would do US no good, while it would annoy him and prevent his sleeping; therefore we had better "grin and bear it" like men until eight bells, when we might stand a chance to get some assistance. He moreover told us that he would not put up with such a disturbance in the forecastle; it was against al rules; and if we did not clap a stopper on our cries and groans, he would turn out and give us something worth crying for he would pummel us both without mercy!

Thus cautioned by our compassionate shipmate, we endeavored to restrain ourselves from giving utterance to our feelings until the expiration of the watch.

When the watch was called our wailings were loud and clamorous. Our sufferings awakened the sympathy of the officers; our condition was inquired into, and assistance furnished. Both my feet were badly frost-bitten, and inflamed and swollen. Collins, my watchmate, had not escaped unscathed from the attack of this furious northwester, but being provided with a pair of stout boots, his injuries were much less than mine. In a few days he was about the deck as active as ever.

The result of my conflict with the elements on "the winter's coast" was of a serious and painful character; and for a time there was reason to fear that amputation of a portion of one, if not both feet might be necessary. Captain Page treated me with kindness, and was unremitting in his surgical attentions; and by dint of great care, a free application of emollients, and copious quantities of "British oil, " since known at different times as "Seneca oil, " or "Petroleum, " a partial cure was gradually effected; but several weeks passed away ere I was able to go aloft, and a free circulation of the blood has never been restored.

A few days after this furious gale, we found ourselves in warm weather, having entered the edge of the Gulf Stream. We proceeded in a south-east direction, crossing the trade winds on our way to the equinoctial line. Were it not for the monotony, which always fatigues, there would be few undertakings more interesting than a sail through the latitudes of "the trades, " where we meet with a balmy atmosphere, gentle breezes, and smooth seas. In the night the heavens are often unclouded, the constellations seem more interesting, the stars shine with a milder radiance, and the moon gives a purer light, than in a more northern region. Often in my passage through the tropics, during the night-watches, seated on a spare topmast, or the windlass, or the heel of the bowsprit, I have, for hours at a time, indulged my taste for reading and study by the light of the moon.

Fish of many kinds are met with in those seas; and the attempt to capture them furnishes a pleasant excitement; and if the attempt is successful, an agreeable variety is added to the ordinary fare on shipboard. The dolphin is the fish most frequently seen, and is the most easily caught of these finny visitors. He is one of the most beautiful of the inhabitants of the deep, and presents a singularly striking and captivating appearance, as, clad in gorgeous array, he moves gracefully through the water. He usually swims near the surface, and when in pursuit of a flying- fish shoots along with inconceivable velocity.

The dolphin, when properly cooked, although rather dry, is nevertheless excellent eating; and as good fish is a welcome commodity at sea, the capture of a dolphin is not only an exciting but an important event. When the word is given forth that "there's a dolphin alongside, " the whole ship's company are on the alert. Business, unless of the last importance, is suspended, and the implements required for the death or captivity of the unsuspecting stranger are eagerly sought for. The men look resolved, ready to render any assistance, and watch the proceedings with an eager eye; and the wonted grin on the features of the delighted cook, in anticipation of an opportunity to display his culinary skill, assumes a broader character.

The captain or the mate takes his station in some convenient part of the vessel, on the bow or on the quarter, or beneath the bowsprit on the martingale stay. By throwing overboard a bright spoon, or a tin vessel, to which a line is attached, and towing it on the top of the water, the dolphin, attracted by its glittering appearance, and instigated by curiosity, moves quickly towards the deceiving object, unconscious that his artful enemy, man, armed with a deadly weapon, a sort of five-pronged harpoon, called a GRANES, is standing over him, with uplifted arm, ready to give the fatal blow.

The fish is transferred from his native element to the deck; the granes is disengaged from the quivering muscles, and again passed to the officer, who, it may be, soon adds another to the killed. It is sometimes the case that half a dozen dolphin are captured in this way in a few minutes. A hook and line over the stern, with a flying-fish for bait, will often prove a successful means of capturing the beautiful inhabitants of the deep.

The dolphin is a fine-looking fish. Its shape is symmetry itself, and has furnished a valuable hint for the model of fast- sailing vessels. It is usually from two to three feet in length, and is sometimes met with of nearly twice that size, and weighing seventy-five or a hundred pounds. One of the properties for which the dolphin is celebrated is that of changing its color when dying. By many this is considered fabulous; but it is strictly true. After the fish is captured, and while struggling in the scuppers, the changes constantly taking place in its color are truly remarkable. The hues which predominate are blue, green, and yellow, with their various combinations: but when the fish is dead, the beauty of its external appearance, caused by the brilliancy of its hues, no longer exists. Falconer, the sailor poet, in his interesting poem of "The Shipwreck, " thus describes this singular phenomenon:

"But while his heart the fatal javelin thrills,
And flitting life escapes in sanguine rills,
What radiant changes strike the astonished sight!

What glowing hues of mingled shade and light!
Not equal beauties gild the lucid west,
With parting beams all o'er profusely drest;
Not lovelier colors paint the vernal dawn,
When orient dews impearl the enamelled lawn,
Than from his sides in bright suffusion flow,
That now with gold empyreal seem to glow;
Now in pellucid sapphires meet the view,
And emulate the soft, celestial hue;
Now beam a flaming crimson in the eye,
And now assume the purple's deeper dye."

The second mate of the Clarissa, Mr. Fairfield, was a veteran sailor, and a very active and industrious man. He was always busy when not asleep; and, what was of more importance, and frequently an annoyance to the ship's company, he dearly loved to see other people busy. He regarded idleness as the parent of evil, and always acted on the uncharitable principle that if steady employment is not provided for a ship's company they will be constantly contriving mischief.

Unfortunately for the crew of the Clarissa, Mr. Fairfield had great influence with the captain, having sailed with him the previous voyage, and proved himself a good and faithful officer. He, therefore, had no difficulty in carrying into operation his favorite scheme of KEEPING ALL HANDS AT WORK. A large quantity of "old junk" was put on board in Salem, and on the passage to Brazil, after we reached the pleasant latitudes, all hands were employed from eight o'clock in the morning until six o'clock in the evening in knotting yarns, twisting spunyarn, weaving mats, braiding sinnett, making reef-points and gaskets, and manufacturing small rope to be used for "royal rigging, " for among the ingenious expedients devised by the second mate for keeping the crew employed was the absurd and unprofitable one of changing the snug pole royal masts into "sliding gunters, " with royal yards athwart, man-of-war fashion.

Sunday on board the Clarissa was welcomed as a day of respite from hard labor. The crew on that day had "watch and watch, " which gave them an opportunity to attend to many little duties connected with their individual comforts, that had been neglected during the previous week. This is exemplified in a conversation I had with

Newhall, one of my watchmates, one pleasant Sunday morning, after breakfast.

"Heigh-ho, " sighed Newhall, with a sepulchral yawn; "Sunday has come at last, and I am glad. It is called a day of rest, but is no day of rest for me. I have a thousand things to do this forenoon; one hour has passed away already, and I don't know which to do first. "

"Indeed! What have you to do to-day more than usual, " I inquired.

"Not much out of the usual way, perhaps, Hawser. But I must shave and change my clothes. Although we can't go to meeting, it's well enough for a fellow to look clean and decent, at least once a week. I must also wash a couple of shirts, make a cap out of a piece of canvas trousers, stop a leak in my pea-jacket, read a chapter in the Bible, which I promised my grandmother in Lynnfield I would do every Sunday, and bottle off an hour's sleep. "

"Well, then, " said I, "if you have so much to do, no time is to be lost. You had better go to work at once. "

"So I will, " said he; "and as an hour's sleep is the most important of all, I'll make sure of that to begin with, for fear of accidents. So, here goes. "

And into his berth he tumbled "all standing, " and was neither seen nor heard until the watch was called at twelve o'clock.

But little time was given for the performance of religious duties on the Sabbath; indeed, in the times of which I write, such duties among sailors were little thought of. Religious subjects were not often discussed in a ship's forecastle, and even the distinction between various religious sects and creeds was unheeded, perhaps unknown. And yet the germ of piety was implanted in the sailor's heart. His religion was simple, but sincere. Without making professions, he believed in the being of a wise and merciful Creator; he believed in a system of future rewards and punishments; he read his Bible, a book which was always found in a sailor's chest, pinned his faith upon the Gospels, and treasured up the precepts of our Saviour; he believed that though his sins were many, his manifold temptations would also be remembered. He manifested but little fear of death, relying firmly on the MERCY of the Almighty.

My description of the uninterrupted labors of the crew on board the Clarissa may induce the inquiry how the ship's company could do with so little sleep, and even if a sailor could catch a cat-nap occasionally in his watch, what must become of the officers, who are supposed to be wide awake and vigilant during the hours they remain on deck?

I can only say, that on board the Clarissa there was an exception to this very excellent rule. Captain Page, like other shipmasters of the past, perhaps also of the present day, although bearing the reputation of a good shipmaster, seldom troubled himself about ship's duty in the night time. He trusted to his officers, who were worthy men and experienced sailors. Between eight and nine o'clock he turned in, and was seldom seen again until seven bells, or half past seven o'clock in the morning. After he left the deck, the officer of the watch, wrapped in his pea-jacket, measured his length on the weather hencoop, and soon gave unimpeachable evidence of enjoying a comfortable nap. The remainder of the watch, emulating the noble example of the officer, selected the softest planks on the deck, threw themselves, nothing loath, into a horizontal position, and in a few minutes were transported into the land of forgetfulness.

The helmsman only, of all the ship's company, was awake, to watch the wind and look out for squalls; and he, perhaps, was nodding at his post, while the brig was moving through the water, her head pointing by turns in every direction but the right one. If the wind veered or hauled, the yard remained without any corresponding change in their position. If more sail could be set to advantage, it was seldom done until the sun's purple rays illumined the eastern horizon, when every man in the watch was aroused, and a great stir was made on the deck. When the captain came up the companion-way, every sail was properly set which would draw to advantage, and the yards were braced according to the direction of the wind.

It was, undoubtedly, owing to this negligence on the part of the officers during the night watches, and not to any ill qualities on the part of the brig, that our passage to Maranham occupied over sixty days. And, undoubtedly, to this negligence may be ascribed the extraordinary length of passages to and from foreign ports of many good-sailing ships in these days.

Chapter XII MARANHAM AND PARA.

As we drew near the equinoctial line, I occasionally heard some talk among the officers on the subject of a visit from Old Neptune; and as there were three of the crew who had never crossed the line, it was thought probable that the venerable sea god would visit the brig, and shake hands with the strangers, welcoming them to his dominions.

A few days afterwards, when the latitude was determined by a meridian altitude of the sun, Captain Page ordered Collins to go aloft and take a good look around the horizon, as it was not unlikely something was in sight. Collins grinned, and went aloft. He soon hailed the deck from the fore-topsail yard, and said he saw a boat broad off on the weather bow, with her sails spread "wing and wing, " and steering directly for the brig.

"That's Old Neptune himself! " shouted Captain Page, clapping his hands. "He will soon be alongside. Mr. Abbot, " continued he, speaking to the chief mate, "let the men get their dinners at once. We must be prepared to receive the old gentleman! "

After dinner, Mr. Fairfield ordered those of the crew including myself who had never crossed the line, into the forecastle, to remove one of the water casks. We had no sooner descended the ladder than the fore-scuttle was closed and fastened, and we were caught like rats in a trap. Preparations of a noisy character were now made on deck for the reception of Old Neptune.

An hour a long and tedious one it appeared to those confined below elapsed before the old gentleman got within hail. At length we heard a great trampling on the forecastle, and anon a gruff voice, which seemed to come from the end of the flying jib- boom, yelled out, "Brig, ahoy! "

"Hallo! " replied the captain.

"Have you any strangers on board? "

"Ay, ay! "

"Heave me a rope! I'll come alongside and shave them directly! "

A cordial greeting was soon interchanged between captain Page and Old Neptune on deck, to which we prisoners listened with much interest. The slide of the scuttle was removed, and orders given for one of the "strangers" to come on deck and be shaved. Anxious to develop the mystery and be qualified to bear a part in the frolic, I pressed forward; but as soon as my head appeared above the rim of the scuttle I was seized, blindfolded, and led to the main deck, where I was urged, by a press of politeness I could not withstand, to be seated on a plank. The process of shaving commenced, which, owing to the peculiar roughness of the razor and the repulsive qualities of the lather, was more painful and disagreeable than pleasant, but to which I submitted without a murmur. When the scarifying process was finished, I was told to hold up my head, raise my voice to its highest pitch, and say, "Yarns! " I obeyed the mandate, as in duty bound; and to give full and distinct utterance to the word, opened my mouth as if about to swallow a whale, when some remorseless knave, amid shouts of laughter from the surrounding group, popped into my open mouth the huge tar brush, well charged with the unsavory ingredients for shaving.

I now thought my trials were over. Not so. I was interrogated through a speaking trumpet on several miscellaneous subjects; but suspecting some trick, my answers were brief and given through closed teeth. At length, Captain Page exclaimed, "Old Neptune, this will never do. Give him a speaking trumpet also, and let him answer according to rule, and in shipshape fashion, so that we can all hear and understand him. "

I put the trumpet to my mouth, and to the next question attempted to reply in stunning tones, "None of your business! " for I was getting impatient, and felt somewhat angry. The sentence was but half uttered when a whole bucket of salt water was hurled into the broad end of the speaking trumpet, which conducted it into my mouth and down my throat, nearly producing strangulation; at the same time, the seat was pulled from beneath me, and I was plunged over head and ears in the briny element.

As soon as I recovered my breath, the bandage was removed from my eyes, and I found myself floating in the long boat, which had been nearly filled with water for the occasion, and surrounded by as jovial a set of fellows as ever played off a practical joke. Old Neptune proved to be Jim Sinclair, of Marblehead, but so disguised that his own mother could not have known him. His ill- favored and weather-beaten visage was covered with streaks of paint, like the face of a wild Indian on the war-path. He had a thick beard made of oakum; and a wig of rope-yarns, the curls hanging gracefully on his shoulders, was surmounted with a paper cap, fashioned and painted so as to bear a greater resemblance to the papal tiara than to the diadem of the ocean monarch. In one hand he held a huge speaking trumpet, and in the other he brandished, instead of a trident, the ship's granes with FIVE prongs!

The other strangers to Old Neptune were subsequently compelled to go through the same ceremonies, in which I assisted with a hearty good will; and those who did not patiently submit to the indignities, received the roughest treatment. The shades of evening fell before the frolic was over, and the wonted order and discipline restored.

It was formerly the invariable practice with all American and British vessels to observe ceremonies, when crossing the line, of a character similar to those I have described, varying, of course, according to the taste of the commander of the vessel and other circumstances. In a large ship, with a numerous crew, when it was deemed expedient to be particularly classical, Neptune appeared in full costume, accompanied by the fair Amphitrite, decorated with a profusion of sea-weed or gulf-weed, shells, coral, and other emblems of salt water sovereignty, and followed by a group of Tritons and Nereids fantastically arrayed. Sometimes, and especially when remonstrances were made to the mandates of the sea god, and his authority was questioned in a style bordering on rebellion, the proceedings were of a character which bore unjustifiably severe on his recusant subjects. Instances have been known where keel-hauling has been resorted to as an exemplary punishment for a refractory individual.

This cruel and inhuman mode of punishment, in former ages, was not uncommon in ships of war of all nations. It was performed by fastening a rope around the body of an individual, beneath the armpits, as he stood on the weather gunwale. One end of the rope was passed beneath the keel and brought up to the deck on the opposite side, and placed in the hands of half a dozen stout seamen. The man was then pushed overboard, and the men stationed to leeward commenced hauling, while those to windward gently "eased away" the other end of the rope. The victim was thus, by main force, dragged beneath the keel, and hauled up to the deck on the other side. The operation, when adroitly performed, occupied but a short time in the estimation of the bystanders, although it must have seemed ages to the poor fellow doomed to undergo the punishment. Sometimes a leg or an arm would come in contact with the keel, and protract the operation; therefore, a severe bruise, a broken limb, a dislocated joint, or even death itself, was not an unfrequent attendant on this kind of punishment!

Many years ago, on board an English East Indiaman, an officer, who had figured conspicuously in perpetrating severe jokes on those who were, for the first time, introduced to Old Neptune, was shot through the head by an enraged passenger, who could not, or would not appreciate the humor of the performances!

The ceremony of "shaving when crossing the line" is not so generally observed as formerly in our American ships; and, as it is sometimes carried to unjustifiable lengths, and can hardly be advocated on any other ground than ancient custom, it is in a fair way to become obsolete.

In those days there were no correct charts of the northern coast of Brazil, and Captain Page, relying on such charts as he could obtain, was one night in imminent danger of losing the brig, which was saved only by the sensitiveness of the olfactory organs of the second mate!

It was about six bells in the middle watch, or three o'clock in the morning; the heavens were clear and unclouded; the stars shone with great brilliancy; there was a pleasant breeze from the southeast, and the ship was gliding quietly along, with the wind abaft the beam, at the rate of five or six knots. Suddenly Mr. Fairfield, whose nose was not remarkable for size, but might with propriety be classed among the SNUBS, ceased to play upon it its accustomed tune in the night watches, sprang from the hen-coop, on which he had been reclining, and began to snuff the air in an eager and agitated manner! He snuffed again; he stretched his head over the weather quarter and continued to snuff! I was at the helm, and was not a little startled at his strange and unaccountable conduct. I had almost convinced myself that he was laboring under a sudden attack of insanity, when, turning round, he abruptly asked me IF I COULD NOT SMELL THE LAND?

I snuffed, but could smell nothing unusual, and frankly told him so; upon which he went forward and asked Newhall and Collins if either of them could smell the land. Newhall said "no; " but Collins, after pointing his nose to windward, declared he "could smell it plainly, and that the smell resembled beefsteak and onions! "

To this, after a long snuff, the mate assented adding that beef was abundant in Brazil, and the people were notoriously fond of garlic! Collins afterwards acknowledged that he could smell nothing, but was bound to have as good a nose as the second mate!

Upon the strength of this additional testimony Mr. Fairfield called the captain, who snuffed vigorously, but without effect. He could smell neither land, nor "beefsteak and onions. " He was also incredulous in regard to our proximity to the shore, but very properly concluded, as it was so near daylight, to heave the brig to, with her head off shore, until we could test the correctness of the second mate's nose!

After waiting impatiently a couple of hours we could get glimpses along the southern horizon, and, to the surprise of Captain Page, and the triumph of the second mate, the land was visible in the shape of a long, low, hummocky beach, and not more than three leagues distant. When Mr. Fairfield first scented it we were probably not more than four or five miles from the shore, towards which we were steering on a diagonal course.

The land we fell in with was some three or four degrees to windward of Maranham. On the following day we entered the mouth of the river, and anchored opposite the city.

Before we had been a week in port a large English ship, bound to Maranham, went ashore in the night on the very beach which would have wrecked the Clarissa, had it not been for the extraordinary acuteness o Mr. Fairfield's nose, and became a total wreck. The officers and crew remained near the spot for several days to save what property they could, and gave a lamentable account of their sufferings. They were sheltered from the heat of the sun by day, and the dews and rains by night, by tents rudely constructed from the ship's sails. But these tents could not protect the men from the sand-flies and mosquitoes, and their annoyance from those insects must have been intolerable. The poor fellows shed tears when they told the tale of their trials, and pointed to the ulcers on their limbs as evidence of the ferocity of the mosquitoes!

It appeared, also, that their provisions fell short, and they would have suffered from hunger were it not that the coast, which was but sparsely inhabited, abounded in wild turkeys, as they said, of which they shot several, which furnished them with "delicious food. " They must have been excessively hungry, or blessed with powerful imaginations, for, on cross-examination, these "wild turkeys" proved to be TURKEY BUZZARDS, or carrion vultures, most filthy creatures, which, in many places where the decay of animal matter is common, act faithfully the part of scavengers, and their flesh is strongly tinctured with the quality of their food.

St. Louis de Maranham is a large and wealthy city, situated near the mouth of the Maranham River, about two degrees and a half south of the equator. The city is embellished with many fine buildings, among which is the palace of the governor of the province, and many richly endowed churches or cathedrals. These numerous churches were each furnished with bells by the dozen, which were continually ringing, tolling, or playing tunes from morning until night, as if vieing with each other, in a paroxysm of desperation, which should make the most deafening clamor. I have visited many Catholic cities, but never met with a people so extravagantly fond of the music of bells as the inhabitants of Maranham.

This perpetual ringing and pealing of bells, of all sizes and tones, at first astonishes and rather amuses a stranger, who regards it as a part of the rejoicings at some great festival. But, when day after day passes, and there is no cessation of these clanging sounds, he becomes annoyed; at every fresh peal he cannot refrain from exclaiming "Silence that dreadful bell! " and wishes from his heart they were all transformed to dumb bells! Yet, after a time, when the ear becomes familiar with the sounds, he regards the discordant music of the bells with indifference. When the Clarissa left the port of Maranham, after having been exposed for months to such an unceasing clang, something seemed wanting; the crew found themselves involuntarily listening for the ringing of the bells, and weeks elapsed before they became accustomed and reconciled to the absence of the stunning tintinabulary clatter!

The city of Maranham was inhabited almost entirely by Portuguese, or the descendants of Portuguese. We found no persons there of foreign extraction, excepting a few British commission merchants. There was not a French, a German, or an American commercial house in the place. The Portuguese are a people by no means calculated to gain the kind consideration and respect of foreigners. They may possess much intrinsic worth, but it is so covered with, or concealed beneath a cloak of arrogance and self-esteem, among the higher classes, and of ignorance, superstition, incivility, and knavery among the lower, that it is difficult to appreciate it. Of their courtesy to strangers, a little incident, which occurred to Captain Page while in Maranham, will furnish an illustration.

Passing, one day, by a large cathedral, he found many persons entering the edifice or standing near the doorway, an indication that some holy rites were about to be celebrated. Wishing to view the ceremony, he joined the throng and entered the church, which was already crowded by persons of all ranks. Pressing forward he found a vacant spot on the floor of the cathedral, in full view of the altar. Here he took his stand, and gazed with interest on the proceedings.

He soon perceived that he was the observed of all observers; that he was stared at as an object of interest and no little amusement by persons in his immediate vicinity, who, notwithstanding their saturnine temperaments, could not suppress their smiles, and winked and nodded to each other, at the same time pointing slyly towards him, as if there was some capital joke on hand in which he bore a conspicuous part. His indignation may be imagined when he discovered that he had been standing directly beneath a huge chandelier, which was well supplied with lighted wax candles, and the drops of melted wax were continually falling, from a considerable height, upon his new dress coat, and the drops congealing, his coat looked as if covered with spangles! Not one of the spectators of this scene was courteous enough to give him a hint of his misfortune, but all seemed to relish, with infinite gusto, the mishap of the stranger.

Captain Page found in Maranham a dull market for his East India goods. His provisions and his flour, however, bought a good price, but the greatest per centum of profit was made on cigars. One of the owners of the Clarissa stepped into an auction store in State Street one day, when a lot of fifty thousand cigars, imported in an English vessel from St. Jago de Cuba, were put up for sale. The duty on foreign cigars, at that time, was three dollars and a half a thousand. These cigars had been regularly entered at the custom house, and were entitled to debenture, that is, to a return of the duties, on sufficient proof being furnished that they had been exported and landed in a foreign port. As there were few bidders, and the cigars were of inferior quality, the owner of the Clarissa bought the lot at the rate of three dollars per thousand, and put them on board the brig. They were sold in Maranham as "Cuban cigars" for fifteen dollars a thousand, and on the return of the brig the custom house handed over the debenture three dollars and a half a thousand! This was what may be called a neat speculation, certainly a SAFE one, as the return duty alone would have covered the cost and expenses!

In the river, opposite the city, the current was rapid, especially during the ebb tide, and sharks were numerous. We caught three or four heavy and voracious ones with a shark-hook while lying at anchor. Only a few days before we arrived a negro child was carried off by one of these monsters, while bathing near the steps of the public landing-place, and devoured.

A few days before we left port I sculled ashore in the yawl, bearing a message from the mate to the captain. It was nearly low water, the flood tide having just commenced, and I hauled the boat on the flats, calculating to be absent but a few minutes. Having been delayed by business, when I approached the spot where I left the boat I found, to my great mortification, that the boat had floated with the rise of the tide, and was borne by a fresh breeze some twenty or thirty yards from the shore. My chagrin may be imagined when I beheld the boat drifting merrily up the river, at the rate of three or four knots an hour!

I stood on the shore and gazed wistfully on the departing yawl. There was no boat in the vicinity, and only one mode of arresting the progress of the fugitive. I almost wept through vexation. I hesitated one moment on account of the sharks, then plunged into the river, and with rapid and strong strokes swam towards the boat. I was soon alongside, seized the gunwale, and, expecting every moment that a shark would seize me by the leg, by a convulsive movement threw myself into the boat.

As I sculled back towards the place from which the boat had drifted, Captain Page came down to the water side. He had witnessed the scene from a balcony, and administered a severe rebuke for my foolhardiness in swimming off into the river, particularly during the young flood, which brought the voracious monsters in from the sea.

On our passage to Maranham, and during a portion of our stay in that port, the utmost harmony prevailed on board. The men, although kept constantly at work, were nevertheless satisfied with their treatment. The officers and the crew were on pleasant terms with each other; and grumbling without cause, which is often indulged in on shipboard, was seldom known in the forecastle of the Clarissa. But it happened, unfortunately for our peace and happiness, that Captain Page added two men to his crew in Maranham. One of them was an Englishman, one of the poor fellows, who, when shipwrecked on the coast, were nearly eaten up by the mosquitoes, and who in turn banqueted on turkey buzzards, as the greatest of luxuries! He was a stout, ablebodied sailor, but ignorant, obstinate, insolent, and quarrelsome one of those men who, always dissatisfied and uncomfortable, seem to take pains to make others unhappy also.

The other was a native of New England. He had met with various strange adventures and been impressed on board an English man-of-war, where he had served a couple of years, and, according to his own statement, been twice flogged at the gangway. He was a shrewd fellow, impatient under the restraints of discipline; always complaining of "the usage" in the Clarissa, and being something of a sea lawyer, and liberally endowed with the gift of speech, exercised a controlling influence over the crew, and in conjunction with the Englishman, kept the ship's company in that unpleasant state of tumult and rebellion, known as "hot water, " until the end of the voyage.

One or two men, of a character similar to those I have described, are to be found in almost every vessel, and are always the cause of more or less trouble; of discontent and insolence on the part of the crew, and of corresponding harsh treatment on the part of the officers; and the ship which is destined to be the home, for months, of men who, under other circumstances, would be brave, manly, and obedient, and which SHOULD be the abode of kindness, comfort, and harmony, becomes a Pandemonium, where cruelty and oppression are practised a gladiatorial arena, where quarrels, revolts, and perhaps murders, are enacted. When such men, determined promoters of strife, are found among a ship's company, they should be got rid of at any cost, with the earliest opportunity.

When our cargo was disposed of at Maranham we proceeded down the coast to the city of Para, on one of the mouths of the Amazon.

Here we received a cargo of cacao for the United States. There was, at that time, a vast quantity of wild, uncultivated forest land in the interior of the province, which may account for the many curious specimens of wild living animals which we met with at that place. Indeed the city seemed one vast menagerie, well stocked with birds, beasts, and creeping things.

Of the birds, the parrot tribe held the most conspicuous place. They were of all colors and sizes, from the large, awkward- looking mackaw, with his hoarse, discordant note, to the little, delicate-looking paroquet, dumb as a barnacle, and not bigger than a wren. The monkeys, of all sizes, forms, and colors, continually chattering and grimacing, as fully represented the four-footed animals as the parrots did the bipeds. We found there the mongoose, but little larger than a squirrel; an animal almost as intelligent as the monkey, but far more interesting and attractive. The hideous-looking sloth, with his coarse hair, resembling Carolina moss, his repulsive physiognomy, his strong, crooked claws, his long and sharp teeth, darkly dyed with the coloring matter of the trees and shrubs which constituted his diet, was thrust in our faces in every street; and the variegated venomous serpent, with his prehensile fangs, and the huge boa constrictor, writhing in captivity, were encountered as desirable articles of merchandise at every corner.

But the MOSQUITOES at the mouth of the Amazon were perhaps the most remarkable, as well as the most bloodthirsty animals which abounded in that region. They were remarkable not only for size, but for voracity and numbers. This insect is a pest in every climate. I have found them troublesome on the bar of the Mississippi in the heat of summer; and at the same season exceedingly annoying while navigating the Dwina on the way to Archangel. In the low lands of Java they are seen, heard, and felt to a degree destructive to comfort; and in certain localities in the West Indies are the direct cause of intense nervous excitement, loud and bitter denunciations, and fierce anathemas. But the mosquitoes that inhabit the country bordering on the mouths of the Amazon must bear away the palm from every other portion of the globe.

Every part of our brig was seized upon by these marauding insects; no nook or corner was too secluded for their presence, and no covering seemed impervious to their bills. Their numbers were at all times incredible; but at the commencement of twilight they seemed to increase, and actually formed clouds above the deck, or to speak more correctly, one continuous living cloud hovered above the deck, and excluded to a certain extent the rays of light.

There being no mosquito bars attached to the berths in the forecastle, the foretop was the only place in which I could procure a few hours repose. There I took up my lodgings, and my rest was seldom disturbed excepting occasionally by the visits of a few of the most venturous and aspiring of the mosquito tribe, or a copious shower of rain.

An incident, IT WAS SAID, occurred on board a ship in the harbor, which, if correctly stated, furnishes a striking proof of the countless myriads of mosquitoes which abound in Para. One of the sailors, who occupied a portion of the foretop as a sleeping room, unfortunately rolled over the rim of the top one night while locked in the embraces of Somnus. He fell to the deck, where he would inevitably have broken his neck were it not for the dense body of mosquitoes, closely packed, which hovered over the deck, awaiting their turn for a delicious banquet. This elastic body of living insects broke Jack's fall, and let him down gently to the deck without doing him harm.

Fortunately it was not necessary to tarry a long time in Para. We took on board a cargo of cacao in bulk, and sailed on our return to Salem. As we approached the coast of the United States we experienced much cloudy weather, and for several days no opportunity offered for observing any unusual phenomena in the heavens. But one pleasant evening, as we were entering the South Channel, being on soundings south-east of Nantucket, one of the crew, who was leaning over the lee gunwale, was struck with the strange appearance of a star, which shone with unusual brilliancy, and left a long, broad, and crooked wake behind.

His exclamation of surprise caused every eye to be directed to the spot, about fifty-five degrees above the eastern horizon, pointed out by our observing shipmate and there in full view, to the admiration of some and the terror of others, the comet of 1811 stood confessed!

The men indulged in wild speculations respecting the character of this mysterious visitor, but all concurred in the belief that it was the messenger of a superior power, announcing the coming of some fearful national evil, such as a terrible earthquake, a devastating pestilence, or a fierce and bloody war. Our country was engaged in a war with a powerful nation within the following year; but to those who watched the signs of the times, and remembered the capture of the Chesapeake, and were aware of the impressment of our seamen, the confiscation of property belonging to our citizens captured on the high seas without even a decent pretence, and the many indignities heaped on our government and people by Great Britain, it needed no gifted seer or celestial visitant to foretell that an obstinate war with that haughty power was inevitable.

A few days after the discovery of the comet furnished such a liberal scope for conjecture and comment in the forecastle and the cabin, about the middle of October, 1811, we arrived in Salem, having been absent between eight and nine months.

Chapter XIII SHIP PACKET OF BOSTON

Having been two voyages to the West Indies and one to the Brazils, I began to regard myself as a sailor of no little experience. When rigged out in my blue jacket and trousers, with a neatly covered straw hat, a black silk kerchief tied jauntily around my neck, I felt confidence in my own powers and resources, and was ready, and, as I thought, able to grapple with any thing in the shape of good or ill fortune that might come along. I was aware that success in life depended on my own energies, and I looked forward to a brilliant career in the arduous calling which I had embraced. Like Ancient Pistol, I could say,

> "The world's mine oyster,
> Which I with sword will open!"

With this difference, that I proposed to substitute, for the present at least, a marlinspike for the sword.

Captain Page invited me to remain by the Clarissa and accompany him on a voyage to Gibraltar, but I felt desirous of trying my fortune and gain knowledge of my calling in a good ship bound to the East Indies, or on a fur-trading voyage to the "north-west coast" of America.

At that time the trade with the Indians for furs on the "north-west coast" was carried on extensively from Boston. The ships took out tobacco, molasses, blankets, hardware, and trinkets in large quantities. Proceeding around Cape Horn, they entered the Pacific Ocean, and on reaching the north-west coast, anchored in some of the bays and harbors north of Columbia River. They were visited by canoes from the shore, and traffic commenced. The natives exchanged their furs for articles useful or ornamental. The ship went from port to port until a cargo of furs was obtained, and then sailed for Canton, and disposed of them to the Chinese for silks and teas. After an absence of a couple of years the ship would return to the United States with a cargo worth a hundred thousand dollars. Some of the most eminent merchants in Boston, in this way, laid the foundation of their fortunes.

This trade was not carried on without risk. The north-west coast of America at that period had not been surveyed; no good charts had been constructed, and the shores were lined with reefs and sunken rocks, which, added to a climate where boisterous winds prevailed, rendered the navigation dangerous.

This traffic was attended with other perils. The Indians were bloodthirsty and treacherous; and it required constant vigilance on the part of a ship's company to prevent their carrying into execution some deep-laid plan to massacre the crew and gain possession of the ship. For this reason the trading vessels were always well armed and strongly manned. With such means of defence, and a reasonable share of prudence on the part of the captain, there was but little danger. But the captain and officers were not always prudent. Deceived by the smiles and humility of the natives, they sometimes allowed them to come on board in large numbers, when, at a signal from their chief, they drew their arms from beneath their garments and commenced the work of death. After they had become masters of the ship, they would cut the cables and let her drift ashore, gaining a valuable prize in the cargo, in the iron and copper bolts, spikes, and nails with which the timbers and planks were fastened together, and in the tools, furniture, clothing, and arms. A number of vessels belonging to New England were in this way cut off by the savages on the "north-west coast, " and unsuccessful attempts were made on others.

The "ower true tales" of disasters and massacres on the "north- west coast" seemed to invest a voyage to that quarter with a kind of magic attraction or fascination as viewed through the medium of a youthful imagination; and a voyage of this description would give me an opportunity to perfect myself in much which pertained to the sailor and navigator.

After a delay of a few weeks the opportunity offered which I so eagerly sought. The ship Packet was preparing for a voyage from Boston to the north-west coast via Liverpool, and I succeeded in obtaining a situation on board that ship before the mast. I hastened to Boston and took up my temporary abode at a boarding house, kept by Mrs. Lillibridge, a widow, in Spring Lane, on or near the spot on which the vestry of the Old South Church now stands. I called immediately on the agents, and obtained information in relation to the details of the voyage, and commenced making the necessary preparations.

Several merchants were interested in this contemplated voyage, but the business was transacted by the mercantile house of Messrs. Ropes and Pickman, on Central Wharf. This firm had not been long engaged in business. Indeed, both the partners were young men, but they subsequently became well known to the community. Benjamin T. Pickman became interested in politics, and rendered good service in the legislature. On several occasions he received marks of the confidence of his fellow- citizens in his ability and integrity. He was elected to the Senate, and was chosen president of that body. He died in 1835. Mr. William Ropes, the senior partner of the firm fifty years ago, after having pursued an honorable mercantile career at home and abroad, occupies at this time a high position as an enterprising and successful merchant and a public-spirited citizen.

I laid in a good stock of clothes, such as were needed on a voyage to that inclement part of the world, provided myself with various comforts for a long voyage, and purchased as large an assortment of books as my limited funds would allow, not forgetting writing materials, blank journals, and every thing requisite for obtaining a good practical knowledge of navigation, and of other subjects useful to a shipmaster.

The Packet was a beautiful ship, of about three hundred tons burden, originally intended as a regular trader between Boston and Liverpool; but in consequence of her superior qualities was purchased on the termination of her first voyage for this expedition to the north-west coast. She was to be commanded by Daniel C. Bacon, a young, active, and highly intelligent shipmaster, who a few years before had sailed as a mate with Captain William Sturgis, and had thus studied the principles of his profession in a good school, and under a good teacher. He had made one successful voyage to that remote quarter in command of a ship. Captain Bacon, as is known to many of my readers, subsequently engaged in mercantile business in Boston, and for many years, until his death, not long since, his name was the synonyme of mercantile enterprise, honor, and integrity.

The name of the chief mate was Stetson. He was a tall, bony, muscular man, about forty years old. He had been bred to the sea, and had served in every capacity. He was a thorough sailor, and strict disciplinarian; fearless and arbitrary, he had but little sympathy with the crew; his main object being to get the greatest quantity of work in the shortest possible time. Stories were afloat that he was unfeeling and tyrannical; that fighting and flogging were too frequent to be agreeable in ships where he was vested with authority. There were even vague rumors in circulation that he indulged occasionally in the unique and exciting amusement of shooting at men on the yards when engaged in reefing topsails. These rumors, however, although they invested the aspect and conduct of the mate with a singular degree of interest, were not confirmed. For my own part, although a little startled at the notoriety which Mr. Stetson had achieved, I determined to execute my duties promptly and faithfully so far as was in my power, to be respectful and obedient to my superiors and trustworthy in every act, and let the future take care of itself. Indeed, this is the line of conduct I have endeavored to follow in every situation I have filled in the course of an eventful life, and I can earnestly recommend it to my youthful readers as eminently calculated to contribute to their present comfort and insure their permanent prosperity.

In a few days the Packet received her cargo, consisting chiefly of tobacco and molasses. It was arranged that she should take on board, in Liverpool, bales of blankets and coarse woollen goods, and boxes containing various articles of hardware and trinkets, such as would be acceptable to the savages on the coast. The ship was hauled into the stream, and being a fine model, freshly painted, with royal yards athwart, and colors flying, and signal guns being fired night and morning, attracted much notice and was the admiration of sailors. I was proud of my good fortune in obtaining a chance before the mast, in such a vessel, bound on such a voyage.

The crew was numerous for a ship of three hundred tons, consisting of eight able seamen, exclusive of the boatswain, and four boys. Besides a cook and steward we had a captain's clerk, an armorer, a carpenter, and a tailor. The ship's complement, all told, consisting of twenty-two. For an armament we carried four handsome carriage guns, besides boarding pikes, cutlasses, and muskets in abundance. We had also many coils of rattling stuff, small rope for making boarding nettings, and a good supply of gunpowder was deposited in the magazine.

The sailors came on board, or were brought on board by their landlords, after we had hauled from the wharf. Some of them were sober and well behaved, others were stupid or crazy from intoxication. It required energy and decision to establish order and institute strict rules of discipline among such a miscellaneous collection of web-footed gentry. But Mr. Stetson, assisted by Mr. Bachelder, the second mate, was equal to the task. Indeed he was in his element while directing the labors of the men, blackguarding this one for his stupidity, anathematizing that one for his indolence, and shaking his fist at another, and menacing him with rough treatment for his short answers and sulky looks.

One of the seamen who had been brought on board nearly dead drunk, showed his figure-head above the forescuttle on the following morning. His eyes, preternaturally brilliant, were bloodshot, his cheeks were pale and haggard, his long black hair was matted, and he seemed a personification of desperation and despondency. Stetson caught a glimpse of his features; even his fossilized heart was touched with his appearance and he drove him below.

"Down with you! " said he, shaking his brawny fist in the drunken man's face, "don't let me see your ugly phiz again for the next twenty-four hours. The sight of it is enough to frighten a land-lubber into hysterics, and conjure up a hurricane in the harbor before we can let go the sheet anchor. Down with you; vanish! Tumble into your berth! Take another long and strong nap, and then turn out a fresh man, and show yourself a sailor; or you'll rue the day when you first tasted salt water! "

The rueful visage disappeared, unable to withstand such a broadside, and its owner subsequently proved to be a first-rate seaman, and was an especial favorite with Stetson.

A circumstance occurred while the ship was in the stream, where she lay at anchor two or three days, which will convey a correct ides of the character of the mate. One afternoon, while all hands were busily employed in heaving in the slack of the cable, a boat, pulled by two stout, able-bodied men, came alongside. One of the men came on board, and addressing the mate, said he had a letter which he wished to send to Liverpool. The mate looked hard at the man, and replied in a gruff and surly tone, "We can't receive any letters here. The letter bag is at Ropes and Pickman's counting room, and you must leave your letter there if you want it to go to Liverpool in this ship. "

"Never mind, " exclaimed the stranger, "I am acquainted with one of the crew, and I will hand it to him. "

Regardless of Stetson's threats of vengeance provided he gave the letter into the hands of any one on board, the man stepped forward to the windlass, and handed the missive to one of the sailors.

At this contempt of his authority Stetson's indignation knew no bounds. He roared, in a voice hoarse with passion, "Lay hold of that scoundrel, Mr. Bachelder. Seize the villain by the throat. I'll teach im better than to cut his shines in a ship while I have charge of the deck. I'll seize him up to the mizzen shrouds, make a spread eagle of him, give him a cool dozen, and see how he will like that. "

The stranger, witnessing the mate's excitement, and hearing his violent language, seemed suddenly conscious that he had been guilty of a terrible crime, for which he was liable to be punished without trial or jury. He made a spring over the gunwale, and eluded the grasp of Mr. Bachelder, who followed him into the main chain-wales, and grabbed one of his coat tails just as he was slipping into his boat!

He struggled hard to get away, and his companion raised an oar and endeavored to strike the second mate with that ponderous club. The garment by which the stranger was detained, fortunately for him, was not made of such firm and solid materials as the doublet of Baillie Jarvie when he accompanied the Southrons in their invasion of the Highland fastnesses of Rob Roy. The texture, unable to bear the heavy strain, gave way; the man slid from the chain-wale into the boat, which was quickly shoved off, and the two terrified landsmen pulled away from the inhospitable ship with almost superhuman vigor, leaving the coat- tail in the hands of the second officer, who waved it as a trophy of victory!

Meanwhile Stetson was foaming at the mouth and raving like a madman. He ordered the steward to bring up his pistols to shoot the rascals, and when it seemed likely the offenders would escape, he called upon me, and another boy, by name, and in language neither courteous nor refined told us to haul the ship's yawl alongside and be lively about it. I instantly entered the boat from the taffrail by means of the painter; and in half a minute the boat was at the gangway, MANNED by a couple of BOYS, and Stetson rushed down the accommodation ladder, with a stout hickory stick in his hand, and without seating himself, seized the tiller, and with a tremendous oath, ordered us to shove off.

Away we went in full chase after the swiftly-receding boat, my young shipmate and myself bending our backs to the work with all the strength and skill of which we were master, while Stetson stood erect in the stern seats, at one time shaking his stick at the affrighted men, and hurling at their heads volleys of curses both loud and deep, at another, urging and encouraging us to pull harder, or cursing us in turn because we did not gain on the chase. The fugitives were dreadfully alarmed. They pulled for their lives; and the terror stamped on their visages would have been ludicrous, had we not known that if we came up with the chase a contest would take place that might be attended with serious, perhaps fatal, results.

The shore boat had a good start, which gave it an unfair advantage, and being propelled by two vigorous MEN, obeying an instinctive impulse to escape from an impending danger, kept about the same distance ahead. They steered for Long Wharf the nearest route to TERRA FIRMA passed the steps on the north side, and pulled alongside a schooner which was lying near the T, clambered to her decks, leaving the boat to her fate, nimbly leaped ashore, took to their heels, and commenced a race up the wharf as if the avenger of blood was upon their tracks!

Stetson steered the boat directly for the steps, up which he hastily ascended, and ordered me to follow. As we rounded the corner of the adjoining store, we beheld the fugitives leaving us at a pace which no sailor could expect to equal. The man who had particularly excited the wrath of the mate took the lead, and cut a conspicuous figure with his single coat-tail sticking out behind him horizontally like the leg of a loon!

The mate, seeing the hopelessness of further pursuit, suddenly stopped, and contented himself with shaking his cudgel at the runaways, and muttering between his teeth, "Run, you blackguards, run! "

And run they did, until they turned down India Street, and were lost to sight.

In a day or two after the occurrence above described, the ship Packet started on her voyage to Liverpool. She was a noble ship, well found and furnished in every respect, and, setting aside the uncertain temper and eccentricities of the chief mate, well officered and manned.

When we passed Boston light house with a fresh northerly breeze, one clear and cold morning towards the close of November, in the year 1811, bound on a voyage of several years' duration, I experienced no regret at leaving my home and native land, and had no misgiving in regard to the future. My spirits rose as the majestic dome of the State House diminished in the distance; my heart bounded with hope as we entered the waters of Massachusetts Bay. I felt that the path I was destined to travel, although perhaps a rugged one, would be a straight and successful one, and if not entirely free from thorns, would be liberally sprinkled with flowers.

It is wisely ordered by a benignant Providence that man, notwithstanding his eager desire to know the secrets of futurity, can never penetrate those mysteries. In some cases, could he know the changes which would take place in his condition, the misfortunes he would experience, the miseries he would undergo, in the lapse of only a few short years, or perhaps months, he would shrink like a coward from the conflict, and yield himself up to despair.

I could not long indulge in vagaries of the imagination. In a few hours the wind hauled into the north-east, and a short head sea rendered the ship exceedingly uneasy. While busily employed in various duties I felt an uncomfortable sensation pervading every part of my system. My head grew dizzy and my limbs grew weak; I found, to my utter confusion, that I WAS SEASICK! I had hardly made the humiliating discovery, when the boatswain hoarsely issued the unwelcome order, "Lay aloft, lads, and send down the royal yards and masts! "

My pride would not allow me to shrink from my duty, and especially a duty like this, which belonged to light hands. And while I heartily wished the masts and yards, which added so much to the beauty of the ship, and of which I was so proud in port, fifty fathoms beneath the keelson, I hastened with my wonted alacrity aloft, and commenced the work of sending down the main- royal yard.

Seasickness is an unwelcome malady at best. It not only deprives a person of all buoyancy of spirit, but plunges him headlong into the gulf of despondency. His only desire is to remain quiet; to stir neither limb nor muscle; to lounge or lie down and muse on his unhappy destiny. If he is urged by a sense of duty to arouse himself from this stupor, and occupy himself with labors and cares while weighed down by the heavy load, his condition, although it may command little sympathy from his companions, is truly pitiable.

In my particular case, feeling compelled to mount aloft, and attain that "bad eminence, " the main-royal mast head, while the slender spar was whipping backwards and forwards with every plunge of the ship into a heavy head sea, and the visible effect produced by every vibration causing me to fear an inverted position of my whole internal system, no one can imagine the extent of my sufferings. They were of a nature that Dante would eagerly have pounced upon to add to the horrors of his Inferno. I felt at times willing to quit my feeble hold of a backstay or shroud, and seek repose by diving into the briny billows beneath. If I had paused for a moment in my work I should, undoubtedly, have failed in its accomplishment. But Stetson's eye was upon me; his voice was heard at times calling out "Main-royal mast head, there! Bear a hand, and send down that mast! Why don't you bear a hand! "

To this reminder, making a desperate exertion, I promptly replied, in a spirited tone, "Ay, ay, sir! "

Diligence was the watchword, and it acted as my preserver.

It often happens that a crew, composed wholly or in part of old sailors, will make an experiment on the temper and character of the officers at the commencement of the voyage. When this is the case, the first night after leaving port will decide the question whether the officers or the men will have command of the ship. If the officers are not firm and peremptory; if they are deficient in nerve, and fail to rebuke, in a prompt and decided manner, aught bordering on insolence or insubordination in the outset, farewell to discipline, to good order and harmony, for the remainder of the passage.

Captain Bacon was a man of slight figure, gentlemanly exterior, and pleasant countenance. Although his appearance commanded respect, it was not calculated to inspire awe; and few would have supposed that beneath his quiet physiognomy and benevolent cast of features were concealed a fund of energy and determination of character which could carry him safely through difficulty and danger.

Mr. Bachelder, the second mate, was a young man of intelligence, familiar with his duties, and blessed with kind and generous feelings. Unlike Stetson, he was neither a blackguard nor a bully. After some little consultation among the old sailors who composed the starboard watch, it was thought advisable to begin with him, and ascertain if there was any GRIT in his composition.

It was about six bells eleven o'clock at night when the wind hauling to the north-west, Mr. Bachelder called out, "Forward there! Lay aft and take a pull of the weather braces. "

One of the men, a smart active fellow, who went by the name of Jack Robinson, and had been an unsuccessful candidate for the office of boatswain, replied in a loud and distinct tone, "Ay, ay! "

This was agreed on as the test. I knew the crisis had come, and awaited with painful anxiety the result.

Mr. Bachelder rushed forward into the midst of the group near the end of the windlass.

"Who said, 'Ay, ay'? " he inquired, in an angry tone.

"I did, " replied Robinson.

"YOU did! Don't you know how to reply to an officer in a proper manner? "

"How SHOULD I reply? " said Robinson, doggedly.

"Say 'Ay, ay, SIR, ' when you reply to me, " cried Bachelder, in a tone of thunder at the same time seizing him by the collar and giving him a shake "and, " continued he, "don't undertake to cut any of your shines here, my lad! If you do, you will be glad to die the death of a miserable dog. Lay aft, men, and round in the weather braces! "

"Ay, ay, sir! Ay, ay, sir! " was the respectful response from every side.

The yards were trimmed to the breeze, and when the watch gathered again on the forecastle it was unanimously voted that IT WOULD NOT DO!

Notwithstanding the decided result of the experiment with the second mate, one of the men belonging to the larboard watch, named Allen, determined to try conclusions with the captain and chief mate, and ascertain how far they would allow the strict rules of discipline on shipboard to be infringed. Allen was a powerful fellow, of huge proportions, and tolerably good features, which, however, were overshadowed by a truculent expression. Although of a daring disposition, and unused to subordination, having served for several years in ships engaged in the African slave trade, the nursery of pirates and desperadoes, he showed but little wisdom in trying the patience of Stetson.

On the second night after leaving port, the ship being under double-reefed topsails, the watch was summoned aft to execute some duty. The captain was on deck, and casually remarked to the mate, "It blows hard, Mr. Stetson; we may have a regular gale before morning!"

Allen at that moment was passing along to WINDWARD of the captain and mate. He stopped, and before Stetson could reply, said in a tone of insolent familiarity, "Yes, it blows hard, and will blow harder yet! Well, who cares? Let it blow and be _____! "

Captain Bacon seemed utterly astonished at the impudence of the man; but Stetson, who was equally prompt and energetic on all occasions, and who divined the object that Allen had in view, in lieu of a civil rejoinder dealt him a blow on the left temple, which sent him with violence against the bulwarks. Allen recovered himself, however, and sprang on the mate like a tiger, clasped him in his sinewy embrace, and called upon his watchmates for assistance.

As Stetson and Allen were both powerful men it is uncertain what would have been the result had Stetson fought the battle single-handed. The men looked on, waiting the result, but without daring to interfere. Not so the captain. When he saw Allen attack the mate, he seized a belaying pin, that was loose in the fife-rail, and watching his opportunity, gave the refractory sailor two or three smart raps over the head and face, which embarrassed him amazingly, caused him to release his grasp on the mate, and felled him to the deck!

The mate then took a stout rope's end and threshed him until he roared for mercy. The fellow was terribly punished and staggered forward, followed by a volley of threats and anathemas.

But the matter did not end here. At twelve o'clock Allen went below, and was loud in his complaints of the barbarous manner in which he had been treated. He swore revenge, and said he would lay a plan to get the mate into the forecastle, and then square all accounts. Robinson and another of the starboard watch, having no idea that Stetson could be enticed below, approved of the suggestion, and intimated that they would lend him a hand if necessary. They did not KNOW Stetson!

When the watch was called at four o'clock Allen did not make his appearance. In about half an hour the voice of Stetson was heard at the forescuttle ordering him on deck.

"Ay, ay, sir, " said Allen, "I am coming directly. "

"You had better do so, " said the mate, "if you know when you are well off. "

"Ay, ay, sir! "

Allen was sitting on a chest, dressed, but did not move. I was lying in my berth attentive to the proceedings, as, I believe were all my watchmates. In about a quarter of an hour Stetson took another look down the scuttle, and bellowed out, "Allen, are you coming on deck or not? "

"Ay, ay, sir; directly! "

"If I have to go down after you, my good fellow, it will be worse for you, that's all. "

Allen remained sitting on the chest. Day began to break. Stetson was again heard at the entrance of the forecastle. His patience, of which he had not a large stock, was exhausted.

"Come on deck, this instant, you lazy, lounging, big-shouldered renegade! Will you let other people do your work? Show your broken head and your lovely battered features on deck at once in the twinkling of a handspike. I want to see how you look after your frolic! "

"Ay, ay, sir! I'm coming right up. "

"You lie, you rascal. You don't mean to come! But I'll soon settle the question whether you are to have your way in this ship or I am to have mine! "

Saying this, Stetson descended the steps which led into the habitation of the sailors. In doing this, under the peculiar circumstances, he gave a striking proof of his fearless character. He had reason to anticipate a desperate resistance from Allen, while some of the sailors might also be ready to take part with their shipmate, if they saw him overmatched; and in that dark and close apartment, where no features could be clearly distinguished, he would be likely to receive exceedingly rough treatment.

Stetson, however, was a man who seldom calculated consequences in cases of this kind. He may have been armed, but he made no display of other weapons than his brawny fist. He seized Allen by the collar with a vigorous grasp. "You scoundrel, " said he, "what do you mean by this conduct? Go on deck and attend to your duty! On deck, I say! Up with you, at once! "

Allen at first held back, hoping that some of his shipmates would come to his aid, as they partly promised; but not a man stirred, greatly to his disappointment and disgust. They, doubtless, felt it might be unsafe to engage in the quarrels of others; and Allen, after receiving a few gentle reminders from the mate in the shape of clips on the side of his head and punches among the short ribs, preceded the mate on deck. He was conquered.

The weather was cold and cheerless; the wind was blowing heavy; the rain was falling fast; and Allen, who had few clothes, was thinly clad; but he was sent aloft in an exposed situation, and kept there through the greater part of the day. His battered head, his cut face, his swollen features, and his gory locks told the tale of his punishment. Stetson had no magnanimity in his composition. He cherished a grudge against that man to the end of the passage, and lost no opportunity to indulge his hatred and vindictiveness.

"Never mind, " said Allen, one day, when sent on some useless mission in the vicinity of the knight-heads, while the ship was plunging violently, and sending cataracts of salt water over the bowsprit at every dive; "never mind, it will be only for a single passage. "

"I know that, " said Stetson, with an oath; "and I will take good care to 'work you up' well during the passage. " And he was as good as his word.

The mate of a ship, especially when the captain is inactive, is not properly acquainted with his duties, or is disposed to let him pursue his own course, is vested with great authority. He has it in his power to contribute to the comfort of the men, and establish that good understanding between the cabin and the forecastle which should ever reign in a merchant ship. But it sometimes, unfortunately, happens that the officers of a ship are men of amazingly little souls; deficient in manliness of character, illiberal in their sentiments, and jealous of their authority; and although but little deserving the respect of good men, are rigorous in exacting it. Such men are easily offended, take umbrage at trifles, and are unforgiving in their resentments. While they have power to annoy or punish an individual from whom they have received real or fancied injuries, they do not hesitate to exercise it.

Every seafaring man, of large experience, has often witnessed the unpleasant consequences of these old grudges, of this system of punishing a ship's company, by petty annoyances and unceasing hard work for some trifling misconduct on the part of one or more of the crew during the early part of the voyage. A master of a ship must be aware that the interest of all parties will be promoted by harmony on shipboard, which encourages the sailors to perform faithfully their manifold duties. Therefore, a good shipmaster will not only be firm, and decided, and just, and gentlemanly himself towards his crew, but he will promptly interfere to prevent unjust and tyrannical conduct on the part of his officers, when they are inexperienced or of a vindictive disposition.

When a man is insolent or insubordinate, the punishment or rebuke, if any is intended, SHOULD BE PROMPTLY ADMINISTERED. The account against him should not be entered on the books, but balanced on the spot. Whatever is his due should be paid off to the last stiver, and there the matter should end, never to be again agitated, or even referred to. This system of petty tyranny, this "working up" of a whole ship's company, or a single individual, in order to gratify a vindictive and unforgiving spirit, has been the cause of a deal of trouble and unhappiness, and has furnished materials in abundance for "men learned in the law. "

Sailors are not stocks and stones. Few of them are so low and degraded as not to be able to distinguish the right from the wrong. They are aware of the importance of discipline, and know they must submit to its restraints, and render prompt obedience to orders from their superiors, without question; yet few of them are so deeply imbued with the meek spirit of Christianity as to forego remonstrance to injustice or resistance to tyranny.

The Packet proved to be a fast-sailing ship. The log often indicated ten, eleven, and eleven and a half knots. We had a quick but rough passage across the Atlantic, and frequently took on board a much larger quantity of salt water than was agreeable to those who had berths in her bows. In four days after leaving Boston we reached the Banks of Newfoundland; in eighteen days, we struck soundings off Cape Clear; and in twenty-one days, let go our anchor in the River Mersey.

Chapter XIV DISAPPOINTED HOPES

The day succeeding our arrival at Liverpool, having disposed of our gunpowder, we hauled into King's Dock, and commenced preparations for receiving the remainder of our cargo. At that period there were only four floating docks in Liverpool. The town was not in a prosperous condition. It had not recovered from the shock caused by the abolition of the slave trade. That inhuman traffic had been carried on to a very great extent for many years by Liverpool merchants, and, of course, the law prohibiting the traffic a law wise and humane, in itself, but injurious to the interests of individuals was resisted in Parliament by all the commercial wealth of Liverpool and Bristol, the two principal ports in which the merchants resided who were engaged in the slave traffic. Even in 1811, many fine ships were lying idle in the docks, which had been built expressly for that business; and their grated air-ports, high and solid bulwarks, peculiar hatchways, large and unsightly poops, all gave evidence of the expensive arrangements and great importance of the "Guineamen" of those days.

It was expected that our cargo would be completed immediately after our arrival at Liverpool, and the ship despatched on her way around Cape Horn; but the tobacco which we had taken on board in Boston, being an article on which an enormous duty was exacted, was the cause of trouble and delay. Consultations with the authorities in London were necessary, and weeks elapsed before Captain Bacon could get the ship out of the clutches of the revenue department. In the mean time the crew remained by the ship, but took their meals at a boarding house on shore, as was the custom in Liverpool. They were all furnished with American protections; but some of them, unwilling to rely on the protecting power of a paper document, which in their cases told a tale of fiction, adopted various expedients to avoid the press- gangs which occasionally thridded the streets, and even entered dwellings when the doors were unfastened, to capture sailors and COMPEL them to VOLUNTEER to serve their king and country.

One of these unfortunate men, after having successfully dodged the pressgangs for a fortnight, and living meanwhile in an unenviable state of anxiety, was pounced upon by some disguised members of a pressgang as he left the boarding house one evening. He struggled hard to escape, but was knocked down and dragged off to the naval rendezvous. He was examined the next morning before the American consul, but, notwithstanding his protection, his citizenship could not be substantiated. He was in reality a Prussian, and of course detained as a lawful prize. The poor fellow lamented his hard destiny with tears. He knew the degrading and unhappy character of the slavery to which he was doomed probably for life, and strongly implored Captain Bacon to leave no means untried to procure his release; but the captain's efforts were in vain.

I was rejoiced when intelligence came that the trouble about the tobacco was at an end, and the remainder of the cargo could be taken on board. On the following forenoon the ship was hauled stern on to the quay, and the heavy bales of goods, when brought down, were tumbled on deck by the crew and rolled along to the main hatchway. I was employed with one of my shipmates in this work, when some clumsy fellows who were handling another bale behind me pitched it over in such a careless manner that it struck my left leg, which it doubled up like a rattan. I felt that my leg was fractured, indeed, I heard the bone snap, and threw myself on a gun carriage, making wry faces in consequence of the pain I suffered.

"Are you MUCH hurt, Hawser? " inquired the chief mate, in a tone of irony, and with a grim smile.

"Yes, sir; badly hurt. I'm afraid my leg is broken. "

"Not so bad as that, I hope, " exclaimed Stetson, with some display of anxiety. "I guess you are more frightened than hurt. Let me look at your leg. "

He found my surmises were correct, and expressed more sympathy for my misfortune than I could have expected. I was carried into the cabin, and after a short delay conveyed in a carriage to the Infirmary or hospital. When the carriage reached the gateway of the Infirmary, the bell was rung by the coachman, and the porter made his appearance. He was a tall, hard-featured, sulky-looking man, about fifty years of age, called Thomas; and having held that office a number of years, he assumed as many airs, and pretended to as much surgical skill, as the professors.

"What's the matter now? " inquired the porter, with a discontented growl.

"An accident, " replied the coachman. "This boy has broken his leg. He is a sailor, belonging to an American ship. "

"Ah, ha! An American, is he? " added Thomas, with a diabolical sneer. "A Yankee Doodle! Never mind; we'll take care of him. "

I was lifted from the carriage and carried by the ship's armorer, very gently, into one of the rooms, the grim-looking porter leading the way. I was placed in an arm chair, and, as the surgeon whose duty it was to attend to accidents on that day was not immediately forthcoming, the porter undertook to examine the fracture. He proceeded to take off the stocking, which fitted rather closely, and the removal of which gave me intolerable pain. I begged him to rip off the garment with a knife, and put an end to my torments. The armorer also remonstrated against his unnecessary cruelty, but in vain. The only reply of the grumbling rascal was that the stocking was too good to be destroyed, and he never knew a Yankee who could bear pain like a man! He then began, in a cool and business-like manner, to twist my foot about, grinding the fractured bones together to ascertain, as he said, whether the limb was actually broken! And I verily believe that my complaints and groans, which I did not attempt to suppress, were sweet music in his ears. It was clear to me that, for some reason which I could never learn, Mr. Thomas owed the whole Yankee nation a grudge, and was ready to pay it off on an individual whenever he could get a chance.

After he finished his examination, I looked around the room, which was not a large one. It was number one of the "accident ward. " It contained six beds, besides a pallet in a corner for the nurse of the ward. These beds, with two exceptions, were occupied by unfortunate beings like myself. As I was brought in among them they gazed upon me earnestly, prompted, I verily believe, not only by curiosity, but commiseration for my unhappy condition. The surgeon made his appearance, and succeeded, without much difficulty, in setting the limb, an operation which, acknowledging its necessity, I bore with becoming fortitude. I was placed on my back in one of the unoccupied beds, with the rather unnecessary caution to lie perfectly still. The armorer returned to the ship, and I was left among strangers.

I now had leisure to reflect on my situation. My hopes of visiting the "north-west coast" were suddenly destroyed. A cripple, in a strange land, without money or friends, a cloud seemed to rest on my prospects. During the remainder of the day and the succeeding night I suffered much from "the blues. " My spirits were out of tune. The scanty hospital fare that was offered me I sent away untouched, and sleep refused to bury my senses in forgetfulness until long after the midnight hour. This, however, might have been partly owing to the involuntary groans and murmurs of unfortunate sufferers in my immediate vicinity. That first day and night wore a sombre aspect, and teemed with gloomy forebodings.

In the morning I fell into a kind of doze, and dreamed that I was walking in a beautiful meadow, which was traversed by a wide and deep ditch. Wishing to pass to the other side I attempted to leap the ditch, but jumped short, and buried myself in mud and mire to the waist! I awoke with a start, which I accompanied with a cry of distress. I had moved the broken limb, and furnished more work for the surgeon and suffering for myself.

My gloomy reflections and disquietude of mind did not last long. In the morning my attention was attracted by the novelties of my situation, and I found much to excite my curiosity and interest my feelings. My "fit of the blues" had passed off to return no more. I had some conversation with a remarkably tall, military- looking man, who moved about awkwardly as if he was learning to walk upon stilts, or was lame in both legs, which I afterwards found to be the case. He appeared friendly and intelligent, and gave me interesting information in relation to the inmates and economy of the establishment.

I learned from him that the bed nearest mine, within a few feet on the right hand, and the one beyond it, were occupied by two boys who were victims of a sad misfortune. Their intense sufferings were the cause of the moans and murmurings I had heard during the night. These boys were apprentices to the rope-making business, and a few days before, while spinning ropeyarns, with the loose hemp wound in folds around their waists, the youngest, a lad about fourteen years old, unwittingly approached an open fire, the weather being cold. A spark ignited the hemp, and in a moment the whole was in a blaze. The other boy, obeying an involuntary but generous impulse, rushed to the assistance of his companion, only to share his misfortune. They were both terribly burned, and conveyed to the hospital.

Every morning the rations for the day were served out to the patients. The quality of the food, always excepting a dark- looking liquid of revolting aspect, known as "beer porridge, " and which I ate only through fear of starvation was generally good, and the quantity was sufficient to keep the patients alive, while they had no reason to apprehend ill consequences from a surfeit.

In the course of the forenoon Captain Bacon came to see me. He expressed regret at my misfortune, and tried to console me with the assurance that I should be well cared for. He said the ship Packet would sail the next day, that my chest and bedding should be sent to the house where the crew had boarded, that HE HAD COMMENDED ME TO THE PARTICULAR CONSIDERATION OF THE AMERICAN CONSUL, who was his consignee, an would see that I was sent back to the United States as soon as I should be in a condition to leave the hospital. He put a silver dollar into my hand, as he said to buy some fruit, bade me be of good cheer, and left me to my reflections.

In the afternoon of the same day, one of my shipmates, a kind-hearted lad, about my own age, called at the hospital to bid me farewell. He regretted the necessity of our separation, and wept over the misfortune that had occasioned it. From him I learned that the key of my chest having been left in the lock when I was carried from the ship, he feared that Allen and one or two others of the crew, who were not liberally supplied with clothing for a long voyage, had made free with my property. He also told me that three of the ship's company had deserted, having no confidence in the amiable qualities of Mr. Stetson, the chief mate; but that Allen, who had been the victim of his vindictiveness during the whole passage from Boston, dreading the horrors of impressment more than the barbarity of the mate, and having a good American protection, had determined to remain by the ship!

He told me, further, he was by no means satisfied with the character of Stetson, and feared that when again on the ocean he would prove a Tartar; and that I had no great reasons to regret an accident which would prevent my proceeding on the voyage.

I subsequently learned that Stetson showed his true colors after the ship left Liverpool, and owing to his evil deportment and tyrannical conduct, there was little peace or comfort for the crew during the three years' voyage.

On the third day of my residence in the Infirmary, the unfortunate boy who occupied the bed nearest mine appeared to be sinking rapidly. It was sad to witness his sufferings. His mother, a woman in the lowest rank of life, was with him through the day. She eagerly watched every symptom of his illness, nursed him with care and tenderness, sought to prepare him for the great change which was about to take place; and, a true woman and a mother, endeavored to hide her own anguish while she ministered to the bodily and spiritual wants of her only child, who nobly risked his life to save that of his companion. I watched the proceedings with deep interest through the day, and when night came I felt no inclination to sleep. The groans of the unfortunate boy became fainter and fainter, and it was evident he would soon be released from his sufferings by the hand of death.

At length I became weary with watching, and about eleven o'clock fell asleep, in spite of the dying moans of the boy and the half- stifled sobs of his mother. I slept soundly, undisturbed by the mournful scenes which were enacted around me. When I awoke the room was lighted only by the rays of an expiring lamp in the chimney corner. No one was moving; not a sound was heard except the loud breathing of the inmates, who, their wonted rest having been interrupted by this melancholy interlude, had buried their pains and anxieties in sleep.

I looked towards the bed where the sufferer lay whose sad fate had so attracted my attention and elicited my sympathies a few hours before. His mother was no longer present. His moans were no longer heard. His form seemed extended motionless on the bed, and his head reposed as usual on the pillow. But I was startled at perceiving him staring fixedly at me with eyes preternaturally large, and of a cold, glassy, ghastly appearance! I closed my own eyes and turned my head away, while a tremor shook very nerve. Was this an illusion? Was I laboring under the effects of a dream? Or had my imagination conjured up a spectre?

I looked again. The eyes, like two full moons, were still there, glaring at me with that cold, fixed, maddening expression. I could no longer control my feelings. If I had been able to use my limbs I should have fled from the room. As that was impossible I called loudly to the nurse, and awoke her from a sound sleep! She came muttering to my bedside, and inquired what was the matter?

"Look at William's eyes! " said I. "Is he dead, or is he alive? What is the meaning of those horrible-looking, unearthly eyes? Why DON'T you speak? "

"Don't be a fool, " replied the nurse, sharply, "and let shadows frighten you out of your wits. "

While I remained in an agony of suspense she leisurely returned to the fireplace, took the lamp from the hearth, raised the wick to increase the light, and approaching the bedside, held it over the body of the occupant. The boy was dead! Two large pieces of bright copper coin had been placed over the eyes for the purpose of closing the lids after death, and the faint and flickering reflection of the lamplight, aided, probably, by the excited condition of my nervous system, had given them that wild and ghastly appearance which had shaken my soul with terror.

For three weeks I lay in my bed, an attentive observer of the singular scenes that occurred in my apartment. I was visited every morning by a student in surgery, or "dresser, " and twice a week by one of the regular surgeons of the establishment while going his rounds. My general health was good, notwithstanding a want of that exercise and fresh air to which I had been accustomed. My appetite was remarkable; indeed, my greatest, if not only cause of complaint, was the very STINTED QUANTITY of daily food that was served out to each individual. No discrimination was observed; the robust young man, with an iron constitution, was, so far as related to food, placed on a par with the poor invalid, debilitated with protracted suffering or dying of inappetency.

In every other situation in which I have been placed I have had abundance of food. Sometimes the food was of a quality deplorably wretched, it is true, but such as it was there was always enough. But in the Liverpool Infirmary I experienced the miseries of SHORT ALLOWANCE, and had an opportunity to witness the effect it produces in ruffling the temper and breeding discontent. It also opened my eyes to the instinctive selfishness of man. Those who were in sound health, with good appetites, although apparently endued with a full share of affections and sympathies, seemed actually to rejoice when one of their companions, through suffering and debility, was unable to consume his allowance of bread or porridge, which would be distributed among the more healthy inmates of the apartment.

Chapter XV SCENES IN A HOSPITAL

At the expiration of three weeks the dresser informed me he was about to case my fractured limb in splints and bandages, when I might quit my mattress, don my garments, and hop about the room or seat myself by the fireside.

This was good news, but my joy was somewhat dampened by the intelligence that I could not be furnished immediately with a pair of crutches, all belonging to the establishment being in use. I borrowed a pair occasionally for a few minutes, from an unfortunate individual who was domiciled in my apartment, and sometimes I shuffled about for exercise with a stout cane in my right hand, and a house-brush, in an inverted position under my left arm, in lieu of a crutch.

I witnessed many interesting scenes during my stay in the Infirmary, and fell in with some singular individuals, all of which showed me phases of human life that I had never dreamed of. The tall, military-looking man, with whom I became acquainted soon after I entered the establishment, proved to have been a soldier. He had served for years in a regiment of heavy dragoons, and attained the rank of corporal. He had sabred Frenchmen by dozens during the unsuccessful campaign in Holland under the Duke of York. He fought his battles over again with all the ardor and energy of an Othello, and to an audience as attentive, although, it may be, not so high-born or beautiful.

There was also present during my stay a young native of the Emerald Isle, who had seen service in the British navy. In an obstinate and bloody battle between English and French squadrons off the Island of Lissa, in the Adriatic, about nine months before, in which Sir William Hoste achieved a splendid victory, his leg had been shattered by a splinter. After a partial recovery he had received his discharge, and was returning to his home in "dear Old Ireland, " when a relapse took place, and he took refuge in the hospital. He also could tell tales of wondrous interest connected with man-of-war life. He loved to talk of his cruises in the Mediterranean, of the whizzing of cannon balls, the mutilation of limbs, decks slippery with gore, levanters, pressgangs, boatswains' calls, and the cat-o'-nine tails of the boatswains' mates.

The patient, from whom I occasionally borrowed a pair of crutches, although a pleasant companion, bore upon his person unequivocal marks of having met with rough handling on the ocean or on the land. He was MINUS an eye, his nose had been knocked athwartships to the great injury of his beauty, and a deep scar, from a wound made with a bludgeon, adorned one of his temples! I learned that this man, who seemed to have been the football of fortune and had received many hard kicks, had never been in the army or the navy, that his wounds had been received in CIVIL wars, battling with his countrymen. I was further told by the nurse, as a secret, that although he was so amiable among his fellow-sufferers in the hospital, when outside the walls, if he could obtain a glass of gin or whiskey to raise his temper and courage to the STRIKING point, he never passed a day without fighting. He was notorious for his pugnacious propensities; had been in the Infirmary more than once for the tokens he had received of the prowess of his opponents. In his battles he always came off second best, and was now in the "accident ward" in consequence of a broken leg, having been kicked down stairs by a gang of rowdies whom he had insulted and defied!

There were also in the Infirmary inmates of a more pacific character. Fortunately for mankind it is not the mission of every one to fight. Among them was a gardener, a poor, inoffensive man, advanced in years, who with a cleaver had chopped off accidentally, he said two fingers of his right hand. The mutilation was intentional without doubt; his object having been to procure a claim for subsistence in the Infirmary for a time, and afterwards a passport to the poorhouse in Chester for life. He had experienced the ills of poverty; had outlived his wife and children; and able to talk well and fluently, entertained us with homely but forcible narratives illustrating life in the lowest ranks of society. When his wounds were healed he was reluctant to quit his comfortable quarters, and was actually driven from the establishment.

Other patients were brought in from time to time, and their wounds dressed. Some were dismissed in a few days; others detained for months. One intelligent young man, an English mechanic, was afflicted with a white swelling on his knee and suffered intolerable pain. His sobs and groans through the night, which he could not suppress, excited my sympathy, but grated harshly on the nerves of my tall friend the corporal of dragoons, who expostulated with him seriously on the unreasonableness of his conduct, arguing, like the honest tar on board the brig Clarissa, that these loud indications of suffering, while they afforded no positive relief to the sufferer, disturbed the slumbers of those who were free from pain or bore it with becoming fortitude.

In the evening, after we had partaken of the regular meal, those of us who were able to move about, and to whom I have more particularly alluded, would gather around the hearth, a coal fire burning in the grate, and pass a couple of hours in conversation, in which agreeable occupations, having read much and already seen something of the world, I was able to bear a part. There are few persons who are unable to converse, and converse well too, when their feelings are enlisted and they labor under no restraint; and very few persons so dull and stupid as to fail to receive or impart instruction from conversation with others.

Notwithstanding the rules of the infirmary to the contrary, the inmates of "number one" were not altogether deprived of the advantages and charms of female society. To say nothing of the old nurse, who was a host in gossip herself, her two daughters, both young and pretty girls, were sometimes smuggled into the Infirmary by the connivance of the grim and trustworthy porter, and remained there days at a time, carefully hid away in the pantry whenever "the master" or the surgeons went their regular rounds, which was always at stated hours. When the wind raged without, and the rain, hail, or snow sought entrance through the casement, while sitting near a comfortable fire, listening to female prattle and gossip, narratives of incidents of real life, discussions on disputed points in politics, philosophy, or religion between my friend with the crutches and the tall corporal of dragoons, who were both as fond of controversy as Mr. Shandy himself; or drinking in with my ears the Irish tar's glowing descriptions.

> "Of moving accidents by flood and field;
> And of the cannibals that each other eat;
> The anthropophagi, and men whose heads
> Do grow beneath their shoulders!"

I was led to confess there were worse places in the world than the Liverpool Infirmary.

After a week's delay I came into possession of a pair of crutches, and could move around the room at pleasure, take exercise in the hall, and even visit an acquaintance in either of the other apartments. The garden attached to the establishment was thrown open to the patients at stated hours on particular days. The season was not inviting; nevertheless, one sunny day, accompanied by my lame friend of pugnacious reputation, I visited the garden, and rejoiced at finding myself once more in he open air. The ramble on crutches through the lonely walks was truly refreshing. Our spirits mounted to fever heat, and as we returned towards the building through the neatly gravelled avenue, my companion proposed a race, to which I assented. I have forgotten which won the race; I know we both made capital time, and performed to our own satisfaction, but not to the satisfaction of others. The gardener grumbled at the manner in which his walks were perforated and disfigured by our crutches. He complained to the authorities, and greatly to our regret a regulation was adopted by which all persons using crutches were forbidden to enter the garden.

I remained six weeks in the Infirmary, and became accustomed to the place, and made myself useful in various ways. I held the basin when a patient was let blood; I took charge of the instruments and bandages when a serious wound was closed by sutures and afterwards dressed; and was particularly busy when a fracture was examined or a dislocation reduced. Indeed I took a strange kind of interest in witnessing and aiding in the various operations, and was in a fair way to become a good practical surgeon, when I was discharged, and found myself a poor sailor, friendless, penniless, and lame. But the surgical knowledge, inaccurate and desultory as it was, which I acquired in the Liverpool Infirmary, and the power to preserve coolness and presence of mind, and minister relief in cases of wounds and dangerous diseases, when no medical adviser could be applied to, has often since been of valuable service to myself and others.

I took an affectionate farewell of my friends and acquaintances in the establishment, not forgetting the nurse and her pretty daughters, and, accompanied by the landlord of the house where the crew of the ship Packet boarded, passed through the gateway without meeting any obstruction on the part of the porter, who, on the contrary, grinned his approbation of my departure.

The distance to the boarding house was about half a mile; nevertheless I accomplished it easily on crutches without being fatigued, and congratulated myself when I passed the threshold and arrived at what I considered my home. But my troubles were not ended. The landlady, who was actually "the head" of the house, did not welcome my return with the cordiality I expected. She expressed a hope that the American consul would lose no time in providing means for my return to the United States, and favored me with the interesting information that while the regular charge for board without lodging was eighteen shillings a week, the American government allowed only twelve shillings a week for board and lodging. The inevitable inference was, that I was an unprofitable boarder, and the sooner they got me off their hands the better.

Another circumstance was a source of greater chagrin. When I reached the house, one of my first inquiries was for my chest and other property which I left in the forecastle of the ship. My chest was safely deposited with the landlord; BUT IT WAS NEARLY EMPTY! To my dismay I found that my stock of clothing for a two years' voyage jackets, boots, hats, blankets, and books had vanished. A few "old duds" only were left, hardly enough for a change of raiment. The officers had neglected to lock my chest and look after my little property; the men were bound on a long and tempestuous voyage, some of them scantily furnished with clothing; the ship was to sail in a day or two after I was carried to the hospital; the temptation was irresistible; they helped themselves freely at the expense of their unfortunate shipmate!

The United States consul at Liverpool was a merchant, of large means and extensive business; a man of great respectability, and it was confidently asserted, of generous feelings. I doubted not that when my case was represented to him he would grant me some relief, especially as Captain Bacon had recommended me to his care. I had heard nothing from him in the Infirmary. He was notified, officially, of my discharge; and as vessels were every day leaving Liverpool for Boston and New York, I expected to be immediately provided with a passage to one of those ports. But when days passed away, and I seemed to be forgotten, I mounted my crutches one morning and hobbled off through the crowded streets to a distant part of the town, in quest of an interview with the consul, intending to solicit that assistance to which every American citizen in distress was entitled.

With some difficulty, for Liverpool is not a rectangular town, I found the counting room of the consul, into which I boldly entered, confidently anticipating not only relief but sympathy for my misfortune. My appearance was not prepossessing, as my garments, although of the true nautical cut, were neither new nor genteel; and although I was in perfect health, my complexion was sallow from long confinement. But these drawbacks on my respectability, I thought, under the circumstances, might be excused. I found myself in a comfortable apartment in which two or three young men were writing at desks, one of whom, a dapper little fellow, dressed with as much precision and neatness as if he had just escaped from a bandbox, came towards me with a stern, forbidding look, and asked me what I wanted.

"I want to see the American consul. "

"The consul is not in. "

"When do you expect him? " I inquired, in a tone of disappointment.

"'Tis uncertain. He may not be here today. "

"I am sorry, as I have some important business with him. "

"What is your important business? " demanded the clerk, in an authoritative manner. "Perhaps I can attend to it. "

"I am the young American sailor, who met with an accident on board the ship Packet, and was sent to the Infirmary. I have recently been discharged, and am in want of some articles of clothing, and particularly a pair of shoes. I also want to know if the consul has taken steps towards procuring me a passage to Boston"

"Very IMPORTANT business, truly! " replied the Englishman, with a sneer. "How does it happen that you are so poorly off for clothing?"

I explained the circumstances connected with the robbery of my chest by my shipmates.

"A likely story! " he exclaimed. "As to giving you a pair of shoes, my fine fellow, that is out of the question. When any step is taken towards sending you to the United States, you, or the man you board with, will hear of it. " Saying this, the worthy representative of our government, after pointing significantly to the door, turned away and resumed his occupation at the desk. Disappointed and shocked at such a reception, I ventured to inquire if I should be able to see the consul on the following day.

"No, " replied the clerk, abruptly, without raising his eyes from the desk; "neither tomorrow nor the day after. "

I left the counting room, hobbled down the steps, and returned to my temporary home, feeling like "the Ancient Mariner, " "a sadder and a wiser man! "

Chapter XVI UNITED STATES CONSULS

Weeks passed, and I remained in Liverpool. I had called several times at the consulate, and each time met with the same ungracious reception. I could never see the consul, and began to regard him as a myth. I did not then know that every time I called he was seated at his comfortable desk in a room elegantly furnished, which was entered from the ante-room occupied by his clerks. Nor could I get any satisfactory information from the well-dressed Englishman, his head clerk. I ventured to ask that gentleman one day if Captain Bacon had not left money with Mr. Maury for my benefit. But he seemed astonished at my audacity in imagining the possibility of such a thing.

After the lapse of three weeks, a messenger came to my boarding house with directions for me to appear at the consulate the next morning at nine o'clock precisely. Full of hope, overjoyed that some change was about to take place in my destiny, I impatiently awaited the hour in which I was to present myself at the office of the American consul, hoping to have an interview with that dignitary. By this time I had thrown aside my crutches, and, although owing to the weakness of my fractured limb I limped as ungracefully as the swarthy deity who, after being kicked out of heaven, set up his blacksmith's shop in the Isle of Lemnos, I managed, with the aid of a stout cane, to pass through the streets without difficulty.

When I reached the counting room of the consul, I found the everlasting clerk at his post, as unfeeling, as authoritative, and haughty as ever. He addressed me at once as follows: "You will go directly to Queen's Dock; find the ship Lady Madison of New York, and put this letter into the hands of Captain Swain. He will give you a passage to New York, where you must take care of yourself. The ship will sail in a day or two. Be sure to be on board when the ship leaves the dock. "

I regretted that a passage had not been provided in a vessel going directly to Boston. Ships were leaving Liverpool every day for that place. Nevertheless, I took the letter with a good grace, told the clerk I was rejoiced at such good news; that I was as much pleased at the idea of leaving Liverpool as he could possibly be at getting rid of my complaints. But I suggested that I was not in a condition to WORK MY PASSAGE as was proposed, at that inclement season, unless I was furnished with some additional clothing, a pea-jacket, a blanket, and a pair of boots or shoes; and I pointed to the shoes on my feet, which were little better than a pair of very shabby sandals.

The little deputy listened with impatience to my suggestions. He then wrote something on a slip of paper. "Here, " said he, "is an order for a pair of shoes; and it is all you will get! A pea- jacket is out of the question; and as for blankets, I suppose you'll find enough on board. Captain Swain will take care of you. Your passage will not be a long one only thirty or forty days. I dare say you will live through it; if not, there will be no great loss! " And conscious that he had said a good thing, he looked at his fellow-clerks and smiled.

I felt indignant at such treatment, but wisely refrained from giving utterance to my feelings, and proceeded directly to the Queen's Dock, where I found Captain Swain, and handed him the letter. He read it, crumpled it up and put it in his pocket, and then stared fixedly at me, exclaiming, "Well, this is a pretty business! What does the consul mean by sending such a chap as YOU home in my ship? Are there not ships enough in port to take you home without singling out mine? "

To this question I could give no satisfactory answer, nor is it probable he expected one. After a further ebullition of wrath he honored me with another stare, surveyed me from head to foot, and with an air rather rude than polite, gruffly remarked, "Well, I suppose I must take you, and make the best of it. The ship will sail the day after tomorrow; " and he turned away, muttering something I could not distinctly hear, but which I suspect was not complimentary to myself or the American consul.

I returned to my boarding house, and gladdened the master and mistress with the intelligence that the consul had at last found a ship to take me to the united States. I packed in my chest the few articles my shipmates had considerately left me, not forgetting the pair of shoes which the mild-mannered and compassionate consular clerk had given me, and made my appearance, a most unwelcome guest, on the deck of the Lady Madison, as the ship was hauling out of dock. And thus, without articles of clothing necessary to supply my actual wants; without bed or bedding; destitute of "small stores, " as tea, coffee, sugar, etc, which were not furnished the sailors, they receiving a certain sum of money instead and supplying themselves, deprived of the little comforts which even the most unthrifty seamen will provide on a passage across the Atlantic; the victim, not of imprudence or vice, but of misfortune; afer a tedious and unnecessary delay, I was sent, a stranger, against whom the captain and officers were unjustly prejudiced, and, in a crippled condition, on board a ship to work my passage to my native land! And this was done by the orders and authority of a man who was bound by his official duties to render all necessary and reasonable relief to Americans in distress!

Were this a solitary instance of the kind I should hardly indulge in a passing remark. But I have reason to believe that such cases, caused by the inhumanity or culpable neglect of American consuls in foreign ports, are not uncommon. If such proceedings take place under the eye and authority and apparent sanction of a man of high character and acknowledged worth, what may we not expect from consuls of a different character; from men who never knew a noble impulse; whose bosoms never throbbed with one generous feeling?

Our government is not sufficiently circumspect in the appointment of consuls. The office is an important one, and should be given to men capable of faithfully executing the duties. It cannot be properly filled by persons whose time is engrossed by business of their own, by political partisans, or men who have no practical knowledge of mercantile affairs. American consuls should also be supposed to have some sympathy with every class of American citizens, and capable of enjoying satisfaction in relieving the sufferings of a fellow-creature. All consular fees should be abolished, and the consul should receive from the government a yearly compensation, graduated on the importance of his duties.

The Lady Madison was considered a large ship, being four hundred and fifty tons burden. She belonged to Jacob Barker, now a resident of New Orleans, but who was at that time in the zenith of his mercantile prosperity, and the owner of ships trading to all parts of the globe. Captain Swain was a native and resident of Nantucket, an excellent sailor and a worthy man; and the ship was navigated by a crew composed mostly of young and active Americans. The Lady Madison had sailed from Cronstadt bound to New York, but met with disasters which compelled her to put into Liverpool for repairs.

On joining the Lady Madison I found there was a very natural but unjust prejudice existing against me on the part of the officers, which it would be difficult to overcome. I was thrust on board by the consul against their wishes, and was entitled to ship room and ship's fare, which was reluctantly granted. I must, however, admit that my appearance, with a costume of the "Persian" cut, pale and sickly visage and a halting gait, an air of dejection caused by misfortune and diffidence, was not prepossessing, but verged strongly on the vagabond order. It is, therefore, not surprising that when I stepped on deck I was looked upon as an intruder, and instead of being greeted with smiles and words of encouragement, of which I was greatly in need, received looks which would have chilled an icicle, and frowns which made me feel all my insignificance.

I should probably have found little sympathy among the sailors had I not met among them an old acquaintance. A young man named Giddings, on hearing my name mentioned, regarded me with a degree of interest that surprised me. After staring at me a few minutes, he inquired if I had not once lived in Rockingham county, New Hampshire. On my replying in the affirmative, he introduced himself as an old schoolmate, a native of Exeter, from which, having chosen a sailor's life, he had been absent for years.

I rejoiced at finding a friend, and soon realized the truth of the good old proverb, "a friend in need is a friend indeed. " Through his influence and representation the crew were disposed to look upon me in a favorable light. He gave me the privilege of using his berth and his blankets during my watch below; he loaned me a monkey jacket in stormy weather, and shared with me his "small stores, " of which he had a good supply. More than all this, he encouraged me to keep a stout heart and "stiff upper lip, " assuring me that all would come right in the end. Had it not been for that kind-hearted young man, my condition on board the ship must have been wretched. I have often witnessed the disgraceful fact, that when a man is DOWN every one seems determined TO KEEP HIM DOWN! If a poor fellow received a kick from fortune, every man he meets with will give him another kick for that very reason!

Captain Swain never deigned to notice me in any way, and the chief mate followed his example so far as was practicable. The second mate's name was Cathcart. He was man of inferior capacity, ignorant, and coarse. As I was looked upon as a sort of "black sheep" in the flock, and was in the second mate's watch, that officer imagined he could, with impunity, make me a target for his vulgar jokes, and practised on me a line of conduct which he dared not pratise on others. A day or two after we left Liverpool, he took occasion, when several of the crew were standing by, to make my rather quaint NAME the subject of some offensive remarks. My indignation was roused at such ungentlemanly conduct, and I retorted with a degree of bitterness as well as imprudence that surprised myself as well as others.

"My name? " said I; "you object to MY name! Look at home! My name is a quiet name, a sensible name, surrounded with pleasant associations, and easily spoken, which is more than can be said of yours. Ca-a-th-ca-r-r-t! There is neither sense, meaning, nor beauty in that name. Why, " continued I, making strange grimaces, "one cannot speak it without twisting the mouth into kinks and cuckold's necks without number. Ca-a-th-c-a-a-rt! I would sooner be called Tantarabogus. "

This turned the laugh against him. He made no reply, but no longer annoyed me with his coarse jokes, and the respectable epithet of "Tantarabogus" stuck to him until our arrival in New York.

The ship Lady Madison left Liverpool about the 17th of March, 1812. The wind had been blowing a long time from the westward, with occasional gales which prevented vessels from getting to sea; and we sailed in company with a large fleet of merchant ships at the commencement of a change of wind. We left the Mersey with a fine breeze and soon passed the headmost vessels in the fleet. Our ship was large, a fine model, newly coppered, well provided with sails, and having left part of her cargo in Liverpool was in good ballast trim, and slipped through the water like a fish.

For eight days this easterly wind continued, the ship sometimes carrying top-gallant sails and a fore-topmast studding sail, and sometimes running directly before the wind under double-reefed topsails and foresail, progressing at the rate of ten, eleven, and eleven and a half knots. Chronometers were unknown in those days, and lunar observations, owing to the cloudy weather and other causes, could not be taken during the passage. It is, therefore, not remarkable that under the circumstances, and with a heavy sea following the ship, the judgment of the navigators was at fault and the ship overran her reckoning.

On the eighth day after the Lady Madison left the dock, the atmosphere being hazy and the temperature unusually cool, I was standing on the lee side of the forecastle when something afar off on the bow caught my eye. It looked like a massive fortress on a mountain rock of crystal. Its appearance, different from anything I had ever seen on the ocean, excited my wonder. Could it be a cloud? I pointed it out to one of my watchmates, who, being familiar with such appearances, instantly called out, "Ice, ho! "

There was a commotion throughout the ship. "Ice! " exclaimed the captain, rushing up the companion-way, spyglass in hand. "Ice! Where-away? 'Tis impossible! We cannot be near the Grand Bank! "

The ice island was now clearly perceptible, looming up through the thin fog, "a fixed fact, " which could not be shaken. We were on the eastern edge of the Bank of Newfoundland. In eight days the ship had run nearly two thousand miles. Although this may not be considered a remarkable feat for a modern clipper of giant proportions, it was an instance of fast sailing and favorable breezes seldom exceeded in those days.

Had the wind continued unchanged in strength or direction after we reached the Bank, we should have made the passage to New York in twelve days. But its force was spent. Instead of feeling grateful and expressing satisfaction at such a noble run, the captain, and I believe every man on board, as is usual in such cases, grumbled intolerably when the change took place! Head winds and calms prevailed, and ten days elapsed before we greeted the highlands of Neversink. We passed inside of Sandy Hook on the 4th of April 1812, having made a passage of eighteen days from Liverpool to anchorage off the Battery!

While beating through the narrows we passed the ship Honestus, which sailed from Liverpool about forty days before the Lady Madison left that port, and had been battling with head winds the whole distance across the Atlantic.

Chapter XVII ADRIFT IN NEW YORK

When the ship Lady Madison arrived in New York there was quite a stir among the mercantile community. Congress was engaged in important deliberations, and it was whispered, that in secret session, an embargo was about to be laid on American vessels in every port in the United States as a preparatory step to a declaration of war against Great Britain.

The passage of an "embargo act" was generally expected; but many persons, who had full faith in the more than Christian patience and forbearance of our government, believed there would be no war, notwithstanding the insults heaped upon American citizens, the piratical aggressions on our commerce, and the contumely and contempt in which our government and our flag, during a series of years, had been everywhere held by British authorities, as shown in the capture of the Chesapeake, and a multitude of kindred acts, each of which, as a knowledge of them travelled through the land, should have produced the effect of a "fiery cross, " and kindled into a fierce and living flame every spark of patriotism existing in the bosoms of our countrymen.

There was great commotion on the wharves. "The embargo is coming, " said one excited individual. "The act is already passed! " said another. Merchants were busy fitting away their ships to every quarter of the globe; the piers and wharves were lumbered with goods and produce of every description; the work was busily carried on night and day; fabulous prices were paid to laborers; in many cases the cargoes were thrown on board, tumbled into the hold, or piled on the decks, and the ship was "cleared" at the custom house, got under weigh, and anchored in the offing, where, beyond the jurisdiction of the United states, her stores and what remained of her cargo were SMUGGLED on board at leisure.

On reaching New York I again found myself in a strange city, without money or friends. I went with Giddings and some of his shipmates to a sailor boarding house in Dover Street, kept by a German named Hansen. At the recommendation of Giddings, the landlord received me, although with reluctance, as I had no visible means of paying for my board. Giddings and his friends shipped the following day for another voyage in the Lady Madison, which ship left the harbor for Liverpool on the evening previous to the reception of the news of the passage of the "embargo act, " which, by some mysterious influence, had been strangely delayed. The Lady Madison remained at anchor, for at least a fortnight, nine or ten miles outside of Sandy Hook, when, having taken on board those portions of her cargo THAT HAD BEEN FORGOTTEN, SHE PROCEEDED ON HER VOYAGE.

My condition at this time furnished a striking contrast with my condition when I left Boston not five months before. Disappointment had laid on my spirits a heavy hand, and there were no particularly cheering scenes in perspective. I would gladly have returned to my home, there to have recovered the full use of my fractured limb before I embarked on any new enterprise. But I had no means of getting from New York to Boston, and through a feeling of pride, far from commendable, I was unwilling to make application to my relatives for pecuniary assistance. I did not even write to inform them of my return to the United States.

The question now came up, "What shall I do to improve my condition and gain a livelihood? Lame as I was, I dared not undertake to ship in a square-rigged vessel, or even a "topsail schooner, " where it might often be necessary to go aloft. I tried to get a berth in a coaster, or small vessel trading to the West Indies, where gymnastic feats would not be required. I applied to many skippers but without success. Even the proud captain of a rusty-looking old craft, that could hardly be kept afloat in the harbor, looked sour and sulky, and shook his head with as much significance as Lord Burleigh himself, when I inquired if he was in want of a hand! Either my looks were unpromising, or this class of vessels were well supplied with men. In the mean time my board bill was running up, and my landlord looked as grave as an oyster, and his manners were as rough as the outside of the shell.

Passing through Maiden Lane one day, I saw a gentleman whom I had formerly known, standing in the doorway of a bookstore. I had boarded in his family several weeks after my recovery from fever and ague. He, as well as his wife, at that time professed a strong interest in my prosperity. When I left them, and entered on my voyage to South America in the Clarissa, they bade me farewell with protestations of an affection as warm and enduring as if I had been a near and dear relative. It is therefore not wonderful that when I spied Mr. Robinson my heart yearned towards him. I had encountered a friend in that overgrown city; I saw a familiar face the first for many months. Without CALCULATING whether he could be of service to me, or whether it was proper to appear before him in apparel more remarkable for its antiquity and simplicity than its gentility, I obeyed the dictates of an honest heart, rushed towards him, and grasped his hand. Perceiving his astonishment, and that he was about to reprove my unauthorized familiarity, I mentioned my name.

"It is no wonder you don't recollect me, " said I; "I have met with the rubbers, and must have greatly changed since you saw me last. Indeed, I am now rather hard up. Nothing to do, and not a cent in my pocket. It rejoices me to meet an old acquaintance.

The smile of recognition with which Robinson received the announcement of my name, vanished like a torch quenched in the ocean when he heard of my penniless condition. He nevertheless put a tolerably good face on the matter, invited me into his store, said he had lived in New York about nine months, asked me several commonplace questions, and at last, turning away as if he had more important business to attend to, desired me to drop in and see him occasionally.

Not dreaming that he would be otherwise than delighted to see me at his house, I bluntly asked him where he lived.

"O, " said he, in a careless manner, "I LIVE away up in the Bowery, but my place of business is HERE; and when you have nothing better to do, give me a call, I shall always be glad to see you! "

And my cold-hearted, calculating friend, who feared I should make an appeal to his pockets, gave me quite a polite bow, and thus taught me a lesson in the fashionable accomplishment of bowing a troublesome acquaintance into the street!

A few days after this, as I was walking in Broadway, musing on my condition, and convinced of the truth of the saying that "there is no solitude so complete as in the midst of a great city, " but firmly believing that something would soon "turn up, " I saw on the sidewalk an elegant and costly breastpin, which must have belonged to a fashionable lady. I gladly seized the glittering prize and bore it away, exulting in my good fortune. Although I intended to spare no pains to find the owner, I trusted the incident might in some way contribute to my advantage. I showed the pin in triumph to the wife of my landlord, a shrewd woman, not over-scrupulous, and well skilled in the art of turning little events to her own profit, and explained the circumstances under which it came into my possession.

"This is indeed wonderful! " she exclaimed, holding up her hands. "How fortunate that you, of all persons, should have found this costly ornament! It belongs to Mrs. Johnson, a dear friend of mine, who lives just over the way! It must be it is the same. I know it. I have seen it a thousand times. She was here not five minutes ago, lamenting the loss of it. How overjoyed she will be when she knows it is found! I will send to her directly, and make her happy with the news. "

Mrs. Hansen disappeared, leaving me, I am afraid, looking rather confounded at this singular and unexpected COINCIDENCE, and almost sorry that the owner of the pin had been so easily discovered. In a few minutes Mrs. Hansen returned, accompanied by "her dear friend, " Mrs. Johnson, who, after examining the pin, said it was her own. She thanked me for having found it, was in raptures with her good fortune, declared she should never forget she was indebted to me, then in a business-like manner placed the rich ornament on her bosom, where it seemed as much out of place "as a rich jewel in an Ethiop's ear, " and hastily walked off with the prize before I could recover from my astonishment! I was a stranger to the ways of the world, and it did not occur to me, until years afterwards, that this was an IMPROMPTU comedy, ingeniously devised and skilfully performed by two capital actresses, for the purpose of swindling me out of the jewel!

A day or two after the adventure of the breastpin, my landlord represented to me, with much gravity, that I had been living with him above a fortnight, had not paid a cent towards my board, and, so far as he could see, there was no prospect that I ever would pay any. This state of things, I must be sensible, could not last forever.

I told him, in reply, that I was every day becoming more able to do a seaman's duty' that, as he well knew, I had tried to find a berth in a coaster, but none was to be had; that I was confident I should at some future time pay him, principal and interest, for all his expense and trouble, and he might rely on my promise.

Hansen rejoined, with a derisive smile, that it was not his custom to give credit, or rely upon promises; that I must find something to do, or he should be compelled to turn me out of his house! "Did you ever do any thing but go to sea? " he asked abruptly.

"O, yes, " said I, "I was brought up on a farm, and understand all kinds of farming work. "

"If that's the case, " continued he, "your business is done. There are fine farms in Brooklyn, within sight of the ferry. All our best vegetables and fruit are raised on those farms. It is now the spring of the year, when farm laborers are wanted. You had better go over to Brooklyn and find work on a farm. "

"That I'll do with pleasure, " said I; "but I have no money to pay my fare over the ferry. "

"Never mind, I'll lend you a couple of sixpences, and charge them in your account. You had better go tomorrow, and take the whole day before you. " Accordingly on the following day I started for Long Island in quest of work as a day laborer on a farm.

At that time Brooklyn was not, as now, a large, populous, and thriving city. It was a small, sparsely-settled village; and the vast extent of land which is now laid out in streets and squares, and covered with costly edifices, was then improved for gardens, orchards, and farms. I landed from the ferry boat and took my way along the public highway which led towards the interior of the island. The rural aspect of a cultivated country, after having my view confined for many months to salt water and the unseemly masses of brick and mortar called cities, gladdened my heart; and I determined, in a spirit of true philosophy, to give vain cares and regrets to the wind, and pass one pleasant day in rambling about that agricultural district.

My efforts to obtain employment were not attended with success. My sailor costume, my pale features, and my constitutional diffidence, which has always been a drag in my efforts to press forward in the world, served me not as a letter of recommendation among the shrewd and money-making farmers and gardeners of Long Island. Indeed, to my mortification, I found that a blue jacket and loose trousers, when worn by a weather-beaten or bronzedvisaged wayfarer, were looked upon as PRIMA FACIE evidence that "he was no better than he should be. " One of the farmers to whom I applied, after questioning me about my ability to work on a farm, came to the conclusion that he did not require any additional help; another wanted a hand, but I was not stout enough for his purpose; a third expressed a belief that I was an impostor, and knew nothing about farming work; and a fourth, after cross-questioning me until I felt assured he was satisfied with my character and capacity, graciously informed me I might stay a week or so on trial, and if I worked well perhaps he would give me my board through the summer! My case was a desperate one, and I might have acceded to his proposal if he had not unguardedly added that I should have to sleep in a cockloft in the shed! And thus I wandered about that part of the island the whole day, and returned to my boarding house towards dark, fatigued, hungry, and unsuccessful. I told Hansen the result of my day's labor. He looked disappointed and angry.

"You did not try! " said he. "I don't believe you said one word for yourself. There is one more shilling gone for nothing. But you must pretty quick find something to do. "

The next day, when I returned home after my daily jaunt around the wharves in search of employment, Hansen met me with a smile, and introduced me to Stephen Schmidt, a thickset Dutchman, with little gray eyes, and capacious cheeks, of a color which proved he was a dear lover of schnapps. Schmidt claimed to be a native of Hudson; his ancestors were Dutch, and Dutch was the sole language of his early days. He had been several years employed in the North River sloops, but for the last six months had been in a coaster. Wearied of this kind of life and afraid of impressment, as his English pronunciation was strongly tinctured with the gutturals of a genuine Knickerbocker, and British ships- of-war swarmed along our coast, he had made up his mind to return to his home on the banks of the Hudson, and try his hand at cultivating cabbages and manufacturing SAUER KRAUT! A man was wanted in his place on board the coasting vessel and Hansen had persuaded Schmidt to use his influence with the captain to procure me the enviable situation.

I cared not a rush what kind of vessel this coaster was, whether old or new, bound on a cruise to New Orleans or Baffin's Bay; nor did I care whether the captain was a gentleman or a clown; a worthy man or an ignorant bully. I was anxious to obtain the vacant situation, and feared that the captain, following the fashion of the Long Island farmers, would not like the cut of my jib. I learned, however, that the schooner was a comfortable vessel, about a hundred tons burden, called the Mary, belonging to Newbern in North Carolina. The name of the captain was Thompson. The schooner was taking in cargo for Newbern, and would soon be ready for sea. Towards evening I accompanied Schmidt to the wharf where the Mary lay, and went on board, my bosom agitated with hopes and fears. The captain was on deck, a sturdy, rough-looking man. Schmidt went boldly up to him. "Captain Thompson, " said he, "this is the man I spoke to you about this morning to take my place. "

"This the man? " said the captain, abruptly. "Why, this is a boy! He's lame, too, and looks sickly. He will never do for me! "

It was time for me to speak; and I made a bold effort to overcome my diffidence. "Sir, " said I, "a few months ago I had the misfortune to break my leg in Liverpool, and was sent home by the American consul. The limb is nearly well; but I don't feel able to ship in a square-rigged vessel. But, sir, I am in good health; I want employment; I can do as good a day's work as any man on board your schooner. You will find me active, industrious, and faithful. You may rely on it, sir, you will never have cause to repent giving me the berth. "

Captain Thompson eyed me sharply a few moments without saying a word. After he had completed the examination of my person, he mildly inquired, "How much wages do you expect? "

"Whatever you may think I am worth, sir, " said I. "I owe my landlord for three weeks board; but he will have to trust me for a part of it until I come back to New York. I am but poorly off for clothes, but that is of no consequence; summer is coming. "

"You seem to be in a tight place, young man, " said the kind- hearted captain. "Come on board with your rattletraps tomorrow. I'll soon find out what you are made of. "

I returned home with a light heart, and rejoiced Hansen with the intelligence that I had become one of the crew of the Mary. I promised him every cent of my advance wages. With this he was obliged to be content, but declared his intention to keep my chest, my books, and other articles of trifling value, as security for the remainder of my board. To this I made no objection, thinking it reasonable enough. But Captain Thompson, the next day, when I received my half month's pay in advance, and informed him of my arrangements, called me a fool, and inveighed in bitter terms against the whole race of sailor landlords.

I took nothing with me on board the Mary but a change of clothing and a few articles of trifling value, packed in an old pillow case, loaned me by my landlady, with strict injunctions to return it if I ever came back to New York. I was overjoyed to think I had found employment, and could gain a subsistence by my own labors. I was sure of a home for a few weeks, until I should recover from the effects of my mishap, when I hoped to be above the necessity of asking favors.

The mate, whose name was Pierce, received me in a surly manner. He evidently thought Captain Thompson did a foolish act in shipping such "a useless piece of lumber" as myself. The crew, however, gave me a hearty reception, which placed me at my ease. I found the crew to consist of two young men, not much older than myself, and a negro boy. The two men were swarthy sons of North Carolina, born near Cape Hatteras; good-hearted, ignorant, lazy, careless fellows, who liked good living and clear comfort better than hard work. The cook was of the genuine African type; and when not employed in serious work about the camboose, was throwing off the exuberance of his good humor in peals of laughter. Taken together, they were a set of jolly fellows, and I rejoiced that my lot was cast among them. My spirits, which had been below zero for some time, in spite of my philosophy, took a sudden rise immediately, notwithstanding the sullen humor of the mate, who, like Cassius, had "a lean and hungry look, " and never even indulged in a smile. He manifested a singular antipathy towards me in all his acts.

Some animals seem to have a bitter hatred against those of their own kind which are the victims of accident or misfortune. A wolf, wounded by hunters, is torn in pieces by the pack; and a porpoise, if struck and mangled by a harpoon, is pursued by the whole shoal, and put to death without mercy. We sometimes find human beings possessed of such savage attributes. They pay court to wealth and power, but when they find a fellow-being stricken to the earth by misfortune or sickness, imbibe a prejudice against him, and instead of stretching forth a kind and open hand to relieve, will be more likely to shake a clinched fist in his face.

Chapter XVIII SCHOONER MARY OF NEWBERN

We cast loose from the wharf the following day, about the 20th of April, 1812, and proceeded down the harbor. But the wind coming from the eastward, we anchored above the Narrows. I was soon convinced that Captain Thompson was no driver. Although originally a Massachusetts man, he had lived long enough in southern climates to acquire indolent habits. When the wind was ahead, if on anchorage ground, he would let go an anchor, rather than take the trouble of beating to windward for what he considered the trifling object of saving a day or two in the passage! "Have patience and the wind will change, " was his motto. He was not the only shipmaster I have met with who was in the habit of looking after his own comfort as well as the interest of his employer.

The wind was favorable the next day, and we glided past Sandy Hook and entered on the broad ocean. Away we went to the southward with the wind abeam, blowing a strong breeze from the westward. The captain took the helm, and all hands were employed in clearing the decks and putting things in order; Mr. Pierce being particularly active in the work, saying but little, and looking unusually solemn.

I was on the weather side of the main deck, securing the lashings of the long-boat, when I heard a splash in the water to leeward; at the same moment the cook shouted out, with all the power of his African lungs, "Goramity! Mr. Pierce is fell overboard! "

"The mate is overboard! The mate is overboard! " was now the cry from every mouth.

"Hard-a-lee! " screamed the skipper, and at the same instant executed the order himself by jamming the tiller hard down to leeward. "Haul the fore sheet to windward! Clear away the long-boat! Be handy, lads! We'll save the poor fellow yet. "

And then the captain shouted to the unfortunate man, as he was seen not far off in the wake, "Be of good cheer! Keep your head up! No danger! We'll soon be alongside! "

I seized the cook's axe and cut away the lashings of the boat, and in a space of time incredibly brief, the boat was lifted from the chocks by main strength and launched over the side. We were about to shove off to the struggling mate, when Captain Thompson, who had not taken his eyes from the man after he had fallen overboard, and kept making signs and giving him words of encouragement, exclaimed, in a mournful tone, "Avast there with the boat! 'Tis no use. He's gone he's sunk, and out of sight. We shall never see him again! Poor fellow poor fellow! May the Lord have mercy on him! "

It appeared that Mr. Pierce had stepped on the lee gunwale for the purpose of grasping a rope that was loose. His left hand was on one of the main shrouds, when a sudden lurch disengaged his grasp and precipitated him into the water. He was not a hundred yards from the schooner when he disappeared. Whether his body struck against the side of the vessel as he fell and he was thus deprived of the full use of his limbs, whether he was panic- struck at the fate which appeared to await him, or unable to swim, we could never learn. The simple, solemn fact, however, was before us in all its terrible significance. The man who, a few moments before, stood on the deck of the Schooner Mary, strong, healthy, and in the meridian of life, was no longer with us. He was removed without warning; buried in the depths of the ocean; cut off by some mysterious agency, "And sent to his account With all his imperfections on his head. "

Soon after this sad accident, when we had taken in the long-boat, trimmed the sails, and were pursuing our way towards Cape Hatteras, the captain, with a solemn look, called me to the helm and went into the cabin, where he undoubtedly found consolation in the embrace of an intimate but treacherous friend. Indeed, on his return to the deck, a few minutes afterwards, I had olfactory demonstration that he and the brandy bottle had been in close communion! Captain Thompson had hardly spoken to me since we left the wharf in New York. He had now got his "talking tacks" on board, and was sociable enough.

"Hawser, " said he, with a sigh, "this is a serious and sad thing, this death of poor Pierce. It might be your fate or mine at any time as easily as his. He was just from Liverpool, having been shipwrecked on the English coast, and on his way home to Washington, expecting to see his wife and children in a few days. Poor fellow! This will be a terrible blow to his family and friends. His fate, so sudden, is enough to make any man who IS a man, think seriously of his 'better end' of what may become of him hereafter! " He clinched this remark, which he delivered with much energy, with an oath that almost made my hair stand on end, and struck me at the time as being singularly out of place in that connection.

With another deep-drawn sigh he dismissed the subject, and did not again allude to it. He spoke of the "embargo act, " of various ingenious modes of evading it, and of the prospect of a war with England; and made some assertion in relation to proceedings in Congress, which, in a respectful manner, but to his great astonishment, I ventured to dispute on the authority of a paragraph I had seen in a New York newspaper a few days before. The captain, after gravely staring me in the face a moment, as much as to say, "What do YOU know about newspapers or politics? " inquired the name of the newspaper I was talking about.

I mentioned the name of the paper. "Well, " said he, "I have that paper, with others, in a bundle in the cabin so that matter can be soon settled. "

Down he went into the cabin, leaving me not a little alarmed at his conduct. Thinks I to myself, "Can he be offended because a vagabond like myself has dared to differ with him on a question of fact? "

He soon appeared on deck with a large bundle of newspapers, which he put into my hands, at the same time taking possession of the tiller. "There, " said he, "find the newspaper you were speaking of and pick out the paragraph, IF YOU CAN. "

From my earliest boyhood I had manifested a strong attachment for newspapers. It may have been that, not finding other means to gratify my thirst for reading, I read every newspaper that came in my way; and as I was blessed with a good memory, I always kept tolerably well posted in regard to the current news of the day. I opened the bundle and promptly singled out the newspaper in question, and pointing to a paragraph with my finger, said, "There, sir, you may see for yourself. "

The captain seemed astonished. He did not take the paper from my hands. "My eyes, " said he, "are not good; they are weak, and it troubles me to read. Let me hear YOU read it. "

I read the paragraph accordingly. The captain, meanwhile, fixed his eyes, which exhibited no signs of weakness, upon me with an earnest expression. When I finished reading, he nodded his head and mused a few moments in silence, then hastily surrendered the tiller, bundled up the newspapers, and vanished down the companion-way.

"What does this bode? " thought I to myself. "The man is evidently angry. I acted like a fool to question anything he said, however absurd. " I did Captain Thompson injustice. He was not long absent, but soon came up the steps, bringing a sack- bottomed chair in one hand and a suspicious-looking pamphlet in the other. He placed the chair in front of the tiller.

"Hawser, " said he, "sit down in that chair, and take this pamphlet, which is one of the most wonderful books that was ever laid before a wicked world. The author shows by figures, facts, and calculations that the world will be destroyed on the 12th of June. Good Lord! The time is close at hand. I have not read the book; my eyes trouble me too much besides, I have not had time. But I have heard much about it, and received orders, when I left Newbern for New York to bring back a dozen copies to enlighten the poor creatures on their fate. Sit right down, Hawser, I tell you, and go to work. I'll steer the schooner while you read. "

I obeyed orders, as was my custom; and a curious picture we must have presented, the captain steering the schooner and listening with greedy ears to every word which fell from my lips, as, seated directly fronting him, my back supported by the binnacle, I read in a clear and distinct voice, and with due emphasis, the crude absurdities of a crack-brained religious enthusiast.

This "wonderful pamphlet" was written by a man named Cochran, a resident of Richmond, in Virginia, who, after poring over the Book of Revelation for years, convinced himself that he had obtained a clew to the mysteries contained in the writings of St. John.

After satisfying himself, as he said, beyond question of the correctness of his views, he published his pamphlet of some thirty or forty pages, notifying the public of the terrible fact that the day of judgment was at hand; and predicting the day, and suggesting the hour, when the world would come to an end! He even went so far as to describe the scene of destruction, when all the elements would be put in motion to destroy mankind, when volcanoes would deluge the land with liquid fire, and earthquakes shake and shatter the world to its centre!

Cochran claimed to PROVE all this by his interpretation of the Book of Revelation; by labored calculations based upon arithmetical principles, and algebraic formulae until then unknown, but which appeared mystical and appalling from the fact that they were incomprehensible. The book was written in a style well calculated to perplex, astonish, or terrify the readers, especially those who were not well stocked with intelligence. It is therefore not remarkable that it caused a commotion wherever it was circulated. The judgment day was the topic of discourse and persons of ungodly lives and conversation were led to think seriously of the error of their ways.

I read the pamphlet through, from title page to "finis, " calculations, figures, and all; and no reader ever had a more attentive listener. Captain Thompson took the book in his hand after I had got through, and gazed upon it attentively.

"Well, " said he, "this beats cock fighting! The man keeps a good log; works out his case like a sailing master; and proves it by alphabetic signs and logarithms, as clear as a problem in plain sailing. This is a great book; a tremendous book! I wish I had two hundred copies to distribute among the poor, ignorant heathens at Newbern and Portsmouth. Won't it make the folks stare like bewildered porpoises! Are you tired of reading, Hawser? "

"No, sir. I will read as long as you wish. "

"Well, if that's the case, I'll bring up the Bible from the cabin, and you may wind up with one or two of the Chapters in Revelation, which are referred to in the pamphlet. "

The Bible was brought up, and I read to his great gratification until about six o'clock, when the supper hour put a stop to our literary and biblical pursuits. But the following day, the day after, every day, I had to read that doomsday pamphlet whenever it was my turn to take the helm, and frequently a chapter in the Bible besides.

One morning, as we were slowly moving along with a light breeze, on soundings between Cape Henry and Cape Hatteras, a large loggerhead turtle was seen a short distance to windward, motionless, and apparently asleep on the water. This caused quite a sensation; every man was on deck in a moment. The schooner was hove to, preparations were making to launch the boat, and the captain was loudly calling for his GIG, a species of three-pronged harpoon for striking small fish, when one of the crew, named Church, remonstrated against this mode of proceeding.

"Hold on, captain, " said he, "or you will lose the lovely crittur. If you go near him in a boat he will open his peepers and vanish as suddenly as an evil spirit sprinkled with holy water But I know a trick to take him that cannot fail. Let me have my own way, and I'll catch that lazy, lubberly chap, and bring him alongside, man fashion, in no time! "

Church, while making this appeal, had been hastily divesting himself of his garments, and by the time he finished his remarks, stood, EN CUERPO, on the gunwale.

"Go ahead, my lad! " said the captain. "But if you let that turtle slip through your fingers, don't you ever come back to the schooner. "

Church grinned, let himself gently into the water, and paddled away noiselessly and swiftly towards the unsuspicious reptile, who was lazily snoozing in midday, without dreaming of danger. The sailor approached him warily from behind; and when sufficiently near, grabbed the astonished animal by the stern flippers, and exclaimed, "Hurrah, the day's our own, boys! Captain, I've got a prize. Run up the stripes and stars. Turtle steaks forever! Victory, hurrah! "

The turtle, although taken at disadvantage, did not at once "give up the ship. " He struggled manfully for that liberty which is the birthright of every living creature, and made a desperate attempt to go down, knowing intuitively that his captor would not dare follow him to the depths below. But whenever he attempted to dive, Church threw the whole weight of his body on the stern flippers, and thus prevented him from executing that maneuver. After being foiled in this manner two or three times his turtleship seemed disposed to abandon this mode of proceeding, and tried to paddle off with his forward flippers, as if to escape from the incumbrance.

Church was now in his glory. By PULLING one hind flipper and PUSHING the other he could guide the reptile in whatever direction he pleased, and soon navigated him alongside the schooner, when a rope was hospitably put around the neck of the captive, and he was hauled on board.

Passing around Cape Hatteras, between the outer shoals and the land, we arrived at Ocracoke Inlet. The wind being ahead, we were unable to cross the bar, but remained two or three days at anchor in its immediate vicinity. Ocracoke Inlet is the main entrance into Pamlico Sound, a large inlet or body of water, some eighty miles long, separated from the sea by low sandy islands, mostly inhabited. On this Sound are situated some thriving towns, and into it the rivers Tar and Neuse empty their waters. The little town or village of Portsmouth is situated on an island in the immediate vicinity of Ocracoke Inlet. The inhabitants, or those who at that time deigned to pursue any regular occupation, were for the most part engaged in fishing and piloting. The sand banks, shoals, and flats in that neighborhood furnish admirable facilities for seine fisheries, and enormous quantities of mullets were taken every year on those sandy shores, packed in barrels, and sent to the West Indies.

There was also at that time carried on with considerable success, a porpoise fishery, after a fashion peculiar, I believe, to that part of the world. Porpoises often made their appearance very near the coast, in shoals not "schools, " for porpoises are uneducated some hundreds in number. They were surrounded by boats and driven into shallow water. When sufficiently near the land, a strong seine was cautiously drawn around them and they were slowly but surely dragged to the beach; the blubber was stripped from their carcasses and converted into oil. Sometimes a shark was found in their company, who, disdaining to be so easily subdued, performed wondrous feats of strength and ferocity, biting and maiming the inoffensive porpoises without mercy, and in most cases rending the seine by his enormous power, and escaping from his persecutors.

When lying at Ocracoke, waiting for a chance over "the Swash, " the crew of the Mary having little to do, were generally engaged in looking after their physical comforts by laying in a stock of shell-fish. Oysters were found in abundance all along shore, and of excellent quality; also the large clam known as the QUAHAUG, which when properly cooked and divested of its toughness is capital food; crabs, of delicate flavor and respectable size, were taken in hand-nets in any quantity; and flounders, mullets, and drum-fish were captured with little trouble. Ducks and teal, and other kinds of water fowl, abounded in the creeks and coves.

The staple articles of food on board the Mary consisted of corn meal, molasses, Carolina hams and middlings, with sweet lard and salt pork, in unstinted quantities. As a drink, instead of Oriental tea and West India or manufactured coffee, we were supplied with the decoction of an herb found in the woods or swamps of the Carolinas, and generally known as YAUPON TEA. It was at first insipid, if not unpalatable, but improved greatly on a more intimate acquaintance.

In the Mary we were stinted in nothing that could be readily procured; and having a cook who prided himself on his skill in manufacturing hoe-cakes, oyster fritters, clam chowders, turtle stews and the like, I am free to confess that so far as related to GOOD LIVING, I never passed three months more satisfactorily than while I was on board the Mary of Newbern. I often compared it with my wretched fare on board the Schooner John, or with my "short commons" in the Liverpool Infirmary, and the result was decidedly in favor of the North Carolina coaster.

The inhabitants of the district bordering on Ocracoke Inlet, as a body, were not remarkable for industrious habits, or sober and exemplary lives. Fishing and piloting, I have already said, constituted their chief business. Many, being too lazy to work, indulged themselves in lounging, drinking, betting, cock- fighting, and similar amusements. One redeeming virtue, however, they possessed, which is not always met with among the sedate, thrifty, and moral portion of mankind hospitality! They were frank, open-hearted, and compassionate; professed no virtues which they did not practise; would throw open their doors to the stranger, welcome him to their dwellings, and freely share their last dollar with a friend.

The news reached Portsmouth by the pilot boat that Captain Thompson had arrived from New York, and had brought the pamphlet which proclaimed the destruction of the world. The people took a deep interest in the subject. The men visited the schooner by scores; and as most of them were unable to read, through the infirmities of ignorance and "weak eyes, " my literary powers were put in requisition, and again and again I was compelled to read aloud, for their edification, the conglomeration of absurdities which the prophet had put forth. They listened with attention; and it was amusing to hear their strange remarks and queer logic in favor of or against the prediction. The effect upon the minds of some of these children of the sandy isles was undoubtedly beneficial. It led them to think; it brought the Bible directly before them, and reminded them that whether the pamphlet was true or false a day of judgment was at hand.

The wind having changed, we crossed "the Swash, " entered the Sound, and soon reached the mouth of the River Neuse. This is a stream of considerable importance, being four hundred miles in length, and draining a large tract of country. It is navigable for boats about one half that distance. An immense quantity of produce is brought down the river from the interior of the state and deposited at Newbern, whence it is shipped to different parts of the world.

Newbern is situated about forty or fifty miles from Pamlico sound, on the south-west bank of the Neuse, and at the junction of that river with the Trent. It was, in 1812, a pleasant and flourishing town, containing about three thousand inhabitants, who carried on a prosperous business to the West Indies, and who employed many vessels in the coasting trade.

On reaching Newbern the crew were discharged, the voyage being terminated. Captain Thompson told me that the schooner would be sent on another voyage without delay, and if I was willing to remain and take charge of her at the wharf, keep an account of the cargo as it was delivered and received on board, I should be allowed the same wages I had been receiving, eight or ten dollars a month. I accepted the proposition without hesitation. Indeed, the arrangement was to the advantage of both parties; he secured at a low rate of compensation the services of one who could perform the duties or shipkeeper and mate combined, and I was provided with an asylum, board, lodging, plenty of work, and pay into the bargain.

Chapter XIX A TRIP TO BALTIMORE

When we arrived at Newbern, the people, having heard of the dreadful prophecies, were prepared to receive the pamphlets and devour their contents. Cochran's name, connected with the day of judgment, was in every mouth. Groups collected at the corners of the streets and on the wharves, composed of persons of various characters and all complexions, and discussed the subject of the prediction with wonderful earnestness and intensity of feeling. Indeed, the excitement in Newbern and vicinity, caused by this pamphlet, was hardly exceeded in sober New England in 1839 and 1840, when the charlatan, Miller, by his ridiculous predictions, spread a panic through the land; when many persons, discarding the modicum of brains they were supposed to possess, abandoned their farms, neglected their families, gave away to wiser persons the little property they owned, and actually prepared their "ascension robes, " to meet with decency and decorum the day of doom.

On the second day after our arrival at Newbern, when I had finished my labors for the day and was preparing for rest, Captain Thompson came hurriedly down the wharf and sprang on board the schooner. "Hawser, " said he, as soon as he recovered breath, "you must rig yourself up a little and go with me to Captain Merritt's. "

"What is going on there, sir, that requires my presence? "

"The boarders want you to read Cochran's pamphlet, and you MUST come. "

"But I have no suitable clothes to rig myself up with, sir. "

"Never mind your clothes. Wash your face, comb your hair, straighten up your collar, look in the glass, and you will do well enough. But bear a hand. They are waiting for you now. "

I arranged my toilet in accordance with the captain's suggestions. When I gave it the finishing touch, by "looking in the glass, " I was not satisfied, believing my costume could hardly reflect honor on the company; and my heart throbbed with emotion as I accompanied Captain Thompson to his boarding house. We entered the dining hall, the centre of which was occupied by a long table, around which were seated some fifteen or twenty well- dressed individuals, chiefly masters of vessels, and very different in their appearance and manner from the Ocracoke pilots. At the head of the table was an empty chair, towards which I was led by my conductor, who told me to be seated.

Naturally bashful, and conscious of my inferior position, I hardly knew whether I was asleep or awake; but was soon restored to my senses by Captain Thompson, who said, in an off-hand manner, "Hawser, these gentlemen are anxious to hear you read Cochran's pamphlet, which tells about the judgment day; " and he pushed towards me a copy of the prediction.

I took the familiar document and commenced my labors. My voice was tremulous at first, but I soon became accustomed to its sound, and as, by this time, I knew the greater portion of the book by heart, I got through the tissue of extravagance with great credit, not only to the prophet Cochran but myself.

My auditors listened with the closest attention, hardly seeming to breathe, and it was curious to mark the various expressions which their tell-tale countenances exhibited as I proceeded. After I had completed my task, the gentlemen breathed more freely, and stared at one another in silence. One or two were inclined to treat the prediction with levity, but their remarks were not well received. It was generally conceded that the subject was not a proper one for a joke. I received the thanks of several of my auditors for the acceptable manner in which I had performed my part in the drama. A few evenings afterwards I was again called upon to lay the contents of this everlasting pamphlet before another set of eager listeners! And I rejoiced when, with a full cargo of naval stores and Carolina notions, the schooner left the wharf, bound on a voyage to Baltimore.

On reaching Ocracoke Inlet, it appeared that the impression which the predictions of Cochran had made upon the minds of the inhabitants was not effaced. We lay at anchor there three days waiting for a wind to cross the bar, and every evening I was called upon to read Chapters in the Bible for the edification of the worthy Ocracoke pilots, who probably had not heard a chapter of Scripture recited for years. The prophecy had taken a deep hold on the minds of some; and ribald jests and disgusting oaths were seldom heard in the neighborhood of "the Swash. "

I was treated with kindness by Captain Thompson, and performed many of the duties of mate without occupying the station or receiving the pay. On the passage to Baltimore the captain exhibited occasional symptoms of piety, and at one time would listen to a chapter in the Bible with commendable gravity, and discourse seriously on serious subjects; half an hour afterwards he would resume his profane and disorderly habits, and chase away reflection by getting drunk! He was not at peace with himself; and he dearly loved whiskey and peach brandy.

It was a pleasant season of the year, and the trip to Baltimore, through the waters of the Chesapeake Bay, was an interesting one. I expected to find in Baltimore a distant relative, who had often visited my father's house; been for a time domiciled in his family, and had received repeated favors. He was now in a respectable position in Baltimore, and in the simplicity of my heart I longed to visit him, talk with him over family matters, and listen to words of advice and encouragement from a friend and relative.

We arrived at Baltimore on a Friday afternoon. I had spoken to Captain Thompson about my relative and my anticipations of a cordial welcome. His experience, however, had led him to entertain an unfavorable opinion of mankind in general, and he expressed a doubt whether a knowledge of my forlorn condition would not repel the advances and freeze the affectionate welcome which under other circumstances I might have expected. I was indignant at such an insinuation, and made known my intention to call upon my kinsman the next day, and put his feelings to the proof. The captain kindly aided my purpose. He received information from the wharfinger of the place of business and position of my relative; and on the following afternoon, after making myself look as respectable as possible, I proceeded, with a guide furnished by the wharfinger, to the counting room or office of my father's friend and protege in a distant part of the city.

I found him alone, writing at his desk, and recognized him immediately. But he stared at me, and inquired my business. I mentioned my name; upon which he seemed greatly astonished, bade me be seated, and questioned me about myself and connections. I told him the tale of my adventures, gave him the name of the schooner to which I belonged, the wharf at which she was lying, and also of the wharfinger, one of his intimate acquaintances, who had directed me to his office.

He expressed gratification that I had called upon him, said he should always be glad to hear of my welfare, and after a pause of a few minutes, rather gravely remarked that he would gladly render me any service in his power; but he was at that time busy, and requested me to visit him at his boarding house the next morning at nine o'clock, when he should have leisure to talk with me further. I returned to the schooner well satisfied with my reception, and recounted to Captain Thompson the particulars of the interview. The captain shook his head, and smiled incredulously.

The next morning, being Sunday, I put myself in what I considered passable trim, and proceeded with a light heart to the boarding house, which I found to be a handsome edifice in a genteel part of the city. I knocked at the door and inquired for my kinsman. The servant ushered me into a hall and left me. He was absent some time, during which I was an object of curiosity to several persons of both sexes who entered or left an adjoining apartment. One very pretty young woman seemed unpleasantly struck with my appearance, and expressed in audible tones her astonishment at my impertinence in entering the front door. The servant at length returned and said the gentleman I wanted was unwell, and could not be seen.

I was thunderstruck at this announcement, and declared it must be a mistake. I bade him return and tell the gentlemen I was the person whom he requested to call that morning at nine o'clock on important business. Some ten minutes elapsed; my pride took the alarm. Could he be inventing some paltry excuse for getting rid of what he might consider my importunities? The young woman again appeared who had before honored me with her notice, and who I presumed was the daughter of the woman who kept the house. She accosted me in a manner by no means flattering to my self-esteem, and told me the gentleman whom I so absolutely persisted in seeing was quite unwell, and unable to converse with any one that day; that I must come tomorrow or the day following, or some other day, when he would be quite well and at leisure! With a contemptuous toss of her pretty head, she showed me the door, and motioned me to depart.

"Tell him, " said I, "that I shall not trouble him again. " She smiled, as if my remark met her hearty approval, and closed the door with a slam!

I slowly returned, through the many magnificent thoroughfares of Baltimore, to the schooner. The streets were thronged with people elegantly dressed, who appeared to be rejoicing in their good fortune and happy in their friends and families. As I pensively wandered along, unnoticed and unknown, I felt all my loneliness, and began to think the prosperous and happy times would never arrive that had been promised in my dreams. The conduct of my relative disappointed me much. It shook my confidence in mankind, and paralyzed my small stock of self- esteem a quality essential to even ordinary success in life.

Captain Thompson, perceiving my dejected air, inquired into the particulars of my interview. I related to him the facts, but suggested excuses, and placed the matter in as favorable a light as the truth would admit. The straightforward sailor, however, saw through it all. He could not contain his indignation: after letting it explode in true sailor fashion, he concluded with this piece of practical philosophy: "Never mind, Hawser; 'tis the way of the world. I have always found it so. As for gratitude, affection, disinterested kindness, and friendship, 'tis all a humbug! RELY ON YOURSELF. Fight the battle of life alone. If you conquer, you will find friends, kind friends, disinterested friends. Ha, ha, ha! Cheer up, my boy. "

I still clung to a hope that there was some mistake, perhaps a blunder on the part of the servant who delivered the message, and that I should receive a note or a visit the next day which would set the matter right. But neither note nor visit came. In a few days the schooner Mary left Baltimore on the return to Newbern.

On the passage, the captain was testy, petulant, and unhappy. The prophecy of Cochran had taken a stronger hold on his mind than he was willing to acknowledge. I was called upon to read aloud chapters in the Bible, and especially in the Book of Revelation, Knotty passages in the pamphlet I was also required to read from time to time. But the oftener they were read, and the more closely they were examined, the greater was the puzzle, the more complete the mystification.

We reached Ocracoke in the evening, and the next morning had a fair wind over the bar and across Pamlico Sound. This was the day on which the dreaded prediction was to be fulfilled. The sun rose in a clear, unclouded sky on the morning of that day, and its beams flashed brilliantly and benignly, as with a gentle breeze from the northward we entered the mouth of the River Neuse. There could not be a lovelier day. Even Captain Thompson felt apparently relieved of his anxiety as he looked abroad upon the beauties of nature and beheld no indications of the day of doom. He saw no anger in the heavens; he heard no moans from the distressed animals instinctively snuffing the near approach of danger and death; he breathed no stifled and sulphurous atmosphere nor witnessed any other sign of the near approach of a terrible calamity. He even ventured to express an opinion that "the prophecy of that old rascal Cochran would not prove true after all. "

We reached Newbern in the afternoon, and found everybody gazing at the heavens with eager looks, in which it would be difficult to say whether fear or curiosity predominated. Many would not venture to bed till their hopes were made certain by the striking of the midnight hour; and then they were so overjoyed at what appeared a new lease of life, that sleep, that "sweet restorer, " was a stranger during the night. In the morning, however, a gloom was again cast over the spirits of some of the most superstitious by the remark of a meddlesome old West India captain, that undoubtedly Cochran, like the seers of olden times, made his calculations according to the "old style" of computing time. Thus twelve additional days were allowed to pass before they dared give a full loose to their joy at the failure of the prediction.

After we had discharged our cargo in Newbern, I indicated to Captain Thompson that I should like to pass a few days on shore, take respite from labor, look around the town, and take note of the place and its inhabitants.

He admitted the reasonableness of my proposition, but took decided measures to prevent my being led astray by bad company. The worthy captain, although addicted to irregular habits himself, and in his own person and character a dangerous exemplar for a young man, watched my proceedings with the closest scrutiny, and lost no chance to impress on my mind correct rules of conduct. He particularly cautioned me against the habit of drinking intoxicating liquors. "It is, " said he with a sigh, "a rock on which many a noble vessel has been wrecked. " So much easier is it to preach than to practise.

With a view to insure my moral safety, Captain Thompson insisted that while I remained on shore I should stay at his boarding house and occupy the same room with himself. I accordingly took up my quarters at Captain Merritt's, where I was heartily welcomed by the landlord and his boarders.

The impression made upon my mind by the good people of Newbern was decidedly favorable. I was advised, by several substantial citizens to whom I was introduced, to make Newbern my home. I was assured that I should meet with success corresponding with my merits. I regarded the suggestion as a compliment; and having agreed to accompany Captain Thompson on another coasting voyage to New York, I determined to take the matter into consideration. I never returned to Newbern. But I have always felt grateful for the kind conduct and encouraging words which I received from the good people of that pleasant and flourishing city. Ever since that time the name of Newbern falls gently on my ear, and conjures up a thousand agreeable associations.

The owner of the Mary, Mr. Jarvis, was an active and enterprising man. He did not allow his vessels to remain idle. In a few days we had another cargo on board, and proceeded down the river on our way to New York. Being detained as usual at the Inlet, several of the pilots and other inhabitants of Portsmouth came on board, and the ribald jest, the oath, and the dram cup passed freely round. Cochran's pamphlet was consigned to oblivion. I was no longer called upon to read passages from the Holy Scriptures. Solemn looks and serious conversation were voted a bore. They laughed at their former fears; a reaction had taken place, and the struggle now seemed to be who should surpass his fellows in wickedness.

So much for Cochran's famous prediction, closely resembling in character that of Miller at a later day, and uttered with as much confidence and believed by as many persons. Morever, it is probable that Cochran was as sincere in his belief as Miller, perhaps more so, for the miserable man, finding his imagination had played him a trick, and that his prediction had not been fulfilled, overcome by mortification, and not supported by a pure religious principle, COMMITTED SUICIDE BY CUTTING HIS THROAT.

It is hardly worth while for man to attempt to solve mysteries in order to ascertain when the day of judgment will arrive. He should strive so to regulate his actions, that, let it come when it will, he need not fear the result.

Chapter XX DECLARATION OF WAR

On our passage to New York we met with no remarkable occurrence, and saw not a cruiser of any nation. On reaching the city, we found that an extraordinary excitement prevailed. War had been declared against Great Britain; an American fleet under Commodore Rodgers had sailed the day before on a cruise. The frigate Essex was at Brooklyn with a complete and gallant crew, and her commander, Captain Porter, was making preparations for an immediate departure. This brave officer made no secret of his intention to bring the enemy to close quarters whenever a chance offered, and proclaimed throughout the frigate that any man who repented having shipped might receive his discharge.

One man only of the hundreds composing the crew availed himself of the captain's proclamation, under the plausible pretext that he was an Englishman. But it having been ascertained that so far from being a loyal subject of the king of Great Britain, he was a native-born Yankee with a cowardly spirit, his shipmates were so indignant that they tarred and feathered him, carried him over to New York, placed a placard on his breast, formed a procession, and paraded him through the streets.

There was a great bustle about the wharves in New York, although of a different kind from that which prevailed two months previous in consequence of the embargo. Clippers of all kinds and sizes were bought up at enormous prices, and rapidly transformed into privateers and letters of marque. Heavy guns, instead of bales of goods, were dragged through the streets by dray horses, and muskets, cutlasses, and boarding pikes met the eye at every turn. Fierce-looking men with juvenile mustachios jostled each other in the streets, and even the dapper clerks and peaceable artisans swore deeper oaths and assumed more swaggering airs. News of naval battles was anxiously looked for, startling rumors of all kinds were afloat, and every vessel which arrived was supposed to be fraught with momentous intelligence respecting the cruisers on the coast. I noted these proceedings, caught the spirit of enthusiasm, and sympathized in the excitement which so universally prevailed. I told Captain Thompson I had made up my mind to join a privateer. To this remark the worthy skipper made no reply but by a smile, which I interpreted as an approval of my determination.

One of my first acts, however, was to call on Hansen, the keeper of the boarding house where I had formerly resided, and discharge my debt. I resumed possession of my chest and books, which I regarded as my greatest treasure. I had recovered from my lameness. I was strong and active, and although poorly off for clothing or worldly goods, was free from debt, and had a couple of dollars which I could call my own. My condition had decidedly improved; the prospect ahead began to brighten, and I felt able and anxious to perform a manly part in any noble enterprise.

I took an early opportunity to look around the wharves, and examine the privateers that were getting ready for a cruise. Two of these vessels particularly commanded my admiration, the Teaser and the Paul Jones. The Teaser was a New York pilot boat of ninety tons burden, a rakish, wicked-looking clipper enough. Her armament consisted chiefly of one long eighteen-pounder amidships. The Paul Jones was a large schooner of two hundred and twenty tons, heavily rigged, with immense spars, a spacious deck, and of a genuine buccaneer model. The armament of this privateer consisted of one long twenty-four-pounder and twelve heavy carronades.

After the deliberation I fixed upon the Paul Jones as the more desirable vessel. The warlike preparations and rakish appearance of this schooner looked like BUSINESS, and I had seen the insolence of John Bull so often exhibited on the broad highway of nations, and had so often listened to his taunts and sneers in ridicule of the prowess of the Yankees, that I longed for an opportunity to lend a hand to give him a drubbing. I stepped on board and inquired of an officer who seemed busy in giving directions, if I could have a chance in the privateer. He asked me a few questions, to which I gave satisfactory answers. He said there were many applications of a similar character, but he thought he could insure me a situation; told me to call next day at two o'clock, when the agent would be on board, and the matter could be arranged.

The important part which the American privateers bore in the last war with Great Britain is well known. They were fitted out in every port, manned by brave and active men, and heavily armed. Managed with seaman-like dexterity, and superior in sailing capacity to vessels belonging to any other nation, they could not be easily captured. The injury inflicted on the commerce of Great Britain by these privateers is incalculable. They carried terror among our enemies in the remotest parts of the ocean, and the desire of the British government to put an end to the war may, in part, be attributed to the activity, courage, and enterprise of our privateers. The principle has been adopted in all ages, that private property, captured on the high seas, is a lawful prize to the captors; also, that the destruction of private property belonging to an enemy is a justifiable act. To a well-constituted mind it must appear, on investigation, that such principles are unjust, belong to a barbarous age, and cannot be advocated on any platform of ethics recognized among civilized nations in modern times.

An attempt was made within a few years on the part of Great Britain, which also met the approval of the French government, TO ABOLISH THE PRIVATEER SYSTEM, on the ground that this mode of warfare is wrong in principle, irregular subject to abuses, and to a certain extent irresponsible. A proposition was made to our government to be a party to an agreement to abolish the system forever. Under the cloak of Christian philanthropy this was a master stroke or policy on the part of the British and French governments. Should the privateer system be abolished and a war unhappily take place between this country and France or Great Britain, either of those nations, with myriads of heavily armed men-of-war, could overrun the ocean, and every American merchantman venturing to sea would be captured or burned; our own commerce would be annihilated, while OUR FEW NATIONAL SHIPS, scattered over a large surface, could offer but little check to the commercial pursuits of an enemy.

Our government met the proposition in a manly manner, and while it declined entering into any agreement which had for its exclusive object the abolition of the privateer system, a measure which would inure chiefly to the advantage of Great Britain or France, it went further, and declared itself ready to accede to any arrangement by which, during a war, private property of every character should be exempted from capture, not only by privateers but NATIONAL VESSELS. This noble suggestion, worthy a great nation in an enlightened age, did not meet the views of our friends across the water. This broad Christian principle, if carried out, would deprive them of many advantages they might reasonably expect to derive from their numerous ships of war.

It must be evident that in case of a war between this country and a mighty naval power, which we trust will never occur, the many large "clipper ships, " which compose a large portion of our commercial marine, will be provided with screw propellers, and transformed into privateers. Armed with guns of the heaviest metal, unequalled in speed, and able to select their distance and position, they will prove a formidable means of defence and aggression; and will do much towards protecting our own commerce while they will destroy that of the enemy.

With a buoyant heart I left the proud and warlike looking privateer, Paul Jones, and proceeded to the slip where the schooner Mary lay. For this vessel, looking so demure and Quaker-like, I very ungratefully began to entertain feelings akin to contempt. She was now taking in cargo and was expected to sail in a few days on her return to Newbern. When Captain Thompson came on board, I told him I had engaged to join the privateer Paul Jones, which vessel was about to sail on a cruise. He seemed greatly astonished, and abruptly asked me what I meant by such conduct. I explained my intentions more at length, and referred to the notice I had given of my wish to join a privateer.

"I had no idea you were serious, " said the captain. "I thought you intended it as a joke. I didn't suppose you were such a confounded fool as to think seriously of joining a privateer. "

"Why, sir, what can I do better? Our merchant ships will be laid up or captured on the high seas. Even the coasting trade will be destroyed by British cruisers stationed along the whole extent of our coast. If I return to Newbern, I shall probably be thrown out of employment; a stranger in a small place, and almost as destitute as when I first shipped on board the Mary. I have pondered on the subject, and am convinced that my best course is to go a privateering. "

"Go to Beelzebub, you mean! " exclaimed the captain, in a rage. "I have no patience with you. You talk nonsense. The schooner will not be laid up on her return to Newbern. And, furthermore, you have signed a contract to perform a voyage from Newbern to New York AND BACK! And I shall hold you to your agreement. Go a privateering! Pah! "

We had some further discussion, in the midst of which Mr. Jarvis, the owner of the schooner, who had arrived in New York a day or two before from North Carolina, came on board. He was a dignified-looking man, greatly respected and esteemed in Newbern. He espoused captain Thompson's side of the argument, assured me it was unlikely his vessels would be laid up on account of the war, and would promise me that in any event I should not be thrown out of employment. If his vessels remained idle at the wharves, he would find business for me in his counting room until more propitious times.

The united remonstrances of the captain and the owner of the Mary came with a force I was unable to resist; with a strong effort I gulped down my disappointment, and gave up my darling project of making a cruise in the Paul Jones. Our fortunes in this life our destinies seem sometimes balanced on a pivot which a breath will turn. Had I accomplished my intention and embarked on a cruise, how different my fate, in all likelihood, would have been!

We left New York about the 2d of July. After having reached the offing, while pursuing our course with diligence towards Cape Hatteras, we were overhauled by a New York pilot boat of the smallest size, apparently bound in the same direction. This little schooner was in ballast, and skimmed over the seas like a Mother Carey's chicken; ranged up on our weather quarter and hailed us. It proved to be the Young Pilot, Captain Moncrieff, bound to Savannah. The mate, whose name was Campbell, was known to Captain Thompson. They had been boarders in the same house. After an interchange of salutations and hearty wishes for a pleasant voyage, the little schooner rapidly drew ahead and passed on her way. There was nothing remarkable in this incident. I little thought at the time that this egg-shell of a vessel was destined to exercise an important influence on the future events of my life.

On the morning of the Fourth of July we were off the Chesapeake Bay, some twelve or fifteen miles from Cape Henry. Captain Thompson was a sterling patriot. He dearly loved his country, and gladly caught at every chance to display the broad flag of the Union. Accordingly, on this memorable day the gorgeous ensign was hoisted at the peak, the American jack waved at the fore-topmast head, and a long pennant fell in wavy folds from the main truck.

"If I had a big gun, " exclaimed the worthy skipper, in a paroxysm of patriotism "a thirty-two-pound carronade, I would fire a genuine republican salute, and make such a thundering noise, not only in the air above but in the depths below, as to wake up the lazy inhabitants of the deep, and make them peep out of their caves to ask the cause of the terrible rumpus over their heads. " At this very moment a suspicious-looking, double-headed cloud was slowly rising in the west, and ere long spread over a large space in the heavens. As it rolled onward, flashes of lightning were seen and a distant rumbling was heard a thunder squall was at hand. The lightning became more vivid, and the thunder more frequent and deafening. Every sail was lowered to the deck, the helm was put hard a-port, and the gust came upon us with terrible fury. The rain fell in torrents, the lightning kept the atmosphere in a constant state of illumination, and the peals of thunder were truly appalling! A grander salute, or a more brilliant and effective display of fireworks on the Fourth of July, could hardly have been wished by the most enthusiastic patriot. Even Captain Thompson's longings for "a thundering noise" were more than realized. He stood firmly on the break of the quarter-deck, surrounded by most of the crew, who seemed to gather near him for protection, astonished and terrified at the sublimity of the scene.

I was standing on the main deck, not far from the rest of the crew at the time, and noticed that when the storm struck the schooner, some ropes that had not been hitched to a belaying pin were flying loose and might become unrove. I stepped forward, and standing on tiptoe was in the act of stretching up my right arm to grasp the end of the peak-halliards, when there came a flash of white lightning which almost blinded every man on deck, accompanied by a peal of thunder that seemed loud enough to shake the world to its centre. We all believed the schooner had been struck by lightning. This was not the case. It was, nevertheless, a narrow escape. I received on my hand and arm an electric shock, which tingled through every nerve and nearly felled me to the deck, and rendered my arm powerless for an hour afterwards.

The captain now seemed really alarmed. He ordered me in a loud voice to come aft, and told the crew to follow him into the cabin, leaving the schooner to manage matters with the thunder storm and take care of herself. He produced a bottle of "old Madeira" from a locker, and filled several glasses; and while the short-lived storm raged fearfully above our heads, he insisted on every man drinking a toast in honor of the Fourth of July, and set the example himself by tossing off a tumbler filled to the brim.

We rounded Cape Hatteras early one delightful morning, and with a pleasant breeze from the northward shaped our course for Ocracoke Inlet. Several coasters were in company, and a small schooner was seen standing towards us from the Gulf Stream. This vessel was soon recognized as the Young Pilot, bound to Savannah, which we had spoken off Sandy Hook. The captain of the little schooner appeared to recognize the Mary, hoisted his colors, and steered directly towards us.

"What can that fellow want? " muttered Captain Thompson. "He should have been in Savannah before this? What has he been doing away there in the Gulf Stream? There is roguery somewhere? "

The Young Pilot soon came within hail, when Captain Moncrieff requested Captain Thompson to heave to, as he wanted to come on board. The boat was launched from the deck of the pilot boat, and, manned by four athletic seamen, brought Captain Moncrieff alongside in handsome style. He jumped on deck, grasped the hand of Captain Thompson, and requested to have some conversation with him in the cabin. They were absent communing together for several minutes, when Captain Thompson thrust his head out of the companion-way, and looking round, caught my eye. He beckoned me to enter the cabin.

"What's in the wind now? " thought I to myself. "What part am I to play in this mysterious drama? Something better than reading doomsday pamphlets, I hope. "

I went down into the cabin. "Here, " said Captain Thompson to Captain Moncrieff, pointing to me, "is the only person on board my vessel who would think of accompanying you on your voyage. I would gladly assist you in your unpleasant dilemma, but I cannot advise him to go with you. Nevertheless, if he is willing I shall make no objection. "

Captain Moncrieff gazed upon me with a look of deep interest. "Young man, " said he, "you are aware I sailed from New York the same day with the Mary. My vessel was cleared at the custom house for Savannah; this was necessary in consequence of the embargo; but I was in reality bound for LaGuayra, on the Spanish Main, being the bearer of despatches of importance to a ship belonging to New York. On egging off to the eastward, to cross the Gulf Stream, my crew, convinced that Savannah was not my destined port, began to murmur. And when I acknowledged I was bound to the Spanish Main, they, one and all, refused to proceed further on the voyage, and insisted on my running into some port on the coast. I have told Captain Thompson that if I can procure ONE MAN from his schooner, I will leave these mutinous fellows with him and proceed on my voyage. Say, then, my good fellow, that you will go with me. I will allow you twenty dollars a month, and a month's pay in advance more if you wish it. You shall receive good treatment, and will always find a friend in Archibald Moncrieff. "

When the captain of the pilot-boat, who seemed much excited, finished his narrative, I quietly answered without hesitation, "I WILL GO WITH YOU. "

He grasped my hand, gave it a hearty shake, and said, "I thank you. You shall have no cause to regret your decision. Pack up your things, my lad, and be ready to go on board when I return. "

He entered his yawl, and was soon on the deck of the pilot-boat. It took me but a few minutes to get ready for my departure. Captain Thompson said not a word, but looked thoughtful and dejected. He appeared already to regret having been so easily persuaded to accommodate Captain Moncrieff, by granting me permission to embark on this uncertain expedition.

It was not long before the yawl returned from the little schooner, laden with chests, bags, and bundles, and having on board the captain, four seamen, and the cook. The luggage was tumbled out of the boat in short order; my chest was deposited in the stern seats. I shook hands with my old shipmates, took an affectionate leave of Captain Thompson, who had always treated me with the kindness of a father, and entered the boat. Captain Moncrieff took one oar, I took another, and in a few minutes I stood on the deck of the Young Pilot. A tackle was hooked on to the yawl, which was, which was hoisted in and snugly stowed on deck; the helm was put up, the fore-sheet hauled to leeward, and, before I had time to realize this change in my situation, I found myself in a strange vessel, with strange companions, bound on a strange voyage to the Spanish Main.

Chapter XXI ON BOARD THE YOUNG PILOT

After the vessels had separated and were rapidly increasing the space between them, I looked back upon the schooner Mary and recalled the many pleasant hours I had passed in that vessel, and asked myself if it would not have been better to have remained on board, trusting to the friendship of Captain Thompson and the promises of Mr. Jarvis. When I looked around, and fully comprehended the situation in which I had so unthinkingly placed myself, I saw little to give me consolation or encouragement. Captain Moncrieff was not prepossessing in his person or deportment. He was a tall, large-limbed Scotchman, about forty years of age, with light blue eyes and coarse, bloated features. He was abrupt in his language, had an exalted opinion of his merits and capacity, was always the hero of his own story; and, although he subsequently proved to be a man of generous feelings, to my unpractised optics he looked more like a bully than a gentleman.

Mr. Campbell, the mate, was also a Scotchman; but his appearance and character differed essentially from those of the captain. He was slightly built, with thin, pale features. There was nothing genial in his looks; and a certain vulpine cast of countenance, a low forehead, and a brow deeply wrinkled but not with age conveyed the idea of a selfish, narrow-minded individual.

With the exception of myself, there was no other person on board the pilot-boat. On acceding to the proposition of Captain Moncrieff, it escaped my notice that the cook was to leave the schooner with the rest of the crew. It now flashed across my mind, communicating any thing but a pleasurable sensation, that in addition to the ordinary duties of a seaman, I was expected to perform the part of that sable functionary. I therefore found myself monopolizing several responsible situations, and held at one and the same time the office of second mate, cook, and all hands.

In the novelty of my situation, however, I found a source of amusement; and the very uncertainty of the expedition, the singular manner in which I joined the pilot-boat, and the abundant cause I had for wondering "what would turn up next, " imparted to the whole enterprise an unexpected charm. My duties, although various, were not arduous, but occupied a large portion of my time. The mate and myself stood watch by turns through the night, each steering the schooner his regular trick of four hours at a time. The captain seldom came on deck during the night, but enjoyed his rest of eight or ten hours undisturbed.

The Young Pilot steered so easily, the helmsman being snugly seated in the cuddy, that it was next to impossible for any one to remain four hours in that comfortable situation, in pleasant weather, with no one to converse with or even to look at, without falling asleep. Aware of the responsibility of my situation, and remembering the lesson I had received when lying at anchor inside of Charleston bar, I strove hard to resist the influence of the drowsy god, but was often compelled to nod to his dominion; and many a sweet and stolen nap have I enjoyed when stationed at the helm, and the vessel left entirely in my charge. Sometimes, on arousing myself from my slumbers, I found the rebellious little vessel running along four or five points off her course. In more than one instance, when the orders were to keep close-hauled, the schooner gradually fell off until she got before the wind, when the sails gibed, all standing, making a terrible clatter, and awakening not only myself, but the captain also, who, on coming on deck, must have divined the true state of things; but, with a degree of consideration which I could hardly have expected, and did not deserve, he never gave me a word of reproof. How these matters were managed by Mr. Campbell, I could never learn. He was one of those nervous, restless mortals who require but little sleep. It can hardly be doubted, however, that he sometimes fell asleep in his watch, and steered the schooner in every direction but the right one. This wild steering during the night will sufficiently account for a long passage, and errors in navigation. Dead reckoning is of little use when the courses and distances are not correctly noted. In the daytime, Captain Moncrieff would sometimes steer hours at a time, especially when I was employed in other business or taking a nap below.

The most unpleasant duty I was expected to perform was that of cooking. I had never been inducted into the mysteries of that art, and was disgusted with its drudgeries. While in the Dolphin, with Captain Turner, I tried my hand at cooking more than once, when the cook had been so badly flogged as to be unable to perform his duties. But I gained no laurels in that department. Indeed, dissatisfaction was expressed in the forecastle and the cabin at the bungling and unartistic style in which I prepared the food on those occasions. In the Young Pilot I succeeded but little better; and the captain, who was something of an epicure in his way, whenever a good cup of coffee was required for breakfast, or a palatable dish for dinner, released me from my vocation for the time, and installed himself in the camboose. And it would have been amusing to a looker-on, to see the big, burly Scotchman steaming over the fire and smoke, rattling the pans and kettles, and compounding various materials, while I sat quietly at the helm, watching his operations, and thanking my stars that I had no genius for cooking.

The greatest cause I had for disquiet on this passage was the want of society. The captain and mate could spin their yarns and discuss subjects of nautical philosophy; but the mate, naturally unsocial and taciturn, seldom spoke to me, and the captain never honored me by entering into familiar conversation, excepting when he had indulged in an extra glass, and Mr. Campbell was not on deck. At such times, being in a garrulous humor, he would, as a sort of "Hogson's choice, " address himself to me, and rattle off narratives of adventures of the most astounding description.

The schooner was easily managed, being a small vessel of only thirty tons burden. In ordinary weather, one man, without leaving his station at the helm, could tack ship, gibe, and trim every sail. The schooner was a good-sailing vessel in light winds; but her chief excellence consisted in ability to beat to windward. When within four points of the wind she progressed at the rate of six or seven knots with a moderate breeze, while with a strong wind on the quarter eight knots was her greatest speed. An opportunity offered of testing her sailing qualities a few days after I had the honor to constitute her whole crew.

One morning, at daylight, as we were steering to the southward on a wind, a sail was made on the lee bow. It proved to be a large ship with two tiers of ports, not more than three or four miles off, steering to the westward. As soon as we were seen, the ship hauled her wind, spread every sail, and seemed determined to ascertain our character and business in those seas. Captain Moncrieff, with perfect propriety, resolved, if possible, to prevent the gratification of such impertinent curiosity. The British cruiser sailed remarkably well; and if we had been under her lee, our voyage would have ended before it was fairly begun. But we made short tacks to windward, shooting into the wind's eye every time we went about, and by three o'clock the ship was hull down to leeward, when she gave up the chase, squared away the yards, and steered to the westward.

A few days after this incident we fell in with a large, rakish- looking schooner on our weather bow. The schooner was heavily armed and her decks were full of men. She crossed our hawse and kept on her course until some distance under the lee bow, then hauled to the wind on the starboard tack, and on reaching our wake tacked within long gunshot and stood directly after us. She now fired a blank cartridge and hoisted the Patriot flag.

If Captain Moncrieff had kept his wits about him, and had not been afraid of cannon balls, we might have escaped, by keeping on our course or making short tacks to windward. This was worth the trial, as it was not unlikely the schooner, although showing Patriot colors, was a Spanish privateer or government cruiser; in which case, it would appear by letters and other documents that we were bound to LaGuayra, which at that time was in possession of the Patriot forces, and could expect little forbearance from the Spaniards, who were waging war to the knife against the patriots. This was forcibly represented to Captain Moncrieff by Mr. Campbell; and we trimmed every sail carefully, and kept close to the wind, with a fair prospect of making our escape.

The piratical-looking craft, perceiving we took no notice of her hint to heave to, yawed off a couple of points and sent a messenger after us in the shape of a twenty-four pound shot, which struck the water a short distance astern, and, playfully skipping along, sank beneath the surface near the weather quarter. Captain Moncrieff said not a word, but looked amazingly sober. Campbell, who cared little for his life, but had great fear of being robbed, and who regarded all privateers as neither more nor less than thieves and pirates, coolly remarked, "O, he may fire away as much as he likes; he cannot hit us at that distance. "

"I don't know that, " replied captain Moncrieff, much agitated. "I believe he is gaining on us. The next shot may take away one of the masts. "

"He is NOT gaining on us, " said Campbell. "If he should hit one of the masts we should be COMPELLED to heave to; it would no longer be a matter of choice. But I don't believe he can do it"

At this moment the schooner yawed, and gave us another gun. The ball came whizzing along, passed just over the mast-head, and fell in the water a couple of lengths off on the starboard bow.

"I'll bet a beaver hat, " said Campbell, "he can't do that again. "

"This will never do, " exclaimed the captain, greatly alarmed, and pale as a ghost. "He will hull us next time, and send us all to 'Davy's locker. ' Haul the foresheet to windward! "

This was done; and the pilot-boat lay like a log on the water, waiting the approach of our pursuer.

"Now, " said Campbell, with a scowl of disappointment, "I will go below and take care of 'number one. ' And Hawser, " continued he, "I know those chaps better than you do. They glory in robbing a sailor's chest when there is anything in it worth taking. I advise you to do as I mean to do clothe yourself in two or three suits of your best garments; for I never knew them strip the clothing from a man's back. "

"I thank you for your counsel, sir, " said I; "but if they overhaul MY chest in expectation of a prize, they will be woefully disappointed. "

Mr. Campbell went below a slight-built, thin-looking man, bearing a closer resemblance to Shakespeare's portrait of Prince Hal than to that of Falstaff. When, fifteen minutes afterwards, he appeared on deck, staggering under the load of three pairs of trousers, an equal number of vests, covering half a dozen shirts, with two or three silk kerchiefs around his neck, he looked, from his chin downwards, more like the "fat knight" than Prince Hal; and his thin face, peaked nose, and chin showing itself above such a portly corporation and huge limbs, gave him an unnatural appearance ludicrous in the extreme. He told me he had stowed away the remainder of his property where it would puzzle the privateersmen to find it, and chuckled over the ingenuity by which he expected to outwit the rascals.

It was not long before the armed schooner ranged alongside. She was a formidable-looking craft, with a "long Tom" and a stout armament besides. We were hailed in broken English: "You capitan, come on board directly, and bring your papers. "

The captain remonstrated, saying we were short-manned, and unable to launch the boat, or to man it afterwards. They did not, or would not, understand his objections, but repeated the order in a style which silenced further remonstrance: "Come on board, Senor Capitan, this minute, and bring your papers, or I shall shoot directly!"

There was no alternative. After much labor and heavy lifting we launched the boat. Captain Moncrieff put his papers in his pocket, and leaving Mr. Campbell in charge of the schooner, followed me into the yawl. Putting his dignity along with his papers, he took an oar, I took another, and we pulled for the privateer, which by this time was out of hail to leeward. We went alongside, and were roughly ordered on deck, where we found a motley set. Some of the crew were savage, desperate-looking fellows:

"As ever scuttled ship, or cut a throat. "

Others were squalid, ragged, and filthy, to a degree I had never before witnessed. There was apparently but little discipline on board, but a great deal of disputation and a continual jabbering. A ruffianly-looking fellow, with a swarthy complexion and big black whiskers, who proved to be the commander, beckoned Captain Moncrieff to the quarter-deck, where he examined the schooner's papers and various letters, all of which proved, beyond a doubt, that the schooner was an American vessel, bound to a Patriot port on the Spanish Main.

Fortunately for us our captor was a Patriot privateer, and our little vessel, under no pretext, could be regarded as a prize. If we had been bound to a port on the Spanish Main where the inhabitants had not thrown off their allegiance to the king or if the privateer had been a Spaniard, the case would have been different, and the pilot-boat would have been taken possession of and confiscated to the benefit of the captors, probably without trial. In those days other nations, following the example of France and England, trampled on the great principles of international law so far as our insulted country was concerned.

As the privateersmen could not take our vessel without avowing themselves pirates, they reluctantly limited themselves to plunder. An officer and half a dozen men, armed with pistols and cutlasses, were despatched in our boat to the schooner, which they thoroughly examined from stem to stern. As we had no goods, hey removed the ballast to find valuable property or money, which we might have concealed. They overhauled chests, trunks, and writing-desks, looking for specie or hidden papers; helped themselves to whatever they particularly fancied, and finally conveyed to the privateer all the water, beef, bread, sugar, coffee, and other provisions and stores which they could find, with the exception of a very scanty supply for our own use!

After a detention of a couple of hours, the last boat load of provisions was transferred to the deck of the privateer, and Captain Moncrieff and myself were about to step into the boat on our return, when the officer who had superintended the piratical operations suggested to the commander of the privateer that our boat was a remarkably fine one; far better and more serviceable than any one in their possession, and THEREFORE it would be right and proper for us the captain and crew of the pilot-boat to return to our own vessel in a skiff belonging to the privateer, and leave our boat for their use.

The case was forcibly put; the logic was unanswerable, and the conclusion inevitable. The stern-boat, a light skiff, was lowered and brought alongside, and then it appeared why the privateersmen did not board us in their own boat, as is usual on such occasions. They had had an engagement the day before with a Spanish government brig; had been roughly handled, had several men killed and wounded, and sustained damage in hull and spars. The boats had been riddled with shot, and, not having been subsequently repaired, were not seaworthy.

When the little skiff was brought beneath the gangway the water was pouring through the bottom in divers places. No time was given for deliberation. We were unceremoniously shoved into the skiff, the painter was cast loose, and a dark, ugly-visaged scoundrel told us, in broken English and with a diabolical grin, to "pull for our lives! " So, indeed, we did. The pilot-boat was not far off, nevertheless we should have swamped ere we could have reached her had not the captain, with admirable presence of mind, ordered me to lay in my oar, and at the same time handed me his hat, a large one and in tolerable good condition, and pointing to the water in which our legs were immersed, bade me "bale away! " Then placing his oar over the stern of the boat, he sculled off towards the schooner like an excited Hercules!

In this way we managed to reach the Young Pilot, and greatly to the amusement of the piratical patriots, scrambled on board in a most undignified manner. In spite of our exertions the skiff was filled with water when we trod the deck of the schooner. Mr. Campbell relieved himself of his superfluous garments, and we went busily to work rigging purchases, with which to hoist in the boat we had received in exchange for our own. We then proceeded on our way.

Any person who has sailed on the Atlantic must have noticed the luminous appearance of the water of the ocean, especially at night and in tempestuous weather. This beautiful phenomenon is witnessed to a greater extent in some parts of the ocean than in others, and in different sections it presents different appearances. In one place it seems uniformly luminous, shining feebly with a pale and sickly light; in another it exhibits bright flashes; again, it appears composed of brilliants of different sizes and shades, and sometimes, like a grand exhibition of the "northern lights, " all these appearances are combined. The most phosphorescent sea seldom exhibits peculiarities by daylight. Nevertheless, sometimes, though rarely, luminous patches and even large tracts of water are seen in the daytime, and at a great distance from ordinary soundings, with the color differing materially from the well-known hue of the ocean, and seeming to indicate to the astonished mariner the existence of banks or shoals.

A few days after we fell in with the Patriot privateer, being in about twenty-six degrees of latitude, in the middle of a clear and beautiful day, Mr. Campbell, who was at the helm, exclaimed, in a tone of alarm, "There's a shoal ahead! "

On looking in that direction, a tract of water embracing several square miles was seen, which was of a light green color inclining to yellow. Its edges were well defined, but irregular, and presented a strong contrast with the general appearance of the ocean. We supposed the water on that spot must be shallow, but as there was a heavy swell and no breakers were seen, it was manifest there was depth of water enough for our little schooner. The deep-sea lead was got ready, and when we had reached what we considered the centre and shoalest part of the bank, no bottom was found with a hundred fathoms of line. The peculiarity in color was undoubtedly owing to luminous particles floating in the water, and if we had remained on that spot until dark we should have seen that whole tract of ocean splendidly illuminated.

The cause of this singular phenomenon has given rise to many theories and much discussion among naturalists. It was for a time contended that this phosphorescence was a quality of the water itself. But later and more accurate observers ascertained beyond a doubt, that some marine worms and other insects were luminous. On pursuing the investigation it is ascertained that the sea water is far less pure than has been supposed, and is often crowded with myriads of minute luminous animals. It is now admitted that the phosphorescence of sea water is a property not belonging to itself, but is produced by animalcula, or microscopic creatures. They are far more numerous in some tracts of ocean than in others, and all possess the power of producing a light, a spark, or flash at will. There can be no doubt that these living, transparent atoms cause the luminous appearance of the ocean, which excites admiration, and has so often been described in glowing language by the poet.

Chapter XXII CAPTURED BY A PRIVATEER

Captain Moncrieff was desirous of entering the Caribbean Sea through the Sail-rock passage, which separates the barren island of St. Thomas from Porto Rico. But when we reached the latitude of those islands we beheld, on our starboard bow, the mountainous country on the eastern part of Hayti. The island of Porto Rico was soon afterwards seen on the other bow, and directly ahead was the little island of Mona, rising abruptly from the sea. Instead of striking the Sail-rock passage we found ourselves in the centre of the Mona passage, a hundred and twenty miles to leeward of Sail-rock, and twenty or thirty miles westward of the meridian of LaGuayra.

Although Captain Moncrieff was glad of an opportunity to ascertain his true position, he was mortified at finding himself westward of his destined port. The Young Pilot was immediately hauled on a wind, and we crossed the Caribbean Sea with a fine breeze, and one morning beheld the Rocas, a cluster of barren rocks, right ahead. We passed over a bank extending from this group of rocks, and with a fishing-line trailing astern and a piece of the rind of pork for bait, caught a quantity of Spanish mackerel, a fish of excellent flavor, weighing four or five pounds each.

And I will here state, for the benefit of those navigators who have little experience in those seas, that on the edge of soundings in all parts of the West Indies, and particularly on the edges of the Bahamas and Salt Key Bank, abundance of fish of excellent quality, as black perch, kingfish, barracooter, and Spanish mackerel, may be taken by trailing during a breeze, in any reasonable quantity.

By steering a course directly from the Rocas to LaGuayra we could have reached that port on the following day, but Captain Moncrieff was impressed with the idea that a strong current was setting to the westward. Therefore, instead of proceeding directly to the Spanish Main, as he should have done, he commenced beating to windward, and continued this absurd process for two days, when, having made the island of Tortuga, he satisfied himself he was far enough to windward, and that there was no current at that time in those seas. The helm was accordingly put up, and with a free wind we now steered to the south-west, to fall in with the coast somewhere near Cape Codera. We made the land about fifty miles to windward of LaGuayra, in the afternoon, about three o'clock. Captain Moncrieff clapped his hands in ecstasy when he saw the land. "If this breeze holds, " said he, "we can run along under easy sail and be off the harbor before daylight tomorrow morning. "

His exultation was moderated by the sight of a large topsail schooner on our starboard quarter, dead to windward, steering towards us under a heavy press of sail, and coming up hand over hand. We hoisted our square-sail and wet our other sails, but the schooner gained upon us rapidly. Ere the darkness of night concealed us from her view, we became aware that the schooner in chase was a Spanish government vessel, termed a Guarda Costa, one of the very few armed vessels stationed on that coast to show that the blockade of the Patriot ports on the Spanish Main was not a mere paper blockade.

A hasty consultation between the captain and the mate was now held, to devise means of keeping out of the clutches of the Spaniard during the night. They both agreed in the opinion that the Guarda Costa would keep on the course she was steering when last seen, with the expectation of soon overhauling us. Therefore, the best mode of disappointing those expectations would be to change our course, run directly towards the shore, dowse every sail, and remain concealed by the darkness until morning.

The stratagem devised by the combined wisdom of the officers was carried into effect. We ran in under the land and hauled down every sail, thus presenting so small a surface to the eye that it was almost impossible we should be seen during the night. It was deemed advisable to keep a good look-out, and Captain Moncrieff volunteered to keep the watch from eight o'clock to eleven. Mr. Campbell was to be on deck from eleven o'clock until three, when I was to be called to keep the look-out until daylight.

Everything passed off well during the first and second watches of the night. At three o'clock I was roused out by the mate, and took my station on deck. I could not divest myself of the idea that the Guarda Costa had divined our intentions and was quietly lying to, somewhere in our vicinity, sure of finding us snugly under her guns at the dawn of the day. There was no moon in the heavens, nevertheless the horizon was well defined, and a large object could be seen at the distance of a couple of miles. I took a careful look around the horizon, waited a short time and looked again. I suffered my eyes to dwell on that quarter, in a north- east direction, where the schooner had been seen the evening before, and after a while I beheld a speck darker than the surrounding atmosphere.

Might it not exist only in imagination? I turned away my eyes and took a survey of the horizon in another direction, and again looked towards the quarter where the dark object had appeared. It was still there. Feeling assured I was not the victim of error, I ventured to call Captain Moncrieff, who hastened on deck followed by the mate. I gave him my reasons for disturbing his slumbers, and pointed to the dark speck which had arrested my attention. They both looked in the direction I indicated, but could see nothing. The captain swept the horizon with his spy glass, then turning to me, said, "Hawser, you have persuaded yourself that the Guarda Costa is still in that direction, than which nothing can be more unlikely, and your fancy has conjured up a vision that is visible to no one but yourself. "

"It is no fancy, sir, " said I, boldly. "I KNOW there is a vessel in that direction. I can see it distinctly; and you may mark my words that the sooner we get the schooner under sail, the greater will be the chance of escaping capture. "

Mr. Campbell, with a sneering laugh, remarked that his eyes never yet deceived him, and that he could see as far in the dark as any one! The captain, however, was staggered by the obstinacy with which I adhered to my statement, and said to the mate, "It is possible that Hawser may see something in that quarter which we cannot see, and as it is nearly daylight it may be well to get the schooner under sail and commence running down the coast. "

We began to hoist our sails; but before the foresail was set, a flash of light appeared in the north-east followed by the report of a gun, thus confirming the correctness of my assertion and establishing the excellence of my eyesight. We lost no time in getting sail on the schooner; and now Captain Moncrieff regretted that instead of running in towards the land he had not adopted means during the night of getting the weather-gage, when he could have laughed at the efforts of the Guarda Costa to interrupt our voyage.

Daylight appeared in the east, when the Spanish schooner was plainly seen; also another vessel which had fallen into her hands whilst she was quietly lying to, hoping to pounce upon us. As soon as objects could be distinctly seen, the boat of the Guarda Costa was returning from a visit to the stranger, and the Spaniard having got a glimpse of the pilot-boat, showed a determination to become better acquainted with the object of our voyage. The affair became exciting. We were close in with the shore, running directly before the wind with a fresh breeze. The schooner had got in our wake and was crowding all sail in pursuit.

It soon became manifest that we could not escape. Our pursuer was hardly a gunshot off, and slowly but surely lessening the space between us. The sagacious Mr. Campbell regarded our capture as inevitable, and, true to his characteristics, repeated the stratagem which had served him so successfully when we were molested by the Patriot privateer. He doffed his old garments, which were not worth stealing, and clad himself from top to toe in two or three complete suits of his best clothing. He came on deck resembling a swathed mummy, and perspiring freely under the heavy load.

When the Guarda Costa had approached within fair gunshot, and we were every minute expecting an iron shower, we saw at a short distance ahead on a projecting point of land, a fort on which several guns were mounted, and the Patriot flag was waving from a tall flagstaff. The masts of some small vessels were also visible over the point.

"There is a snug harbor, " exclaimed Captain Moncrieff, "defended by a fort and in possession of the Patriots. We will run in under the guns of our friends and come to anchor. Hurrah, we are all right at last! " And he cut a pigeon-wing with a dexterity of which I had hardly believed him capable.

And now an armed felucca shot out from the harbor beyond the fort with the Patriot flag flying at the peak. She was full of men, evidently a privateer, and with long sweeps pulled swiftly towards us. When within hearing, a fierce-looking fellow, with pistols in his belt and a sabre at his side, stepped upon the gunwale and hailed us in tolerable English.

"Captain, " said he, "that Spanish schooner is one great rascal. If he should board your vessel, HE WILL CUT ALL YOUR THROATS! "

"Can I enter that harbor? " inquired Captain Moncrieff, greatly alarmed at such a sanguinary piece of intelligence.

"Certainly, certainly! There, and there only you will be safe. Follow the felucca, and we will pilot you in. "

The felucca rounded the point, closely followed by the pilot-boat. We entered a snug little bay, well sheltered from the regular winds and waves, and agreeably to the directions of our new and zealous friends let go an anchor; at the same time the Guarda Costa fired a gun, hauled down her colors, gave up the chase, and steered away to the northward.

We were boarded by the commander of the felucca and the officer who had so kindly told us of the bloody intentions of our pursuers. They shook Captain Moncrieff by the hand, and congratulated him on having baffled the enemy.

"But, " asked Captain Moncrieff, "will not the blood-thirsty Spaniards return at night, send in an armed boat and cut us out from under the guns of the fort? "

"O, no! There's no fear of that, " replied the commander of the felucca, with a savage smile which I did not half like. "Be not alarmed. WE will take good care of you, " and he clapped his hand significantly on the hilt of his sabre!

I was an attentive observer of every event which took place, and was by no means satisfied with the proceedings. The sudden apparition of the felucca, the departure of the Guarda Costa without firing a shot, and the exultation of the officers who boarded us, and which they tried in vain to conceal, all convinced me there was some mystery which it was not in my power to fathom.

"Where are you bound, captain? " inquired the officious commander of the felucca.

"To LaGuayra, if it still belongs to the Patriots, " replied Moncrieff.

"That is right, " exclaimed the grinning corsair. "You are a good patriot, and have letters and intelligence which will be valuable to our friends in LaGuayra! "

"Certainly, replied Moncrieff. "I have letters in abundance, and any thing in my power to aid in establishing the independence of the Spanish Provinces on the Main I will do with pleasure. "

The commander of the felucca expressed satisfaction at such noble sentiments, and added, "I will, with your permission, go below and examine your papers. "

Hardly had the two captains left the deck, when the loud report of a gun from the fort echoed across the water, and down came the Patriot flag from the flagstaff! It was immediately replaced by the sickly emblem of Spain. A musket was fired from the felucca, and the Spanish ensign waved also at her peak! Moncrieff heard the firing and rushed on deck just as an ill-looking fellow, who had for some time been busy about the signal halliards, near the taffrail, was running up a Spanish flag, WITH THE STARS AND STRIPES BENEATH! He saw at a glance that he was the victim of an ingenious trick. He was terribly agitated his features, usually florid, were as pale as death. "What is the meaning of all this? " he exclaimed, in a husky voice.

"A BUENO prize, captain! A BUENO prize! " replied the exulting commander of the felucca, patting him affectionately on the shoulder.

The affair required but little explanation. The fort was a Spanish fort. The felucca was a Spanish privateer, belonging to Porto Cabello, and her commander had adroitly managed to capture the pilot-boat just as we were about to fall into the jaws of the Guarda Costa. The commander of the felucca had furthermore wormed out of the unsuspecting Moncrieff all the secrets of his mission, and paved the way for the confiscation of our little schooner.

Moncrieff stormed and raved like a madman; but there was no remedy. The Spaniards were too well pleased with the success of their stratagem to notice his anger, and the captain on reflection was somewhat consoled by the idea that if he had missed the felucca he could not have escaped the Guarda Costa. On conversing further with his captors, he ascertained that the ship, to reach which was the object of his mission, was now at Porto Cabello, which place had been recently captured by the royalists after a hard battle. He further learned that it was the intention of his captors to proceed directly to Porto Cabello with their prize.

A prize-master and eight men, armed to the teeth, were put on board. Mr. Campbell was ordered into the felucca without an opportunity of relieving himself of his extra clothing. The rays of the sun in that sheltered harbor seemed endued with a tenfold degree of calorie; and the poor fellow, as he stepped over the side, bowed down by the weight of his garments and sweltering with heat, was a legitimate object of pity, although a martyr to his selfish propensities.

We left the harbor on our way to Porto Cabello; but our progress was slow, being interrupted by calms. The prize crew of the Young Pilot were attentive to their duties and faithful and vigilant during the night. They were divided into two watches, and four of them, armed with pistols and cutlasses, paced the deck at all hours. Nevertheless, on the third day after leaving port, the felucca being out of sight in the north-east chasing a suspicious- looking vessel, Captain Moncrieff, having raised and fortified his courage by an extra portion of cogniac, called me into the cabin and broached the subject of retaking the schooner!

"Hawser, " said he, "I cannot reconcile myself to the loss of my vessel; the idea of being tricked out of her by a set of garlic- eating ragamuffins puts me out of all patience. I have as good a pair of pistols as were ever manufactured, which I concealed when the schooner was searched. With these, and a good cutlass in my hand, I would face a dozen of these cowardly Spaniards at any time. If you will stand by me we will drive every mother's son of them overboard! "

I saw that Moncrieff was so drunk he could hardly stand. Indeed, it was only at such times his courage was roused to fighting heat. I attempted to calm his excitement by representing the slender chance of success we should have in open combat with eight or ten men completely armed; that it was far more likely we should be thrown overboard than the prize crew. I also argued that even if we should be successful in the desperate contest we should gain nothing, but on the contrary lose the opportunity of proceeding to Porto Cabello where the ship Charity was now lying; that in every point of view his design was objectionable, as well as impracticable; and furthermore, the attempt would be an ungrateful return for the civilities and indulgence we had received from the prize-master and his associates.

My remonstrances only served to increase the fury of Moncrieff, who swore that single-handed he would retake the schooner. With his back against the mainmast and a good claymore in his hand, he would cut down every man one after another!

I found he was too far gone to listen to reason; and it is possible he might have staggered on deck, pistol in hand, and been shot down for his pains, if the prize-master, attracted by his loud and threatening language, had not listened to a part of the conversation; and as the captain was on the point of sallying forth, like a doughty champion of old, in search of hard knocks, his collar was grasped by a couple of stout men; and he was roughly laid on his back and handcuffed in a trice. His pistols were found and appropriated to the use of the prize-master as spoils of the vanquished, and he would have been treated with great harshness had I not interfered and pointed out the brandy bottle as the guilty originator of the plot. The brandy was promptly secured, to be punished hereafter. The captain was relieved of his manacles and shoved into his berth, where he slept off his valorous propensities, and awoke a few hours afterwards a different man, who could hardly be drubbed into a plot which would endanger his own life.

In spite of calms, and light winds, and Patriot cruisers, we reached Porto Cabello on the fifth day after leaving the little harbor where we were so handsomely entrapped. The felucca entered the port at the same time, and Mr. Campbell was permitted to join us once more; and he did it with an alacrity which, I confess to my shame, furnished me with no little amusement. The sufferings of the poor man while in the felucca can hardly be imagined. He was exposed in that hot climate, and during the prevalence of calms, to the fiercest rays of the sun, while loaded with clothes enough to keep him uncomfortably warm during a polar winter. And he felt compelled to bear his burden without murmuring or seeking to be relieved, lest his companions should suspect his reasons for bearing his whole wardrobe on his back, and take umbrage at such a reflection on their honor!

Chapter XXIII PORTO CABELLO

The ship Charity was lying in the harbor of Porto Cabello, but under seizure of the Spanish government. Captain Moncrieff, Mr. Campbell, and myself, with no longer a home in the pilot-boat, transferred our quarters to the ship. The officers took up their abode in the cabin, while I was thrown on the hospitalities of the forecastle. The prize-master of the pilot-boat honored me with a pressing invitation to join the crew of the felucca, assuring me there was "good picking" along the coast, and he would put me in the way of doing well. I felt flattered by his good opinion; but under the circumstances thought proper to decline the invitation.

The ship Charity was a vessel of about three hundred and fifty tons burden, moored at this time in the centre of the harbor, awaiting the decision of the Admiralty Court. The ship was commanded by a man of very ordinary capacity. The mate was a mere sailor, wanting in intelligence and worth, and a fit associate for the captain. The ship and her valuable cargo were actually n charge of the supercargo, a Mr. Parker, of New York, who was also part owner. He resided on shore and seldom visited the ship. It was at his instance I found an asylum in the Charity along with the officers of the pilot-boat.

The crew of the Charity consisted of some eight or ten men, Dutchmen, Swedes, and Italians, as brutal and ignorant a set of men as it was ever my misfortune to fall in with. With such officers and such a crew, it may be imagined there was little discipline on board. Liquor could be easily obtained; and drunken rows and fighting among themselves, and occasionally with the captain or mate, were of frequent occurrence. None of the crew gave me a welcome when I went on board, and I saw at once there could be no good fellowship between us. I found a space in the forecastle for my chest, and in that warm climate it mattered little where I slept. I performed my duties regularly with the crew, and for the first two days led an unsocial, almost a solitary life, in the midst of a large ship's company. Captain Moncrieff, like an honest man, paid me the month's pay to which I was entitled, in advance. This money I kept about my person, and carefully concealed from every one the prosperous sate of my finances. I was thus enabled to indulge in little comforts which, to some extent, counterbalanced the inconveniences to which I was subjected.

On the morning of the third day after I had taken up my quarters in the ship, another person was received on board in accordance with a mandate from the supercargo. His name was Frederick Strictland. He was an Englishman, a veritable cockney, about nineteen or twenty years of age, a strong-built and rather good- looking young man. His countenance, although intelligent, was not prepossessing; there was a sort of nameless expression about the eye which repelled confidence and invited suspicion. But it was no time for me to entertain prejudices which might be unfounded, or indulge in surmises unfavorable to the character of my new shipmate. He could talk English, and talk it well. He was the victim of misfortune, being destitute of friends and money in a strange country. Finding ourselves accidentally thrown together in the same ship, it is not remarkable that we became constant companions from the commencement of our acquaintance, and intimate friends.

Strictland's story was calculated to excite compassion. His father was a respectable trader in London, and Frederick had been a clerk in his counting room. He frankly acknowledged he had been a little wild and extravagant, and having expressed a desire to go abroad, his father allowed him to proceed to Curacoa on a visit to a brother in that island. His brother received him coldly and could not or would not find him employment. He induced him to take passage for Porto Cabello, with assurances that he would there find some desirable means of getting a living. Disappointed in this, and having spent the little money given him by his brother, and sold or pawned the greater part of his clothing, his next project was to proceed to the United States, and he applied to Mr. Parker for a passage in the only American vessel in port. He was told that the ship might not leave the harbor for months, if ever. But as he was suffering from want, he was permitted to make it his home until he could find some other resource. I did not allow myself to doubt the truth of any portion of Strictland's narrative. I confided to him the particulars of my own situation. We conversed freely in regard to the future, and formed a resolution to keep together, and embrace the first opportunity of getting to the United States.

When I had been about a week in Porto Cabello, I was attacked by a severe and dangerous illness. I suffered severe pains incessantly, which deprived me of sleep. I was losing my strength daily, and at length, without any relaxation of the symptoms, was hardly able to crawl about the ship. I received no sympathy or medical aid from the captain or mate, and could not even obtain a little rice or gruel, or any other food than the coarse viands that were served out to the ship's company.

Strictland was with me whenever he could be spared from his regular duties, and gave me encouragement and aid. But I could not conceal from myself that my illness was becoming a serious matter. I accidentally heard two or three of the crew conversing about my sickness one day, and, to my great consternation, they came to the conclusion that I was rapidly sinking, and they would soon be rid of my company.

"Yaw, " muttered in thick guttural tones a thick-headed Dutchman, who had manifested towards me particular dislike, "in one or TWO days more, at farthest, we shall help to carry him ashore in a wooden box. " And a pleasant smile for a moment lighted up his ugly features.

"You lie, you heartless vagabond! " I exclaimed, giving a loose to my indignation; "you won't get rid of me so easily as you think. I will live and laugh at you yet, were it only to disappoint your expectations. "

Nevertheless, the opinion which my unsympathizing shipmates thus volunteered came over me like an electric shock. It sounded in my ears like a sentence of death. I crawled along the lower deck into the forecastle, and from the bottom of my chest took a small looking-glass which I had not used for weeks. I saw the reflection of my features, and started back aghast. The transformation was appalling. The uncombed locks, the sunken eyes, the pallid, fleshless cheeks, the sharp features, and the anxious, agonized expression caused by continual pain, all seemed to have been suddenly created by the spell of some malignant enchanter. I did not venture to take a second look, and no longer wondered at the gloomy prediction of my companions.

The next day I found myself growing worse, and the pain increasing; and, notwithstanding my determination to recover and falsify the prediction of my unfeeling shipmates, I should undoubtedly have followed the dark path which thousands of my young countrymen, sick and neglected in a foreign land, had trod before, had I not received aid from an unexpected quarter. I was crawling along the main deck, near the gangway, when Mr. Parker, the supercargo, came on board. As he stepped over the gunwale, my appearance, fortunately for me, arrested his attention. He inquired my name, examined my condition, and seemed greatly shocked at the brutal neglect I had experienced. He told me to be of good courage; that it was not yet too late to arrest the progress of my disease. He commenced his healing operations by administering a copious dose of laudanum, which immediately relieved my pain and threw me into a refreshing sleep. He furnished me with other medicines, ordered me food suitable to my condition, and in a few days, owing to his humanity, care, and skill, I no longer suffered excepting from debility.

When Porto Cabello was recaptured by the Spaniards, in 1812, there was a number of French families in the place, who, having sympathized with the Patriots, received an intimation that their presence would be no longer tolerated; that they must shift their quarters forthwith. They accordingly purchased a small schooner, called "La Concha, " put all their movable property on board, procured a French captain and mate, and prepared to embark for St. Bartholomew. When I heard of the expedition, two men were required to complete the crew. I conferred with Strictland; we both regarded it as an opportunity too favorable to be neglected, imagining that if we could reach St. Bartholomew, a neutral port, there would be no difficulty in getting a passage to the United States. We lost no time in calling on the captain, and offered to work our passage to St. Bartholomew an offer which was gladly accepted.

I expended a few of my Spanish dollars in providing necessaries for our voyage, which might be of two or three weeks' duration, and when the time appointed for the departure of the schooner arrived, we bade farewell to the Charity, and in a few hours, while sailing close-hauled on a wind to the northward, beheld the fortifications at the mouth of the harbor lessening in the distance.

The entrance to the harbor of Porto Cabello was once the theatre of one of the most gallant exploits recorded in the annals of naval warfare. A mutiny took place on board the British frigate Hermione, in 1799, while on the West India station, in consequence, it was said, of the harsh treatment which the crew received. The officers were murdered and thrown overboard. Captain Pigot, who commanded the frigate, after receiving several wounds, retreated to his cabin, and defended himself desperately with his dirk until he was bayoneted by the mutineers.

The frigate, thus taken possession of, was carried into Porto Cabello and delivered up to the Spanish authorities; Spain at that time being at war with Great Britain. The red-handed mutineers dispersed, and many of them subsequently returned to their native country, but were from time to time arrested, tried by court martial, and executed.

Indeed, no pains or expense were spared by the British government to bring these mutineers to punishment. They were sought for in every part of the world; hunted out of their hiding-places, and hanged. No false philanthropy interfered in their behalf, and threw obstacles in the swift and sure career of justice. Very few, if any, escaped the terrible punishment due to their crimes MUTINY AND MURDER ON THE HIGH SEAS. The effect of the EXAMPLE, which is the object of capital punishment was most salutary. No mutiny has occurred in the British navy since that time.

The Hermione was regarded as a lawful prize by the Spaniards, notwithstanding the extraordinary manner by which the ship fell into their hands. She was refitted; a crew of four hundred men, including marines, were put on board, and, ready for a cruise, she lay at anchor near the entrance of the harbor and within musket shot of the principal fortifications, which mounted two hundred cannon.

These facts became known to Captain Hamilton, who commanded the British frigate Surprise, cruising on the coast, and that gallant officer conceived the daring design of boarding the Hermione with a portion of his crew, and cutting her out in spite of opposition, while she was lying under the guns of this heavy fortification. Such an enterprise could only have been conceived by a man of unusual intrepidity; but it was planned with a degree of prudence and cool calculation which insured success.

After having well observed the situation of the frigate, Captain Hamilton with one hundred men left the Surprise in boats soon after midnight on the 25th of October, 1800. On approaching the Hermione the alarm was given by the frigate's launch, which, armed with a twenty-four pounder, was rowing guard around the ship. After beating off the launch, Captain Hamilton, at the head of fifty chosen men, armed chiefly with cutlasses, boarded the Hermione on the bows. As soon as he and his bold companions obtained foothold, the boat's crews cut the cables and commenced towing the Hermione into the offing. Thus, while the battle was raging on the ship's decks, she was rapidly towed further from the batteries which had now commenced firing, and nearer to the Surprise, which ship stood close into the harbor.

A bloody contest for the possession of the ship took place on her decks. The Spaniards fought bravely; but the English, forming a front across the main deck after they got possession of the forecastle, drove them aft, where, after a desperate struggle on the quarter-deck or poop, the Dons were all killed or driven overboard. The fight was still continued on the gun-deck, where a dreadful carnage took place; and it was only after an obstinate combat of an hour and a half from the commencement of the action, that the Spaniards called for quarter, being entirely subdued.

In this action the British had no men killed, and only fourteen wounded among whom was Captain Hamilton, who fought boldly at the head of his men. The Spaniards had ninety-seven men wounded, most of them severely, and one hundred and nineteen killed! It would thus seem that while the courage of both parties was about equal, the English had a vast superiority in physical power. The Spaniards, unable to oppose to their fierce enemies other than a feeble resistance, bravely SUBMITTED TO BE KILLED; and the English sailors hacked and hewed them down until they cried for quarter.

The little La Concha, in which I was now embarked, was a dull-sailing vessel with poor accommodations, but crowded with living beings; and when beneath the deck, they were necessarily stowed away in the most miscellaneous manner, resembling herrings packed in a barrel. In addition to the officers and crew, we had about thirty passengers, men, women, and children, exiles from the land of their adoption; driven forth by the hand of power to seek a place of refuge in unknown countries. In this case, there was a great loss of property as well as of comfort, and the future must have presented to this little band of exiles an uninviting picture.

The feelings of people born in any other land than France, would have been deeply affected by such a change; and unavailing regrets, bitter complaints, and gloomy speculations in regard to the future, would have cast a cloud over their spirits, and repressed aught like gayety or cheerfulness during the passage. But our passengers were truly French; and "VIVE LA BAGATELLE" was their motto. Although subjected to many inconveniences during a long and tedious passage, and deprived of comforts to which they had been accustomed, yet without resorting for consolation to the philosophy of the schools, there was no murmuring at their unhappy lot. They seemed not merely contented, but gay; they even made a jest of their misfortunes, indulged in practical jokes, fun, and frolic, and derived amusement from every occurrence which took place.

On this passage, Strictland, who entertained the prejudices of his nation against the French, lost no opportunity to manifest his contempt of the passengers, and commented on their proceedings in a manner ill-natured and unjust.

He more than once exhibited a surliness and incivility in his demeanor, which is supposed to be a prominent feature in the character of a burly Briton; and was far from being a favorite with any of the passengers or the captain. On more than one occasion a misunderstanding occurred between Strictland and myself, and at one time it approached an open rupture.

We were both familiar with Smollet's "Adventures of Roderick Random, " and compared ourselves, with our rambles about the world in quest of a living, to the hero of that celebrated work and his faithful friend Strap; with this difference, however, that while each of us applied to himself the part of Roderick, neither was willing to assume the humble character of the honest but simple- minded Strap. In the course of our discussion Strictland lost his temper, and indulged in language towards myself that I was not disposed to pass lightly over. The next morning, the little uninhabited island of Orchilla being in sight, the wind light and the weather pleasant, the boat was launched, and the mate with several passengers, urged by curiosity, embarked, and were pulled ashore by Strictland and myself. While the other parties were rambling about, making investigations, we, more pugnaciously inclined, retired to a short distance from the shore, and prepared to settle all our disputes in a "bout at fisticuffs, " an ungentlemanly method of settling a controversy, but one which may afford as much SATISFACTION to the vanquished party as a sword- thrust through the vitals, or pistol bullet in the brain.

After exchanging a few left-handed compliments with no decided result, our pugilistic amusement was interrupted by the unauthorized influence of two of the passengers, who had been searching for shell-fish among the rocks. What the result of the contest would have been I will not venture to conjecture. I was but a tyro in the art, while Strictland prided himself in his scientific skill, and gave an indication of the purity of his tastes by boasting of having once acted in the honorable capacity of bottle-holder to a disciple of the notorious Tom Crib, on a very interesting public occasion.

After we had been about a fortnight on our passage, daily beating to windward in the Caribbean Sea, we were fallen in with by a British sloop-of-war. The sight of this vessel, and a knowledge of her character, caused a sensation throughout the schooner. Doubts were very naturally entertained in regard to the treatment the passengers would receive at the hands of their much-dreaded enemy. They were Frenchmen, and all the property on board was French property; and notwithstanding they sailed under Spanish colors, it was predicted by some, who entertained exaggerated notions of the rapacity of Englishmen and their hatred of the French, that the flag of Spain would not serve as a protection; but that their little property would be seized upon, and themselves detained and confined as prisoners or war. Others, however, cherished a different opinion, and had confidence in that magnanimity which has always been claimed by the English as one of their national attributes.

It was an anxious moment; and a general council of war was held among the passengers on the deck of the schooner, in which, as at a conclave of parrots, few seemed to listen while every one was eager to speak. The consultation, however, produced no result. Indeed, nothing could be done, excepting to wait, and bow submissively to the decrees of the conqueror.

My friend and companion, Strictland, was really in greater jeopardy than either of the Frenchmen. If his name and station had been discovered, he would have found snug quarters during the term of his natural life; nothing could have saved him from impressment. The French passengers, aware of the fact, with the kindest feelings took active measures to prevent such a misfortune. They changed his name, clad him in Frenchified garments, bound a many-colored handkerchief around his head, put a cigarette in his mouth, and cautioned him against replying in his native tongue to questions that might be asked. Thus travestied, it was boldly predicted that he would not be taken for an Englishman.

The sloop-of-war sent a boat alongside, commanded by a lieutenant, who seemed surprised at the singular group by which he was surrounded on reaching the schooner's deck. To his questions, replies were received from a dozen different mouths. He was a pleasant, gentlemanly officer and seemed greatly amused at his reception. At length he inquired for the captain, and on his being pointed out, addressed his questions to him, and repressed the officious interference of others until he received a full explanation of the character of the vessel and the intent of the voyage. The statements of the captain were confirmed by papers and documents, which left no doubt of their truth. The lieutenant, after obtaining all necessary information, returned to the ship to report the result of his visit. He did not tarry long, and when he came back relieved the apprehensions of the passengers by assuring them that the commander of the sloop of war, far from seeking to injure or embarrass them, felt for their misfortunes and would gladly render them any assistance in his power. He then went among the passengers, conversed with them, asked each one his name and country, and took other means to prevent deception. When he came to Strictland, and asked his name, the reply was, "Jean Fourchette, " in a bold tone.

"Are you a Frenchman? " asked the officer.

"Yes, SIR, " was Strictland's reply, in a most anti-Gallican accent.

The officer stared at him for a moment, but without asking more questions passed on to others.

I felt somewhat apprehensive that the British ship was short-manned, and that the officer might cast a longing look on me, and consider me worthy of serving his "most gracious majesty"; in which case I intended to fall back on my American protection, which I regarded as my richest treasure, and insist upon going to an English prison rather than sling my hammock in a man-of-war. But no questions were asked, as I was looked upon as one of the crew, which, without counting Strictland, consisted of only three individuals; and the idea of reducing that small number by impressment was not entertained.

The officer, before he left the schooner, with great glee communicated to our passengers an important piece of intelligence, which was more gratifying to British than to French ears. A great and decisive battle had been fought at Salamanca, in Spain, between the combined armies under Wellington and the French army under Marmont. It resulted in the signal defeat of the French marshal, who was severely wounded. The officer left some English newspapers on board the schooner containing the details of the battle.

The difficulty which had occurred between Strictland and myself, and which at one time threatened to sever forever all friendly ties, was amicably settled before we arrived at St. Bartholomew. Policy undoubtedly pointed out to the Englishman the importance of continuing our friendly relations while my money lasted; and he apologized in a handsome manner for what I considered his rude and uncivil conduct. Again we became sworn friends and brothers, and resolved that the same fortune, good or evil, should betide us both.

We arrived at St. Bartholomew about the 20th of September, 1812, and landed our passengers in good order, well-conditioned, and in tip-top spirits, after a passage of twenty days.

Chapter XXIV HARD TIMES IN ST. BARTHOLOMEW

We found the harbor of St. Bartholomew full of vessels belonging to almost every nation. Among them were several American clippers taking in cargo for the United States; also vessels under Swedish colors bound in the same direction. From these facts we anticipated little difficulty in procuring a passage to that country, on whose shores my friend, the young Englishman, as well as myself, was anxious to stand. But, although there were many vessels in port, there were also many sailors; far more than could be provided with employment; men, who by shipwreck or capture, had been set adrift in different parts of the Windward islands, and had flocked to St. Bartholomew with a view to get a passage to "The land of the free and the home of the brave. "

Strictland and myself remained in the schooner La Concha a couple of days, until the cargo was discharged, when the French captain, taking me aside, told me he was making arrangements to proceed on a trip to Point Petre, in Guadaloupe, and was desirous I should remain with him as one of the crew on regular wages. But as he positively refused to receive my companion on the same terms, or on any ter0ms whatever, and, moreover, expressed an opinion of his character by no means favorable, and which I believed to be unjust, I declined his proposition as a matter of course.

It now became necessary to seek some abiding place on shore until we could find means of getting from the island. But on inquiry I ascertained that thee expenses of board, even of the humblest character, were so great that our slender resources, the few dollars remained of my single month's pay, would not warrant such an extravagant proceeding as a resort to a boarding house. I convinced Strictland of the importance of the strictest economy in our expenditures; succeeded in persuading a good-natured Swede, who kept a small shop near the careenage, to allow my chest to remain with him a few days, and we undertook to "rough it" as well as we could.

In the morning we usually took a survey of the vessels in the harbor, hoping to find employment of some kind or a chance to leave the island. When hungry, we bought, for a small sum, a loaf of bread and a half dozen small fish, jacks or ballahues, already cooked, of which there was always a bountiful supply for sale about the wharves, and then retiring to the outskirts of the town, seated in the shade of one of the few trees in that neighborhood, we made a hearty and delicious repast. The greatest inconvenience to which we were subjected was a want of water. There was a great scarcity of that "necessary of life" in the island, and a drink of water, when asked for, was frequently refused. More than once, when hard pressed by thirst, I entered a grog shop and paid for a glass of liquor in order to obtain a refreshing draught of the pure element.

At night, after walking through the streets and listening to the gossip of the sailors collected in groups in the streets, we retired to some lonely wharf, and throwing ourselves down on a pile of SOFT pine boards, and gathering our jackets around us, and curtained by the starry canopy of heaven, we slept as soundly and sweetly as if reposing on the most luxurious couch.

But even this cheap mode of lodging was attended with inconveniences. One night a shower of rain came suddenly upon us. This was an event unfrequent and consequently unexpected, and our garments were thoroughly soaked before we could realize our misfortune. As this happened about three o'clock in the morning, there was nothing left but to wait patiently several hours, wet to the skin and shivering in the night air, until our clothing was dried by the rays of the sun and warmth restored to our frames.

One night an unprincipled knave undertook to rob us while we slept. Fortunately for us he began his work with Strictland, and took possession of the few effects which his pockets contained before my companion awoke and gave the alarm. On hearing his cry, I started to my feet and seized the fellow, who, being nearly naked, eluded my grasp and ran. We chased him the length of a street, when he entered an alley and disappeared among a row of dilapidated buildings.

After these events we considered it expedient to change our capacious lodging house for one of more limited dimensions, where we might be screened from a shower and concealed from the prying eyes of a robber. We proceeded the next day in quest of such an accommodation, and after a careful survey of various localities, our labors were crowned with success. We found on the northern side of the harbor an old boat that had been hauled up on the beach and turned bottom upwards. This furnished us with a capital lodging house. We took up our quarters there every night without asking permission of the owner, and were never disturbed in our snug domicile after we laid ourselves down to rest.

It may be asked why I did not apply to the American consul for assistance. The treatment which I received from the agent of our government, when in distress, at Liverpool, created on my mind an unfavorable impression in regard to that class of officials, and the reluctant aid and little encouragement which those of my countrymen met with who applied for advice and assistance to the consul at St. Bartholomew, were calculated to prevent any application on my part. Besides, I had entwined my fortunes with another an Englishman; and we had resolved to partake of weal or woe together.

On more than one occasion I could have procured a passage for myself to my native land if I had been willing to leave Strictland, My "protection, " as well as appearance, furnished indisputable evidence that I was an American; but Strictland had no testimony of any kind to offer in favor of his citizenship, and to every application for a passage he received a decided shake of the head, from which there was no appeal.

About this time an excitement prevailed among the web-footed gentry in St. Bartholomew in relation to the impressment of seamen by British authorities. The cruisers on the West India station were deficient in men; and all kinds of stratagems were regarded as justifiable which would be likely to supply the deficiency. British ships and brigs of war were often seen cruising off the harbor of St. Bartholomew, and their boats were sent ashore for intelligence and provisions. It became known to some of the officers that there was a large number of seamen in the town destitute of employment, and a plot was devised to kidnap a few of them, and do them a good turn against their will, by giving them board and lodging gratis, and an opportunity to display their courage by fighting the enemies of Great Britain.

A shrewd and intelligent English office, who could tell a good story and make himself agreeable in a grog shop, disguised in the plain dress of a common sailor, one day got admittance to a knot of these unsuspecting "old salts, " and by his liberality and good humor acquired their confidence. Under some plausible pretext he induced a dozen or fifteen Dutchmen, Swedes, Britons, and Yankees to accompany him to a wharf on the opposite side of the harbor, where an alarm or cries for succor could hardly be heard by any of the sailors on shore. Instead of the sport which was expected, they found themselves surrounded by the boat's crew of a man-of- war! After a brief, but unsuccessful struggle, they were all, with the exception of two, hustled into the boat and carried off in triumph on board an English frigate. Those two effected their escape by making good use of their legs, and their account of this most unjustifiable but successful case of man-stealing created a feeling of hatred against the officers of British men-of-war, which manifested itself on several occasions, and was near being attended with serious results.

One pleasant morning, an American clipper brig arrived at St. Bartholomew from the United States. The event was soon known to every person in the island, and caused quite an excitement. When a boat from the brig, with the captain on board, reached the landing-place, a crowd was assembled to hear the news and inquire into the results of the war. Englishmen and Americans met upon the wharf upon the most friendly footing, and jocularly offered bets with each other in regard to the nature of the intelligence brought by this arrival.

The captain stepped on shore and was besieged on every side. "What is the news, captain? " eagerly inquired half a dozen individuals in the same breath.

"Is Canada captured by the Americans? " shouted an undoubted Jonathan, one of those persevering, restless mortals of whom it has been said by a Yankee girl,

> "No matter where his home may be,
> What flag may be unfurled;
> He'll manage, by some cute device,
> To whittle through the world!"

"Has there been any naval engagement? Any American frigates taken, hey? " inquired a genuine native of Albion, his eyes sparkling with expectation.

The captain, although thus suddenly surrounded, captured, and taken possession of, seemed more amused than annoyed by these inquisitorial proceedings, and, with a clear voice and a good-humored smile, replied, while the tumult was hushed and every ear expanded to catch the interesting intelligence, "I know of no battles that have been fought on the land or sea; but just before I left New York, intelligence was received that General Hull, the commander of the American forces on the frontiers, had surrendered his whole army to the enemy at Detroit, with all his guns, ammunition, and stores, WITHOUT FIRING A GUN! "

It is impossible to describe the scene which followed the announcement of this unexpected intelligence, the exultation of the British, and the mortification and wrath of the Americans. Hull was stigmatized by his country-men as the basest of cowards. Curses, both loud and deep, were heaped upon his hoary head. Had he been within the grasp of those who listened to the story of his shame, a host of armed Englishmen could not have saved him from the fury of the Yankees.

Occasionally an American privateer was seen in the offing; and the boldness, enterprise, and success of this class of vessels in crippling the commerce of Great Britain among the islands, created astonishment and indignation among the loyal subjects of "his majesty. " Rumors were afloat every day sometimes false, but more frequently true of some deed of daring, or destruction of British property, committed in that quarter by American private- armed vessels.

One day, a small drogher arrived from the English island of Antigua, bringing as passengers four or five seamen, the only survivors of a terrible disaster which befell one of those privateers while cruising to the windward of Antigua. One of the men was boatswain of the vessel. The tale which he related was a sad one, and its correctness was confirmed by the deep emotion which the narrator and his shipmates manifested and by the tears they shed.

The captain of the privateer was a man of violent and ungovernable temper and drunken habits. He had a quarrel every day with some of his officers or some of his men; and one Sunday afternoon a wordy contest took place between the captain and his first lieutenant, both being well primed with alcohol. The language and conduct of the insulted officer was such as to provoke the captain to madness. He raged and raved, and at last struck his lieutenant, and gave peremptory orders to "put the rascal in irons. "

On hearing this order given, but before it could be executed, the lieutenant seized a loaded pistol. Instead of shooting his brutal commander on the spot, he rushed down the steps into the after part of the vessel, and undoubtedly discharged his weapon among the powder in the magazine! A tremendous explosion followed, which blew the privateer to fragments, scattering the timbers and planks, and the legs, arms, and bodies of the crew, in every direction! The shrieks of the wounded, the struggles of the dying, and the spectacle of horrors which those men witnessed, made a lasting impression on their minds.

After having been on the water a few minutes, almost stunned by the explosion, the boatswain and some of his companions succeeded in constructing a raft from the floating planks; and after days of suffering and exposure, without food, and almost without clothing, the survivors were driven ashore on the island of Antigua, where they were kindly treated, and subsequently sent to St. Bartholomew, with the expectation that they would there find a chance to get to the United States.

Strictland and myself led the vagabond kind of life I have described for a couple of weeks. My purse was gradually growing lighter, and it became evident that we must soon find employment or starve. We formed various plans for improving our condition, neither of which proved practicable when put to the test. One of these was to proceed to Tortola, and join a band of strolling players that were perambulating the islands, and attracting admiration, if not money, by the excellence of their dramatic representations. Strictland, it seemed, besides having been a hanger-on at the "Fives Court, " had served occasionally as a supernumerary at Covent Garden Theatre. He could sing almost any one of Dibdin's songs in imitation of Incledon, in a manner to astonish an audience; and he flattered my vanity by assuring me that I should make a decided hit before an intelligent audience as "Young Norval. " But this project failed for want of means to carry us to the theatre of action.

One morning, while looking about the wharves, we learned that the brig Gustavus, a vessel under Swedish colors, supposed to belong to St. Bartholomew, was making preparations for a voyage to the United States. We lost no time in finding the captain of the brig, a chuckle-headed, crafty-looking native of Sweden, who had been long a resident of the West Indies. I represented our case in the most forcible language I could command; and already aware that some men will be more likely to do a kind act from motives of self-interest than the promptings of a benevolent heart, I told him we were anxious to proceed to the United states, and if he would promise us the privilege of working our passage, we would go on board forthwith and assist in taking in cargo and getting the brig ready for sea.

The captain listened to my eloquence with a good-natured smile and accepted our offer. He promised us a passage to some port in the United States if we would go on board the brig and work faithfully until she sailed. We abandoned our convenient, I had almost said luxurious lodgings beneath the boat on the beach, and, with my chest and what other baggage we possessed, joyfully transferred our quarters to the forecastle of the brig Gustavus.

We remained on board the brig about a fortnight, faithfully and steadily at work, stowing cargo, repairing and setting up the rigging, and bending sails. We congratulated ourselves, from time to time, on our good fortune in securing such a chance, after so much disappointment and delay.

But one morning I was alarmed at finding Strictland had been suddenly attacked with violent headache and other symptoms of fever. The mate gave him some medicine, but he continued unwell. In the afternoon the captain came on board, and after a conference with the mate, called me to the quarter-deck, and told me my companion was sick; that he did not like sick people; and the sooner I took him ashore, the better for all parties. "The brig, " he continued, "is now ready for sea. I can find plenty of my countrymen who will go with me on the terms you offered, and of course I shall not give either of you a passage to America. If I should be overhauled by an English man-of-war while my crew is composed in part of Americans and Englishmen, my vessel will be seized and condemned. Therefore, you had better clear out at once, and take your sick friend along with you. "

I was disgusted with the cold-blooded rascality of this man, who could thus, almost without a pretext, violate a solemn obligation when he could no longer be benefitted by its fulfilment.

"As for taking my friend ashore in his present condition, " said I, "with no place in which to shelter him, and no means of procuring him medical advice or support, that is out of the question. He must remain where he now is until he recovers from his illness. But I will no longer trouble you with MY presence on board. I will gladly quit your vessel as soon as you pay me for the work I have done during the last fortnight. "

"Work!! " said the skipper; "pay! I didn't agree to pay you for your work! You've got your food and lodging for your work. Not one single rix dollar will I pay you besides! " And the skipper kept his word.

After giving him, in very plain language, my opinion of his conduct, I went into the forecastle and had some conversation with Strictland. I found him more comfortable, and told him my determination not to sleep another night on board the brig, but that I would visit him the next morning. I called a boat alongside, and, swelling with indignation, went ashore. I proceeded immediately to an American clipper brig which was ready to sail for a port in the Chesapeake Bay. I represented to the captain the forlorn situation of myself and companion, and urged him to give us a passage to the United States. He listened patiently to my representations, but replied that he had already consented to receive a larger number of his distressed countrymen as passengers than he felt justified in doing, and that he had neither room nor provisions for any additional number. Seeing that I was greatly disappointed at his refusal of my application, he finally told me he would give ME a passage to America if I chose to go, but he would not take my companion. This was reasonable enough; but I could not think of abandoning Strictland, especially while he was sick and destitute, and resolved to forego this opportunity and wait for more propitious times. I was convinced that when I got to the bottom of Fortune's constantly revolving wheel, my circumstances must improve by the revolution, whichever way the wheel might turn.

Fatigued, disappointed, and indignant withal, as soon as the shades of evening fell I proceeded leisurely around the harbor to the beach on the opposite side of the bay, and again took possession of my comfortable lodgings beneath the boat. For hours I lay awake, reflecting on my awkward situation, and striving to devise some practicable means to overcome the difficulties by which I was surrounded.

I awoke at a somewhat late hour the next morning, and heard the unwonted sounds of the wind whistling and howling around my domicile. It was blowing a gale, the beginning of a hurricane. I hastened with eager steps to the other side of the harbor, where I found everything in confusion. The quays were thronged with people, and every man seemed busy. Boats were passing to and from the vessels, freighted with men to render assistance; carrying off cables and anchors, and in some cases, where the cargoes had been discharged, stone ballast, which was hastily thrown on the decks and thence transferred to the hold, fears being entertained that as the hurricane increased, the vessels in port might be forced from their anchors, and wrecked on the rocks at the entrance of the haven, or driven out into the Caribbean Sea.

The vessels were thickly moored, and cables already began to part and anchors to drag. Sloops, schooners, brigs, and ships got foul of each other. The "hardest fend off! " was the cry, and cracking work commenced; and what with the howling of the hurricane gusts as they swept down the mountain side, the angry roar of the short waves, so suddenly conjured up, as they dashed against the bows of the different vessels, the shouting of the seamen mooring or unmooring, the orders, intermingled with fierce oaths and threats, of the masters and mates as they exerted all their energies to avert impending disasters, the crashing of bulwarks, the destruction of cutwaters and bowsprits, and the demolition of spars, a scene of unusual character was displayed, which, to a person not a busy actor, was brim full of interest, and not destitute of sublimity.

The mate of the Gustavus, with a number of men, was employed in carrying off from the shore a cable and anchor, the small bower having parted at the beginning of the gale. The mate represented the situation of the brig as somewhat critical, and urged me to render assistance. Anxious to see Strictland, I acceded to his request. It was not long before we were under the bows of the brig. Men were engaged in carrying out the anchor ahead to haul her away from a cluster of vessels which were making sad havoc with her quarter rails, fashion pieces, and gingerbread work on the stern.

I entered the forecastle, shook hands with Strictland, whose health had greatly improved, with prospect of a speedy recovery, and bade him be of good cheer, that he would be well enough on the morrow. I threw on a chest my jacket and vest, containing what little money still remained on hand, and my "protection, " and thus airily equipped, reckless of the clouds of mist and rain which at times enveloped the whole harbor, went on deck and turned to with a will, notwithstanding the scurvy treatment I had received from the captain the day before. When I reached the deck, some of the men were engaged in heaving in the new cable; others were just then called aft by the captain to assist in bearing off a sloop on one quarter and a schooner on the other, and in disengaging the rigging which had caught in the spars. The sloop had the appearance of a wreck. The laniards of the shrouds had been cut away on both sides, and the tall and tapering mast was quivering and bending like a whipstock, from the action of the wind and the waves. One of the cables, it was supposed, had parted; the sails, not having been properly furled, were fluttering and struggling, not altogether in vain, to get loose; and the deck on both sides was filled with shingle ballast, which had been brought from the shore early that morning, in the fear that the sloop might be driven out to sea, and had not been thrown into the hold.

The captain, mate, and crew of the sloop, finding their vessel in such a helpless condition, and entertaining wholesome fears for their own safety, ABANDONED THE SLOOP TO HER FATE, and embarked, with all their baggage, in the last boat that had brought off ballast. But with the last boat there came from the shore a young man, who, as supercargo, had charge of the vessel and cargo. Aware to some extent of the perilous condition of the sloop, he had been actively engaged during the morning in efforts to prepare his vessel to encounter the disasters incident to a hurricane. As he stepped on the deck of the sloop, and before the ballast had all been discharged from the boat, the officers and crew were eager for their departure. The captain urged the supercargo to accompany him on shore, and, when he refused, pointed out the desperate condition of the sloop, assuring him that in a few minutes that vessel, held by a single anchor, would break adrift and be wrecked on the rocks, when probably no individual could be saved.

The name of the supercargo was Bohun, a native of the "Emerald Isle. " He peremptorily refused to quit the vessel, saying, as he stamped his foot on the deck, "Here I stand, determined to sink or swim with the sloop. "

"Shove off! " exclaimed the captain; "it is useless to parley with a fool! "

At this moment the crew of the Gustavus were summoned aft to disengage the brig from the sloop, and the captain was issuing orders in his most effective style. "Bear off! Why don't you bear off! Cut away the laniards of those shrouds, and clear the main chainwales! Bring an axe here, and cut away that fore-stay which is foul of the main yard! "

Calling now to Bohun, who stood in the forward part of the sloop with a most rueful visage, the captain said, "Why don't you pay out cable, you lubber, and drop astern, clear of the brig? "

Bohun stood near the windlass, and his appearance struck me as being singularly interesting. He was dressed like a gentleman; wore a green frock coat and a white fur hat; but his garments were saturated with rain and the spray. He seemed resolute, nevertheless, and anxious to do something, but he knew not what to do. When roughly accosted by the captain of the brig, he replied, "If you'll send two or three men to help me, I will soon get the sloop clear of your vessel. My men have all deserted, and I can do nothing without assistance. "

The captain of the Gustavus shook his head and his fist at the young Irishman, and discharged a double-headed oath at him, within point-blank shot. Nevertheless, Bohun continued, "If you will let me have one man, only ONE man, I may be able to save the sloop. "

"One man! " replied the Swedish captain, screaming with passion, "how do you expect me to spare even one man, when my own vessel may strike adrift at any moment? Pay out cable, and be hanged to you! Pay out cable, and drop astern! " And he aimed another ferocious oath at the unfortunate supercargo.

Poor Bohun was no sailor. He hardly knew the difference between the cable and the cathead. He looked the picture of distress, almost of despair. But I, being under no obligations to the brutal captain of the brig, was at liberty to obey the impulse of my feelings. I stepped over the quarter rail, grasped the topmast stay of the sloop, swung myself on the jibboom, and in the space of a few seconds after the captain had concluded his maledictions I was standing on the sloop's forecastle, alongside of Bohun.

Chapter XXV TREACHERY AND INGRATITUDE

As soon as I reached the deck of the sloop, Bohun eagerly grasped me by the hand. "My good fellow, " said he, "tell me what to do, and I will go about it at once; only tell me what to do first. "

I cast my eye around, and comprehended in a moment the exact condition of the little vessel. I felt that a great responsibility had suddenly devolved upon me, and I determined to be equal to the task. The sloop, pitching and rolling, and jammed between two much larger vessels, was awkwardly situated, and riding, I supposed, at a single anchor. About half the cable only was payed out; the remainder was coiled on the forecastle, and the end was not secured.

"In the first place, " said I, recollecting the scene near Charleston bar, "we will clinch the end of the cable around the mast, and then we can veer out as much as we like, without risk of its running away. "

This was soon done, and by veering cable, the sloop dropped astern, until clear of all other vessels. I then found, to my satisfaction, that neither of the cables had parted. It subsequently appeared that the small bower anchor had merely been dropped under foot. By giving a good scope to both cables, the sloop was as likely to ride out the gale, so far as depended on ground tackling, as any vessel in port. The sails, which had been loosed by the force of the wind, were next secured. The foresail was furled in such manner that it could be cast loose and the head of it hoisted at a minute's notice. I greatly feared that some light vessel might be forced from her moorings, and drift athwart our bows, and thus bear the sloop away from her anchors. I therefore got an axe, and placed it by the windlass, with the design of cutting both cables when such an act might be considered necessary for our safety, hoist the head of the foresail, and run out to sea.

In the mean time, the decks were in a deplorable condition, lumbered up with barrels, boxes, and ballast. The supercargo commenced on one side, and myself on the other, to throw the ballast into the hold. The miscellaneous articles were then tumbled down in an unceremonious manner, and the hatchways properly secured. Our attention was now turned to the mast, which had no support on either side, and was in an awkward and uneasy position. Bohun looked at it as it swayed from starboard to port and from port to starboard, and then looked inquiringly at me.

"We can co it! " said I, without hesitation. "Have you any spare rigging on board? "

"Yes, plenty! Down in the forward part of the sloop, "

I went below, and found a coil of rope which I believed would answer my purpose. I brought it on deck, and began to reeve laniards for the shrouds. I then procured a handspike and heaver, and went to work setting up the rigging by a "Spanish windlass. " I had only once seen an operation of this kind performed; but having closely watched the process, I knew I could perform it successfully. In this matter Bohun rendered me valuable aid. We worked diligently, for we felt that every minute was of importance; and it was not long before the shrouds on both sides were set up, and the mast rendered safe. By the time this work was accomplished and the vessel put in good condition, the forenoon had nearly expired; but the hurricane continued. Several vessels had already been driven from their anchors, and blown broadside on, through the whole length of the harbor, and dashed to pieces against the rocks.

Through the mist and rain I kept a good lookout ahead, lest some of those unfortunate craft should come down upon our little sloop. And at one time, in the middle of the afternoon, I thought the crisis had come, and we should be obliged to go to sea. A large schooner which had been lying snugly at anchor at the extremity of the harbor for months, with no person on board, parted her cable, and was driven by the wind among the vessels already tossing about in that fearful gale, rubbing against one, crushing in the bulwarks of another, and carrying alarm and terror throughout her whole route. This hulk had passed through the great body of the shipping without causing much serious or irremediable damage, and now, broadside to the gale, was rapidly wafted towards the sloop. My heart beat violently, as, axe in hand, I watched her approach.

I raised the axe above my head to give the fatal blow, when I perceived the stern of the schooner swinging round. I dropped the axe, and called upon Bohun to lend me a hand to bear off. The schooner came down almost with the force of an avalanche, cleared the bowsprit, as I anticipated, but struck our larboard bow, swung alongside, caught by our chain-wale for a moment, was freed by a violent gust of wind, dropped astern, and was soon pounding upon the ledges.

Bohun, who had never before been an actor in such scenes, was completely exhausted with excitement and fatigue. He loaned me a pea-jacket, for, after my severe labors, and ablutions in fresh and salt water, I was shivering with cold; and requesting me to keep a good lookout, went below long before the gale abated, and buried his inquietudes in sleep.

The tempest began to diminish in violence soon after the shades of evening fell; but I continued on my watch until nearly midnight, when no longer doubting that the fierce hurricane had exhausted its wrath, I also left the deck, turned into one of the cabin berths, and slept soundly until the sun was above the horizon.

When Bohun came on deck he assured me he felt under great obligations for the assistance I had rendered in saving the sloop from destruction, and would cheerfully make me any compensation in his power. He requested as an additional favor that I would remain by the sloop, as there was valuable property on board, until he could make some necessary arrangements. I gave him my promise. He then called a boat alongside, and proceeded on shore.

I was anxious to visit the Gustavus to inquire about Strictland's health, and consult with him in relation to future proceedings. But there was no boat at this time attached to the sloop; the small boat broke away at the commencement of the gale, and was never afterwards seen; and the long-boat was taken possession of by the dastardly creoles who composed the officers and crew. I knew, however, that Strictland was well provided for, and being determined to visit him at the earliest opportunity, gave myself no further anxiety, but patiently awaited the return of the supercargo. I waited in vain; he did not arrive that day, but about eight o'clock in the evening a boat came off bringing a new captain, mate, and a couple of men. My short-lived reign was at an end! I had tasted the sweets of despotic authority for two delicious days. I was now deposed, and about to be resolved into my original elements.

It was too late to visit Strictland that night; but the next morning after breakfast, I obtained permission from the new captain to use the boat for a short time, and with a light and joyous heart for I was proud of my successful exertions during the gale sculled away for the Gustavus. I stepped gayly on board, and encountered the mate as I passed over the gangway. He greeted me kindly, but expressed surprise at my appearance.

"How is Strictland? " I exclaimed. "Has he entirely recovered? "

"Strictland! " replied the mate. "Have you not seen him? Don't you KNOW where he is? "

"Certainly not, " said I, somewhat alarmed at his manner, "if he is not on board the brig! "

"He left the brig this morning, " said the mate, "and is now on board that vessel in the offing, " pointing to a rakish clipper brig under American colors that was outside the harbor, and seemed to be flying away under a cloud of canvas. "He has taken his chest and everything belonging to you both, " continued the mate, seeing my astonishment. "I thought you were with him, and that the whole thing was arranged by mutual agreement. "

I was thunderstruck at this intelligence; but after a moment's reflection, I refused to believe it. "It must be a mistake, " said I; "Strictland would not go off to America, and leave me here without means or employment. He cannot be so ungrateful. "

The mate looked as if he thought such a thing were possible.

"And if he HAS availed himself of a chance to go to the United States, he has undoubtedly left the chest, which is mine, and other property belonging to me where I can easily find it. "

"I hope you MAY find it, " said the mate dryly, "but I don't believe you will. "

I went forward and conversed with the men who had taken Strictland on board the brig, and from them learned the particulars of the transaction. It appeared that Strictland, who had quite recovered his health, on coming on deck that memorable morning, perceived the clipper brig, which two days before I had visited without a successful result, making preparations for immediate departure. He borrowed the boat, and accompanied by one of the crew of the Gustavus, went on board the American brig, where he represented himself to the captain as an American, in great distress, and anxious to get home. He exhibited a "protection, " mine undoubtedly, as evidence of his assertions. The tale of his misfortunes, told in eloquent language, albeit it must have smacked strongly of cockney peculiarities, melted the heart of the worthy and unsuspecting sailor, who told him to bring his things on board at once, and he would give him a passage to the United States.

Strictland returned to the Gustavus, gathered together not only everything which belonged to him, but every article of my property besides, not even excepting the garments I had thrown off on the morning of the hurricane. He took with him the money belonging to me which was still unexpended, and also what I regarded as far more valuable than the rest of my property my American protection. He told the crew this was done in pursuance of an arrangement made with me the day previous to the hurricane. He reached the brig with his "plunder" just as the anchor was hauled to the cathead, and the brig was hanging by a single line attached to a neighboring vessel until the topsails were sheeted home. My chest was transferred to the deck of the clipper, and five minutes afterwards the brig was leaving the harbor under full sail, bound home.

It was some time before I could realize the extent of my misfortune, and persuade myself of the melancholy fact that I was a stranger in a foreign port, without friends, while every item of my goods and chattels consisted of an old pair of patched canvas trousers, a checked shirt, and a dilapidated straw hat; I had not even a pair of shoes, a kerchief, a jack-knife, or the value of a stiver in cash.

I stood a moment gazing earnestly at the brig as she was rapidly sinking beneath the horizon. I was more disappointed and shocked at the ingratitude of Strictland than grieved at the loss of my goods and chattels. And when I saw that I had been deceived, cajoled, and swindled by an unprincipled adventurer, so far from rejoicing at such an opportunity to "come out strong, " as Mark Tapley would have done under similar circumstances, I could hardly control my indignation. But conscious that my wrongs could neither be remedied nor avenged, I repressed my feelings, and amid the well-meaning condolence of my friends in the Gustavus, entered my boat and returned to the sloop.

I was rejoiced to find Bohun on board. He seized my hand and greeted me with much kindness. His countenance, open, frank, and honest, emboldened me to explain to him my situation. When I had concluded my narrative of facts, "Now, " said I, "if you consider yourself indebted to me, and are willing to do me a favor, all I ask is, that you will give me a situation on board this sloop as one of the sailors, until I can find an opportunity to do something better. I shall expect the same rate of wages as others, of course and have also to request that you will advance me a few dollars, with which I can supply myself with some necessary articles of clothing.

Bohun graciously acceded to my wishes, and told me I might henceforth consider myself one of the crew of the sloop. I then ascertained what had hitherto escaped my knowledge, that the sloop was called the "Lapwing" of St. Bartholomew; but really belonged to Mr. Thomas, an opulent merchant residing in St. George, Grenada, and was about to proceed to that port with a cargo of flour and other articles of American produce. Bohun was a clerk with Mr. Thomas; and he assured me that on his representations of my conduct to his employer, and the unfortunate consequences of it to myself, that gentleman would undoubtedly show his appreciation of my services in a manner highly proper and acceptable.

This consideration, however, had no weight with me. All I asked for was employment. I wanted to be placed in a situation where by my labors I could earn my living. This I then regarded as independence; and I have never since seen cause to change that opinion.

As the Lapwing belonged nominally and officially to a Swedish port, it was necessary she should have Swedish officers and in part a Swedish crew. The captain was a tall, stiff-looking man, whose name was Lordick. He was a native of the little island of Saba; and two of the crew belonged to the same place. The mate was a native of St. Bartholomew. All belonging to the sloop were creoles, and assumed to be subjects of the king of Sweden, excepting Bohun and myself; and I had been so much exposed to the sun in that hot climate, that I looked as much like a creole as any person on board.

The island of Saba is in sight of St. Bartholomew a level, precipitous rock, nine miles in circumference, highest in the enter, appearing like a mound rising out of the sea, and covered with no great depth of soil. Saba was first settled by a colony of Dutch from St. Eustatia towards the close of the seventeenth century. It is a place of no trade, having no harbor, and is but little known. It is accessible only on the south side, where there is a narrow, intricate, and artificial path leading from the landing-place to the summit. Frequent rains give growth to fruit and vegetables of large size and superior flavor, which are conveyed to the neighboring islands in open boats and sold. It contained in the early part of the present century about fifty families of whites, and probably double that number of slaves. The chief employment of the inhabitants consisted in cultivating the soil, and raising, besides vegetables and fruit, cotton, which the women spun and manufactured into stockings, of a very delicate fabric, that readily commanded a high price in the neighboring islands. The people, living in a village on the top of a rock between the sky and the sea, enjoy the benefits of both elements without dreading their storms. Indeed, Saba is one of those quiet secluded nooks, which are sometimes unexpectedly discovered in different parts of the world, where the people, generation after generation, live in a sort of primitive simplicity, and pride themselves upon their peculiarities and seclusion from mankind. The traveller in quest of novelties would do well to visit Saba.

In a few days after I became one of the crew of the Lapwing, that vessel was ready for sea. Captain Lordick manifested toward me a friendly feeling; he sympathized with me in my misfortunes; made me a present of some articles, which, although of trifling intrinsic value, were highly useful; and inveighed in severe terms against the villainy of Strictland.

The day before we left port, Captain Lordick called me into the cabin. "Hawser, " said he, "you are an American, but you have no evidence of that fact. The trading vessels among the islands are often boarded by English men-of-war, with a view to get men to supply a deficiency in their crews. If an Englishman is found, he is sure to be impressed. As you have no "protection, " and the burden of proof lies with you, you will be regarded as an Englishman, a proper person to serve the king of Great Britain. Even if you state the truth, and claim to be an American, there will be no means of escape from this terrible species of servitude. I have a plan to propose, which may save you from the clutches of John Bull. The natives of St.

Bartholomew, and also of Saba, which is a dependency on Holland, are exempted from impressment, provided they can exhibit proofs of their citizenship. Therefore every sailor belonging to those islands is provided with a document, called a 'burgher's brief, ' which, like an American protection, gives a minute description of the person of the bearer, and is signed and sealed by the official authorities. Now, Hawser, " continued the generous creole, "I had a younger brother who died of yellow fever in St. Kitts some six months ago. He was about your age, and resembled you in appearance. His 'burgher's brief, ' as a citizen of St. Bartholomew, is now in my possession. Therefore you shall no longer be a citizen of the United States, but a native of Saba. I assure you there are very good people in Saba; and your name is no longer Hawser Martingale, but John Lordick; remember this; I shall so enter your name in the ship's papers.

The captain's reasons for a change in my identity were powerful. Besides, a "purser's name" was a common thing among sailors. And although I felt unwilling to forego my claim to American citizenship, even for a brief period, I convinced myself that no evil to anyone, but much good to myself, would be likely to result from such a course. Expediency is a powerful casuist; the captain's kindness also touched my heart, and conquering an instinctive repugnance to sacrifice the truth under any circumstances, I rashly told him that in accordance with his suggestion, I would adopt the name of his brother for a short time, and endeavor not to disgrace it.

"I have no fear that you will, " said he.

Chapter XXVI COASTING AMONG THE ISLANDS

We left St. Bartholomew in the Lapwing and proceeded on our way towards Grenada. I was treated with kindness by every person in the sloop, and found my situation far more agreeable than when loafing and vagabondizing about the wharves.

Mr. Bohun was a light-hearted young man, intelligent, high- spirited, and impulsive. He conversed with me about the events of the war, and speculated freely in relation to the future. He spoke of the defeat of General Hull as an event which might have been expected. When I expressed an opinion that our national vessels would be more successful on the sea, he appeared amused, laboring under the error which was universal among the British at that time, that an American frigate of the first class could hardly be considered a match for an English sloop-of-war.

I spoke of the action between the President and the Little Belt, where one broadside, fired through mistake by the American frigate, transformed the proud and defiant sloop-of-war into a sinking wreck. But my argumentative fact was met by a reference to the unfortunate affair between the Leopard and the Chesapeake. I urged that the Chesapeake, although rated and officered and manned as a frigate, was merely an armed STORE-SHIP carrying out supplies in a time of peace to our ships in the Mediterranean. But Bohun, like every other Briton I have met with, would not admit the efficiency of the excuse. I next recurred to the Tripolitan war, and alluded to the many deeds of daring performed by my gallant countrymen. But Bohun contended that their feats of valor in a war against barbarians could not be regarded as a test of their ability to battle on equal terms against the most accomplished seamen in the world. Bohun said that the Shannon and the Guerriere, two of the finest frigates in the English navy, had recently been fitted out and ordered to cruise on the American coast, with the expectation that a single-handed contest between one of these vessels and an American frigate of the first class would humble the pride of the Yankees, and decide the question of superiority. I could only reply that I hoped the meeting would soon take place, and when it did, he would be as much astonished as I should be gratified at the result.

The next morning after the above conversation, we were passing along the westerly side of the island of Dominica, and Mr. Bohun expressed a wish to touch at Rosseau, the principal port in the island, in order to obtain some desirable information. When off the mouth of the harbor, orders were given for the sloop to lie off and on, while the supercargo was conveyed on shore in the yawl, pulled by one of my Saba countrymen and myself. On reaching a landing place, Bohun directed us to remain by the boat until he should return, which would be in the course of half an hour, and tripped gayly up the wharf.

The town of Rosseau is pleasantly situated in a valley near the seashore. The harbor is little better than an open roadstead, and is defended by strong fortifications overhanging the city. The town has been three times destroyed; once by an inundation from the mountains after heavy rains which swept away many of the dwellings and caused the death of numerous inhabitants. Some ten or twenty years afterwards, when the town had been rebuilt, a destructive fire raged through the place, laid it in ashes, and destroyed an immense deal of property. A third time it was destroyed ay a furious hurricane, when nearly all the houses were demolished or unroofed, and hundreds of the inhabitants were killed or seriously wounded. Having thus been at different times a victim to the rage of three of the elements, air, fire, and water, many were led to believe that the final destruction of the place would be caused by an earthquake.

It was about two o'clock in the afternoon when Bohun came down to the boat, having been absent between three and four hours. His countenance was lighted up with a smile of gayety, and his eyes sparkled as if he had joyful news to communicate.

"Well, John, " he shouted as he came within hail, "there has been an arrival from Halifax, and a piece of important intelligence has been received. "

"Indeed, sir, " said I, with a faltering voice, as from his cheerful bearing I anticipated unfavorable tidings; "what is the character of the news? "

"A desperate battle has been fought between the British frigate Guerriere, and the American frigate Constitution. What do you think of that? " added he, with a light laugh.

"Which gained the victory, sir? " said I, almost afraid to make the inquiry.

"One of the frigates, " said he, without replying to my question, "was thoroughly whipped in short order and in handsome style, dismasted and sunk, with one half of her crew killed and wounded, while the injury the other received was hardly worth mentioning. Which do YOU think gained the day? "

"The American frigate, of course, " said I. "You are right, John, " exclaimed Bohun with a laugh. THE CONSTITUTION HAS SUNK THE GUERRIERE. Brother Jonathan is looking up. He is a worthy descendant of John Bull. I find you understand the character of your sailors better than I do. "

After having imparted this interesting piece of intelligence, and telling my shipmate and myself to remain by the boat until he should return, which would be in a few minutes, he again walked nimbly up the street, and was soon lost to sight.

As in duty bound we remained at the wharf in expectation of the return of Bohun, but hour after hour passed and he did not return. He was "enjoying life" among some boon companions, and over a decanter of good wine, as he afterwards acknowledged, lost for a time all recollection of the existence not only of the boat, but also of the sloop.

When the company broke up about nine o'clock in the evening, he came staggering down the wharf, rolled himself into the stern seats of the boat, and ordered us to shove off and pull towards the sloop. We represented to him that the night was dark and cloudy, and it would be next to an impossibility to find the sloop in the broad bay at that hour; that the attempt would be attended with risk, and consequently it would be wiser to wait until morning before we left the quay.

Our remonstrances were of no avail. He insisted on going off immediately. Nothing, he said, would induce him to wait until morning; he knew exactly where to find the sloop, and could steer the boat directly alongside.

It was useless to argue with him, and we dared not disobey his orders. The motto of Jack, like the submissive response of a Mussulman to an Eastern caliph, is "To hear is to obey. " We left the wharf and pulled briskly out of the harbor. But no sloop was to be seen. We stopped for a moment to reconnoitre, but Bohun told us to keep pulling; it was all right; we were going directly towards her. In a few minutes he dropped the tiller and sank down in the bottom of the boat, where he lay coiled up like a hedgehog, oblivious to all that was passing around him.

By this time we were broad off in the bay; the lights in the town glimmered in the distance, the stars shone occasionally through the broken clouds, the wind was light, and the sea comparatively smooth. On consultation with my shipmate, we came to the conclusion it was hardly worth while to pull the boat about in different directions on a bootless quest after the sloop. We also rejected the idea of returning to the town. We laid in our oars, composed ourselves as comfortably as we could beneath the thwarts, and with clear consciences resigned ourselves to sleep.

We must have slept for hours when we were awakened by an unpleasant and alarming noise. It was some minutes before we could recollect ourselves and ascertain the cause of the hubbub. It proved to be the roaring of the wind, the pattering of the rain, and the angry dash of the waves. While we slept a severe squall had been gradually concocted among the mountains, and now burst upon us in all its fury. How long the wind had been blowing we did not know; but we did know we were some miles out to sea in a cockle-shell of a boat, and rapidly drifting farther from the land. No lights could be seen in any quarter; but all around was dark and drear. We supposed that as a matter of course the wind blew from the land, and therefore got out our oars and pulled dead to windward, thus preventing further drift, and lessening our danger by laying the boat head to the sea, which was now rapidly rising.

The squall continued for an hour after we were conscious of its existence; we were thoroughly drenched, but exercise kept us warm; while Bohun still maintained his snug position beneath the stern seats in a happy state of unconsciousness of the jarring of the elements and the peril to which he was exposed. The first streaks of dawn were hailed with delight, and at broad daylight we beheld the sloop, which had been driven to leeward during the night; and although eight or ten miles from the land, she was not more than a couple of miles to windward of the boat, and beating up towards the harbor. We awakened Bohun, whose garments were saturated by the shower, and who seemed greatly amused with our account of the night's adventure. The wind was fortunately light, and by dint of hard rowing, we soon got near enough to the Lapwing to make signals, and were recognized. The sloop then bore away and ran down, and we were truly rejoiced, fatigued, wet, hungry as we were, to stand again upon the deck.

Proceeding along to leeward of Martinico and St. Lucia, we came to St. Vincent, an island about twenty miles in length from north to south, which was chiefly remarkable at that time as being the only abiding place of the once numerous and warlike tribe of the Caribs, who inhabited the Windward Islands when the American continent was discovered, and were doomed, like all other tribes of their race, to wilt and die beneath the sun of civilization.

The Caribs, although described by historians as fierce and unpitying cannibals of the lowest grade of human organization, undoubtedly possessed moral and intellectual faculties by no means inferior to the great body of American Indians; but, like the tribe of savages which inhabited the island of Hispaniola, and other tribes on the continent, they observed the custom of flattening their heads, which gave to their features an unnatural and sinister expression, by no means calculated to gain the good will and confidence of strangers. The head was squeezed, soon after birth, between two boards, applied before and behind, which made the front and back part of the head resemble two sides of a square. This custom is still retained among the Caribs of St. Vincent.

The flattening of the head among the natives of Hispaniola was performed in a different manner, and produced a different effect. The forehead only was depressed, almost annihilating the facial angle, and swelling the back part of the head out of all proportion. The early Spanish settlers complained of this savage custom, as subjecting them to much inconvenience. In the course of their HUMANE experiments, they ascertained that, owing to the thickening of the back part of the cranium caused by this process, the broadsword of the strongest cavalier could not cleave the skull at a single blow, but would often snap off in the middle without serious damage to the owner of the cranium!

When I passed along the shores of the island of St. Vincent, in 1810, I was particularly struck with the wild and uncultivated appearance of the northern section, a huge mountain, or combination of mountains, rudely precipitous, covered with luxuriant vegetation even to the summit, but containing deep chasms or gorges, down which sparkling streams were rushing, forming numerous waterfalls, and all constituting a wild, picturesque, and attractive landscape.

When I passed St. Vincent in the Lapwing, in October, 1812, a mighty change had taken place. Every trace of vegetation had vanished from this part of the island; not a tree or a shrub remained. The rivers were dried up, and even the deep and dark chasms and gorges no longer existed. Cinders and ashes covered the mountain sides, and beds of lava were pouring down from the summit, and hissing as they entered the ocean. On the 30th of April, about one month after the terrible earthquake by which the city of Caraccas, three hundred and sixty miles distant, was destroyed, and twelve thousand of the inhabitants buried in the ruins, an eruption took place from an old crater on the summit of this mountain in St. Vincent, at which for more than a century had shown no symptom of life. The eruption was sudden and over whelming. Stones and ashes were scattered over the island; vessels more than a hundred miles to the eastward had their decks covered with cinders, and the crews were terrified at the noises which attended this fierce ebullition of the warring elements beneath the earth's surface. At St. Bartholomew, distant from St. Vincent about three hundred miles, the explosions were distinctly heard, and through the whole night were so continuous and loud as to resemble a heavy cannonading from hostile fleets. Indeed, it was believed for several days that a desperate action between English and French squadrons had been fought within the distance of a few miles. By this eruption the vegetation on the north part of the island, comprising one third of the whole territory, was destroyed, and the soil rendered sterile, being covered to a great depth with cinders and ashes. All the lands in the immediate vicinity were also rendered unfit for cultivation. What is remarkable, but few lives were lost. The unfortunate Caribs, however, who comprised about one hundred families, dwelt in this ungenial and unproductive district, and were driven from their homes to find elsewhere and nearer to the habitations of the whites, some desolate spot, shunned by all others, where they could again set up their household gods.

Proceeding past St. Vincent we came to the Grenadines, a cluster of small islands and rocks lying between St. Vincent and Grenada; two of which only, Bequia and Curriacou, are of any importance. These two islands are fertile, and produce a considerable quantity of cotton. Others, although small, are cultivated; and the isle of Rhoude, which lies within a few miles of Grenada, is in itself a large cotton plantation. One of these islets, or, more properly speaking, isolated rocks, lying not far from the shores of Grenada, and at a distance from the cluster is remarkable as having been the scene of an event which tradition seems to have carefully, if not faithfully, recorded. In the obstinate wars between France and Holland, in the middle of the eighteenth century, a Dutch frigate, commanded by a burly and brave officer, a genuine fire-eater, especially when he had his "schnapps" on board, was cruising under the lee of Grenada, and fell in with a large ship, to which the frigate gave chase. The ship answered no signals, but hoisted a white flag and fired a gun to windward, and was thus recognized as a French frigate or heavy sloop-of-war.

Night was coming on, and the chase, with a pleasant breeze, stood on a wind to the northward and eastward. The valiant "mynheer, " whose courage, by means of schnapps, had been screwed up to the sticking point, made all sail after the enemy, and caused a double portion of the stimulating article to be served out to his crew. Under this invigorating influence he made a speech, in which he promised a rich reward to all who would manfully assist in giving the enemy a double dose of "donner and blitzen. " He further promised that, to give his crew a good chance to distinguish themselves, he would lay the ship alongside the enemy, and fight the battle yard-arm and yard-arm. The gallant crew gave three hearty cheers, and swore to do their duty as became the countrymen of Van Tromp.

Darkness soon came on. The night was cloudy, and the wind was moderate. The chase was lost sight of, though it was believed the Dutchman was losing with the enemy hand over hand. The decks were cleared for action, the deck lanterns lighted, the guns double-shotted, and men with eyes of preternatural brilliancy stationed on the lookout.

Hours passed in anxious expectation, and another allowance of schnapps was served out to keep up the spirits of the crew; when, to the great gratification of every man on board, a lookout on the end of the flying jib-boom shouted, "Sail, ho! " The chase was soon distinctly visible, looming up, not like a speck, but like a LARGE BLACK SPOT on the dark horizon. A bloody battle was now certain to take place, and mynheer, combining discretion with valor, took in his light sails, and got his ship into a condition to be easily handled..

The Frenchman was apparently lying to, waiting for his antagonist to come up. He did not have long to wait. The Dutch frigate luffed up on his weather quarter, ranged alongside within musket shot, and poured in a tremendous broadside, then shooting ahead, peppered the astonished enemy in a truly scientific manner. The frigate then wore short round athwart the Frenchman's bows, sweeping his decks with another terrible broadside. The Dutchman kept up the combat with a degree of courage, energy, and spirit that was a marvel to behold; sometimes lying athwart the enemy's wake and raking the decks with terrible effect; sometimes crossing the bows and sending the devastating iron shower the whole length from stem to stern; and sometimes lying bravely alongside, as if courting, as well as giving, hard knocks; and displaying, under these critical circumstances, specimens of seamanship and maneuvering which would have commanded the admiration of the great DeRuyter himself.

But a combat fought with such desperation could not last forever. One of the frigate's guns, being overcharged, burst, killing several men and wounding others; and just as the first signs of daybreak were seen in the east, the Dutchman hauled off to repair damages and count his losses. The enemy apparently had not lost a spar, notwithstanding the terrible hammering he had received, but continued doggedly lying to, preserving, to the great indignation of his opponent, a most defiant attitude.

When daylight shone on the scene of battle, and the doughty Dutchman, having repaired damages, was ready to renew the combat, it suddenly became manifest to every man on board the frigate who had the proper use of his eyes, that the French ship-of-war which had so nobly sustained a tremendous cannonading through the night, was neither more nor less than A HUGE ROCK, which, with its head high above the surface, like the Sail-rock near the island of St. Thomas, marvellously resembled a ship under sail. The captain of the frigate rubbed his eyes on beholding the unexpected vision, as much astonished as the chivalrous Don Quixote, who, after an unsuccessful contest with a squad of giants, found his enemies transformed into windmills. This rock was afterwards known as rock Donner or Donnerock, and will stand forever an imperishable monument commemorative of "Dutch courage. "

The principal town in Grenada is St. George, which is situated on a bay on the south-west side of the island, and is defended by heavy fortifications. On arriving at the mouth of the harbor in the Lapwing, we fell in with a large brig-of-war, called the Ringdove, and was boarded before we came to anchor in the bay. When the boat from the brig was approaching, it was strange to see the trepidation which seized every one of our crew. Although all, with the exception of myself, were in possession of genuine legal documents that should have served as impregnable barriers against impressment, yet they had witnessed so many facts showing the utter disregard of human or divine laws on the part of the commanders of British ships-of-war when in want of men, that they awaited the result of the visit with fear and trembling.

A lieutenant came on board and conversed pleasantly with the captain and supercargo. The men were mustered and called aft to the quarter-deck, and carefully scrutinized by the boarding officer. Our protections were examined, but being printed or inscribed in the Swedish language, were not read. Every thing appeared according to rule. The lieutenant looked hard at me as John Lordick, and asked some questions of the captain, to which the captain replied, "He is my brother, " which seemed to settle the matter. The boat returned on board the Ringdove, and I, as well as the others, rejoiced in having eluded impressment in a man-of-war.

The sloop was brought to anchor, and the cook and myself were ordered into the boat for the purpose of setting the captain and supercargo on shore. We pulled around the principal fort, which is situated on a point of land, and entered a beautiful land- locked harbor, or careenage, where a number of vessels were lying at the wharves. The captain and supercargo landed on one of these wharves, and the captain directed the cook to accompany him to the market square for the purpose of procuring fresh provisions; I was ordered to remain by the boat.

When the captain was gone, and I was left standing alone, my thoughts again recurred to the subject of impressment, which had so completely engrossed the minds of the crew that morning; and I thought to myself, "Suppose some crafty, determined, unscrupulous officer of the Ringdove, or some other British vessel, should be at this very time on shore, lounging about the wharves, disguised as an inoffensive citizen, but watching an opportunity to pounce upon a poor unfortunate fellow, like myself, and bear him off in triumph, to become a victim of the cat-o'-nine-tails at the gangway, or food for gunpowder. " While I was shuddering at the idea of such a climax to my adventures, I saw a man coming towards me, whose countenance and demeanor aroused all my suspicions. He was a thick-set, swarthy individual, with enormous black whiskers and sparkling black eyes. He was dressed like a gentleman, but I thought his garments hung loosely about him; indeed, his whole appearance, in my eyes, was that of the leader of a press-gang or the captain of a band of pirates. He eyed me closely as he advanced towards me with what I conceived to be a regular man-of- war swagger. Being driven to bay, I stood my ground firmly, and confronted him.

"Do you belong to the sloop which is anchored in the bay, my lad? " inquired he, with a mild voice and pleasant smile, affected, of course, to conceal his real intentions.

"Yes, " was my rather curt reply.

"What is the name of the sloop? "

"Lapwing. "

"Where does the Lapwing belong? "

"To St. Bartholomew. "

"Where are you from last? "

"St. Bartholomew. "

"Hum! What is the name of your captain? "

"James Lordick. "

"Ah, James Lordick? " exclaimed he, with vivacity. "Indeed" Then addressing me abruptly, he inquired, "Where do YOU belong? "

"Now for it, " thought I to myself; "the time has come when I must plunge headforemost into the sea of falsehood; so here goes. " And I answered boldly, "To Saba. "

"To Saba? Do you, indeed? " And he gazed at me with his piercing eyes, as if he could read my very soul. "To Saba. You belong to Saba? What is your name? "

"John Lordick. "

"Is it possible! " exclaimed my black-whiskered friend. "Are you REALLY John Lordick, the brother of James? Good Lord! Who would have thought it! "

Thus strongly appealed to, I felt unable to reply except by an affirmative nod.

"So you are John Lordick? I heard you were dead. How the world is given to lying! I should never have known you. You have changed amazingly since I left Saba six years ago, John. "

As this remark did not necessarily require any reply, I made none. I now began to suspect that I was mistaken in the estimate of the character of my interrogator that he was neither the captain of a band of pirates nor the leader of a press-gang; and it being my first essay at carrying out a system of falsehood, I was terribly frightened at the dilemma in which I was involved. I lost my presence of mind, and instead of frankly avowing the truth, as policy, as well as principle, would have dictated, I came to the conclusion to stick by my story, and carry out the deception to the end of the Chapter. But my mortification, my confusion, my chagrin, at being subjected to this unforeseen cross-examination, can hardly be conceived. I envied the condition of the wretch standing by the gallows with a noose around his neck. After a brief pause, my tormentor continued "Do you recollect me? "

"No, " said I, promptly; and glad of a chance to speak a little truth, I added, "To the best of my knowledge, I never saw you before in my life. "

"Ha! Ha! Ha! " My friend seemed greatly amused. "Can it be that I have changed so much within a few short years? You knew me well enough once, John, when I lived opposite your father's house. I am Lewis Brown. " And in a friendly, but somewhat patronizing manner, he held out his hand.

"Indeed, " said I, grasping his proffered hand, "Lewis Brown! I never should have recognized you. "

"Yes, " said Brown, "six years WILL make a change in one's appearance. I should never have recognized you as John Lordick. How is your sister, Bertha, and all the rest of the folks? "

"Well, quite well. "

"Whom did your sister marry? "

"She is not married yet, " said I.

"Not married yet! Why, she must be at least twenty years old. When I left home, she was a beautiful girl even then a belle. Not married, and in Saba! But she will be, soon, I suppose. "

"Perhaps, " said I.

"Ah! Ah! She is engaged, I see. Who is the happy man? "

"Indeed, I don't know, " I exclaimed, wishing the inquisitive fellow at the bottom of the Red Sea, with a twenty-four pound shot fastened to his feet.

"What has become of your cousin, Mark Haraden? Is he as lively and good-humored as ever? "

This Lewis Brown, delighted at having met with an old acquaintance, seemed bent on getting all the information and gossip about his old cronies, that chance had thrown in his way. Fearing I might perpetrate some palpable absurdity in my fabulous statements, as in the case of my "sister Bertha, " I resolved to kill off all his friends and relations in detail, without ceremony or remorse. And therefore I replied to the question about Mark Haraden by saying,

"O! Mark was capsized by a squall while going in a boat from St. Martin to St. Bartholomew with a load of sugar, and all hands were lost. "

"Poor fellow! Poor fellow! I am sorry to hear this; but life's uncertain. Where is Nicholas Ven Vert now? "

"Nicholas Van Vert? He happened to be at St. Kitts last year when the yellow fever broke out there, and was attacked with it the day after he reached home, and lived only three days. "

"Indeed! Indeed! Well, we should all be prepared for whatever may happen! How is old Captain Wagner as hale and hearty as ever? "

"The old man slipped and fell over a precipice on the north side of the island a few weeks ago, and broke his neck. "

"Good Lord! What a terrible mortality among my best friends in Saba! I am almost afraid to inquire after my old flame, Julia Hoffner. What has become of her? "

While I was considering in what way I should dispose of the fair and interesting Julia, a grinning darkey, who had approached the wharf in great haste, shouted, "Captain Brown, massa mate wants you on board, right off, directly"

I felt grateful to the dark-complexioned youth for the seasonable interruption, and secretly resolved that if it should ever be in my power to do him a good turn, I would do it. Unfortunately for him, I never saw him more.

Captain Brown seemed annoyed at the summons, and turning to me, said, "I suppose I must go, John, but I'll be back in a minute. It's a real treat to talk to a Saba man. But you have told me some sad news don't go away. " And the inquisitive gentleman walked off, looking as sad and forlorn as if he had really "lost all his friends, " and leaving me half dead with terror lest my falsehoods should be detected, and perspiring with remorse at having made such a rectangular deviation from the strict line of truth.

I breathed more freely. I had obtained a respite from my sufferings. I cast a searching look up the street, to see if the captain or the cook was coming, and on finding no signs of aid from that quarter, I fairly turned my back upon the boat, and ran off to some distance, where, concealed behind an old building, I could, by peering round a corner, note every transaction which took place on the wharf.

A few minutes only elapsed when the inquisitive Captain Lewis Brown returned with hurried steps to the spot where our conference was held. He seemed disappointed, and, I thought, somewhat hurt at not finding his old acquaintance, John Lordick. He looked around inquiringly in every direction, but apparently convinced that I had absconded, again walked away, but this time slowly, as if pondering on the startling information I had given him. Soon afterwards the cook came down loaded with fresh provisions. He brought orders from the captain to go on board immediately, and return for him at twelve o'clock.

At the hour appointed, the boat, with myself pulling the bow oar, approached the wharf, where, to my confusion, I found Captain Lordick in close conversation with my big-whiskered friend, Lewis Brown. That gentleman gave me an angry look, but said not a word. It was clear that Captain Lordick had betrayed the secret of my citizenship, and had given him information in regard to his old friends and gossips, which differed materially from my extemporaneous effusions; so that so far from being rejoiced, as a reasonable man would have been, at finding his friends alive and well, he seemed greatly provoked, and eyed me with the ferocity of a cannibal on learning that they had not shuffled off this mortal coil in the manner I had so feelingly described.

This gentleman proved to be the captain of a three-masted schooner, which traded between Cumana and the Islands, bringing over cargoes of mules. He had resided in Saba in early life and bore the reputation of a worthy and respectable man. I saw him several times after our memorable interview; but he always regarded me with a grim look, as if he owed me a heavy grudge, and would rejoice in an opportunity to pay it off.

Chapter XXVII CROSSING THE MOUNTAINS

In the afternoon the sloop was hauled into the inner harbor, and on the following day we commenced discharging cargo. I took an early opportunity to hold some conversation with Captain Lordick on the subject of my change of name. The Lesson I had received in my agonizing interview with Captain Brown made a deep impression on my mind, and doubtless had an effect in shaping my character in future life.

I expressed my gratitude to Captain Lordick for the interest he took in my welfare, but frankly told him I could no longer sail under false colors; that falsehood, in any shape, was alien to my character; that I was determined to fall back on the name to which I was rightfully entitled, a very good and quiet name in itself, and acknowledge myself in all times and places a native citizen of the United States. If I should be involved in trouble by this straightforward and honest mode of proceeding, impressed on board a man-of-war, or detained as a prisoner, in my tribulations I should be able to bear a bold front and enjoy the glorious consciousness of telling the truth and being no imposter.

The captain stared. Although a worthy and upright man, he could hardly appreciate the line of conduct I had determined to adopt. He urged that if I remained in those seas, and avowed myself an American without evidence of the fact, I should beyond all doubt be impressed, and under such circumstances I should not only be justified by the strictest code of morality in eluding the grasp of the kidnappers by changing my name, but be a great fool for rejecting such a simple and harmless means of safety. Nevertheless, I remained firm in my determination.

In a few days the cargo was discharged, and I learned that the sloop was about to proceed on a trip to Barbadoes, and that Mr. Thomas, the owner, intended to go in the sloop as a passenger and take charge of the business. I had seen Mr. Thomas, who was a fine-looking, portly gentleman, when he visited the sloop; but he had never spoken to me, and I had no longer any communication with Mr. Bohun. Not a syllable had been lisped in relation to further compensation for my services in St. Bartholomew, which, I supposed, had been undervalued or forgotten, as a matter of course. But in this supposition I was unjust; for, on the day on which it was expected the Lapwing would sail, Bohun came on board, and, referring to my conduct during the hurricane, said he felt uneasy in regard to my situation in the sloop, especially as the Lapwing was bound to a port which was much frequented by English men-of-war. He suggested that some business on shore would be preferable to a voyage to the Island of Barbadoes.

I heartily assented to this view of the subject, but added, that having neither money, clothing, nor friends, I felt rejoiced at procuring employment of any kind; but if I could obtain the means of living in the island until I could meet a favorable opportunity to return to my native country, this would be altogether more desirable than to be compelled to serve on board a man-of-war.

"Well, " said Bohun, "I will represent your case to Mr. Thomas, and perhaps he will be able to make some satisfactory arrangement. "

In two hours afterwards the Lapwing was ready for sea, being confined to the wharf by a single fast, when Mr. Thomas came on board accompanied by Bohun. Mr. Thomas, with a dignified and patronizing air, said, "Young man, Mr. Bohun has just informed me that you rendered valuable aid in saving my vessel from shipwreck in St. Bartholomew. It is a service that I cannot forget; and I shall be happy to bestow upon you a suitable recompense. In the mean time you had better go ashore. Mr. Bohun will take care of you, provide for your wants, and endeavor to procure you a proper situation.

I accordingly went below, gathered together all my worldly effects, which were confined within a very small pocket handkerchief, took an affectionate farewell of my worthy friend and QUONDAM brother, Captain Lordick, and my Saba countrymen, and, lightly clad and barefooted, cheerfully stepped on shore, somewhat amused at the sudden change in my destiny, and wondering what new figure would be presented by the next shake of fortune's kaleidoscope.

Bohun said that the first step should be to find a cheap and comfortable boarding house, where I could remain for a few days; that a widow woman kept a house of that description, he believed, not far from the wharves. He pointed out the place, and suggested that I should call upon her immediately, make use of his name, and ascertain her price for board, and afterwards proceed to the counting room of Mr. Thomas, in a different part of the town, where we would confer together further.

The boarding house to which Bohun directed my attention was an ordinary-looking abode; but I cared little for its character, provided the price would suit. It was kept by a round-faced, jolly-looking, middle-aged woman, whose complexion bore unmistakable evidence of her African extraction. I told my errand. She threw a suspicious glance upon my person and on the diminutive bundle I held in my hand, and the result was unfavorable.

Putting her arms akimbo, and assuming a stately manner, which appeared to be far from natural, she told me she had no spare room for boarders her house was already full.

"Very well, " said I, "I must then apply elsewhere. Mr. Bohun said he thought you would accommodate me, and he would be responsible for the pay. "

"Mr. Bohun! O, that's another thing. I can always find room for a friend of Mr Bohun; " and the whole broad expanse of her face was brightened by a smile.

On inquiry I found that the price for board was two dollars and a half a day! I was startled at this announcement. The amount struck me as exorbitant when compared with the accommodations. I had a secret misgiving that the good woman had not scrupled in this case to add at least a hundred and fifty per centum to her customary charges. I told her I would consult Mr. Bohun, and be guided by his advice.

I lost no time in proceeding to Mr. Thomas's counting room. I communicated to Bohun the result of my inquiries, expressing an opinion that the price for board was exorbitantly high. To my astonishment he seemed well satisfied, pronouncing it reasonable enough. Being unaccustomed to the usages of the place, I supposed it must be all right, and made no further objections.

Bohun took me to a clothing shop, and rigged me out from head to foot in a suit of decent garments a luxury to which I had for some time been a stranger. He also bought me an extra supply of clothing, and a variety of other articles which he assured me I should need.

I was amazed at his liberality; but knowing Mr. Thomas was a rich man, I presumed that Bohun, by ministering to my wants in a manner not altogether offensive to my pride, was seeking to cancel obligations on the part of his employer, and perhaps at the same time was obeying the dictates of a benevolent heart, by rendering important assistance to a stranger in adversity.

Week after week passed away. I saw Bohun from time to time, but he could not procure me a desirable situation. In the mean time the expenses for my board seemed to me a serious matter. My pride took the alarm, and I could not rest easy under the idea that I was all the while living like a price at the expense of Mr. Thomas. When I mentioned this to Bohun, he told me to keep quiet and give myself no anxiety; that my expenses, which I regarded as so heavy, were in reality trifling, and Mr. Thomas would never miss the amount.

A few days after this conversation, Bohun called at my lodgings, and seemed quite excited. "Hawser, " said he, "I have pleasant news to communicate. I have been so fortunate as to secure you an excellent situation on a plantation in the north part of the island. Mr. Church, the attorney for the Pearl estates, was in town yesterday, and on my recommendation has consented to take you to fill a vacancy, in preference to several young men who are applicants for the place. "

"I should much prefer a situation as clerk on a wharf or in a counting room, " said I.

"O, " replied Bohun, "this chance with Mr. Church is far better than a simple clerkship with a trader; the duties are not so arduous, and it will give you a better opportunity to rise in the world; besides, Mr. Church is an excellent man, a whole-souled Irishman, who has been in the army, and has great influence in the island. He will send a mule and a guide over the mountains tomorrow; so you must prepare for the journey on the following day. "

"Very well, " said I, hardly knowing whether to be pleased or dissatisfied with this arrangement, which I decided, however, to accept, with a mental determination, if I found my situation objectionable, to abandon it at once, and if I could do no better, try my fortunes again on the ocean. In the mean time, I should see a new and perhaps interesting phase in life.

"The Upper Pearl estate, where you will reside, " continued Bohun, "is one of the healthiest estates on the island. On some of the sugar plantations, 'fever and ague' prevails at certain seasons of the year, but is unknown on the Pearl estates. Your situation will be a pleasant one in every respect. "

I shuddered at the idea of fever and ague, with the name of which disease the most pleasant associations were not connected, and congratulated myself on the fact that the Pearl estates were exempted from this and almost every other evil in the shape of sickness. The next day I completed my preparations for a journey across the mountains to the opposite side of the island. Agreeably to a suggestion from Bohun, I procured from my accommodating landlady her bill for my board and lodging; to this she added another item for washing, swelling the amount to the very respectable sum of sixty-six dollars.

I handed the bill to Bohun with an innocent and confiding look. He cast his eye over it, and started back aghast. "What is all this? " said he. "What does it mean? Why, the woman is crazy. "

"It is right, sir, " I replied. "Twenty-five days at two dollars and a half a day come to sixty-two dollars and a half; and the washing, at one dollar a week, she says she cannot do it for less, makes a sum total of sixty-six dollars. It is the amount agreed on, although you recollect I expressed an opinion more than once that the price for board was extravagantly high. "

"Two dollars and a half a DAY! " shouted he. "Why, I understood the price to be two dollars and a half a WEEK, and supposed that half a doubloon would pay the whole debt. "

He seemed quite indignant at "the imposition, " and indulged in severe remarks on the character of the woman with whom I boarded. He threatened to give her a regular reprimanding, and swore he would cut down her bill to less than one third of the amount.

On the following morning, at about seven o'clock, I again went to the counting room, and found opposite the entrance a mule already bridled and saddled, with a negro guide to show me the way, over the mountains by the Grand Etang route, to the Upper Pearl estate. I took leave of Bohun, who wrung my hand affectionately at parting, and taking the direction indicated by my guide, entered on my journey.

The road was rough and muddy, for there had been heavy rains, the mule was lazy, and I was unaccustomed to this kind of travelling; besides, I found much on the route to excite my attention; much which was novel and highly interesting. My progress was consequently slow. The road passed among the sugar plantations, which were confined to the comparatively low lands near the sea shore; then ascending towards the mountains, winded through coffee and cacao estates, the successful cultivation of which articles of commerce requires a cooler and moister region than the sugar-cane.

During this journey, I often stopped my mule on the summit of a commanding height, and gazed admiringly around on the beautiful and extensive prospect. The well-cultivated plantations, each appearing like a village in itself, scattered among the many hills and valleys and intervals even to the very sea coast; the sea beyond, which at that distance seemed as smooth and polished as a mirror, encasing the island in a frame of silver; the luxuriant tropical foliage, whose beauty I had often heard described; the cocoanut, orange, tamarind, and guava trees, loaded with fruit, with plantains, bananas, pineapples, aloes and cactuses on every side, all filled my heart with wonder and delight.

Taking the road leading over the mountains, which is impassable for carriages, I passed through vast tracks of forest, where the lofty trees were covered with stout vines reaching to the tree tops, rendering it difficult for man to penetrate those sylvan recesses. Near the highest part of this mountain road, at a height of several thousand feet above the sea, is situated a romantic lake, called by the French the Grand Etang, or Great Lake, which fills the crater of an extinct volcano. Near this spot, where the atmosphere is always cool and humid, we were suddenly enveloped in a cloud, and soon experienced the peltings of a tropical shower. I received conclusive evidence that my garments were not water-proof before we could find shelter in a negro hut by the wayside.

After passing the Grand Etang, we began to descend the mountains on our way towards the north side of the island. The sun again shone brightly, and again a beautiful and expanded prospect met my view. To the eastward was the little town of Greenville, situated at the head of a beautiful bay, in which several ships and quite a number of small vessels were riding at anchor. Far to the north was seen the high and rugged island of St. Vincent, rising like a blue and jagged cloud out of the sea; and between that island and the shores of Grenada, a birdseye view could be obtained of the little islands and rocks, some cultivated and some barren, known as the Grenadines. Among the plantations which appeared afar off, nearest the sea coast, my guide pointed out the Pearl estates, which, he said, with a degree of pride that caused me some astonishment, produced more sugar than any two estates in that part of the island.

In the course of the route, I asked a thousand questions of my guide, who was an intelligent slave belonging to the Upper Pearl estate, and seemed delighted with an opportunity to display his knowledge. He gave me much information, which I subsequently found to be correct, in relation to the mode of managing estates in the West Indies, and conducting the economy of those establishments, each of which, although of course subjected to the general laws of the colony, was in those days a community of itself, under the government of an absolute despotism, the best government in the world provided "the head man" possesses the attributes of goodness, wisdom, and firmness, and is exempt from the imperfections which seem inseparably attached to human nature. But when a despot can boast of none of those attributes, woe to the people who are obliged to submit to his oppressions and obey his behests!

The island of Grenada, as is indeed the case with most of the Windward Islands, is well watered by rivers running from the mountains. Some of the streams are of considerable size, and are never dry in seasons of the greatest drought. The water, conducted by canals from these rivers, constituted the chief motive power for the machinery on the sugar estates, although in a few cases windmills were used for that purpose. The estates comprised each an area of some two to five hundred acres, a considerable portion of which was planted with the cane. The remainder was improved as sites for the various buildings, gardens for the slaves, fields of corn and "guinea grass, " and other purposes. The "sugar works" were placed as near the centre of the estate as convenience would admit. The manager's house, which was a large, inconvenient, one-story building, with numerous out- houses, was generally situated on an elevated spot of land in the vicinity. Another house of smaller size was occupied by the overseers.

At no great distance from the "sugar works, " and sometimes in close proximity, was a collection of huts, thirty or forty in number, cheaply constructed, with thatched roofs, and huddled together without any regard to order, or even convenience. These were known as "negro houses, " the dwellings of the slaves, where, when their daily tasks were ended, they could rest from their labors, and enjoy, without restraint, the few comforts which shed a gleam of sunshine over their condition.

In their houses and families, the slaves made their own regulations. Their enjoyments consisted chiefly in social gatherings and gossip. The women derived gratification from showy dresses and decorations, and sometimes displayed their barbarian tendencies by indulging a love for scandal and mischief-making. They seemed constitutionally gay and cheerful, as was seen by their merry jokes and songs; and a loud, ringing, contagious, African laugh, in the jocund chorus of which many joined, was elicited on very slight provocation.

In their habitations the slaves were greatly influenced, and sometimes controlled, by one or more intelligent individuals, who held superior positions, as is often the case in other communities. The most important person among them was the "head field-driver, " who held that position on account of his superior intelligence and fidelity. The "head boiler" was also a man of consequence among them, also the head carpenter, cooper, and mule- driver. These and others filled situations of responsibility, which required more than ordinary capacity. Of these trusts they were proud.

The manager or overseer on a plantation seldom interfered in the domestic arrangements of the slaves. Their religious and moral instruction was neglected. The marriage tie was not regarded as an indissoluble knot, but as a slender thread, to be broken by either party at will. It is therefore not remarkable that the habits and conduct of these children of bondage were not of the most exemplary character. Each family, who wished it, had a small lot of ground set apart as a garden in some district bordering upon the mountains, where those who were frugal and industrious cultivated yams, cassava, plantains, and other varieties of vegetables or fruit, which were sold to managers of estates, or carried to the nearest town on a Sunday and sold in the market place. In this way some of the most thrifty could supply all reasonable wants, and even indulge in luxuries, which made them the envy of their neighbors; for even in the lowly negro houses of those plantations, as in every other assemblage of human beings, without regard to CASTE or color, were exhibited all the passions, virtues, and weaknesses incident to human nature.

Sunday in the island was generally regarded as a holiday. The slaves on the plantations on that day passed hours in cultivating their gardens, as well as in disposing of their produce and attending to their other concerns. The planters visited each other on the Sabbath, gave dinner parties, made excursions to the neighboring towns to supply their wants at the stores, attended militia musters and shooting matches, indulged in games of quoits and other sports. But religious services and religious instruction were almost entirely unknown. Young men often came to the island who were educated in the strictest Presbyterian faith; lineal descendants of the old Scottish Covenanters; they were scandalized at the little attention given to religious duties and the habitual and open violation of the Sabbath. A few months, however, of familiarity with the customs of the island produced a striking change in their ideas and acts; and their consciences, which were troublesome at first, were soon in a state of quiescence.

A small amount of salted provisions, ling, stock fish, or salt fish was served out every week to the slaves on the plantations as a relish for their vegetables; and a limited, indeed scanty, supply of coarse clothing was annually distributed among them. For other articles of food and clothing, the slaves were compelled to rely on their own industry and management, excepting in "crop time, " when the sugar works were in operation, and every person was allowed an unlimited amount of sirup, which is highly nutritious and wholesome.

On every plantation might be found some wretched-looking, thriftless, or lazy negroes, of the vagabond order. These miserable beings formed the lowest caste, and were despised and often persecuted by those of their fellow-slaves who were orderly and industrious, and cherished habits of self-respect. These were the "pariahs" of the plantation, constituting a class of runaways, who, to avoid work or punishment, or the gibes and jeers of their more RESPECTABLE companions, took refuge in the mountains, and in some of the islands became formidable by their numbers and ferocity. In Dominico, at one period, these run-away negroes, MAROONS, as they were called, amounted to more than a thousand.

They were organized and armed, and subsisted by committing depredations and levying contributions on the plantations. They were subdued only after a desperate and protracted struggle.

The owners of plantations in the English West India Islands, as I have already intimated, usually resided at "home, " in "Merry England, " or the "Land of cakes; " and if they realized a handsome yearly profit from their estates, seldom interested themselves in the condition or welfare of the slaves. Their agents in the islands were called ATTORNEYS, and were vested with almost unlimited power in the management of the property. The trust was an important one, and the labors of an attorney were well compensated, which made the situation desirable. It was sometimes the case that a person who bore a high character for shrewdness and efficiency acted as attorney for several estates. This gave him great power and influence, moral and political, in the island.

The ATTORNEY, holding a grade higher than that of MANAGER, kept a separate establishment, and lived in a loftier style. He often resided in a pleasant and healthy location, some miles, perhaps, distant from the estate whose interest he was appointed to look after, and revelled in tropical luxury and aristocratic grandeur. The details of operations on the plantations were left to the manager, who was appointed by the attorney; and this situation being one of great importance, the manager being intrusted with the management of the slaves and the cultivation of the estate, required an incumbent of superior administrative abilities and large experience.

The manager had generally two assistants to aid him in his arduous task, and direct the operations on the plantation. During half the year, while the canes were planted and growing, these assistants superintended the agricultural labors and attended to various other matters, and in "crop time, " in addition to their usual duties, one had charge of the distillery and the other looked after the manufacture of sugar.

These assistants were called BOOKKEEPERS or OVERSEERS. They were principally young men, of good characters, steady habits, and well educated, who had left their homes in Scotland to seek their fortunes in the West Indies. Those who were not swept off by malignant diseases incident to tropical climates, and who continued correct in their conduct which was not always the case after a few years would be promoted to the situation of manager; and perhaps in time, if they evinced sufficient capacity, would reach the highest object of their ambition and become an attorney. It will be recollected that the poet Burns passed a whole day in taking leave of his "Highland Mary, " when he had made his arrangements for going to the West Indies and obtaining a situation as overseer on a sugar plantation. Very few cases ever came to my knowledge where a creole, a white person born and "brought up" in the West Indies, was engaged on an estate in any capacity. The creoles were reputed lazy, loose in their morals, ignorant and unfaithful agents. They were seldom employed, unless on a plantation which was notoriously unhealthy; where no man, unless he was born in the torrid zone, could expect to resist successfully the poisonous effects of the miasma.

From what I have said it will be inferred that the manager of a plantation possessed great power, and that the treatment of the slaves was regulated in a great measure by the promptings of his head and heart. A manager with a clear understanding, equable temper, and elevated principles, could reconcile his duty to the proprietor with justice and even kindness towards the slaves. So far from treating them with cruelty or even severity, he allowed them every reasonable indulgence, and while he exacted the full quota of labor, looked after their condition, and made them as comfortable and contented as can be expected in a state of bondage. Such managers were seen in Grenada, and where they ruled, the estates were prosperous, and the slaves cheerful and happy.

Some managers, however, were of a different character, and, instigated by whim, liquor, an evil temper, hatred to the African race, or a desire to get an impossible amount of work, acted the part of tyrants and oppressors, and made the slaves feel that they were trodden beneath the foot of a master.

But policy, a regard for the interest of the owner of the estate, generally prevented the infliction of ill treatment and privations which bore severely on the slaves; and public opinion, as well as the laws of the colony, restrained the manager from the commission of extraordinary acts of cruelty. In the British island of Tortola, only a few years before my sojourn in Grenada, the manager of a plantation was arrested for causing the death of a slave by inhuman punishment. He was tried, convicted of murder, and hanged. The penalty exacted met the sanction of public opinion. A full report of the trial was published in a pamphlet form and circulated among the islands, and was doubtless the means of preventing similar acts of monstrous cruelty.

Chapter XXVIII SCENES IN GRENADA

Owing to the many delays on my route across the mountains, it was twilight when I reached an ordinary looking house, situated on an elevated piece of land surrounded on every side by fields of sugar cane. The lands in the vicinity appeared low, and there were indications of swamps at no great distance. About a mile off, in a northerly direction, was the broad ocean. A mule, saddled and bridled, stood at the door. My guide told me, with an air of triumph, that this was the Upper Pearl estate.

As I alighted from my mule, a tall man, with a sad countenance, thin and pallid cheeks, and a tottering frame, came out of the house leaning upon the arm of another person. This sickly-looking gentleman, who proved to be the manager, welcomed me to the plantation, and expressed satisfaction at my arrival. He was on the point of leaving the estate for a few days, he said, on a visit to a friend near the mountains. In the mean time Mr. Murray, the gentleman by whom he was supported, was to look after the plantation and attend to my comforts. This spectral-looking object then, with difficulty, mounted his mule, and accompanied by an able-bodied negro on foot, slowly rode away from the estate.

Mr. Murray received me with cordiality, and tendered me the hospitalities of the mansion. He was a man of pleasing address and more than ordinary intelligence. I afterwards learned that he was the secretary of Mr. Church, the attorney for the Pearl estates. After some little conversation, he abruptly asked me what quarter of the world I came from.

"I am an American, " was my not very definite reply.

"O, " he remarked, with a significant wink, which was evidently intended as a good-natured hint, "you are from Canada, or Nova Scotia, I suppose. "

"No, sir, " said I, emphatically, determined that my position should be distinctly understood, "I was born in the town of Tyngsboro, in the state of Massachusetts, and am a citizen of the United States. "

Having a vague suspicion that the Pearl estate was not the paradise described by Bohun, I inquired why the manager had left the estate so abruptly.

"Because he is attacked with fever, and would not live forty-eight hours if he remained here. "

I was shocked at this announcement, and pursued my inquiries. "Is fever a common occurrence on this plantation, or is this sickness of the manager an extraordinary case? "

"Common enough, in all conscience, " replied Murray, with a laugh. "Mr. Orr is the second manager who has been driven off by sickness within the last six months. Two overseers have died within a year, one after the other, and until Mr. Church met with YOU, no one could be found to take the place, which has been vacant several weeks. "

This was interesting intelligence, but I continued my inquiries. "If the estate is so unhealthy as you represent, why are YOU willing to remain here? "

"O, my stay here will be only a few days, or weeks, at most. Besides, I am well seasoned, having resided ten years in the island; and I make it a rule to keep my system well fortified against fever by the liberal use of generous liquors; and if you hope to LIVE here, you will do well to follow my example. "

"Mr. Bohun told me that the upper Pearl estate was one of the healthiest on the island. How could he have been so grossly deceived? "

"Deceived? Not he; all humbug. "

"But he surely does not know the estate is so unhealthy? "

"Not know it? Bohun not know it? Certainly he does. Every body knows it. Every estate has its reputation, and the reputation of the Pearl estates, both of them, is NOTORIOUSLY BAD. No man, unless his courage or his fortune is desperate, will take a situation on either of these plantations. "

I was astonished, dumbfounded at this intelligence, which effectually silenced further inquiries. After a short pause, Murray proceeded: "The fact is, Mr. Church told me all about the matter yesterday afternoon. Bohun found it difficult to procure you such a situation as you wanted, and was anxious to get you off his hands. Meeting Mr. Church in town, he asked him to take you. Mr. Church objected, telling him it would be a pity to place you on the Pearl plantation, where you might drop off in less than six weeks. But Bohun urged the matter; requested it as a personal favor; and they being countrymen, you know and so and so you see your business was done, and here you are. "

I undoubtedly looked grave at the interesting information thus frankly given; and Murray, remarking it, continued, in a consolatory tone: "Never mind, my good fellow; keep up your spirits. I thought it best to tell you the worst at once, and let you know what you have to expect. You will have to go through a regular seasoning; and if you can stand that on the Pearl estate, you may take your degree of M. D. as Doctor of Malaria, and bid defiance to yellow fever forever after! "

I was not ambitious of such a distinction, and would gladly have declined it, were it possible; but, on calmly surveying my position, there appeared no alternative. Relying on the correctness of Bohun's suggestions and the disinterestedness of his counsels, I had taken a step which could not, for a time at least, be retraced. I therefore determined to go forward and make the best of it; look on the bright side of my situation, if it had any bright side, faithfully perform the duties of my office, and trust to my constitution and regular habits, in spite of the counsels of Murray, for the rest.

I felt hurt at the conduct of Bohun, which from Murray's version was not such as I was prepared to expect, notwithstanding my experience in the dark side of human nature. I still hoped that Murray's statements might be exaggerated, and that Bohun was actuated in his conduct towards me by feelings of grateful kindness.

On the following day Mr. Church visited the estate. He was a middle-aged man, had held a captain's commission in one of those British West India regiments which, after having been reduced to mere skeletons by battles with the French and yellow fever, were unjustly and inhumanly disbanded, at a long distance from "home, " leaving the brave men, who were thus rewarded for their services, to return to their native country as they could, or struggle for a precarious existence in a tropical climate.

Mr. Church chose to remain in the island and engage in the planting business. Possessing energy of character and rectitude of principle, and having influential connections, he became in a few years the attorney for the Pearl estates, married the daughter of a Scotch planter, and resided very pleasantly and happily at a beautiful seat called Bel-Air, situated a few miles from the Upper Pearl. He entered into conversation with me, instructed me in my duties, regretted the absence of the manager, which might unpleasantly affect my comforts, and gave me some precautionary hints in relation to my health. I felt somewhat reassured by my conversation with that gentleman, and erroneously believing it would be in my power to leave the island if I should think proper, at no distant period, indulged in no unavailing regrets, but philosophically resolved to make myself as comfortable as circumstances would allow.

The treatment I met with among the planters, during my whole residence in the island, was that of unvarying kindness; many of them were well educated and cultivated a literary taste; had well-furnished libraries, which were not kept for show; and the history and writings of Ramsay, Ferguson, Burns, Beattie, Robertson, Blair, and other distinguished Scottish authors, were as familiar with some of the planters in Grenada "as household words. " The early novels of the "Wizard of the North" were then exciting much interest, which was shared by the inhabitants of the English West India Islands.

The mildness of the climate seemed to have a tendency to melt away that frigidity which is a characteristic of people of the north, and the residents of the island were as frank, free, and hospitable as if they had never been out of the tropics. I soon formed many pleasant acquaintances and acquired many friends. And this, with the aid of books in abundance, enabled me to pass my leisure hours agreeably. Notwithstanding the heat of the climate, and the prevalence of the erroneous idea that violent physical exercise in the tropics is injurious to the health of strangers, I indulged often in recreations of a kind which excited the surprise and called forth the remonstrances of my friends.

From my earliest recollection, I was a devoted disciple of good old Izaak Walton, and the rivers on the north side of the island, rushing down from the mountains, with deep pools, and rocky channels, and whirling eddies, being well stocked with finny inhabitants, furnished me with fine opportunities to indulge in the exciting sport of angling. My efforts were chiefly confined to the capture of the "mullet, " a fish resembling the brook trout in New England in size and habits, although not in appearance. It is taken with the artificial fly or live grasshopper for bait; and to capture it, as much skill, perseverance, and athletic motion is required as to capture trout in the mountain gorges of New Hampshire.

I also occasionally indulged my taste for rambling in the mountains. In these excursions, which, although exceedingly interesting, were solitary, for I never could persuade anyone to accompany me, I always took a gun, making the ostensible object of my rambles the shooting of RAMEES birds of the pigeon species, of beautiful plumage, nearly as large as a barnyard fowl, and of delicate flavor. These birds inhabited the deepest recesses of the woods, and, although seldom molested, were exceedingly shy.

Few animals are found in the forests and mountains of Grenada. The agouti, the armadillo, and the opossum, are sometimes, though rarely, seen. The only quadruped I ever met with in my rambles was an opossum, which I shot as it was climbing a tree. Of reptiles there are none in the mountains. There are several kinds of snakes in the island, some of which have never been described by naturalists. The species which is most common is a black snake (constrictor) of large size, being frequently eight or ten feet in length, and three or four inches in diameter. These snakes are treated not only with forbearance but kindness by the planters, and in return render important service on the sugar plantations, being most persevering and successful RAT CATCHERS; rats are abundant, and exceedingly destructive to the sugar cane, on which they subsist during a considerable portion of the year. None of the serpents in Grenada are poisonous, but in some of the islands, particularly St. Lucia, there exists a snake which resembles the rattlesnake in the ferocity of its attacks and the deadly venom of its bite. Having no rattles, no warning of danger is given to the unwary traveller until the snake darts from its ambush and inflicts a fatal wound; hence the name given to this dangerous reptile is the LANCE DE FER.

In penetrating those mountain gorges, and climbing those mountain ridges, steep and thickly covered with forest trees and vines of many kinds, and of luxuriant growth, I sometimes passed hours without meeting any sign of life, except the flitting and hum of the humming-bird, and the loud and musical coo of the ramee. That mountain wilderness seemed the chosen home of the humming-bird. I there met with many varieties, some of which were exceedingly beautiful. My appearance in those forests caused them much surprise, and to gratify their curiosity they sometimes flew towards me, and hovered within a few feet of my face, as if eager to examine my appearance and learn what object led me to intrude on their mountain haunts.

There were, however, other and less interesting inhabitants in that region, as I one day discovered to my great consternation. I was passing up the bed of a small stream, where the water, by attrition during many ages, had worn a chasm or "flume" through the solid basaltic rock, the walls of which rose at least a hundred feet nearly perpendicularly, when I found an obstacle to my further progress in the shape of some large rocks, which had fallen from above and blocked the passage. I was unable to scale the CHEVAUX-DE-FRISE; but the whole body of water poured through an aperture three or four feet above the bed of the stream; and although it looked dark and dreary within, instead of retracing my steps to find another route through the woods to the spot I wished to reach, I determined to force my way into the gloomy cavern, with the expectation of being able to emerge on the opposite side.

I listened for a moment at the mouth of the aperture, but heard only the murmuring of the stream as it swept along through the uneven channel. I then thrust in my head, when I heard a rushing noise as of the flapping of a thousand wings, and the next moment I was sprawling on my back in the water, having been summarily capsized, partly by force and partly by an involuntary start of terror!

I raised my head and beheld a legion of BATS, some of them of uncommon size, issuing in a stream from the mouth of the cave. These animals in the tropics are numerous, and seclude themselves from the light of day in caverns or other dark and lonely recesses, where they attach themselves to the roof, and clinging to each other are suspended in large pyramidal clusters or festoons. When disturbed, they take wing, and hastily quit their abodes. By unthinkingly intruding on their territories, which had probably never before been invaded, great alarm was excited among the inmates; a terrible confusion ensued, and the general rush to the aperture caused my unceremonious overthrow.

In one of my mountain excursions, I lost my way while enveloped in a dense mist, and, after descending a steep ridge, came upon a platform or terrace of several acres' extent, which at first view seemed to have been formed by artificial means on the mountain side. This plain was level, and thickly covered with coarse grass, which, finding a genial soil and region, grew to a height of five or six feet. Near the centre of the prairie stood the only tree which flourished on this fertile spot. It was a silk cotton tree. I made my way through the grass with difficulty to the tree, which by measurement I found to be twenty-five feet in circumference larger than any other tree I ever saw in the island. Immense branches shot out horizontally about twenty feet from the ground, extending to a distance in every direction from the trunk sixty or eighty feet. Indeed, the gigantic size of the tree, its rich and luxuriant foliage, and its noble and majestic appearance, were in perfect keeping with the place. I tarried some time beneath its branches, and gazed with interest on the picturesque scene, regretting that I had no companion to share my admiration, and thinking that as doubtless no human being, unless some wild Carib in days of yore, had ever previously visited that singular spot, so it was likely centuries would pass away before any other individual would chance to behold and admire that beautiful terrace on the mountain side. I then plunged among the trees and vines growing upon the steep declivity on the further side, and, after a precipitous retreat of two or three hundred feet, heard the murmuring of a stream below, by following which I at length reached a cultivated district.

The clouds on those mountain tops often collect with extraordinary quickness, and, while the sun is shining brightly on the cultivated lands, pour down the rain in deluging showers, which, rushing in cataracts through the gorges, swell the rivers unexpectedly, sometimes causing fatal disasters by sweeping away horsemen or teams when fording the streams. The rise of a river from this cause is sometimes alarmingly sudden; the water comes down in solid phalanx, six or eight feet in perpendicular height, and extends from bank to bank; and with irresistible force sweeps down rocks and trees, shaking the earth on the banks, and making a loud and rumbling noise like distant thunder.

The vicinity of Grenada to the continent causes this island, as well as Tobago and Trinidad, to be exempt from the hurricanes which have proved a terrible scourge in several of the Windward Islands, and from time to time have been terribly destructive to life and property.

In Barbadoes, on the 10th of October, 1780, nearly all the plantations were ruined by a hurricane of inconceivable fury, and between four and five thousand persons lost their lives. Grenada has only once been visited by a hurricane since its first settlement by a French colony from Martinico, in 1650. But this hurricane was the means of removing a far greater evil, the circumstances attending which were of an extraordinary nature, and which I shall relate as I learned them from the lips of many who were witnesses of their occurrence.

It was about the commencement of the present century that this island suffered much from a visitation, which threatened to bring famine and desolation, and destroy, not only the present, but the future hopes of the planter. There suddenly appeared, simultaneously in different parts of the island, a great number of BLACK ANTS, of large size, being fully an inch in length, and of a kind until then unknown in Grenada. They probably belonged to the species known as "the large black ant of Africa, " remarkable for its boldness and voracity. Although the inhabitants of that fruitful island were wont to treat strangers with hospitality, they were inclined to depart from their usual habit so far as related to these new and strange visitants, who seemed inclined to be more troublesome than was consistent with the welfare of the old residents.

In the course of a couple of years the number of these invaders increased to an incredible amount; they attacked the fruit on the trees and the vegetables in the gardens; and the fields of sugar cane, once so green and flourishing, soon looked as if a fire from heaven, the scourge of an offended deity, had passed over them. Not only the fields, but the trees, the roads, and the dwelling houses, were covered with these ants; and when all sustenance was destroyed in one quarter, they took up their line of march in immense armies and proceeded elsewhere in search of food. In these migratory excursions, if they came to a brook or small river, their progress was not stayed. Those in front were impelled into the stream by the pressure from behind; and, although myriads were swept away and drowned in the rushing waters, many were borne to the other side and continued their journey. In some cases, where the current was not strong, a sort of living bridge was formed, over which immense numbers of these pestiferous insects passed in safety and dry shod. Nothing seemed to check their progress or reduce their numbers.

The inhabitants, both white and black, as may be conceived, were in great consternation, and were about to make preparations to move to some more favored soil, when a furious hurricane was experienced. The destruction of property was great; dwelling houses and sugar works were destroyed, and lives were lost. The inhabitants who survived the tempest were in despair, believing their calamities would never cease. But they soon found, to their great joy, that this hurricane was a blessing, rather than a curse. THE BLACK ANTS WERE EXTERMINATED, and none have since been seen in the island.

Chapter XXIX INSURRECTION IN GRENADA

I have already stated that the French established their first settlement in the island of Grenada in 1650. They found the island inhabited by the Carib Indians, who, regarding the white men as beings superior in goodness as well as intellect, gave them a cordial welcome, and treated them with kindness and hospitality. The French, well pleased with their reception, gave the cacique a few hatchets, knives, and beads, and a barrel of brandy, and very coolly took possession of the island they had thus purchased. Their conduct in this respect reminds one of the language of the ill-treated Caliban to the proud Prospero:

"This island's mine,
Which thou tak'st from me. When thou camest first,
Thou strok'dst and made much of me; wouldst give me
Water with berries in't; and teach me how
To name the bigger light, and how the less,
That burn by day and night; and then I loved thee,
And showed thee all the qualities of the isle
The fresh springs, brine pits, barren place and fertile;
Cursed be I that did so."

The remonstrances of the Caribs against the wrongs they were doomed to suffer were as little heeded by the colonists as the complaints of Caliban by Prospero. The French were resolute, powerful, and rapacious, and treated the red men with inhumanity. The Indians, unable to contend with their oppressors by open force, fled to their mountain fastnesses, and commenced an obstinate predatory warfare upon the whites, murdering without discrimination all whom they found defenceless. This led to a bloody and protracted struggle for the mastery; and a reenforcement of troops having been sent from France to aid the infant colony, it was decided, after mature deliberation, that the most expeditious and effectual mode of ending the war, and establishing peace on a permanent basis, was TO EXTERMINATE THE CARIBS.

These original "lords of the soil" were accordingly driven from their fastnesses, hunted by parties of soldiers, shot down like wild beasts wherever found, until their number was reduced from thousands to about one hundred. Bing cut off from the mountains by a military force, this remnant of a powerful band fled to a promontory on the north part of the island which overlooked the ocean, and, hard pressed by their civilized foes, more than half their number leaped over the rocky precipice into the sea which dashed against its base. The others were massacred.

This promontory has ever since been known as "Morne des Sauteurs, " or the "Hill of the Leapers. " I have stood upon the extreme point of this promontory, where I could look down some eighty or a hundred feet into the raging abyss beneath, and listened to the mournful tradition as detailed by one of the oldest inhabitants of the island. This is only ONE of the vast catalogue of cruelties and wrongs that have been inflicted on the Indians by the whites in constant succession, from the first settlement of the New World to the present time.

The French, who were long in possession of the island of Grenada, established on the plantations French customs, the French language, and the Roman Catholic religion. When the island fell into the hands of the English, although no organized plan was adopted to interfere with the customs of the slaves, or change their language, the English failed in acquiring the attachment of the negroes, who lamented the absence of their French masters, and sighed for their return.

Early in the year 1795, during the French revolution, a plan was conceived by some white men and five mulattoes, in Guadaloupe, who were aware of the existence of this discontented feeling, to create an insurrection among the slaves in Grenada, and take possession of the island. Emissaries were sent among the plantations, who conferred with the principal negroes, and secretly made arrangements for the work they contemplated. In the month of August, two or three sloops, each containing thirty or forty men, with a supply of arms and ammunition, arrived in the harbor of La Baye, on the eastern side of the island. The expedition was commanded by an active and intelligent mulatto named Fedon, and landed in the night, captured the small fort which overlooked the harbor, took possession of the town, murdered a number of the white inhabitants, and plundered the houses and stores. Runners were employed to convey the news to the different plantations, and the insurrection of the slaves was complete.

Some of the white men of the plantations received secret intelligence of the rising among the blacks, and lost no time in fleeing to a place of safety; others remained unconscious of the approach of danger, and were murdered. Deeds of cruelty were perpetrated on this occasion by the negroes, a relation of which would chill the stoutest heart.

It unfortunately happened that when this insurrection broke out, the acting governor with several members of the council, and some merchants and planters of great respectability, were on a visit to the eastern part of the island. As soon as they heard of the attack on La Baye, and the progress of the insurrection, they left the quarters where they had been hospitably entertained, and, accompanied by their host and some other gentlemen, proceeded to the sea shore, and embarked in a sloop, with the intention of proceeding to St. George, which was the seat of government, and was strongly fortified and garrisoned.

As the sloop was passing the little village of Guayave, some negroes appeared on the shore, bearing a flag of truce, and indicated by expressive gestures a wish to hold a conference with the governor. This functionary, not aware of the dreadful atrocities that had been committed, and hoping that some means might be agreed upon to heal the disturbances, imprudently ordered the vessel to be anchored in the roadstead, and himself and a number of the most influential of his friends went ashore in a boat, and were landed on the beach. A party of armed blacks, who until that moment had been concealed, immediately surrounded them, pinioned them, and marched them away. The boat was seized by the negroes, and a party pushed off for the purpose of boarding the sloop, and securing the remainder of the white men; but they, having witnessed the capture of the governor and his companions, suspected the object of this maneuver, cut the cable, and with a fine breeze, distanced the boat which had started in pursuit, and proceeded to St. George with the mournful news.

The rebel chief, Fedon, collected around him, as it were by a single tap of the drum, an army of some thousands of blacks, and distributed among them a considerable number of fire-arms. Others were armed with weapons hastily prepared; and the great body of the insurgents, being desperate men, stimulated by the hope of freedom and the desire of vengeance, with leaders of ability and some military skill, the insurrection assumed a formidable appearance.

Fedon took possession of Mount Quaqua, a high, steep, and somewhat bald mountain in the interior, and there encamped with his army. The base of the mountain was cultivated, and furnished excellent pasturage for the many cattle which were driven thither from the various plantations to furnish subsistence for his army. This place he fortified, determined to make it his stronghold in case of adversity; and he went vigorously to work in organizing and disciplining his army with a view to make an attack on St. George before the government could receive reenforcements, and thus get possession of the whole island.

The governor and his friends, and other prisoners, principally planters, having been strictly confined for several days, and treated with many indignities, were conveyed under a guard to the camp of the rebel chieftain. Fedon caused them to be brought before him, and after exulting over their capture, and heaping upon them insults and abuse, ORDERED THEM TO BE SHOT. This sentence was executed on the following day. Only one of the number escaped to tall the sad tale. This was Mr. Bruce, a merchant residing at St. George, who had acted as attorney for the Pearl plantations. When led out with others to be executed, a negro whispered in his ear, "Massa, my capen tells me, shoot you! But I no shoot you! Only make b'live. You stand up straight when I fire, you fall to ground, and scream, and twist, all same as if you be dead! "

The deception was successful. The negro, whose name was Quamina, and belonged to the Lower Pearl estate, was stationed opposite to Bruce. The word was given. Bruce fell with the rest, and imitated to admiration the agonies of a dying man; and Quamina, at the risk of his life, succeeded in saving that of the white man. That night, he contrived to get him outside the lines, conducted him on the road leading to St. George, and left him. Mr. Bruce, after much fatigue and several hair-breadth escapes, reached the town, being the only one among the prisoners carried to the camp who escaped from the clutches of the monster.

I may as well state here, that after the insurrection was quelled, Mr. Bruce manifested towards his preserver a grateful spirit. He wished to give him his freedom, but Quamina, who was a negro of consequence on the estate, refused to accept it. Quamina was elevated to the situation of head-boiler; and Mr. Bruce every year made him a visit, gave him a sum of money, clothing, and valuable presents for himself and wife.

The military forces in the island were not more than were needed to occupy the forts and defences of St. George, where the white population had fled, with the little property they could take with them on the breaking out of the rebellion. Parties of insurgents, commanded by chiefs appointed by Fedon, who exercised absolute power, had the range of the rest of the island. The rebels made a desperate attempt to capture St. George, but were repulsed with great loss.

Affairs remained in this condition for nearly a year, before any efficient measures were adopted by the British authorities to regain possession. At length General Abercrombie, with a large military power, landed, and, joined by the regular forces in St. George, and some companies of militia, succeeded in driving the insurgents from the sea coast to the mountains. He then invested Mount Quaqua, cut off all supplies from the army of Fedon, and compelled him to fight, surrender, or starve. The insurgent chief, with some of the leaders of the insurrection, and a portion of the rebels, attempted to cut their way through the English army, and some of them succeeded, among whom was Fedon. He proceeded to the sea coast, embarked in an open boat with a few companions, and was probably drowned, as he was never heard of afterwards.

The plantation negroes, generally, returned to the estates to which they had been attached, and, with a few exceptions, were forgiven, and work on the plantations was resumed. A number of the colored persons, slaves and freemen, who were chieftains under Fedon, or had signalized themselves by extraordinary acts of cruelty, were arrested and hanged.

One of the most efficient officers among the rebels was named Jack Shadow. He was a free mulatto, a shrewd, intelligent creole, and previous to the insurrection, had resided in the town of Guayave, and exercised the trade of carpenter. With the assistance of his wife, a mulatto, he also cultivated a garden, and contrived to gain a comfortable living. When the insurrection, instigated by the French revolutionists, broke out in the eastern part of the island, Jack hastened to join the insurgents, and was cordially received by Fedon, who intrusted him with an important mission, which he executed with such adroitness as to gain the confidence of the chief, who appointed him to a high command in the army. Jack was one of Fedon's most efficient officers, and signalized himself by his bitter hatred to the whites, and the zeal with which he abetted his chief in the horrid scenes of cruelty that were enacted.

When the insurrection was quelled, Jack Shadow, although wounded, made his escape, with some others of the most obnoxious rebels, to the woods and mountains in the interior of the island. They endeavored to conceal themselves from the pursuit of the whites, but in the course of one or two years were all, with the exception of Jack, ferreted out and shot when apprehended, or taken to jail, tried, and hanged.

Jack, however, remained in the mountains. A large reward was offered for him, dead or alive; and parties of armed men often scoured the woods, hoping to find his lair and shoot or capture the rebel chief. But though it was known he was hid in a certain part of the island, he eluded all endeavors to arrest him for ten or twelve years, and might perhaps have died of old age, had he not been betrayed by his wife.

It was subsequently ascertained that Jack had erected a hut by the side of a ledge of rocks, which was almost inaccessible to a stranger; and this hut, being surrounded with bushes and undergrowth, and covered with vines, could not be recognized as a habitation by any one unacquainted with the fact. His wife, Marie, remained in her humble cottage in Guayave, and, it appeared still cherished affection for her husband. He was visited in the wilderness by Marie at certain times, and supplied with necessaries and whatever she thought might conduce to his comfort in that wretched abode. At his urgent request, she also furnished him, occasionally, with a JUG OF RUM, with which to cheer his spirits and solace his solitude. He gradually acquired an insatiable fondness for spirituous drinks, and insisted on being supplied, even to the exclusion of articles vastly more suitable to his condition.

The consequence of the indulgence of this habit was soon exhibited. He became gloomy, sullen, and ferocious. He no longer treated his wife, to whom he was so much indebted, and the only being with whom he associated, with his wonted kindness and affection, but, when maddened with liquor, often abused her. Marie bore this for a long time with patience. She still sought his hiding-place at times, and bore him the poisonous beverage, probably unconscious that she was thus indirectly the cause of the changed conduct in her husband. He continued his ill treatment, especially when under the influence of liquor, and after a time the affection of Marie for her husband was extinguished. She began to regard him as the fierce outlaw and murderer, who cherished no gentle affections, but took pleasure in abusing the woman who held his life in her hands, and had labored hard and risked much to screen him from capture and cheer him in his concealment. Her visits became more seldom, and the ill temper of her husband increased.

One night, Marie pursued her devious way to the mountains to furnish Jack with the accustomed supplies. He snatched form her hand the liquor, and took a deep draught. The poison did its work. He became excited, and quarreled with his wife; and, roused to fury by her reproaches, struck her with his hand, seized her by the shoulder and thrust her from the hut, tumbling her over the ledge. Marie rose, groaning with pain, being severely bruised. The cup of her indignation, which had long been full, was now overflowing. She slowly returned to her home in Guayave, brooding over schemes of revenge, and formed the determination to betray her husband into the hands of justice. She called upon Dr. Duncan, a rich planter and a magistrate, and offered to guide him to the spot where Jack Shadow, the daring rebel, was concealed.

Within a couple of hours after the magistrate received the welcome information, he was on his way to the mountains, accompanied by Marie and a guard of soldiers. They entered the thicket on the side of the mountain, where Jack Shadow had taken up his abode. They came to a precipitous ledge of rocks. "Move gently, now, " said Marie, in a low voice; "we are close upon his hut. "

The soldiers could see nothing resembling a hut. With their muskets loaded, and bayonets fixed, they with difficulty made their way through steep, rugged, and crooked passes, and, after a toilsome march, stood by the side of Jack's habitation.

The sergeant was now quietly arranging his men in such a manner as to insure the captivity or death of the outlaw, when one of the soldiers stumbled, and his musket struck the ground with a ringing noise. Jack, who had just awakened from his drunken nap, heard the ominous sound. He had no weapons, but relied on the security of his retreat and his activity and strength. He cautiously opened the door, in front of which stood a soldier with his musket pointed towards him. The sergeant cried, "Surrender, or you are a dead man! "

Jack made one last desperate struggle for life. He sprang down the ledge, turned aside with one hand the bayonet which was thrust at his bosom, and felled the soldier with the other; but ere he could clear the guard, his shoulder was transfixed by another bayonet, which disabled him, and in a few minutes he was stretched at the feet of the soldiers, a wounded, pinioned captive. Before the sun had set that afternoon he was securely lodged in the prison at Guayave, heavily ironed, and the prison was guarded by a detachment of soldiers.

The trial of Jack Shadow soon came on before a bench of magistrates. His identity was proved; also the conspicuous part he had taken in the insurrection, and the bloody acts which he had committed. The outlaw was condemned to death. His deportment was sullen and dogged to the last. He refused to see his wife, who, when too late, regretted the steps which, prompted by anger and a short-lived desire for revenge, she had taken for his arrest. He was hanged on a gallows, about a quarter of a mile outside the village of Guayave.

Chapter XXX WEST INDIA LIFE

I remained on the Upper Pearl estate, and found much to interest an inquiring mind. Murray, although there were some good points about him, was not considered trustworthy. In his cups he was quarrelsome and as choleric as a Welshman; and a fondness for liquor was his besetting sin. He was an excellent accountant and an efficient clerk, but could hardly be relied on when a clear head and cool judgment were required.

A short time before I became acquainted with Murray, he had quarreled at a dinner party with a Mr. Reed, the manager of a coffee plantation. The lie was exchanged, a blow was struck; a challenge was given and accepted on the spot. The next morning the parties met, with their seconds, firmly bent upon shooting each other. There was no flinching on the part of the principals; no desire evinced to give or receive an apology. The seconds, however, were made of milder stuff; and neither of them being Irishmen, thought they would be justified in rendering the duel a bloodless one, and transforming a grave matter into a harmless joke. They accordingly loaded the pistols with powder only, keeping the bullets in their pockets; probably taking the hint from the well-blazoned proceedings in the duel fought at Chalk farm, a few years before, between Jeffries and Moore,

> "When Little's leadless pistol met the eye,
> While Bow Street myrmidons stood laughing by."

The word was given, and both parties fired. No harm was done; but apologies were out of the question, and "another shot" was loudly and peremptorily called for, and the distance, eight paces was shortened to six. The farce was again repeated, when Murray, wondering at the bloodless result, espied a smile on the features of his second, which did not seem in keeping with the gravity of the occasion. His suspicions were aroused; and the seconds, on being charged with duplicity, acknowledged the fact, adding that it would be worse than folly to shoot each other, and suggesting that they should shake hands, take a good breakfast together, and, in a Christian spirit, banish all enmity from their hearts.

This advice, so wise in itself, was not taken in good part by either of the principals. They were indignant at having been imposed upon, and made a laughing-stock to the community. Murray could not control his temper, but threw his pistol at the head of his second, cutting him badly in the face, and knocking him over; he chased the second of his antagonist off the field, and then offered his hand to the man whom he had twice attempted to shoot, which in a kind spirit was heartily grasped; and the two principals in the duel, who, five minutes before, eagerly thirsted for each other's blood, rode off together sworn friends and brothers, and were afterwards as great cronies as the Irish Bard and the Scotch reviewer.

Mr. Orr, the manager of the Upper Pearl, who left the estate, bowed down by disease, on the evening of my arrival, had a narrow escape from death. When he recovered, after a severe illness of several weeks, he refused to resume his situation, declaring he had got enough of the Pearls to last him his lifetime.

Mr. Church rode over from his residence every morning, and gave instructions, which I carried out to the best of my ability. The reputation of the Pearl estates for fevers was such, it was difficult to find a respectable person who would take the station of manager, or, if he accepted the situation, relying on the strength of his constitution, he was not wont to occupy it long. One of that description was engaged after Orr's resignation was received, but he was driven off in a few weeks by an attack of fever and ague, which nearly shook him to atoms. Another, of more doubtful character, was subsequently engaged, but he was found by the attorney tipsy before eleven o'clock in the forenoon. Had it been in the afternoon, it might have been excused; but to get drunk in the morning was an unpardonable offence. In vain he pleaded that he had taken only a few drops to neutralize the effects of the malaria; he was discharged.

After a few months' residence on this plantation, breathing by night and by day the foul and noxious miasma from the swamps, and just as I began to flatter myself that my constitution would weather the storm, I experienced an attack of headache, chills, and fever. By dint of resolution and nerve, which will accomplish much, I succeeded in throwing it off, being determined not to succumb through imagination or fear. A few days afterwards the attack was renewed with greater violence, and I was compelled to admit its reality, and acknowledge the supremacy of remittent fever. Mr. Church manifested much interest in my behalf. He caused a skillful physician to attend me, and promptly provided me with every thing the occasion required, excepting a salubrious atmosphere; and on being told that this was indispensable to my recovery, he generously caused me to be transported on a litter to "Bel-Air, " the beautiful and healthy villa in which he resided. Here I was provided with a comfortable apartment, and received the kindest attention from Mrs. Church. After a severe struggle the fever left me in a weak and emaciated condition, and weeks elapsed before I was permitted to resume my duties of the estate.

My wardrobe, although it had been replenished by Bohun, in a style which I thought unnecessarily liberal was still far from approaching what, by persons of simple tastes, would be called genteel. As I was now liable to be thrown into the company of the WELL-DRESSED visitors to Bel-Air, it was thought by Mr. Church perhaps at the suggestion of his wife that some improvement in my external appearance might be desirable. Accordingly, one day, on returning from a journey to St. George, he brought me, greatly to my astonishment, a dress coat, of bottle-green hue, much too large, which he had purchased ready-made; a pair of stockinet pantaloons, too tight for even my slim shanks, and a flashy- looking vest, which, for aught I know, may have been made of the stuff called "thunder and lightning; " so that, when rigged out in my genteel habiliments, I must have looked not unlike Moses, in the "Vicar of Wakefield, " going to the fair, but far more ridiculous!

I cared less about the effect I might produce in my unaccustomed finery than the expense of such luxuries, which I knew I could not afford, and which would inevitably subject me to much inconvenience. My salary, I found on inquiry, was a nominal one, barely sufficient to furnish me with ordinary comforts. I had already incurred a serious debt in the purchase of a saddle and bridle and other articles which I could not dispense with; and although I fully believed Mr. Thomas would never call upon me to refund his disbursements on my account in St. George, I knew human nature too well to suppose that Mr. Church would not deduct from my salary the price of those genteel articles of dress, which were of no more use to me than a marlinspike to a dandy. Indeed, had I indulged in such unreasonable hopes, I should have been undeceived when a bill for sundries from a trader came to hand, of an amount far exceeding my expectations, with a polite request that I would transmit the money at the earliest convenience!

There was no help; I had put my hand to the plough, and must go forward. I thus found myself enchained to the island for at least twelve months. Indeed, a longer period than that must elapse before I could expect, by the closest economy, to pay off the debts I had incurred. I now, too late, regretted that I had listened to the representations of Bohun, and allowed him to manifest his GRATITUDE for my services, the consequences of which served to embarrass me, and place me in a position which I did not covet; for which I was not calculated by habit or inclination, but from which I could see no means of escaping.

I returned to the Pearl estate and resumed my avocations. Months passed away; and although an occasional chill, followed by fever, reminded me that I was continually breathing an unhealthy atmosphere, I felt a sanguine hope that I should not again be affected by diseases incident to the climate, and that I had already qualified myself for the honorary degree which was referred to by my friend Murray. My hopes were fallacious. I was again attacked by a remittent fever of an obstinate character. I was again conveyed to Bel-Air. The doctor was again summoned, and he had a difficult task in restoring me to health. But he protested against my return to the Pearl estate, declaring that another attack would place me beyond the reach of medical assistance.

It chanced that Mr. Coxall, a rich merchant of St. George, who had a lumber yard and depot of stores in Greenville, was in want of a clerk to look after his affairs in that place, and in consequence of Mr. Church's recommendation he gave me the situation. My duties were pleasant; and I often visited the plantations in the neighborhood, where I acquired a number of friends. My emoluments, however, were inconsiderable; I was in debt, and the amount of my pecuniary obligations was not lessened by the repeated visits of a popular physician during my sickness.

During this time I had not heard a word from Mr. Thomas, or Bohun, his clerk. I supposed they had forgotten me; but I did those gentlemen injustice. I had hardly been a year in the island when I received a letter from Mr. Thomas, enclosing a bill in the handwriting of Bohun, of every article with which I had been furnished in St. George, not omitting my board at two dollars and a half a day, which Bohun so roundly swore should be reduced at least two thirds. The sum total of the bill amounted to more than one hundred dollars, an enormous sum in my then straitened circumstances; and the letter contained an intimation that, having been a year in the island, and in regular employment, it was expected that I was able and willing to settle the accompanying bill!

Although I entertained faint hopes of being able at some future day to reimburse Mr. Thomas for his expenses on my account, I never expected that he would make out this bill, including even the most trifling item, or hold me responsible for the unpardonable blunder of Bohun in relation to my board, and subject me to the mortification of a dun. It appeared, however, that he considered all obligations, on his part, discharged, when an unenviable situation was procured for me on a plantation, where the chances were nine out of ten that I should find my grave within three months! I made a brief reply to this letter, in which I expressed my feelings without reserve; assured him he need not trouble himself further about his money; that if I lived he should receive the full amount, principal and interest, as soon as I could earn it.

This unexpected demand on my resources troubled me greatly. It had the effect to postpone, almost indefinitely, the time when I should leave Grenada, and return to the occupation I preferred, that of a mariner. I could not quit the island honorably or openly without paying my debts; and I could not for a moment entertain the idea of sneaking out of it in a clandestine manner. I was the only citizen of the United States in the island, and I persuaded myself that the honor and reputation of my country were identified, to a certain extent, with my conduct while exercising a humble employment in that secluded portion of the globe. It would be well if others, exercising duties of a more important nature, would recollect this fact; and when their consciences or sense of propriety are not sufficient to restrain them from unworthy acts, let them summon patriotism to their aid, and remember that the disgrace is not confined to themselves, but is shared by the land which gave them birth. By acting on this principle, our country would be more honored abroad than it now is.

After I left the Pearl estate I enjoyed excellent health, with the exception of an occasional attack of intermittent fever, a malady which, although distressing and debilitating, is seldom regarded as alarming. Those only, who were liberally dosed some forty years ago with the powder of Peruvian bark, the sovereign remedy for fever and ague, can duly estimate the value of the services rendered to suffering humanity by the discovery of a mode of administering it in a concentrated form, that of QUININE.

Although some estates were regarded as healthy while others were notoriously the reverse, on no part of the island could persons be secure from those fatal diseases, most dreaded in a tropical climate, such as dysentery, and malignant or yellow fever. It was really startling to notice the sudden deaths which sometimes took place even among those who considered themselves acclimated, and were habitually in the enjoyment of excellent health. This may have been in part, owing to the irregular mode of living in a climate where the humanizing influence of female society was but little known. Dinner parties among the planters were frequent, where the most tempting liquors were produced, and excesses on such occasions, when fun and frolic were rife, were considered not only excusable but laudable.

I had been two years in the island, when I received an official notification that I was appointed one of the constables or civil officers of the district in which I resided, and was expected to qualify myself forthwith to perform my duties. Being well known as a citizen of the United States, I was greatly surprised at this event; and believing that I could not legally discharge the duties of any office of trust, honor, or emolument, however humble, under the British government, I hastened off at once to Mr. Lumsden, an old, and highly respectable planter, who resided on his own estate, and had acted as a magistrate for many years.

"Mr. Lumsden, " said I, exhibiting the document, "I have been appointed a constable for this district. "

"Well, what of that? The appointment is a good one. I recommended you myself. "

"I am obliged to you for your good opinion, " said I, "but you know very well that I am a citizen of the united States; have never taken the oath of allegiance to the British government, and never intend to; consequently I am not eligible. "

"Pooh, pooh! Nonsense! That makes not a farthing's difference. You will do well enough. "

"And more than that, " I continued, "I am only nineteen years of age; that alone is sufficient to incapacitate me. "

"Young man, " said the magistrate, with all the solemnity and wisdom of a Dogberry, "whether you are a Yankee or a Calmuck, whether your are sixty years old or sixteen, it matters not. You have been appointed a constable for this district, AND A CONSTABLE YOU SHALL BE. So no more frivolous excuses. If you do not prepare yourself to act in that capacity when called upon I will cause you to be reported and fined. "

There was no more to be said; the argument relating to the fine was unanswerable; and I caused myself to be qualified forthwith. The duties were not arduous. The only official duty required of me, during my term of office, was to summon a coroner's jury, on one occasion, to sit on the body of a runaway slave, who was stabbed by a watchman while committing depredations on some "negro gardens" in the night time.

Mr. Coxall finally gave up his establishment in Greenville, and I was obliged to look elsewhere for employment. A newspaper was published at St. George, owned and edited by an Englishman, who had been a non-commissioned officer in the regiment which was disbanded in the island a few years before. I had then, even at that early age, some indefinite hankering after newspaper life, and having picked up a crude mass of knowledge, incongruous and undigested, perhaps, from the many books I had devoured, I flattered myself that I could render good service as assistant editor of the St. George Chronicle. I accordingly offered my services to the proprietor, but found him less liberal in his opinions than the worthy sons of Scotia with whom I had been intimately associating. His prejudices against the Yankees were unconquerable. He did not even reply to my letter, but stated to a friend of mine that he must be very hard pushed before he would take a YANKEE into his office to assist in printing and editing an English newspaper.

I again turned my attention to the planting business. A vacancy having occurred on the Hermitage estate, owing to the sudden death, by yellow fever, of a very promising young man from Aberdeen, who had been in the island only a few months, I succeeded, through the kind exertions of Mr. Church, in obtaining the situation.

The Hermitage was one of the finest plantations in Grenada. It was pleasantly situated on elevated ground, a few miles from the sea shore, and was the residence of Mr. Houston, a gentleman of great respectability, who was attorney for the estate, and also for the plantation adjoining, called Belmont. Some years previously the Hermitage had been the residence of the owner of these estates, an Englishman named Bailey. He had spared no expense in stocking the grounds with fruits of various kinds, had planted bread-fruit and bread-nut trees, which, besides proving ornamental, furnished nutritive food for the slaves. Mr. Houston found, however, that the fruit orchards required more labor and care to keep them in good condition than could be profitably spared from other duties; and the beautiful and umbrageous bread- fruit and bread-nut trees shaded some portions of the fertile land capable of producing good sugar cane. The axe was, therefore, freely used, and, one after another, nearly all the trees which produced this excellent fruit were cut down. Other fruit trees, as the orange, the guava, pomegranate, avocado pear, golden apple, water lemon, soursop, etc. grow spontaneously on almost every plantation, and furnish an abundance and a variety of refreshing, nutritious food, at different seasons. Plantains, peas, cassava, kalliloo, yams, and several other kinds of esculent vegetables, some of which bear a close resemblance to the potato in every thing excepting the form, are raised in abundance with very little labor. The calabash tree is also found growing wild on every estate. It resembles an apple tree of moderate dimensions, and bears calabashes of every size, from those which contain several gallons to those which hold only half a pint. These calabashes are of great value on a plantation, being used as vessels for all purposes and occasions except for cooking.

It is hardly necessary to say that my debt to Mr. Thomas was liquidated as soon as I could obtain the means, even by anticipating my salary; and I eagerly looked forward to the time when, by exercising the strictest economy, I should be able to quit a place where, notwithstanding many things which were unpleasant, I had found valuable friends and enjoyed many comforts, and had been treated by all with whom I came in contact with confidence and kindness. During my stay, my feelings were never hurt by ungenerous allusions to my native country. Whatever unpleasant associations were produced, from time to time, among the planters by the passing events of the war, they were restrained by a feeling of delicacy, which I could duly appreciate, from indulging in offensive remarks in my hearing. On one occasion their forbearance, politeness, and respect for myself were put to a severe test.

The war between Great Britain and the United states deprived the inhabitants of the British West India colonies of many comforts and luxuries which they enjoyed when free intercourse was maintained between the United States and the different ports in the English islands. During the war, all the stores and provisions, lumber, and other important materials required on the plantations, were conveyed thither from ports in Great Britain in ships sailing under convoy of men-of-war. The arrival of these ships, which took place at certain seasons, when the produce was ready for shipping, was anxiously expected, as they were freighted not only with useful articles for the estates, but also contained generous lots of hams, porter, cheese, wines, and other delicacies and condiments, ordered by the planters themselves for their especial benefit and enjoyment. It was a day of jubilee and rejoicing when a ship known to be freighted with these "good things" and "creature comforts" arrived safely in port.

At the proper season, in 1814, the good ship Corunna, of Bristol, was expected at Greenville. This ship was an old trader, and the captain had been intrusted with many commissions, which, as he was an honest and faithful man, it was not doubted he would execute satisfactorily. Most of the planters in that part of the island were looking out anxiously every day for the arrival of the Corunna. Their private stores had been long exhausted, and they longed to have them replenished. The ship was an unreasonable time on her passage.

It was Sunday afternoon. I was dining with Mr. Stevenson, the manager of the Tivoli estate, in company with several planters. The house was situated on an elevated spot, and commanded a fine view of the sea, extending nearly from the Grenadines to LaBaye, the port of Greenville. It was distant from the sea shore not more than a couple of miles. Suddenly, on looking out of the front windows of the dining hall, a large ship was seen under full sail, coming with a fair wind from the direction of the Grenadines and steering towards LaBaye.

"That is the Corunna, " shouted one of the gentlemen present. "Hurrah! "

"Not the Corunna, " remarked Mr. Stevenson. "The Corunna is not so good looking and is of a different model. The West India fleet, however, must have arrived at Barbadoes, and the Corunna will soon be along. "

At that moment another ship appeared, carrying a cloud of canvas, coming round the point. This vessel was not the Corunna, and kept close in with the land, running also for LaBaye. A shade of disappointment rested on the features of some of the planters; but all continued to gaze eagerly in the direction of the sea, hoping that the long expected ship, bearing, not the Golden Fleece from Colchis, but treasures from England, of far greater value in the estimation of their owners, would next make her appearance. Their expectations were realized. Another ship came into view, with every sail set which would draw; royals, skysails, and studding sails, from the truck to the deck, and the British ensign was waving at her peak.

"There comes the Corunna, at last! " exclaimed Mr. Stevenson.

"The Corunna! The Corunna! " was the responsive cry.

"I declare, " said Mr. McInnis, the manager of the Carriere estate, "I feel greatly relieved. I began to think the ship had been picked up by some Yankee privateer, and my Stilton cheese and 'brown stout' gone in another direction. "

"I was suspicious, myself, that some accident of that kind had happened, " replied Mr. Stevenson; "but she is safe enough now, and will be at anchor in an hour or so. Therefore, let us fill our glasses, and drink the health of her successful commander. "

The glasses were filled; but before their contents were quaffed, the company were startled by the loud report of a cannon, which came booming across the land. At this moment another vessel, which had fired the gun, was seen coming round the point, following closely in the wake of the Corunna.

This vessel was of a model widely different from those which first came along. She was a long, low, black hermaphrodite brig, with tall, raking masts, and a row of ports, evidently intended for use rather than ornament. Every plank in her hull, every rope at her mast-head, and every cloth of her canvas looked as if they meant MISCHIEF.

Her national flag, which bore the stars and stripes, was not necessary to proclaim the presence of one of the much dreaded American privateers. The company looked as if the angel of destruction was hovering over the island.

"A privateer! An American privateer! " exclaimed Stevenson. "The Corunna is nabbed after all. "

"Not so! " said Mr. McCrimmon of Belmont. "Not so! The Corunna will show fight. Her captain is a brave man, and will not strike his flag without good reason. Look there, he fires a broadside! Huzza! "

The Corunna now changed her course, keeping away before the wind, and running directly for the land. She discharged three or four guns from her starboard ports, which were replied to by the "long Tom" of the privateer. The captain of the ship, apparently, considered it useless to fight, and made an attempt to run the ship ashore; but his object being perceived by the Yankee, he also kept off, and sailing much faster than the Englishman, placed his brig between the ship and the beach, hammering away in the mean time with his "long Tom. " The Corunna fired no shot in return, and in a few minutes hauled down her flag in token of surrender.

It subsequently appeared that the three ships had left England and came to Barbadoes with the large outward bound West India fleet; but being well armed, and stoutly manned, had concluded not to wait for convoy to Grenada, and the risk being small, agreed to keep together, stand by each other, and combine their forces if menaced by an enemy. They passed the Grenadines, came in sight of their port, and were exulting in having accomplished the passage in safety, when the Yankee privateer brig Chasseur, of Baltimore, Captain Boyle, shot out from behind the promontory of Sauteurs and gave chase. A harbor was in sight ahead and the enemy astern. It is perhaps not remarkable that under these circumstances discretion outweighed valor; that the two headmost vessels FORGOT THE AGREEMENT, and, adopting the memorable order which was acted on by the "Grand Army" after the burning of Moscow, "SAUVE QUI PEUT, " ensconced themselves, as quickly as possible, in the snug harbor of Greenville. The captain of the Corunna was a brave man, as had been truly said. He was anxious to fight, but his men, after one ineffective broadside, left the guns. He then attempted to run his ship ashore, but was foiled by the superior sailing of the enemy. The Corunna had a miscellaneous cargo of considerable value, and a successful attempt was made to carry her into an American port. She reached Wilmington in safety, and the North Carolina cotton planters doubtless ate and drank with a keen relish the good things which were intended for the sugar planters of Grenada.

It may be easily imagined, that the news of a treaty of peace having been signed at Ghent, was received with great and sincere delight by the inhabitants of the English islands. Far from their native homes, and in a great measure free from political excitement, they manifested no great interest in the results of the war, indulging only a vague desire and expectation that British arms would prevail. The war had caused them great inconvenience, and deprived them of many comforts; and it was difficult to say whether my friends or myself derived the most gratification from the fact that peace was established between the two countries.

Time passed on. I had nearly cleared myself from debt, and had even fixed the period when I should be able to leave Grenada and engage in other pursuits. My friends combated the resolution I had taken, assuring me of success, even to the extent of my wishes, if I would remain on the island. Indeed, I was more than half promised the management of a plantation near Guayave, called Grosse Point, by Mr. McQueen, the Receiver General. Fearing I might be tempted to remain, by offers which I should be unable to withstand, I was anxious to hasten the period of my departure.

About this time a bill, providing for a registry of the slaves in every British colony, was passed by the Parliament of Great Britain, with a view to put a more effectual barrier to the African slave trade. This bill was not understood by the blacks. They were aware that some law intended for their benefit, perhaps favoring their emancipation, had been enacted, and not experiencing any advantageous results, after waiting patiently some weeks they began to consult together, to murmur, and exhibit signs of discontent, which caused great alarm. On several estates the field laborers in a body, including the head drivers and other magnates, left their homes and went to St. George. They demanded to be put in possession of those indulgences and rights to which they supposed they were entitled by the law which had just been passed.

The planters, recollecting the bloody scenes that had been enacted, years before, at the beginning of the insurrection headed by Fedon, were greatly alarmed. Military organizations were formed in different districts, and a regular night patrol, and a well-devised system of espionage, were kept up for several weeks. The governor of Grenada and the Grenadines, at this period, was Major General Riall, who had distinguished himself while commanding the British army on the Canada frontiers, and was wounded and taken prisoner at the battle of Niagara. Acting with judgment, firmness, and discretion, he succeeded in pacifying those bodies of slaves who sought him, and explained the true character of the act. They slowly returned to the plantations and resumed their labors; but were evidently dissatisfied, and more than half convinced that even the governor was deceiving them.

To add to the excitement, a rumor was spread abroad, and obtained belief, that a number of aliens had arrived in the island, with the intention of stirring up another insurrection; and a sort of panic prevailed among the whites. The governor issued a proclamation, declaring that every free person who was not a native citizen of Great Britain, or who had not taken the oath of allegiance, must appear forthwith before the executive authorities of St. George, and report himself and state his object in being on the island.

I felt myself included in the list of aliens, and in spite of the remonstrances of friends, who insisted that the proclamation did not apply to me, I determined to comply with its directions, and go immediately to St. George. Accompanied by a gentleman who was connected with the government, and to whom I had a letter of introduction, I called upon his excellency. The governor was a thick-set, ruddy-faced man, with a decidedly military air, of simple habits and courteous manners. He received me with great politeness. On being informed that I was an American, he waived all desire for an explanation in regard to the cause of my residence in the island; and further remarked, that should it at any time be in his power to render me service, it would give him pleasure to do it.

When peace was established between the two countries it was expected the ports in the English islands would be thrown open for trade, as before the war. In this expectation the planters were disappointed. In order to protect the trade in the British American provinces, the importation of produce in American bottoms was prohibited. Consequently there was no direct communication between English ports in the West Indies and ports in the United States. Our vessels landed and sold their cargoes in St. Thomas, St.

Bartholomew, or some other free port, where they were shipped in English bottoms, and thence conveyed to the English islands.

There being no opportunity to go directly to the United States from Grenada, I sought the means of proceeding to some other port, where I should be likely to fall in with an American vessel. I called on Mr. Budge, a merchant of St. George, with whom I had some acquaintance, to make inquiries. He informed me he was on the point of chartering a small vessel in which to proceed to St. Pierre in Martinico, should sail in the course of a few weeks, and would cheerfully give me a passage to that port.

I returned to the interior of the island in fine spirits, and commenced making the necessary arrangements for my departure. In due time, having received information from Mr. Budge that his sloop would sail on a certain day, I took leave of my numerous friends, bade farewell to the plantations; to the lonely glens and deep gorges in the mountains, which for me, had many charms, and took the "Grand Etang" route for the capital. I could not bid adieu to my kind Scotch friends without emotion. Several of them expressed an intention to visit the United States before the lapse of many years, perhaps to settle there for life, and promised to look me up. But I have never seen them since. With the sight of a Scotchman, however, is associated many pleasing recollections; and a Scotch accent has ever sounded grateful in my ear since I left the shores of Grenada.

During my residence in Grenada my duties were neither arduous nor difficult. Had I complied with the advice of friends and remained, I might have succeeded as a planter, and led for a number of years a lazy, monotonous, vegetative kind of life. Nevertheless, my stay was not unproductive of advantages. I found much to interest and occupy an inquiring mind; and my situation gave me an opportunity to gratify a thirst for information, to gain an intimate knowledge of tropical life, usages, and productions which has often since proved of signal service. I was brought into communication with people of different nations, different characters, and different modes of thinking; of different politics, philosophy, and religion; all of which has a tendency to eradicate or weaken early prejudices, liberalize opinions, and inculcate charitable views of human nature. While such a relation with people of other countries can never diminish the feeling of patriotism in a well-balanced mind, it will lead a persons to discover, acknowledge, and respect, in other communities and other nations, much that is good and worthy of commendation.

After paying my debts and supplying a few pressing wants I found remaining in my pocket fifty Spanish dollars. I had emerged from a state of poverty and dependence. I was rich, having the means, without much doubt, of procuring a passage from Martinico to some port in the United States.

Chapter XXXI SORROWFUL SCENES

It was about the middle of September in the year 1816 that I embarked with Mr. Budge in a little sloop bound to St. Lucia and Martinico, after having resided in Grenada nearly four years. We had a few other passengers, one of whom was a French gentleman named Chambord, who had fought a duel with an Englishman in St. Lucia a few months before. This duel grew out of a fierce dispute in relation to the battle of Waterloo, and the comparative merit, in a military point of view, of Napoleon and Wellington. The Frenchman, being an adroit swordsman, got the best of the argument by running his antagonist through the body, and leaving him senseless, and apparently lifeless, on the field. He made his escape to Grenada. Having learned that the champion of Wellington was in a fair way to recover from his wound, he was now on his return to his home.

We tarried but a short time at St. Lucia, merely lying off and on at the mouth of the port of Castries, or Carenage, which is one of the most beautiful and safe harbors in that part of the world; the entrance being so narrow that two ships cannot pass through it abreast; but inside, the extent of the harbor and depth of water are sufficient to furnish good anchorage and shelter from hurricanes for a large fleet of ships of the largest class.

On arriving at St. Pierre I found a fearful hurricane had raged in that quarter only a week or ten days before. The wind, blowing from the eastward directly into the open roadstead with irresistible fury, had driven every vessel in port ashore on the beach. The ship Cato, of Portsmouth, New Hampshire, having all her cargo discharged, and presenting a large surface of hull to the wind and the waves, was found, after the tempest had subsided, high and dry in one of the streets, in a condition which precluded the possibility of getting her into the water, and was broken up. Others were launched on "ways" constructed for the purpose; while some sustained but little injury, and were easily got afloat. One English brig, built of the red cedar of Bermuda, a material greatly in favor at that time on account of its remarkable resistance to DECAY, was crushed like an egg-shell the moment it struck the shore, and the fragments were strown along the beach.

At the time I arrived at St. Pierre the yellow fever was prevailing to an alarming extent among the inhabitants. The same epidemic prevailed in Point Petre, Guadaloupe, and the numerous immigrants from France, in some cases whole families, who sought those shores with the hope of improving their condition, were cut off by this terrible disease soon after their arrival. Some cases of yellow fever appeared among the shipping in St. Pierre, and nearly every one proved fatal, showing the malignant type of the disease. Great alarm was manifested lest the epidemic should spread among the vessels, and sweep off whole crews, and I subsequently learned that these apprehensions were realized.

I engaged lodgings on shore, and was there an eye witness to the ravages of this plague of the West Indies. Young and healthy men, full of hope and gayety, with rich prospects in the future, were visited by this grim messenger soon after they set their feet on those shores; and few, very few, recovered. Death was doing a mighty business at Martinico at that time; and during my brief stay I listened to many a thrilling tale of hopes blighted, ties of affection sundered, and sorrows awakened by the remorseless action of the "King of Terrors. " The strong man was cut down while boasting of his strength; and youth, beauty, or worth furnished no protection from the attack of this West India pestilence.

After my long residence in Grenada I had no fear of yellow fever in Martinico; and in several cases at my boarding house I was able to render valuable assistance. I was now anxious to get temporary employment of some kind, or procure a passage to the United States. I was every day getting nearer the bottom of my purse; and I trembled at the idea of finding myself penniless in the town of St. Pierre. I could hardly hope to meet with the sympathy and kindness from the Frenchmen of Martinico that I found in Grenada among the natives of Scotland.

Owing to the shipwrecks, caused by the hurricane, there was no want of seamen; and I could not even get an opportunity to work my passage to an American port before the mast. I had been so long in the West Indies that I had lost the distinguishing marks of a Yankee. And my broad accent, my swarthy complexion, my unseamanlike costume, adapted to the climate, all seemed to contradict my statement that I was an American sailor.

At Martinico I fell in with an Englishman, Captain William Parker, who had resided in the islands for many years, and was thoroughly acquainted with the trade in that part of the globe. He was then making preparations to engage in a sort of wholesale smuggling business, and had obtained possession, by hook or by crook, of two registers of American vessels. One was a BONA FIDE register of a privateer which had been captured during the war, and the other a forgery neatly executed by an artist in Martinico, having the signatures and seals duly arranged and perfected, but leaving blank the description of the vessel.

With these registers, valuable documents, in his estimation, having cost him no trifling sum, it was his wish to proceed to New York, and with the aid of some unscrupulous capitalist, purchase an English schooner, answering nearly to the description in the register of the privateer; or, failing in that, procure an English vessel of any kind suitable, and fill up the blanks with a description of the same in the other American register. Then with two captains, one English and one American, each acting as mate alternately, and with a crew who could be confided in, HE PROPOSED TO CARRY ON A DIRECT TRADE WITH THE ENGLISH ISLANDS, securing all the advantages, in the way of port charges and duties, of an American vessel in an American port and an English vessel in an English port! A few voyages successfully performed on this plan, he plausibly urged, would be productive of immense profit to all concerned.

Parker was desirous that I would embark with him in this enterprise, and act as the nominal American commander. But I had an instinctive repugnance to proceedings of such an underhand, unlawful character. This of itself would have been enough to lead me to reject his proposition; and furthermore I had no confidence in the man, or his ability to carry his project into operation. I thanked Parker for his friendly offer, and the COMPLIMENT it conveyed, but declined to enter into any engagement of the kind. Whether he succeeded in carrying his project into effect I never learned; but the same plan was successfully put into execution by an enterprising rogue about the same time, who undertook to run a vessel between Baltimore and Barbadoes, carrying out flour and bringing back coffee and sugar. He performed two trips successfully, but on the third got into trouble. One of the crew, who had been unadvisedly punished for insubordination, gave information to the authorities in Barbadoes, which put a period, for a time at least, to his enterprising pursuits.

A few days before I landed in St. Pierre, the brig Betsey, Captain Blackler, arrived in the harbor from Marseilles. A large portion of her cargo was discharged, and Captain Blackler concluded to send the brig with the remaining portion, consisting of wine im casks, to New Orleans, while he remained behind to transact important business for the owner of the brig, William Gray, of Salem. Accordingly the mate, Mr. Adams, an intelligent and highly deserving young man, belonging to Marblehead, was placed in charge, and the mate of the unfortunate ship Cato, which forsook her proper element to explore the streets of St. Pierre, and could not get back, was engaged as mate of the Betsey.

I applied to Captain Blackler for a passage to New Orleans. The brig was fully manned, with six stout, able-bodied seamen before the mast, and cook, mate, and captain, nine in all. Captain Blackler demanded forty dollars for a passage in the cabin; by no means an exorbitant charge. Nevertheless this was a poser, as after paying for my board, I had only twenty dollars remaining. This matter, however, was satisfactorily settled by a COMPROMISE, a happy way of getting rid of a difficulty. I proposed to advance twenty dollars before quitting Martinico, and give an obligation for twenty more when the brig should arrive at New Orleans; and he agreed to the proposition. But HOW I should raise twenty dollars on reaching New Orleans, was a question I could not answer, and did not like to consider. I strove hard to convince myself I should never be called upon for payment, or if called upon, that fortune would favor me by furnishing, in some way, the means.

Captain Blackler was a gentleman much respected and esteemed. He was a good specimen of an American shipmaster. When we got under way he came on board, apparently in good health and spirits, to bid us farewell. I shook hands with him as he stepped over the side. He gave some final instructions to Mr. Adams, who had assumed the command of the Betsey. They mutually wished each other continued health and prosperity, expressed a hope to meet before long in Marblehead, and parted NEVER TO MEET AGAIN! Before another week had passed they were both summoned before their God. It was afterwards ascertained that Captain Blackler was attacked by yellow fever a few days after the brig left Martinico, and was quickly added to the numerous band of victims to that disease.

The brig Betsey was about two hundred and twenty tons burden; a clump, dull-sailing craft, of rather venerable appearance, with no pretensions to youth or beauty, having braved the dangers of the seas for thirty years; nevertheless she was now apparently as sound, safe, and tight as any vessel that crossed the ocean. Captain Adams was a worthy man, of an amiable character, who had been educated to his business; and the mate, Mr. Ricker, had been commander of a ship, and was strongly recommended as an able and faithful officer. The crew were Americans, resolute-looking, powerful fellows, in robust health. There had been no sickness on board during the voyage; and all of them, including the captain and mate, were rejoiced to leave the island of Martinico. As the mountains faded in the distance they fancied they had left the yellow fever far behind, and congratulated each other on their good fortune.

Our route, as will be seen by examining a chart or a map, was a remarkably interesting one. It extended through the Caribbean Sea, where the trade winds blow unceasingly from the eastward, in a direction south of some of the most beautiful and picturesque islands in the world, as Porto Rico, St. Domingo, and Cuba, and ranged along in sight of Jamaica and the Caymans, then rounded Cape Antonio, once the notorious haunt of pirates, and entered the Gulf of Mexico. Leaving the harbor of St. Pierre under such auspices, I anticipated a delightful trip and being a passenger, with no duties to perform, and no responsibility resting on my shoulders, I was prepared to enjoy the POETRY of a seafaring life.

The night following our departure there was a gentle breeze from the eastward, the sea was smooth, and everything in the atmosphere, on the ocean, or in the vessel gave promise of a pleasant passage. I remained on deck that night until twelve o'clock, in conversation with Captain Adams. He seemed in a particularly pleasant and communicative mood; spoke of his past life, which had been but little clouded with misfortune, and indulged in the most cheerful anticipations with regard to the future.

The next day I learned that one of the seamen, named James Smith, belonging to Wiscasset, in Maine, was unable, from illness, to do his duty. I found that Smith was not a favorite with the crew, being a lazy fellow, who would act the part of an "old soldier" when an opportunity offered. As he did not seem very sick, and some thought he was feigning illness to avoid work, no alarm was excited in consequence.

There was a man on board the Betsey whose name was Gaskell; a tall, stalwart fellow, belonging to Greenbush, New York. He showed in his words and actions that he was unprincipled, a thorough reprobate, whose soul had been case-hardened in crime. This man ridiculed the illness of Smith; tried to rouse him from his berth in the half-deck; declared that he was "shamming Abraham, " and threatened him with a rope's end unless he gave over skulking. Gaskell spoke of the mortality among the Frenchmen in Martinico, and this furnished him with an inexhaustible source of amusement. Indeed, human suffering, lingering death by shipwreck or disease, always moved him to mirth and laughter. And yet he was not deficient in intellect and education; but had used them for evil purposes. He was coarse, sensual, intemperate, and terribly profane. He boldly avowed a disbelief in a God, and sneered at the idea of punishment for crime in the future. He loved to talk of the yellow fever; he set that fearful disease at defiance, and said he never enjoyed himself so gloriously as he had done the year previously at Savannah, when the yellow fever was sweeping off the crews of the shipping in that port by hundreds, and he found employment as a carpenter, and cleared ten dollars a day by making coffins for the "Yankee" sailors. I felt from the outset that this Gaskell was a bad man, and a further knowledge of him confirmed my impression and increased my disgust.

In the course of the day I visited the half-deck, at the request of Captain Adams, to examine the condition of Smith. I found him in a feverish state, languid, his spirits much depressed, and with a slight headache. At the time I had no suspicion that he was visited with yellow fever, the disease appeared in so mild a form. Some medicine was given him, and it was expected that in a day or so he would recover his health.

The next morning, being the third day after leaving Martinico, I was awakened soon after daybreak by a succession of groans which came from the captain's stateroom. I entered the room, and was greatly alarmed at finding Captain Adams laboring under a severe attack of illness. He was seized with pains in the head and back, accompanied with scorching fever. His pulsations were strong, quick, and irregular. He said he must have caught a violent cold the night before, by remaining on deck without his coat or hat. I did not contradict him; but I had seen persons in a similar condition, and I knew he was suffering from yellow fever in its most alarming form.

All the medical skill I possessed was put in requisition; but the captain grew worse, and before night he was aware of the true character of the disease, and seemed to feel there was no chance for his recovery. I strove to minister consolation and inspire him with hope, but in vain. He acknowledged that life had charms of the most attractive description; fortune had favored him beyond his expectations; he had relations and friends whom he dearly loved; and there was one bright being in his native town to whom he had plighted his vows of affection, and to whom he hoped to have been united for life if Providence had willed his return. But he was resigned to the will of the Almighty. He did not even murmur at the fate which he knew awaited him. He prayed to his God to pardon the sins he had committed, and looked forward with hope to a glorious immortality.

The breeze had been light and the sea remarkably smooth since we left St. Pierre; and the brig, steering to the north-west, had made slow progress. On the morning after the captain was taken sick we expected to be in sight of Porto Rico; and Captain Adams asked Mr. Ricker, the mate, if any land was in sight. The mate thoughtlessly replied, "'The Dead Man's Chest' can just be seen off deck. " This was the English name of a small island, or cluster of rocks, some five or six miles south of Porto Rico, resembling in appearance a coffin, and called, in Spanish, "Moxa del Muerta. "

Captain Adams remarked, in a soliloquizing strain, "The Dead Man's Chest? Already in sight? Well, it will soon be wanted; I am ready. "

The sufferings of this excellent man were intense. The pains in his head and back kept increasing; yet his mind was tranquil, and he retained command of his mental faculties until the last moment of his life. During his illness he expressed kindness for others, and made suggestions to the mate about sailing the brig and carrying on the work. As he grew weaker, he gave explicit directions to Mr. Ricker in regard to the duties which would devolve upon him at his death, and intrusted me with a solemn message to his dearest friends, which I afterwards faithfully delivered.

On the third day after the fever commenced the BLACK VOMIT set in. This is generally regarded as a fatal symptom, being almost always the precursor of death. But the fortitude of the captain never for a moment forsook him. He was sustained in that dread hour by a guiltless conscience and a steadfast, deep-rooted, religious principle.

A few hours after this alarming prognostic made its appearance, he died, while I was bathing his forehead; and a prayer hung upon his lips, even as the spirit left the earthly tabernacle. He died as became a Christian; and his features in death were tranquil as those of a sleeping infant.

His body was soon afterwards brought on deck, where the whole ship's company were assembled. The funeral rites were simple, but solemn and impressive; and far away from the friends of his youth, with no heart-stricken relatives to gather around the coffin, and form a mournful procession to the grave, and hallow the burial spot with the tears of affection, the mortal remains of our worthy commander were launched into the deep. They were committed, not to the silent tomb, but to that vast burial place, that "God's Acre" of almost illimitable extent, where deep caves, and recesses invisible to mortal eye, have served for ages as the last resting place of myriads of human beings, cut off untimely, without warning note of preparation, from the hopes and disappointments, the joys and sorrows, of this world; where, without headstone or monument, inscription or epitaph, to mark the place, with only the rushing winds to mourn their departure, and the murmuring waves to chant their requiem,

"After life's fitful fever, they sleep well. "

It is remarkable that in no part of the world, in any age, has the sea been selected as a burial place for the dead. Indeed, the idea of being drowned at sea, or dying on shipboard to be intombed in the fathomless ocean, is so abhorrent to many individuals that it is with fear and trembling they trust themselves on the water. It was a belief of the ancients, that to insure happiness hereafter, the dead body of a human being must be covered with earth; otherwise the departed spirit would never enter the Elysian Fields, but wander restless on the nether banks of Styx, in full view of delights and joys which it could never expect to realize.

Mr. Ricker, the mate, now took command of the brig. This man possessed a warm and affectionate heart, and was deeply moved by the death of the captain. He wept aloud when the interment took place, and sought to alleviate his grief by copious draughts of spirituous liquors. He wept and drank himself to sleep while reclining on a hen-coop. In a few hours he awoke, and wept again; then told the cook to bring the brandy bottle, which soon acted as an opiate, and banished his sorrows. He pursued this course, crying and drinking for more than a week; and during the greater part of this time, while I was witnessing scenes of sadness and death enough to chill the stoutest heart, he incapacitated himself, by intoxication, from performing his duties as commander of the ill-fated vessel.

Smith was still lingering under the attack of a disease which we now knew to be yellow fever. He was gradually growing worse. Others of the crew were also visited by this dreadful pestilence, and the deck of the brig resembled one of the fever wards of a hospital. The groans of the poor fellows were enough, one would think, to create sympathy in the coldest bosom. But they had no effect upon Gaskell, excepting to excite derision; and when he spoke to his sick or dying shipmates with a ribald jest on his lips, and a scornful grin on his features, I longed to fell him to the deck. I rebuked him for his want of feeling, and suggested that, proud as he was of his strength and immunity from sickness, he might, notwithstanding, become an object of sympathy to his shipmates, and need their assistance. The answer I received was a boisterous laugh, as if the idea was too absurd to be entertained.

Many years have passed since these events occurred, but even now I cannot recur to them without a feeling of sadness. And no one, not familiar with such scenes, can form an idea of the distress which a mortal sickness produces on board a ship at sea. The captain had died, and the mate, who should have taken his place, was constantly in a state of beastly intoxication. Three of the crew were struggling with yellow fever, and, to add to our troubles, Gaskell made his way into the hold, and broached a cask of wine; and those who were not sick followed the example of the mate, and got drunk, and drowned in vociferous shouts and songs the groans of their suffering shipmates. Under these circumstances, I had no alternative but to take on myself the responsibility of navigating and sailing the vessel. And while proceeding along the fruitful shores of St. Domingo, and the picturesque coast of Jamaica, I passed whole nights on deck, engaged in tending the sick, trimming the sails, and steering the brig. It was truly fortunate that the wind continued light and the weather pleasant.

Smith, who was the first man taken sick, did not recover. His illness gradually increased; for several days his mind wandered, but he was not troublesome, and died on the tenth day after we left St. Pierre.

On the day of the captain's death, a young man, belonging to Connecticut, was seized with a fever, and died five days afterwards in a state of delirium. His case required constant care and attention, as he made more than one attempt to throw himself overboard, in order, as he believed, to embrace his parents and friends in his own native village. Two others were taken alarmingly ill, but after suffering severely for several days gradually recovered. The cook, a stout black fellow, inured to warm climates, rendered me great assistance in taking care of the sick. But on the morning on which we beheld the mountains of Jamaica he also was visited by yellow fever. The symptoms were alarming, and there seemed no prospect of his recovery; but on the third day of his sickness, AND AFTER THE BLACK VOMIT HAD COMMENCED, and while I sat watching by his berth, expecting that in a few minutes he would breathe his last, he seemed to revive, and I put some rice-water to his lips. He swallowed a small quantity; the terrible forerunner of a speedy dissolution disappeared, and from that moment his strength gradually increased, the fever left him, and before we reached New Orleans he had recovered.

While the cook was still dangerously ill, one morning early, as we were slowly sailing along towards the Grand Cayman, Gaskell came crawling up the steps leading to the half-deck, and tottered along towards me. I was appalled at the change which a single night had made in his appearance. The defiant, rollicking ruffian no longer stood before me; the sneer was no longer on his countenance, his eyes no longer sparkled with mischief, and his language was not interlarded with disgusting profanity. His eyes were glassy, his cheeks ghastly pale, and a cold sweat, produced by FEAR, stood on his forehead. The workings of suffering and terror were imprinted on his features, and he looked as if twenty years had been added to his life in one short night.

And he had cause for alarm; the yellow fever had fastened upon him with a vice-like grasp, and he felt it in his inmost soul. The man was a coward, after all. He thought himself secure from the scourge, and put on a mask of defiance. He now knew that he had deceived himself, and all his daring vanished. HE WAS AFRAID OF DEATH; AND THE DREADFUL CONVICTION WAS FORCED UPON HIM THAT HIS DYING HOUR WAS AT HAND.

In tremulous accents, Gaskell described the symptoms of the disease. The shooting pains in his head, neck, and shoulders were insufferable, and he entreated me to do something, any thing, to relieve the pain, and restore him to health. He urged me to bleed him, which I undertook, and opened a vein in each arm, but the blood would not flow; the vital current seemed to be congealed by fear. He then begged me to bathe his back with camphor and opodeldoc, and although I knew the operation would produce no effect, I consented to his wishes, and for more than an hour rubbed his back as he desired, and bathed his head with vinegar and lime juice.

But the disease could not be removed. It seized upon his vitals, and he rapidly grew worse. His pains were great, but his mental agonies were greater. For worlds I would not suffer what that man suffered while rushing into the fearful embraces of death. His mind was clear and unclouded, while madness would have been mercy. His life had been loose and depraved. He had been guilty of many crimes, and in the day of death the stings of conscience pierced him to the soul. His evil deeds came back to him in that hour; they were stamped on his heart as with a red-hot iron. I tried to console him, but in vain. He would not listen when I spoke of death, and fiercely motioned me away when I attempted to read aloud a chapter from the Bible. He said but little; but what he did say were words of bitterness and despair. He declared, with an awful oath, that he would not die, and struggled fiercely for life to the last. I never shall forget the wild and ghastly countenance and distorted features of that dying man, who, only a few days before, while in the full flush of health, declared, with a diabolical grin, that he feared neither God nor man.

The fever had now run its race, but our ship's company was greatly reduced in number and in strength. The captain and three of the seamen had been committed to the waves, and others had not fully recovered from the effects of the fever. Mr. Ricker was the only person on board, with the exception of myself, who had entirely escaped. Whether drunkenness acted, in his case, as a preventive, I will not undertake to say; neither will I advise any one to try the hazardous experiment.

We were now in sight of the Isle of Pines, fourteen days having elapsed since we sailed from Martinico, when I observed indications of one of those severe gales not unusual in the Gulf of Mexico and vicinity, and known at "northers. " Light-handed as we were, and without an efficient head, I was aware that our situation was a critical one. I then felt justified in doing what I should have done sooner; I threw overboard every drop of spirit I could find, and then applied myself to rouse Mr. 'Ricker from his drunken inactivity; I explained to him my apprehensions of a gale of wind, and the necessity for making preparation for the coming tempest. This brought him to his senses; and after grumbling somewhat at the loss of his liquor, and taking a deep draught of water, he entered with energy on the sphere of his duties.

Ricker was a man of large stature and great physical strength. He was also a thorough seaman, and, when not stupefied with liquor, was an active, energetic man. By his powerful aid, and under his direction, the brig was soon put in a condition to withstand the heavy gale from the north, which soon came upon us, and completely ventilated the steerage and cabin, which had so long been the depository of a pestilential atmosphere. The "norther" lasted two days, the greater part of which time we were lying to, under a close-reefed main-topsail; and when the gale abated, we found ourselves further north than at its commencement, and not far from Cape St. Antonio, the western extremity of Cuba, a fact which illustrates in a striking manner, the force of the current which at certain times sets north, like a sluice-way, between Cuba and Yucatan, into the Gulf of Mexico, and is the origin of the Gulf Stream.

We entered the Gulf of Mexico, and with a fair breeze sailed for "the Balize. " In a few days we struck soundings near the mouth of the Mississippi, and soon fell in with the turbid waters that are swept far out to sea by the strength of the current of that mighty river. We steered for a lighthouse, constructed of granite, on the eastern extremity of a point, and which, resting on a quagmire, was hardly completed before it assumed an attitude resembling the leaning tower of Pisa, and in six months afterwards it took a horizontal position. It is hardly necessary to say it was never lighted. We took a pilot and entered the river by the Balize or "South-east Pass, " which was the deepest channel at that time, and navigable only for vessels drawing not more than fifteen feet of water, and, by dint of hard labor, steam towboats being then unknown, worked our way to the city of New Orleans.

Chapter XXXII NEW ORLEANS IN 1817

I have already stated that the owner of the Brig Betsey was Mr. Gray, of Salem, a merchant of great enterprise, probity, and wealth. He soon afterwards removed to Boston, and was known throughout this country and the maritime cities of Europe by the name of "Billy Gray. " His agent in New Orleans was Nathaniel Ware. Mr. Ricker explained to him the mournful events which had taken place on the passage from the West Indies, and Mr. Ware exhibited deep sympathy while listening to the tale of suffering. Ricker, prompted by a feeling of gratitude which showed the goodness of his heart, gave me full credit for the services I had rendered during the passage; explained the nature of my connection with the brig, and placed in the hands of Mr. Ware the written obligation I had given Captain Blackler, and which was found among the papers of Captain Adams. This document, which had caused me much anxiety, Mr. Ware returned, along with the twenty dollars I had previously paid towards my passage. He also thanked me for the assistance I had rendered Mr. Ricker, and added something more substantial, in the shape of twenty-five dollars, "as a trifling compensation, " he said, "for my services, " although, for obvious reasons, he was not aware of their full extent. He suggested that, if I designed to follow the sea, I could remain in the brig on pay, and that the command of the vessel would be given to Mr. Ricker. He further said he would represent my conduct in a favorable light to Mr. Gray, which he did, and years afterwards it was remembered to my advantage. Mr. Ricker himself urged me to remain, and occupy the situation of mate. It was in vain I assured him that my practical knowledge of seamanship was limited, and what little I once knew I had forgotten during my residence in the West Indies. He said he knew me better than I knew myself; he would excuse all imperfections, as he had seamanship enough for both, and to spare. I was not convinced; I had also some misgivings in regard to the weakness which he had exhibited, amid danger and death, on the passage through the Caribbean Sea; and I feared he had contracted a habit which would render any man unfit for a situation involving great responsibilities, not only in relation to property but also of life. Nevertheless, I gladly embraced the opportunity to remain on board for a time. The brig would probably be several weeks in port, and my future course could be guided by circumstances.

The moral condition of New Orleans at this period the year 1816-1817 was deplorable. For vice and immorality, it doubtless bore away the palm from every city in Christendom or heathen lands. Gaming houses, and vile, disgusting receptacles of vice and infamy, were thickly scattered over every part of the city. Midnight brawls and robberies were frequent; and hard-fought fisticuff encounters, sometimes between two individuals, and sometimes between two squads of half a dozen on-a-side, were taking place on the levee, or in its neighborhood, almost every hour in the day.

The population of the city was of the most heterogeneous character. Frenchman and Spaniards, of all complexions, native- born citizens, formed the basis. To them were added a thin sprinkling of Yankees, mostly enterprising business men; and an influx of refugees, adventurers, smugglers, pirates, gamblers, and desperate scoundrels from all parts of the world. The large number of ships waiting for freight, and constantly arriving, furnished a formidable body of sailors, many of them old men-of- war's men, who, keeping themselves well primed with whiskey, were always ready for a set-to, a riot, or a row. And if we add to these the boatmen of the Mississippi, not only those who came down the river in flatboats, but that numerous class, now extinct, of hardy, powerful, reckless, quarrelsome fellows who managed the KEELBOATS, the only craft that could stem the current of the Mississippi before the introduction of steamboat navigation, it will be easily imagined that vice struggled hard to exercise full and uncontrolled dominion over the capital of Louisiana.

Ineffectual efforts were made to repress tumult and establish order. The police regulations were in a wretched condition. The police officers were more inclined to look after the blacks than the whites; and the calaboose was filled every night with unfortunate darkies, who in a humble way were imitating the vices of the more enlightened CASTE. When symptoms of a serious riot appeared, the military were called out. On more than one occasion, the sailors on one side to the number of two or three hundred, and the Kentucky and Tennessee boatmen of equal or superior numbers on the other, were drawn up in battle array, and commenced a desperate contest with hard knuckles, bludgeons, and missiles of every description, revolvers and bowie-knives had not at that time been introduced into such MELEES, when the military made their appearance, and the belligerents were dispersed.

Fighting on the levee became an established custom, and was sometimes resorted to as an exciting pastime. If a couple of "old salts" quarrelled under the stimulus of a glass of grog, instead of bandying words, and pouring into each other a broadside of vulgar epithets, they quietly adjourned to the levee and took it out in hard knocks, and after having fought with desperation, and pummelled each other out of all resemblance to human beings, they would go on board their ship and cheerfully attend to their duties.

One day I watched with no little interest a pitched battle between a wooden-legged sailor and a French stevedore. The sailor, although he was wanting in one of his limbs, was said to be a valuable seaman one who would never shrink from work of any kind. He would go aloft in a gale or in a calm, and lend a hand at reefing or furling as promptly as any man in the ship. His wooden leg was so constructed, with iron machinery, at the extremity, that he could stand on a ratline or a hawse without difficulty. The stevedore, who was a powerful fellow, expected to make short work of the cripple, taking it for granted that Jack could not stand firm on his pins; and indeed, almost at the beginning of the combat, the man with the timber toe was capsized. His opponent, flushed with success, and disregarding the rules of honorable warfare, determined to give Jack a drubbing while he lay sprawling on his back. But as he approached him with mischievous intent, his fist clinched and his eyes flashing fire and fury, Jack watched his opportunity, and gave him two or three kicks with his iron-shod wooden leg in swift succession. They were so strongly and judiciously planted that the astonished Frenchman was compelled to measure HIS length on the ground, from which, to is great pain and mortification, he was unable to rise, and wooden- leg hobbled off with the palm of victory.

The most savage and revolting contest which I witnessed was a "rough and tumble" fight between two Mississippi boatmen. One was a young man, of slight frame, and rather prepossessing appearance; the other was a burly, broad-shouldered ruffian from Tennessee. The quarrel originated in a gaming house, over a pack of cards, and the parties adjourned to the street to settle the matter in regular style. But few words were interchanged. They grasped each other firmly by the waist, and after a severe struggle for the mastery, both fell heavily to the earth, when the real battle commenced. In a close, but not loving embrace, they rolled over and over again. No blows were given; they seemed to be clutching at each other's faces, but their motions were so quick, violent, and spasmodic that I could not see how their hands were occupied. The struggle was soon over; the Kentuckian released himself from the relaxed grasp of his prostrate antagonist, and sprang to his feet. He looked around on the spectators with a smile of triumph, then entered the miniature Pandemonium, apparently without having received injury. His vanquished opponent was assisted to his feet. He was groaning, quivering in every limb, and manifesting symptoms of insufferable agony. I pressed forward, eager to ascertain what injury he had received in this strangely conducted combat, when, to my great horror, I saw the blood streaming from his cheeks, and shuddered as I witnessed other and unmistakable proofs of a successful attempt at gouging.

Nor were these pugnacious propensities, which seemed epidemical, confined to the lowest classes in society. They were manifested by those who moved in a higher sphere, and who, looking with contempt on vulgar fisticuffs and gouging, settled their difficulties satisfactorily according to the established rules of the DUELLO with sword, pistol, or rifle. Hostile meetings on the levee, below the city, where the population was sparse, and no impertinent interruptions could be apprehended, were frequent. Indeed, the intelligence, some pleasant morning, that a duel had just been fought, and one of the parties lamed in the sword arm, or scientifically run through the body with a small sword, or bored through the cranium with a pistol-bullet, excited little attention or remark, excepting among the friends and relatives of the parties.

One duel, however, was fought while I was in New Orleans, which, being attended with some unusual circumstances, caused considerable talk. The principals were a French gentleman and a lieutenant in the navy of the United States. A dispute occurred in a billiard room; the Frenchman used some insolent and irritating language, and, instead of being soundly drubbed on the spot, was challenged by the naval officer. The challenged party selected the small sword as the medium of satisfaction, a weapon in the use of which he was well skilled. The American officer was remonstrated with by his friends on the folly of fighting a Frenchman, a noted duellist, with his favorite weapon, the small sword; it was rushing on certain death. But the challenge had been given, accepted, and the weapons agreed on; there could be no change in the arrangement; and, indeed, the Yankee, who was a fine, determined-looking young fellow, showed no disposition to "back out. "

"I may fall in battle, " said he, "by the sword or shot of a brave Englishman, but never by a thrust from a spit in the hands of a spindle-shanked Frenchman! Dismiss all fears on my account; I will give this 'PARLEZ-VOUS FRANCAIS' a lesson in fighting he little dreams of. "

They met on the duelling ground at the appointed hour. There were more spectators present than usual on such occasions. The Frenchman affected to treat the matter with indifference, and made some frivolous remarks which excited the laughter of his countrymen. Indeed, the chances seemed to be a hundred to one against the lieutenant, who could handle with terrible effect a cutlass or a boarding-pike, but was almost a stranger to a weapon, to excel in the use of which, a man must be as loose in the joints as a posture maker, and as light in the heels as a dancing master. And yet there was something in the cool, resolute, business-like bearing of the Yankee which inspired his friends with some confidence in his success; and they watched the proceedings under an intense degree of excitement.

The parties took their places, assumed the proper attitudes, and crossed swords. The Frenchman grinned with anticipated triumph. It was clear that, confident in his skill, and richly endowed with feline propensities, he intended to amuse himself and the bystanders for a few minutes, by playing with his intended victim. His antagonist, however, stood firm, until the Frenchman, with a nimble caper, changed his ground, when the officer bounded forward, got within the guard of his opponent, and with a thrust, the force of which nothing could withstand, sent his sword, apparently, through the body of the Frenchman to the hilt!

The poor fellow was hurled to the ground by the violence of the shock, and supposed to be mortally wounded. That he was not KILLED outright was certain, for, owing to surprise and grief at this unlooked-for result, the fear of death, or extreme physical pain, he discharged a volley of screams that could be heard a mile off, writhed and twisted his body into all sorts of shapes, and manufactured, gratuitously, a continuous and ever-changing series of grimaces, for which the younger Grimaldi would have pawned his cap and bawble.

The wails and contortions of the wounded man were such, that it was some time before his friends and a surgeon who was present could examine his condition, which appeared deplorable enough. Indeed, an examination seemed hardly necessary, unless for the purpose of gratifying curiosity, as the wretched man, amid his groans and screams, kept repeating, with much emphasis and pathos, the terrible words, "JE SUIS ASSASSINE! JE SUIS ASSASSINE! (I am killed! I am killed!) But as his voice grew stronger, instead of weaker, at every repetition of the phrase, doubts were entertained of his veracity; and a surgical inspection showed beyond cavil, that he was laboring under a hallucination, and asseverating with needless energy what was not strictly true.

That he was not killed on the spot, however, impaled on a rapier as an unscrupulous entomologist would impale a beetle, could hardly be regarded as the fault of his opponent. The thrust was directed to the place where the centre of the body of the Frenchman should have been, BUT IT WAS NOT THERE. The sword passed only through the muscles of the abdomen, from the right side to the left, perforating his body, it is true, and grazing, but not injuring, the larger intestines. The wound in itself was not a dangerous one, although the disturbance among the bundle of integuments threw the discomfited duellist into almost mortal agony, and led him to believe he was a dead man, while experiencing in his own person a liberal share of the pain he was so ready to inflict on others.

Chapter XXXIII A VOYAGE TO HAVRE

The Betsey remained some weeks at the levee at New Orleans before Mr. Ware could fix upon a voyage. In the mean time Ricker remained on board as master of the brig; and for several days after our arrival in port his habits were correct and his conduct without reproach. Gradually, however, he strayed from the paths of sobriety. He was of a social turn; frank, honest cheerful, and liberal-minded. He possessed other valuable traits of character; was a good sailor and a skilful navigator, but he could not resist the fascinations of the intoxicating cup.

Intemperance disqualifies a man from employments where the exercise of cool judgment, and clear, undisturbed reasoning faculties are required; and no person addicted to habits of intemperance should be intrusted with the command of a ship, where property to a large amount and lives of incalculable value, are, as it were, given into his hands. If records of disasters could be faithfully (here the page is torn and cannot be read) and unfolded, we should have an appalling list of easy (torn page) quarrels, mutinies, and shipwrecks which have (torn page) caused by intemperance on the part of the (torn page.)

Mr. Ware, the commercial agent of Mr. Gray (torn page) the brig had seen Ricker more than once intoxicated which roused his suspicions that all was not (torn page) unlucky afternoon he found him in a helpless condition, which convinced him that Mr. Ricker, notwithstanding his excellent qualities, was not a (torn page) could be safely given the control of (torn page) the high seas.

Ricker was mortified at losing, through (torn page) the command of the brig. He (torn page) however, of harsh or unjust treatment on the part of Mr. Ware; and consented to remain as mate, promising to refrain entirely from the use of spirituous liquors. The command was given to an officer in the United States navy, Lieutenant Rapp; and in this way I was ousted from the berth which Ricker was so desirous I should fill. There was no longer a home for me in the cabin of the Betsey, and I shipped as an ordinary seaman on board the brig Casket, of New York, Captain Mott, bound on a voyage to Havre.

The Casket was a large and handsome brig, and besides the captain, mate, boatswain, and cook, carried six hands before the mast. The chief mate was a hard-looking customer, somewhat advanced in years, rough in his manners, and profane and coarse in his language. But the captain was a fine-looking man, about thirty years old, rather dignified and reserved. His appearance spoke volumes in his favor, and the crew who joined the ship in New Orleans rejoiced in this opportunity of shipping in a fine vessel, with a whole-souled captain, and bound on a European voyage!

Before we reached the Gulf of Mexico, however, the (torn page) sang a different tune. They found the mate more (torn page) unreasonable, and every way disagreeable, if (torn page) than he looked; and the captain evidently re- (torn page) sailor as a piece of machinery to be wound up (torn page) for the performance of certain duties, but (torn page) human attributes. Whether a heart beat (torn page) bosom, and his head was furnished with (torn page) Mott knew not, neither did he care. The (torn page) of any one of the crew were never (torn page) If a man was sick and incapacitated (torn page) was told, with an oath, to "bear a hand (torn page) not be skulking in the forecastle; " and (torn page) his duties, he was regaled with stern (torn page) language, and sent upon missions at times, and under circumstances, which showed that Captain Mott thought a few sailors, more or less, in the world, were of no manner of consequence.

In former days every Yankee shipmaster was not a live, wide-awake, pushing, driving, web-footed Jehu, who disregarded fogs, was reckless of collisions with ships, fishing vessels, or icebergs, and cared little whether he strained the ship and damaged cargo, provided he made a short passage, as is the case in this enlightened age when "Young America" is in the ascendant. An "old fogy" was occasionally met with, who, being well paid for his services by the month, prided himself more upon the STRENGTH of his ship's sailing than her rapidity. This appears from the following scene which once took place on board a Boston ship:

Captain Jarvis was lying in his berth, dreaming of a long passage and plenty of money at the end of it, when he was awakened by the unwonted noise of water under the counter, giving rise to the suspicion that the officer of the watch was carrying more sail than was expedient. He jumped out of his berth, rushed up the steps, popped his head out of the companion-way, and sharply exclaimed,

"Mr. Popkins, heave the log. "

Mr. Popkins: Ay ay, sir!

Captain Jarvis: How fast does the old ship go, Mr. Popkins?

Mr. Popkins: Nine knots, sir!

Captain Jarvis: Nine knots! Julius Caesar! I am astonished. Take in some of that canvas immediately, Mr. Popkins. I can't afford to sail so fast as nine knots.

Mr. Popkins: Ay, ay, sir.

The studding sails were hauled in, and the main royal and fore and mizzen top-gallant sails furled.

Captain Jarvis: How fast does she go now, Mr. Popkins?

Mr. Popkins (after heaving the log.) Seven knots and a half, sir!

Captain Jarvis: Too fast, sir much too fast! Take in more sail. Why, Mr. Popkins, we shall be at the end of our voyage before we know it, at this rate.

Mr. Popkins, with the men of the larboard watch, went to work, and in a few minutes the ship was running along quietly under her three topsails, jib, and spanker.

Captain Jarvis: Throw the log, Mr. Popkins.

Mr. Popkins: She is now going six knots, sir.

Captain Jarvis: Six knots! Very well very well indeed, Mr. Popkins. Always bear in mind that we are not paid by "the run, " or the voyage; and six knots is very fair sailing between man and man. It is better to sail strong than to sail fast. Don't let me catch you running off at the rate of nine knots again. Stick to six and you will do, otherwise there will be no wages coming to us when we get home. Do you hear, Mr. Popkins?

Mr. Popkins, gruffly, (he had a sprinkling of Young America in his composition.) Ay, ay, sir!

Although Captain Mott was sometimes deficient in judgment, and on more than one occasion narrowly escaped losing overboard some of the crew, or wrecking the brig, he was, nevertheless, an excellent seaman, managed his vessel with skill, and navigated her with unusual correctness. Not being paid by the month but by primage on the freight, he was a veritable "driver, " and lost no opportunity to urge his vessel ahead, even at the risk of starting a butt, springing a spar, or losing a man. Being always willing to work, on hand in any emergency, and never shrinking from danger, I was often a sufferer from his go-ahead instincts, as well as from his arbitrary mandates and unfeeling disposition. And were it not that there is,

> "A sweet little cherub which sits up aloft,
> And looks out for the life of poor Jack,"

I should have become food for fishes long before we reached the longitude of the Western Islands.

One afternoon, before we left the Gulf Stream, a thunder squall arose from the south-east. It came towards us rapidly, as if borne on the wings of the Genius of Storms. Its whole aspect was "wicked" in the extreme, and every man on board knew that prudence required sail to be taken in and preparations made for the reception of the tornado. The captain was on deck, but the boatswain unfortunately remarked, "That squall looks like an ugly customer, sir, and it will soon be necessary to shorten sail. "

This remark, made in the most respectful manner, roused the captain's ire. He chose to consider it an unauthorized and impertinent interference on the part of the petty officer; the squall, as well as the boatswain, was denounced in language not often heard in a drawing room, and both were consigned to a hotter place than the craters of Mauna Loa.

The clouds spread over the zenith, the thunder rattled as if it would rend the welkin, the wind began to blow in short-lived puffs, as if making preparations for a regular "blowout; " the men were stationed at the halliards, fore and aft, waiting with intense anxiety the result, and the captain was pacing the quarter-deck, looking as savage as a hungry bull-dog, and determined to show that he was not to be frightened by squibs, but would carry sail in spite of the squall.

At that time we were under courses, topsails, top-gallant-sails, and a main-royal; our fore-royal mast was snugly stowed alongside the long-boat on deck, where, at that tempestuous season, the main one should also have been. The order at length was given, "Clew up the main-royal! Let a hand go aloft and furl it. "

The sail was clewed up, and in a few seconds I was clinging to the sliding gunter royal mast, and gathering in the canvas, while the captain was denouncing me for a lubber, for not accomplishing impossibilities. The lightning was flashing around ne, and the peals of thunder were deafening; the rain was beginning to fall, and the wind to blow with alarming violence, before I could spill the sail and pass the gaskets. Suddenly I heard a tumultuous noise as of the roar of angry breakers. I cast my eye to windward, and beheld the whole surface of the sea covered with a sheet of snow-white foam. At the same moment I heard the voice of the captain, who was now really alarmed, in a tone which could be heard above the roar of the hurricane, shouting, with frantic energy, "Hard up your helm! Hard up, I say. Let go all the halliards, fore and aft! Haul up the mainsail! Lower away that try-sail! Clew down the top-gallant sails! Why don't you put the helm hard up? "

I was sensible of the danger of my situation, standing on "the hounds" of the top-gallant mast, and almost within reach of the truck, while the brig, with all sail set, was exposed to the fury of this terrible thunder gust. Obeying an irresistible impulse to take care of "number one, " I slid down the topmast cross-trees, caught hold of the weather top-gallant backstay, and came on deck much faster than I went aloft! My feet had hardly touched the deck when a gust struck the brig with a fury which I have seldom seen surpassed. It rushed upon us like an avalanche on a hamlet in an Alpine valley. Halliards, sheets, and tacks were let go, but the yards were still braced up, and the sails could not be clewed down. Before the vessel could get before the wind her lee side was buried in the water. The conviction seized every mind that a capsize was inevitable, and there was a general rush towards the weather gunwale, and a desperate clutching at the shrouds. At this critical moment the main-topmast snapped off like a pipe stem, just above the cap, and carried with it the fore-top-gallant mast. The brig righted, fell off before the wind, scudded like a duck, dragging the broken spars, and her sails torn to ribbons; and a cold shudder crept over me when I thought of the appalling danger from which by sliding down the backstay, I had so narrowly escaped.

When we struck soundings off the English Channel, the word was given to the boatswain to bend the cables and get the anchors over the bows. The wind was blowing hard from the northward, with violent squalls and a short head sea, and Captain Mott showed no disposition to reduce the canvas in order to lighten our labors, but carried sail and drove the vessel as if he was running from a pirate. The brig frequently plunged her knight-heads under water, deluging every man on the forecastle with sheets of salt water. In the mean time the captain, and also the mate, dry-shod on the quarter-deck, grinned, and winked at each other, at witnessing our involuntary ablutions, with the mercury at the freezing point, while subjected to this severe course of hydropathic treatment, and doing work which, under ordinary circumstances, could have been accomplished in a few hours.

Reefing a topsail in a gale is an evolution simple in itself; and when the sail is placed by the skill of the officer of the deck in a proper condition, the work aloft can be accomplished in five minutes, even by a bungling crew. But Captain Mott seemed to take pleasure in placing obstacles in the way of the ready performance of any important duty, and held the crew accountable for any extraordinary delay. Thus in reefing topsails, the men were sometimes half an hour on the yard, endeavoring in vain to do a work which his own obstinacy or ignorance rendered impracticable, and he, all the while, cursing and swearing at the crew for their inefficiency, in a style which would have done credit to the leader of a press-gang.

The men, generally, were good seamen, and able and willing to do their work, and with proper treatment would have proved first rate sailors; but it is an old and true saying that bad officers make a bad crew. When a man's best efforts are rewarded with abuse, it is unreasonable to expect that he will perform his various duties with alacrity and cheerfulness. It was customary, at that period, for rum to be served out to the crew, and the minimum allowance, in nearly all American vessels, was a glass of rum at dinner, with an extra glass during exposure to inclement weather, or when engaged in unusually fatiguing labors. This extra glass was generally served out by the steward at the companion-way, and the men were summoned to partake of this indulgence by a call to "splice the main brace. "

Captain Mott, however, refused to furnish the crew of the Casket with the usual daily allowance of grog. This refusal, there was reason to believe, was caused, not by a commendable wish to promote temperance, and break up habits of intoxication, but from a desire to gratify a surly and unamiable disposition, and deprive the men of an enjoyment which they highly prized. With such a captain and mate, and regulations of the most arbitrary and stringent character, it may be imagined that the grumbling at hard treatment, and the muttered curses against the inmates of the cabin, were neither few, nor far between.

But the captain, while he refused the DAILY allowance of grog, did not deem it advisable to withhold the usual allowance on Saturday night, when every true sailor loved to meet his shipmates around a flowing bowl, and pass a happy hour in lively conversation, singing sea songs, spinning yarns, and drinking with heartfelt emotion the toast of all others the dearest and best "Sweethearts and Wives. "

> "Of all the nights that grace the week,
> There's none can equal this;
> It binds the mind in friendship's bonds;
> It heightens social bliss.
> For though far distant from the land,
> At home our thoughts shall be,
> Whilst, shipmates, joining heart and hand
> Hail Saturday Night at Sea."

No one can imagine the tender, thrilling, and holy associations which cluster round those words, "Sweethearts and Wives, " unless he has been long separated from those he loves, a wanderer on a distant sea. That Saturday night toast came home to the bosom of every man who carried a heart beneath a blue jacket. The gallantry of the sailor has often been spoken of. His devotion to woman is proverbial. With few opportunities to mingle in female society, he can, nevertheless, truly estimate its value, and appreciate its advantages. Indeed, I have known old sailors, whose rough and wrinkled visages, blunt and repulsive manners, coarse and unrefined language, were enough to banish gentle Cupid to an iceberg, exhibit the kindest and tenderest feelings when speaking of

WOMAN, whom in the abstract they regarded as a being not merely to be protected, cherished, and loved, but also to be adored.

I shall never forget the well-deserved rebuke I once received from a sturdy old tar for an ill-timed comment on a woman's personal appearance. It was in St. Salvador. The captain of a Portuguese ship was going on shore accompanied by his wife. The boat crossed the bows of the ship I was in; the feminine garments attracted the attention of all hands, who suspended their work and gazed upon the charming object as if they beheld something more than mortal. As the boat passed onward, and we resumed labors which the glimpse of a petticoat had interrupted, with a want of gallantry which I trust is foreign to my character, for which I cannot even now account, and of which I was afterwards heartily ashamed, I casually remarked, "Well, there's nothing wonderful about her, after all; she's HOMELY enough, in all conscience! "

"Hawser, " said my old shipmate, in a solemn and impressive manner, gracefully waving the marlinspike which he held in his hand, "THERE IS NO SUCH THING IN NATER AS A HOMELY WOMAN! "

"Saturday Night" in olden times was not only devoted to reminiscences of home and affectionate associations, but was also the time selected for indulgence in the songs of the forecastle. After the usual toast, "Sweethearts and Wives, " had been drunk with enthusiasm, some one of the crew was called on for a song, and the call was responded to without affected reluctance; and the beams, carlines, and bulkheads of the old forecastle rang again with stirring songs or ballads poured forth from manly and musical throats, in praise of beauty, descriptive of life at sea, recording deeds of heroism, or inculcating lessons of patriotism.

To these songs of the forecastle, sung on the land as well as on the ocean, in beauty's bower as well as in the sailor's sanctuary or the stifled cabin, in days when accompaniments to vocal music were not considered necessary, when the full melodious sound of the human voice, THE NOBLEST MUSIC IN THE WORLD, was not strangled, drowned, or travestied by the noise of the everlasting piano, played with artistic skill to these spirit-stirring songs of the forecastle was commerce indebted for many of the finest and best sailors ever sprinkled with salt water.

The well known songs of "the Bay of Biscay, " "Black Eyed Susan, " and "Cease, Rude Boreas, " once listened to with emotion and delight at the cottage fireside, or the fashionable drawing room, and the many songs long since forgotten of a similar character, written by salt water poets, and sung by mariners at home and abroad, have transformed enthusiastic and adventurous landsmen into sailors by scores, as by the touch of an enchanter's wand. Dibdin did more to man the "wooden walls of old England" with brave and effective men than all the press-gangs that ever infested the banks of the Thames.

There was one man on board the Casket who, more than all others, aided to keep the crew cheerful and happy. He was the life and soul of the forecastle. Not all the oppressive and unfeeling acts of the captain, and rough and unjust treatment from the mate, which would naturally excite indignation and a discontented spirit, such as sometimes will lead to insubordination on the part of the crew, followed by the free use of handspikes, rope's ends, and manacles, on the part of the officers, could repress the spirits of Jonas Silvernail, spoil his jokes, or lessen the volume of his hearty and sonorous laugh. Jonas was a native of Hudson, in New York; a young, active, intelligent sailor, who, always good-humored, was never more happy than when singing a sea song, spinning a merry yarn, or playing off a practical joke. Jonas was one of those jovial mortals who seemed determined to make sure of present enjoyment, and let the future take care of itself; to bask in the sunshine of life, while others despondingly wilt in the shade.

Good humor is contagious; and it was owing to the cheerful, contented spirit, infused among the crew of the Casket by Silvernail's example, that they forbore from insolent remonstrances, and wisely resolved to bear the ills they had, rather,

"Than fly to others which they knew not of. "

Such a man in the forecastle of a ship and in my seafaring days such men were not rare is a treasure. He lightens the labors of a crew, adds to the harmony and happiness of all on board, shortens a passage, and, as a natural consequence, promotes the interests of the owner.

On one occasion, however, Silvernail's fondness for fun threatened to disturb the harmony which was wont to reign in the forecastle. Among the crew was a big, clumsy Dutchman, through whose thick cranium no joke could penetrate, and whose feet were of proportions as huge as his head, each resembling, in size and shape, a Brazilian catamaran. The men conversing one day of the dangers of the seas, and the best means of preserving life in cases of shipwreck, or when accidentally falling overboard, Hans, who cherished a strong attachment to his own dear person, expressed a regret that he had no cork jacket, by whose aid he could float above the waves.

"Be under no concern on that account, " remarked Jonas. "If you were in the water, a cork jacket would be of no more use to you than a pair of curling tongs to Cuffy, the black cook. But don't try to swim. TREAD WATER lustily with those mud scows (pointing to his feet) and you will never go to the bottom. "

"You just let my foot alone, " said Hans, his face glowing with indignation. "You are always poking fun at my foot, and I don't half like it. My foot is one very good foot, (holding it up, and swaying it backwards and forwards;) just fit to kick an impudent vagabone with and teach him better manners. "

"That may be true, " said Silvernail, with a provoking grin; "but if you should chance to miss the vagabone, as you call him, YOUR FOOT WOULD FLY OFF! "

This, and the loud laugh from his shipmates, with which it was attended, was more than even the phlegmatic Dutchman could bear. He made a furious pass at Jonas with his much-abused foot, which, if it had taken effect, would have demolished the joker in a twinkling. But Jonas stepped aside, caught the ponderous foot in his hand, and the next moment Hans was sprawling on his back. He arose, breathing guttural but incomprehensible denunciations against his tormentor, who escaped from his clutches by nimbly running up the ratlines to the foretop, where he could safely indulge his merriment over the wrath of the Dutchman.

I was often amused at the ingenious manner in which Jonas managed to get over a difficulty. One day when, with the wind abaft the beam, blowing a strong breeze, we were carrying a main-topmast studding sail, the boatswain very properly undertook to get up a preventer-brace on the weather main yard-arm. A rope was procured, which had already been considerably worn, and the boatswain expressed some apprehension that it was hardly strong enough for the service required. "O, " said Jonas in an off-hand, decided manner, "it will hold on until it breaks; and if it was ever so strong it could do no more. "

The boatswain appeared favorably struck with the unanswerable logic embraced in the remark, and made no further objection to the rope.

On this voyage I had one source of pleasure, of an elevated character, which was denied to the rest of my shipmates. This was my attachment to books. Before I left New Orleans, I purchased a variety of second-hand volumes; a miscellaneous collection, which enabled me to pass many pleasant hours on our passage to Havre, and at the same time lay in a stock of information which might prove of great value at a future day.

In books I found biographies of good men, whose example fortified my mind against the temptations to vice and immorality, which beset the sailor on every side. They furnished me with an interesting occupation in an idle hour, acted as a solace for disappointment, and a faithful friend and consoler in anxiety and trouble; inspired me with a feeling of emulation, and bade me look forward with hope. Many is the hour when, after a hard day's work, or an exciting scene of peril or suffering, by the dim light of a tallow candle, or a lamp manufactured by my own hands, while others were lamenting their hard fate, or pouring out their indignation in unavailing grumblings, I have, while poring over a book, lost all sense of unhappiness, and been transported far away to other and happier scenes; sometimes exploring with Barrow the inhospitable wastes of Africa; accompanying Christian on his journey to the Celestial City; sympathizing with the good Vicar of Wakefield in his domestic misfortunes; sharing the disquietudes of Rasselas in the "Happy Valley; " tracing, with almost breathless interest, the career of some ancient hero whom Plutarch has immortalized, or lingering over the thrilling adventures and perils of "Sindbad the Sailor. "

A sailor before the mast, as well as the inmates of the cabin, has many hours on every voyage, which may be and should be, devoted to reading and study. When a resident of the forecastle, I have by my example, and by urgent appeals to the pride, the ambition, and good sense of my shipmates, induced them to cultivate a taste for reading, and awakened in their minds a thirst for information. Some of these men, by dint of hard study, and a determination, even at a late day, to shake off all profligate habits, and be something more than a common sailor, qualified themselves for a different station, and eventually became respectable shipmasters and merchants.

We lost one of our crew overboard, on this passage, in a manner somewhat singular. He was an Italian, called Antonio, and remarkable for a love of cleanliness a priceless virtue, when not carried to excess. He was continually washing his face and hands, as if to get rid of impurities communicated by the atmosphere. One Sunday afternoon, with a strong breeze on the quarter, the brig was reeling it off at the rate of eight or nine knots, and a rough and turbulent sea was helping her along. Notwithstanding the wind was three or four points abaft the beam, Captain Mott insisted on carrying main-topmast and middle staysails, and occasionally when the vessel was a little off of her course, the main-topmast staysail sheet, which was fastened to a cleat in the main deck, would give a "slat, " with great violence. Antonio had just left the helm, and, according to his usual custom, proceeded to draw a bucket of water from alongside, in which to immerse his face and hands. But while he was stooping, in the very act of performing his ablutions, the brig, through the inattention of the helmsman, was run off her course nearly before the wind, the staysails were becalmed and the main-topmast staysail sheet, that is, the rope which kept the sail in its proper position, give a terrible jerk, caught the unfortunate Italian behind, lifted him from his feet, and actually tossed him over the gunwale. The thing was so sudden, he had not time to struggle, or even to scream, as he sank beneath the billows, while the brig swept onward, leaving him far astern. The cry, "A man's overboard! " was instantly raised by those who witnessed the sad event. One man sprang into the weather main shrouds in order to keep an eye on the poor fellow who became a martyr to cleanliness. The helm was put down, the brig rounded to, and sails laid aback. But attempts to rescue him were fruitless. He was not seen after he struck the water.

After having been about forty-five days at sea, we got sight one morning of "the Caskets, " in the middle of the English Channel, about thirty miles west of Cape LaHogue, and on the following day entered the harbor of Havre, the seaport of Paris, situated at the mouth of the Seine.

Chapter XXXIV THE GENERAL ARMSTRONG

Nothing remarkable happened during our stay in Havre, excepting an unpleasant affair in which our good-humored shipmate, Jonas Silvernail, played a principal part. The master of an English brig, an ignorant man, but excessively arrogant and presuming, one day took some of our men to task on the quay, accusing them of having taken a portion of his crew to a grog-shop, where they plied them with liquor until they were drunk, and then left them alone in their glory.

Jonas, in behalf of the crew of the Casket, stoutly but respectfully denied the correctness of the statement, so far as himself or his shipmates were concerned, and was about making an explanation, which must have been satisfactory, when he was interrupted by the excited Briton, who not only gave him the lie direct, but went so far as to define, in coarse and profane language, the particular character of the lie.

Jonas, although a model of subordination on shipboard, nevertheless possessed the spirit of a man, and would not brook abuse or insolence from any one who had no rightful authority over him. His eye sparkled, his lip quivered, and his fingers convulsively contracted, while he remarked, in a tone somewhat emphatic, "When a blackguard gives a gentleman the lie, he is, of course, prepared to defend himself! "

Acting upon this supposition he levelled a blow at the Englishman's face, which laid his cheek open to the bone, and stretched him on the wharf in double-quick time, as flat as a halibut!

Here was a pretty business! The affair looked serious for Jonas, as the Englishman swore vengeance against the Yankee ruffian, if there was any law or justice among a frog-eating people! Jonas was arrested, but by the kind agency of Mr. Beasley, the American consul, he was relieved from restraint on payment of a moderate fine. The choleric Briton was taught a valuable lesson, and in all likelihood put a curb on his tongue ever afterwards when talking to strangers, especially if the stranger happened to be a Yankee!

After having discharged our cargo of cotton, we sailed from Havre in ballast. We encountered a strong head wind in the chops of the

Channel, and were beating about for several days. One night we were steering a course about north-north-west, under single-reefed topsails, courses and spanker, with the wind at west, while the fog was so thick that the jib-boom could hardly be seen from the forecastle, and supposed ourselves at least thirty miles to the southward of the Scilly Islands. Jonas and myself, who were walking the main deck, while the boatswain was leaning lazily against the quarter rail, and the captain and mate were sleeping in their berths below, were startled by a dull, moaning sound, which, ever and anon, seemed to come up from under the lee bow. The noise became more distinct. "What can it be? " said I, alarmed.

"I know it now, " exclaimed Jonas. "It is the ROTE of the breakers dashing against the rocks, and we must be lively, or we shall soon be in kingdom come. Boatswain! " shouted he, "Breakers! Breakers ahead! Call up the captain! " and hastening forward he made such a noise on the forecastle as to rouse out all hands, who rushed on deck marvellously lightly clad, but prepared to encounter some mighty evil.

The captain was awakened by the word "breakers, " a word which sounds ominous in a sailor's ears, and was on deck in a trice. He heard the rumbling noise, the character of which could not be mistaken. "Ready about! ": he screamed. "Stations, men! Hard down the helm! "

The brig came up into the wind, the sails shivered, but owing to the head sea or some other cause, she would not come round, and soon gathered stern way. But captain Mott was a good seaman. "Brace round the head yards! " he exclaimed. "Lower away the spanker peak! "

The brig, by the action of the helm, the head sails being thrown aback, fell off rapidly on her heel, and soon gathering headway, barely cleared the dark and rugged cliffs of St. Agnes in the north, which now, as well as the powerful beacon light by which they were surmounted, broke through the dense fog.

It was a narrow escape. Fifteen minutes more would have carried us among the sunken rocks and ledges which are piled together in admirable confusion on the southwest side of the Scilly Isles, and the vessel and all hands would have been among the things which were.

The wind came round to the eastward on the following day, and we shaped our course across the Atlantic, bound for Savannah, whither we arrived, without the occurrence of any remarkable incident, about the first of May, 1817.

Having passed a couple of months in Savannah a few years before, I was aware from personal inspection of the wretchedly low character of the sailor boarding houses in that city; and I shuddered at the idea of passing the few days or weeks of my sojourn in Savannah at one of these "omnium gatherums" of intemperance and iniquity.

I gave to my shipmates such a graphic but faithful description of the sailor boarding houses in Savannah, that the boatswain of the brig, with Jonas Silvernail and William Jones, agreed to join me in trying to secure quarters of a character somewhat more respectable than the dens of iniquity frequented by sailors. We flattered ourselves there would be no difficulty in finding such a boarding house as we wished, knowing there were many mechanics at that time in Savannah, temporary residents, who were accommodated with board in well-regulated families at a reasonable rate, and we saw no reason why we should not be treated with equal favor.

Accordingly, the day after our arrival in port, having received our discharge, we carefully removed from our hands all stains of tar, rigged ourselves out in our neatest apparel, put on our most sober and demure faces, and started off on a cruise after a boarding house. We had received some desultory information from persons we had fallen in with about the wharves, which in a measure influenced our course.

We were not particularly successful in our quest. The simple fact which we could not deny, that "WE WERE SAILORS, " was sufficient to bar every door against our entrance. It was in vain we represented ourselves as remarkably staid and sober sailors, possessing amiable dispositions, not given to liquor or rowdyism, and in search of quiet quarters in a respectable family.

To all this the one fatal objection was opposed, "WE WERE SAILORS, " and of course could not reasonably expect to be received into any respectable house. No faith was given to our professions of sobriety. The term "sailor" in the minds of those good people was synonymous with "blackguard" or "drunken vagabond. " It comprehended everything which was vile or wicked. After applying at more than a dozen different places, and finding the estimate of a sailor's character every where the same, and that exceptions to the general rule in this case were not allowed, we reluctantly abandoned our exploring expedition, disgusted and mortified at finding such unfounded prejudice existing against sailors, whom WE not only believed to be human beings, and entitled to rights, privileges, and indulgences as such, but a class of men which actually included many worthy, honest, well-behaved individuals, as well as those of an opposite character. We could not but doubt the policy as well as justice of a line of conduct which represses every effort on the part of seafaring men to cultivate a self- respect, and elevate themselves in the scale of society; a line of conduct which is calculated to thrust them contemptuously back, and plunge them deeper in the slough from which, perhaps, they are striving to emerge.

In those days there was no "Mariner's House" or "Sailor's Home" established in our large seaports by true philanthropists for the benefit of seamen, where this useful but too long neglected and condemned class might find a quiet, well-regulated, and respectable house, with its doors thrown open to receive them.

We returned, crestfallen and disheartened, to the brig, and passed another night in the forecastle; and the next morning, being compelled to find an asylum on shore, we inspected several of the sailor boarding houses, with a view to select the least objectionable for our temporary home. There was little room for choice. The landlords were all swaggering foreigners; their rooms were filled with a dense effluvia arising from a combination of odors, in which the fumes of tobacco and rum constituted a prominent part; and drinking grog, playing cards and dominoes, swearing, quarrelling, and fighting seemed to be the principal occupation and amusements of the main portion of the boarders.

Such were the scenes I was destined to witness in Savannah; such were the men with whom I was compelled to associate; such were the temptations to which I was subjected, and which few could pass through unscathed; such were MY "schools and schoolmasters" in early life.

After much hesitation and many misgivings, we finally established our quarters at the sign of the "General Armstrong, " which was kept by John Hubbard, a tight little Irishman, a regular "broth of a boy, " illiterate, not being able to write his name, with a tongue well steeped in blarney, with a conscience as elastic as a piece of India rubber, and a consummate adept in the art of wheedling a sailor out of his money.

The sign which was placed conspicuously over the door of this boarding house was a popular one, and well calculated to attract. It was not intended to represent General Armstrong of revolutionary memory, the avowed author of the treasonable "Newburg Letters, " but the American privateer of that name, riding at anchor, and in the act of battling with the British boats in Fayal. Hubbard had been a petty officer in the privateer, and prided himself on the part which he took in that memorable affair, and on which he dearly loved to dwell, to the great admiration of his half-drunken auditors.

The General Armstrong privateer was a brig belonging to New York, mounting a battery of eight long nines and a twenty-four pounder amidships. The brig, a remarkably fast sailing vessel, was commanded by Samuel C. Reid, a young and gallant sailor, who displayed much courage, activity, and skill in harassing the enemies of his country on the high seas, and had been successful in capturing many valuable British ships.

While cruising off the Western Islands in the autumn of 1814, the privateer being short of water, to procure a supply put into Fayal on the morning of the 26th of September. On the afternoon of the same day three English ships-of-war arrived, anchored at the entrance of the harbor, and received from the pilots and fishermen intelligence that the far-famed American privateer General Armstrong was then in port, and lying beneath the guns of the fortifications.

Captain Reid, witnessing the arrival of these ships, did not consider himself altogether safe from attack. He knew that his vessel was particularly obnoxious to the British, who would be likely to disregard neutrality laws, spare no pains, and overcome almost any scruples in order to insure her destruction; also, that Portugal was a feeble power, which existed only by the sufferance and protection of Great Britain. Therefore Captain Reid, instead of relying on international law as a barrier against aggression, determined to rely on himself and the brave men with him; and when the British ships appeared in the offing, he commenced making vigorous preparations for defence. As soon as it was twilight he commenced warping his vessel nearer the shore. This manoeuver was seen from the decks of the English squadron, which consisted of the Plantagenet ship-of-the-line, the Rota frigate, and the Carnation gun-brig; and four boats were immediately sent off, filled with armed men, who pulled directly towards the privateer.

But Captain Reid was watching the movements of the enemy. He ordered his men to pause in their labors, and stand ready to give their visitors a warm reception. When the boats arrived within speaking distance, he hailed, but received no answer; the boats pulled on in gloomy silence. He hailed again, but there was no reply, but the men redoubled their efforts at the oars. Captain Reid, aware there was no time to be lost, hailed a third time, ordering the boats to keep off, or he would fire into them. The boats kept on. The word was given to "FIRE, " and a volley of musketry was poured into the densely crowded boats, causing great confusion and killing and wounding a large number of the crews. The fire, however, was returned by the British, and the first lieutenant of the privateer was severely wounded and one man was killed. After a sharp, but severe contest, in which the enemy made desperate attempts to get alongside, the boats hauled off and returned to their respective ships.

Captain Reid knew this was only the beginning of the drama. He encouraged his men, and got in readiness for a more serious engagement. He moored his vessel close to the shore, loaded his large guns to the muzzle with grape and canister, and every musket with bullets and buckshot. His men were all on deck ready and eager to meet the foe.

The moon had risen, and lighted up the bay, so that objects could be distinctly seen at a considerable distance. And soon after midnight, twelve boats, carrying nearly four hundred men, and armed with carronades, swivels, and blunderbusses, as well as muskets, pistols, and cutlasses, left the squadron and pulled directly for the privateer. The crisis was at hand, and although the brave commander of the privateer knew that his vessel must eventually fall into the hands of his unscrupulous enemy, he determined to defend her to the last.

A fierce and desperate engagement ensued. As soon as the boats came within range, they were greeted with the contents of "long Tom; " and the nine pounders also faithfully performed their work. The guns were served with almost incredible skill and activity, and aimed with the nicest precision. The fire was returned by the boats, although it was evident that some of them suffered severely from the effects of the first broadside. Others, however, dashed alongside, with the expectation of carrying the privateer by boarding; but here, again, they were disappointed. Pistols and muskets flashed from every porthole, and boarding-pikes and cutlasses, wielded by strong hands, presented a CHEVAUX-DE-FRISE which the enemy could not overleap. The carnage was terrible; the contest lasted over half an hour, and resulted in the total defeat of the British, who, with bull-dog ferocity and obstinacy, although foiled in their desperate effort to take the privateer, were unwilling to abandon the enterprise, and were shot and hewn down by scores. Only three of the officers escaped; several of the boats were destroyed, and two of them, after the action, were found alongside the brig, literally filled with the dead and dying!

The boats which survived the conflict, crushed and discomfited, pulled slowly back to their ships, bearing with them many of the wounded. Of the four hundred who left the ships an hour and a half before, full of health, high in spirits, and eager for the battle, hardly one hundred and fifty returned unharmed.

The attack on the boats by Captain Reid and his brave men was so sudden and overwhelming, that the enemy, notwithstanding the convulsive efforts of a few, seemed incapable of making any effective resistance. Instead of being the attacking party, their efforts were mainly confined to ineffectual attempts to defend themselves. Thus, on the part of the Americans, the loss in the two engagements was only two killed and seven wounded. One of those who fell was Mr. Williams, of New York, the second lieutenant. The first and third lieutenants were among the wounded. Thus, early in the action Captain Reid was deprived of the services of his most efficient officers, but he was equal to the emergency, and his cool and intrepid conduct secured the victory.

On the following morning, soon after daybreak, the Carnation gun-brig was hauled in within point blank gun-shot, and opened a fire on the General Armstrong; but the gallant commander of the privateer, being determined to submit to no other than a superior force, returned the fire with his long twenty-four pounder so effectually, boring the brig through and through at every shot, that she was soon glad to haul off to avoid being sunk at her anchors. Preparations were now making to bring in the frigate; and aware that to prolong the contest would be worse than useless, Captain Reid ordered the brig's masts to be cut away, a hole blown through her bottom, and with all his men, trunks, chests, and baggage, took to his boats and safely reached the shore. They had not been landed fifteen minutes when the dismasted sinking vessel was boarded by the British boats without resistance, and immediately set on fire. Such was the fate of the General Armstrong privateer!

It is perhaps not strange that, before my shipmates and myself had been a week at the boarding house, around whose attractive sign clustered such patriotic associations, Downes, the boatswain of the Casket, and Jones both became acclimated to the noxious atmosphere redolent of alcohol and other disgusting compounds, succumbed to the temptations by which they were surrounded, and drank as much grog, were as noisy and unruly, and as ready for a quarrel as any dissolute old Irishman in the whole circle of Jim Hubbards' household. Indeed the boatswain, a young fellow possessed of many excellent qualities, and who had made a resolution to reform some bad habits in which he had indulged, got drunk before he had been three days an inmate of the establishment, quarrelled with an English sailor, fought with him, was severely whipped and furnished with a couple of magnificent black eyes. So true is the sentiment, beautifully expressed in the language of the poet,

"Vice is a monster of so frightful mien,
As to be hated needs but to be seen;
But seen too oft, familiar with the face,
We first endure, then pity, then embrace."

The generality of Jim Hubbard's boarders were what may be technically termed "a hard set. " Among them were many foreigners, who seemed to have been the off-scourings of their native countries, and whose manners and morals had not been improved by the peculiar discipline and lessons in ethics they had become familiar with on board English men-of-war or Patriot privateers. In truth they were a band of roistering blades, and by day and by night, when not dead drunk, were restless, noisy, vociferous, and terribly profane. Flush with their money, and acting from generous impulses, they would urge a stranger to drink with them in good fellowship, and if the invitation was declined, were equally ready to knock him down or kick him into the street, as unworthy the society of good fellows.

Whole crews came to the house, from long voyages, with pockets overflowing with cash. They were received with smiles of welcome by Hubbard, and the treasures of his bar were placed before them. At the proper time they were told by their obliging landlord that it was a praiseworthy custom among new comers to "treat all hands. " Then commenced a course of unrestrained dissipation, which was not interrupted so long as their money held out. They became uproarious, and took a strange pleasure in enacting scenes, which should never be witnessed out of Bedlam. But as their money diminished their landlord gave them the cold shoulder; their love of frolic and fighting was sensibly lessened, and their spirits at last fell to zero on being told by their sympathizing host, who kept a careful watch over their finances, and kindly aided them in spending their money by making fictitious charges, and exacting double prices for what they actually had, that THEIR CASH WAS ALL GONE; that it was not his custom to give credit, and the sooner they found a ship, and cleared out, the better.

Such, I am sorry to say, was the character of most of the sailor landlords in "days lang syne. " And notwithstanding the efforts which have since been made to elevate the condition of the sailor, and provide him with a comfortable house on shore, I greatly fear the race is not extinct; and that Jack, even in these days, often becomes the prey of one of these crafty, plausible, smiling, unprincipled scoundrels, who hands him a bottle of rum with one hand and picks his pocket with the other; who, under the guise of friendship, bears towards the sailor the same kind of affection he is prepared to expect from the man-eating shark which is seen prowling round a ship. If he falls into the clutches of either, he is sure to be taken in and done for.

But among Jim Hubbard's boarders, there were a very few of a different character from those I have described; some who kept sober, and had a due regard to the rules of propriety. These, sometimes, sought to restore order out of chaos, but soon abandoned the attempt as a bootless task, and bowed submissively to the storm whose force they could not arrest. Among these was a young man named Catlin. He was rather below than above the medium size, but had a broad chest and a muscular frame. He was evidently a thorough sailor; his countenance was open and intelligent; he was quiet and unobtrusive in his manners, and often seemed disgusted with the unruly conduct of the major part of the boarders, some of whom had been shipmates with him in a former voyage. Catlin was troubled with an impediment in his speech, and it was doubtless owing to this, as well as to his sober habits, that his voice was seldom heard amid the vocal din which shook the walls of the General Armstrong.

One morning a large ship arrived in Savannah from Boston, with a choice crew, consisting of the boatswain and ten fine-looking, athletic young men. After the ship was made fast at the wharf, and the decks cleared up, the crew received permission to go ashore; and, neatly rigged and headed by the boatswain, a splendid looking, symmetrically built native of Connecticut, who stood six feet two inches in his stockings, and wore a feather in his hat like a Highland chieftain, they paraded through several of the streets of Savannah, singing, laughing, and cheering, bent on a regular frolic. They occasionally stopped at hospitable houses, where "for a consideration" they could be accommodated with liquor to assuage thirst and enliven their already lively spirits.

It was about nine o'clock in the evening when this jovial crew came to Jim Hubbard's boarding house, entered the public room, and called for something to drink. Some of these men were disposed to be quarrelsome, and were insolent to the landlord; clearly wishing to provoke a fight; and a considerable number of the boarders instantly threw off their jackets, ready to take the part of their host. The parties being nearly equal, there was a very distinct prospect of a neat little row, or a regular pounding match.

Just as the parties were coming to blows the boatswain interposed, requesting his shipmates to keep quiet and close their clamshells; and then in an arrogant and defiant tone, stretching himself to his full height, he exclaimed, "If there is any fighting to be done here, I am the man to do it. " And, with a dash of that spirit of chivalry which animated the Paladins of old, he added, "I challenge any man in the house to step into the street, and face me in a regular boxing match. "

His large stature, big whiskers, insolent tone, and menacing gestures were calculated to inspire awe, and those who had shown themselves most eager to take part in the MELEE, shrank instinctively from the idea of meeting this son of Anak in single combat. But Catlin, the meek-looking, quiet, inoffensive, stuttering Catlin, who had been an attentive looker-on without evincing any disposition to take part in the proceedings no sooner heard the challenge, so vain-gloriously given, than he bounded from his seat in a corner of the room, and stood before the doughty champion.

"I ca-ca-ca-nt stand th-th-at, " said Catlin, his eyes flashing with indignation. "I am your m-m-man! "

The affair became interesting. A ring was immediately formed in front of the boarding house, into which the champions of the respective parties, denuded of all unnecessary covering, and each attended by his second, entered. The crew of the ship, the boarders of the General Armstrong, and the inmates of various boarding houses in the vicinity, formed quite a numerous body of spectators. The combatants very properly dispensed with the absurd custom of shaking hands before they came to blows. After glowering at each other for a moment, they went vigorously to work. The boatswain seemed determined to demolish his puny antagonist at once by some well-directed blows, and might possibly have succeeded if the blows had taken effect. But Catlin parried or avoided them with surprising skill and agility, until the boatswain losing patience, grasped his antagonist in his sinewy arms, and after a brief struggle, Catlin was thorn heavily upon his back.

He rose from the earth, like a second Antaeus, with renewed vigor, and when the boatswain attempted to repeat the operation, Catlin dealt him a blow in the body which fairly lifted him from his feet, and, doubling him up, dropped him motionless on the ground.

By the aid of his second, the boatswain was soon again on his feet. The fight was renewed, and continued with but little cessation for fifteen or twenty minutes, during which time Catlin had been twice thrown, but had received no visible injury; and the boatswain's features had been knocked out of all shape, and he had been several times felled to the earth by the terrible blows given by his antagonist. His endurance was wonderful; he submitted to his pounding like a hero, but he was rapidly losing strength; was evidently suffering much from pain, and another round would probably have finished the fierce contest, crowned Catlin with the victor's wreath, and led to a general tumult and row, when some new actors entered on the scene and changed the order of the performances.

These actors appeared in the guise of a squad of police officers, the city patrol, who had received intelligence of the row. They broke through the ring, without regard to ceremony, and made a dash at the men who were striving so hard to maul one another. The boatswain unable to resist or flee, was easily captured, and also his second. But Catlin, having heard the cry of "the watch! the watch! "

as these vigilant preservers of the public peace broke through the ring, gave his antagonist a parting blow which he long remembered, forced his way through or leaped over the dense throng which obstructed his progress, and with the speed of a race horse rushed into the house, and almost before the officers of the law were aware of his escape, he had donned his garments, and without a scratch on his person, mingled unsuspected with the throng of spectators. The boatswain, notwithstanding the woeful plight he was in, for he was dreadfully punished, was marched off to the guard house, accompanied by his faithful second, and on the following day was mulcted in an exemplary fine for disturbing the peace.

The most singular battle between two-legged brutes that I ever beheld, was fought one day between two stout negroes in the neighborhood of my boarding house in Savannah. They had cherished a grudge against each other for some time, and accidentally meeting, a war of words ensued, which attracted a crowd of spectators, who kindly used all possible efforts to induce them to break the peace, in which charitable enterprise they finally succeeded.

Much to my surprise, and greatly to the amusement of the bystanders, the darkies made no use of their fists, neither did they grasp each other by the waist, or resort to the worse than savage practice of gouging. They retreated from the spot where they had been standing, until the space between them would measure some ten or twelve paces, a good duelling distance, and then instead of throwing tomahawks or javelins at each other's heads, or discharging bullets of lead from the mouths of pistols or blunderbusses, they bowed down their heads, as if overcome with humility, and rushed at each other with inconceivable fury.

Like knights of ancient days, they met half way in the lists; but instead of shivering their spears right manfully, their heads came in contact, like a collision between two locomotives, making a noise like a clap of thunder. As they rose from the ground from which they were both thrown by the violence of the shock, fire seemed actually to flash from their eyes, and they shook their heads from shoulder to shoulder for several seconds, apparently to know if all was right within.

The result being satisfactory, they retreated a short distance, not so far as at first, and again tried the terrible experiment of seeing which head was the hardest. After giving several of these practical illustrations of the noble art of butting, in a fashion that would have cracked, crushed and demolished the thickest craniums belonging to the Caucasian family, but which seemed to produce little effect on these hard-headed sons of sires born on the banks of the Niger, one of the belligerent parties watched an opportunity when his opponent was off his guard, dexterously evaded the favor intended for him, and drove his own head with tremendous force against the bosom of his antagonist.

This of course finished the engagement, for the poor fellow was thrown backwards with violence to the ground, where he remained for some time senseless, while the grinning victor received the congratulations of his friends.

Chapter XXXV VOYAGE TO GOTTENBURG

I passed nearly three weeks in Savannah at Jim Hubbard's boarding house, mingling freely with the different characters who frequented that establishment, making my observations on men and things; and if at times I felt humiliated and uncomfortable, I solaced myself by the reflection that my sojourn in that place would be brief, and in the mean time would open to my inspection a newChapter in the book of life; and being constitutionally of a hopeful disposition, and seldom troubled with despondency, instead of suffering my thoughts to dwell on present perplexities, I looked forward to more prosperous scenes and happier times.

At length I found an opportunity to quit Savannah, of which I shall ever retain a vivid recollection, by shipping before the mast in a good wholesome-looking brig, known as the Joseph, of Boston, and bound to Gottenburg, with a cargo of tobacco.

The name of the brig was not a very attractive one, but I had learned long before that the names of merchant vessels, being bestowed according to the taste, fancy, or whim of the owner, should never be regarded as indicative of character, any more than the names of individuals. The first vessel I sailed in, although named after the most beautiful and swift fish that swims the ocean, the dolphin, was one of the ugliest and dullest sailing crafts that ever floated on salt water.

Some ship-owners have a great partiality to animals; hence we find noble ships bearing the names of creatures of every description, from the most ferocious beast to the most unsightly reptile. Other ships carry on their sterns the names of heroes and heroines, gods and goddesses; satyrs, nymphs, civilians, poets, artists, statesmen, and demagogues; of kings, warriors, buccaneers, philanthropists, and brigands. It is thus we count among our ships a Hercules and a Joan of Arc; with Apollos, Minervas, Canovas, Hogarths, John Howards, and Robin Hoods, with a dense sprinkling of Mammoths and Mosquitoes, Tigers and Humming Birds, Whales and Butterflies, Nondescripts, Demons, volcanoes and Icebergs.

Some names of ships are ingenious and quaint, others commonplace or ridiculous; some are expressed in a phrase consisting of a few words, others in a word of one syllable, and sometimes of one letter. Thus we have the INO, and the GUESS; awkward names to repeat when asked, "What is the name of that ship? " and the "Catch me if you can, " and the "What d'ye think 'tis like? " which, by their respective godfathers, are thought to be extremely witty. Thus, we have the "Ay, ay, sir, " the "Tom, " the "A No. 1, " the "Tallyho, " and the "W. "

During the last war with Great Britain two privateers were built by the same individuals, and were intended to cruise in company; they were called the "United we stand, " and the "Divided we fall. " A number of years since, three large and elegant ships constituted a line of English packets between Liverpool and Charleston, in South Carolina. They were, with commendable taste, named after three celebrated poems by three distinguished British poets, the "Lalla Rookh, " the "Corsair, " and "Marmion. " An opulent merchant in Rhode Island, having been repeatedly disappointed in his wish to have a male descendant, although he was the father of half a dozen cherry-cheeked GIRLS, gave the name of "Boy" to a ship of his, which was launched a few weeks after the birth of his youngest daughter. This ship was a fortunate one, and a great favorite of the owner, but never arrived at man's estate, continuing "a boy" to the end of the chapter.

Some ship-owners give to their vessels names of individuals distinguished for talent or worth, or who have served their country nobly by sea or by land. Some bestow on their ships those names that are dearest to them; those of their sweethearts, their wives, their children, brethren, sisters, or friends, as the case may be. Thus we have the "Three sons, " "Ten Brothers, " "Four Sisters, " "Sally Anne, " "Aunt Hitty, " and "Huldah and Judy; " and thus we may account for the euphonious name of a vessel, once belonging to Windsor, in Virginia, the "Jonathan Jacocks. "

Some years ago two Boston merchants were engaged in building a ship for the freighting business. When finished, there was a difference of opinion in regard to the selection of a name. One proposed the name of a distinguished southern statesman, Mr. Poinsett; the other, an old shipmaster, remonstrated against giving the ship the name of any living person; and he carried his point. "The man you mention, " said he, with energy and emphasis, "is a good fellow enough now; but before two years, he may change his politics, or do some other shabby act that will stamp his name with infamy. And then how foolish we shall look when hailing our ship. No! Never while you live, call your ship, or your child, after any living great man; but take the name of some one whose excellence is vouched for by a tombstone. "

A line of packet ships was projected, and in part established some thirty-five years ago, between Boston and Liverpool, by some public-spirited merchants. The project, however, after a time was abandoned. Three new and beautiful ships were built for this enterprise, and plied regularly between the two ports; they were named the Emerald, the Topaz, and the Amethyst. If the undertaking had been successful, other ships would have been added with names of a similar stamp, as the Diamond, the Ruby, the Coral, or the Pearl.

The government of the United States has, for many years, adopted the plan of naming ships-of-the-line after the different states in the Union, the frigates after the rivers, and the sloops of war after the principal cities; thus we have the Vermont, Ohio, Pennsylvania, etc., the Brandywine, Raritan, Merrimac, etc., and the Jamestown, Portsmouth, Hartford, etc. As no more ships- of-the-line will probably be constructed, comparatively few of the states will receive the honor originally intended.

The introduction of large clipper built ships, within a few years, has been attended with a new and distinct class of names, some of which are of a decidedly poetical character, and fill the largest speaking trumpet to its utmost capacity; thus the ocean is traversed in every direction by "Winged Racers, " "Flying Arrows, " "Sparkling Seas, " "Shooting Stars, " "Foaming Waves, " "White Squalls, " "Sovereigns of the Seas, " and "Thunder Showers; " and we may soon see launched the "Almighty Dollar. "

The brig Joseph was commanded by Ezra Allen, a very worthy, well-meaning man, of moderate capacity, and an indifferent sailor. The mate, Mr. Bowen, was an energetic, down-east Yankee, with a drawl as long as the deep sea line, and almost as much twisted. He was one of those queer mortals, manufactured nowhere but in New England, who, restless, inquisitive, ingenious, and bold, can readily adapt themselves to any situation, and, under a very raw and green exterior, conceal an inexhaustible mine of practical good sense and available intelligence on almost every subject. Mr. Bowen, although deferential in his deportment towards the captain, and ever treating him with a good show of respect, was in reality master of the brig;

his advice being solicited on the most trivial occasion, and every suggestion he made in relation to the management of the vessel was eagerly seized upon by the captain. Indeed, Bowen was a model of a mate; industrious, economical, and faithful, treating the crew with kindness and consideration, yet exacting their full quota of labor. No "bread of idleness" was consumed where he had the direction of affairs. Under his management there was perfect subordination, without the necessity of resorting to heavers and handspikes as a means of enforcing authority.

The second mate, Mr. Conners, was a little, weasel-faced man, of uncertain extraction, who had a great idea of his importance, and like other mates I have seen, bustled about the decks, as if to make up in noise and bustle deficiencies in merit; forgetting that a quiet, decided, straightforward manner is more effective in enforcing authority, and establishing discipline, than the roughest language breathed through iron lungs. We had but a brief opportunity to test his worth, for, on the second day after leaving port, Mr. Conners was attacked with illness, stricken down and confined to his state-room, where he lay, suffering much pain, and uttering moans of a character not unfamiliar to my ears. The chief mate came on deck while I was at the helm, and in answer to my inquiries, gave me the particulars of his illness.

"Mr. Bowen, " said I, "that man has got the yellow fever, and it is a severe case. It will probably go hard with him. "

"Do you think so, Hawser? Said Mr. Bowen, slowly drawling out his words; "well, I don't know but you are more than half right. There have been some deaths from yellow fever in Savannah already this season, and who knows but" and turning to the captain, who at this moment came on deck, carelessly handling his toothpick, he exclaimed, "Captain Allen, Mr. Conners has got the yellow fever! "

The captain started back, aghast, at this terrible announcement. His face was as white as a sheet. "The yellow fever, Mr. Bowen! God forbid! What makes you think so? "

"Why, " replied the mate, "the symptoms are precisely those of yellow fever; and you know there were some fatal cases among the shipping before we left Savannah. "

"That's true, Mr. Bowen true as a book. Perhaps it IS the yellow fever. O Lord! The yellow fever on board the Joseph! What SHALL we do, Mr. Bowen? Had we not better put back? Who knows whose turn it may be next? The yellow fever! Why, this is dreadful! "

And the yellow fever it proved to be. The unfortunate man was seized with delirium in less than twelve hours after he was attacked, and died on the following day. The captain was terribly frightened, and was half disposed to make for the nearest port and resign command of the brig. But Mr. Bowen succeeded in calming his fears, and convince him, that by sprinkling the cabin and forecastle freely with vinegar, and burning brimstone, tobacco- leaves, and tar several hours in a day for several successive days, the infected atmosphere would be rendered pure and innoxious. The experiment was tried; and for more than a week the captain, to the great annoyance of the sailors, was every day busy in devising means of salutary fumigation, and carrying them into effect, or, in other words, trying to drive out one poison by introducing another a hundred times more offensive to our olfactories, and attended, if possible, with more unpleasant associations.

We pursued our course towards Gottenburg; steering nearly in the direction of the Gulf Stream, passing to the southward of the Bank of Newfoundland, and then standing away to the northward and eastward, with a view to pass north of Scotland and enter the Skager-rack through the broad passage which separates the Orkneys from the Shetland Islands. On the passage we fell in with the little islet, or huge rock, known as Rockal, which lies almost in mid-ocean, being about two hundred miles west of the coast of Scotland. This rock is only a few hundred feet in length, and rises abruptly to a height eighty or a hundred feet. It is craggy and precipitous, and is the resort of seals, and myriads of birds, as osprays, gulls, and gannets, which abound in that part of the ocean, and there, undisturbed by the presence of man, lay their eggs and rear their young. Rockal has the appearance, when first seen, of a large ship under sail, and is of a dark gray color, being covered in some parts, probably to the depth of many feet, with birdlime, or guano, the accumulation of ages. But as this rock is exposed to the peltings of the pitiless storms, which are frequent in this part of the world, and is subject to the extremes of heat and cold, it is possible that the rich beds of guano with which it is covered are not of the best quality; besides, as it can boast of no bay or nook in which a vessel, or even a boat, can ride in safety, but is exposed on every side to the constant succession of waves rolling onward eternally across the ocean, but not always in the same direction, forbidding the landing of any human being on its craggy sides, its treasures, however valuable, will probably remain undisturbed forever.

This restlessness of the ocean, creating an undulating surface, even during long-continued calms, excites the wonder of all who, never having been abroad upon the waters, imagine its surface is always smooth and unruffled unless disturbed by a gale of wind. This "tramp of the ocean waves" is beautifully described by Charles H. Brown, one of the "Bowdoin Poets":

> "Roll on, old Ocean, dark and deep!
> For thee there is no rest.
> Those giant waves shall never sleep,
> That o'er thy billowy breast
> Tramp like the march of conquerors,
> Nor cease their choral hymn
> Till earth with fervent heat shall melt,
> And lamps of heaven grow dim."

The next land we fell in with was Fair Isle, which lies about half way between the Shetland and the Orkney Islands, being about twenty-five miles south of Sumburgh Head, the southern extremity of the principal of the Shetland Islands. Fair Isle, as is indeed the case with all these islands which are susceptible of cultivation, is inhabited by a rude and hardy race of beings; the men being engaged a large portion of the time in the ling and cod fishery, which is extensively carried on in this part of the world. Taking advantage of their locality in mid-channel, the boatmen from Fair Isle also board vessels which pass to an fro, going "north about, " and exchange fish and a slender variety of vegetables for tobacco and rum; those articles, so unnecessary to happiness or comfort, being greedily coveted by the rude and semi- barbarous inhabitants of those regions, who also, be it said to their credit, will not object to receive a dozen of biscuit, a piece of beef or pork, or a goodly portion of any other palatable article of food.

We were boarded by two of these boats from Fair Isle, well filled with stalwart and sturdy beggars; and dealing with such a man as Captain Allen, good natured and wanting in decision and energy, their solicitations for favors almost took the shape of peremptory demands, and the brig was virtually laid under a heavy contribution.

Some of the most bold and importunate visited the forecastle, and manifested such an inquisitive and rapacious spirit in their quest after tobacco, that we were provoked to treat them in a manner most inhospitable, and drive them on deck.

Proceeding across the head of the North Sea, and running for the "Naze of Norway, " the weather being pleasant and the sea smooth, I persuaded Mr. Bowen to throw a fishing-line over the stern and let it trail, with the expectation of catching some mackerel. We succeeded in capturing several of those excellent fish, and also two or three gar-fish; a kind of fish I have never met with elsewhere excepting in the tropical seas. These gar-fish of the North Sea were of comparatively small size, about fifteen inches in length, but of most delicious flavor. Their long and slim backbone being of a deep emerald green color, Captain Allen, with characteristic sagacity, concluded that these fish were poisonous and unwholesome, and banished them from the cabin. They were heartily welcomed in the forecastle, however, their qualities fully tested, and the skipper was pronounced the most verdant of the two!

Passing the Naze, a high bluff point at the south-western extremity of Norway, and then losing sight of the rough, mountainous coast, intersected by innumerable arms of the sea, called FIORDS, penetrating inland for miles, we crossed the Skager-rack and entered the Cattegat Sea, which divides the western shores of Sweden from the coast of Jutland, and which is about a hundred miles in length and fifty miles in breadth. We soon got sight of Wingo Beacon, a high pyramidal monument, built on a rock at one of the entrances of the fiord on which the city of Gottenburg is situated, and procured a pilot, who took us through a narrow, winding channel among the rocks, into a snug haven surrounded by barren islets, and brought the brig to anchor.

Here we were obliged to remain until visited the next morning by the health officer; for the quarantine regulations of Sweden, although not so vexatious and absurd as in many other ports of Europe, were nevertheless very strict. A case of plague or yellow fever was never known in Gottenburg, or in any other port in Sweden, yet it was the universal belief among medical men that both diseases were contagious, and could be imported in ships from the Mediterranean and the West Indies. Therefore, an elaborate code of sanitary regulations was established, and precautions of the most useless, yet annoying character to persons engaged in commerce, were taken to prevent the introduction of diseases, which could not exist an hour in that northern climate.

The health officer, a grave and dignified personage, with a formidable posse, was rowed alongside the brig in an eight-oared barge. He asked the question, "Are you all well on board? "

"Yes. "

The crew were summoned to the side of the vessel, and their phizzes critically examined by the doctor. We were then ordered up the rigging as high as the tops, to exhibit our activity, and prove that our muscles were in good working condition.

"Where is your roll of equipage? " asked the doctor.

This document, containing a list of the crew as shipped in Havana, and certified at the custom house, after having undergone an unpleasant process of purification, was passed to the health officer, by the aid of a pair of tongs with legs of extraordinary length.

On counting heads, and comparing the actual number of those who were anxiously looking over the gunwale with the list of the ship's company, that vigilant functionary shook his head. One of the number was missing! An explanation was demanded. Captain Allen was embarrassed. He trumped up a clumsy story about a bad cold, ill health of long standing, consumption, etc., but whispered not a syllable of yellow fever. He was a poor hand at deception; but he might as well have stated the whole truth, for as in all places abroad where strict quarantine laws are established, if one or more of the crew is missing, it matters not whether he died of accident or disease, the health officers take it for granted, and insist upon it in spite of evidence to the contrary, that he died of plague if the vessel is from the Mediterranean, or of yellow fever if from a southern American port or the West Indies.

Greatly to the mortification of Captain Allen, and to the loudly expressed dissatisfaction of the crew, the brig was ordered to remain TEN DAYS IN QUARANTINE.

Nor was this all the trouble and annoyance consequent on the deficiency in the "roll of equipage. " Fumigations in the cabin and the forecastle, of a character stronger and more disagreeable than Captain Allen ever dreamed of, were carried on, under the direction of the pilot and a revenue officer, several times a day. They were attended with a most inodorous effluvia, and caused such a general concert of sneezing and coughing, by night as well as by day, that one would have thought influenza, in its most fearful shape and with giant power, had seized every man by the throat.

Chapter XXXVI SANITARY LAWS MUTINY AND MURDER

Laws for the preservation of the health of a community have been established among civilized nations in every age. And when these laws are based on reason and intelligence, they undoubtedly subserve a noble purpose. But the quarantine laws all over the world, with some rare exceptions, being the offspring of ignorance and terror, are not only the climax of absurdity, but act as an incubus on commerce, causing ruinous delays in mercantile operations, much distress, and unnecessary expense.

The PLAGUE was formerly universally regarded as a contagious disease, and to prevent the horrors which attend its introduction in large cities, the most stringent laws have been enacted for ages. But the contagiousness of the plague is now doubted by many enlightened physicians. Whether it be so or not, it never made its appearance in countries bordering on the North Sea or the Baltic, or on the American continent. Although many vessels every year, almost every month, arrive in our principal ports from the Levant, freighted with rags and other articles, constituting a medium through which this disease, if contagious, would surely be propagated, yet this dreadful scourge of cities, in ancient and modern times, has never been brought across the Atlantic.

The small pox is another disease against the introduction of which quarantine laws have been established. That it is contagious there is no question; but by the blessed discovery of vaccination, this disease, once so dreadful, is robbed of its horrors, and rendered as harmless as the measles or the whooping cough, insomuch that laws, formerly enacted in different states to protect the people from the dangers of the small pox have generally been repealed.

The Asiatic cholera, when it first made its appearance in Europe, was believed to be contagious. Quarantine laws, of the most stringent character, were adopted to prevent its introduction into seaports, and military CORDONS SANITAIRE were drawn around the frontiers of nations to shut it out of villages and towns, until it was ascertained to be an epidemic disease, the germs of which were in the atmosphere, and could no more be controlled than the winds which sweep the earth.

The YELLOW FEVER, however, has for many years been the most terrible bugbear, and to prevent its introduction into the seaports of Europe and the United States has been the chief end and aim of the absurd and ridiculous quarantine regulations to which I have referred. It has never been regarded as contagious by well-informed men in countries where it is most prevalent, and now, in spite of long-existing and deeply-stamped prejudices, it is generally admitted, by enlightened physicians, that the YELLOW FEVER IS NOT CONTAGIOUS. NOT A SINGLE WELL-ESTABLISHED FACT CAN BE ADDUCED TO SHOW THE CONTAGIOUS CHARACTER OF THE DISEASE, OR THAT IT CAN BE CONVEYED IN CARGOES OF ANY DESCRIPTION FROM ONE COUNTRY TO ANOTHER.

Persons in good health may leave a port where yellow fever prevails, and carry within them the seeds of the disease, and on arriving at another port several days afterwards, or on the passage thither, may be attacked with the disease in its most appalling character, and die; BUT THE DISEASE IS NOT COMMUNICATED TO OTHERS. Indeed, the yellow fever is not so INFECTIOUS as the typhus or scarlet fever, which prevails every season in northern climes.

When the yellow fever broke out in New York, and caused much alarm, nearly forty years ago, the first cases occurred in the vicinity of Trinity Church, and until destroyed by a black frost, it spread gradually in every direction from this common centre, insomuch that the "infected district" was clearly defined and marked out from day to day. Persons, who had been in the "infected district, " and left it for other parts of the country, were subsequently attacked by this disease hundreds of miles from New York, and died; but not a single instance occurred in which it was communicated to others. And so in the West Indies: the yellow fever sometimes rages fearfully in one city or town, while in another, on the same island, not a single case exists, although there is a daily and unobstructed intercourse between the two places. And whenever, owing to some mysterious agency, it makes its appearance, precautions to prevent its extension seem useless. It overleaps all barriers, and attacks with equal severity the inmates of a palace or a filthy hovel, the captain of a ship in a splendid cabin, surrounded with phials and pills, and Jack in the forecastle, redolent of tobacco, and destitute of ventilation.

The quarantine regulations in Boston formerly partook of the unreasonable and absurd character, which, to a greater or less extent, has marked these regulations in all maritime countries. Vessels arriving from certain ports where yellow fever was supposed to prevail, were not allowed to haul to a wharf and discharge cargo, or hold any direct personal communication with the city, until the expiration of twenty-five days after leaving port. Thus a vessel from the West Indies, having perishable commodities on board, might reach Boston in twelve days, the vessel and cargo in good condition, and every man stout and hearty. But it was supposed that yellow fever might lurk among the crew, or lie concealed among boxes of sugars or cigars, and, therefore, thirteen additional days were allowed to give it an opportunity to escape. At the expiration of that time, when the patience of the men, kept so long in durance vile without the shadow of a cause, in sight of their homes, was exhausted, and the perishable portion of the cargo in a most unwholesome state of decomposition, caused by the delay, the vessel was pronounced pure, in a fit condition to receive PRATIQUE, and allowed to haul alongside the wharf, receive visitors on board, and discharge cargo.

The reader, inexperienced in the mysteries of sanitary regulations, may smile at the absurdity of such proceedings, but the system of guarding the public against the horrors of the yellow fever, adopted by the health department of Boston, was in those days remarkably judicious and indulgent, when compared with the regulations in other cities, and which exist at the present time, not only on the other side of the Atlantic, but in this country. And, to the credit of Boston, and as an illustration of the intelligence of her citizens, it should be recorded that this seaport, the principal one in New England, WAS THE FIRST IN THE CIVILIZED WORLD TO EXPRESS AN OPINION THAT THE YELLOW FEVER WAS NOT CONTAGIOUS, and to repeal those ridiculous, useless, and burdensome "quarantine laws, " which, originating in panic terror, have been instituted from time immemorial, to prevent the introduction of plague and yellow fever, and establish in their stead sanitary regulations, which are in accordance with the dictates of common sense.

Infectious diseases are sometimes caused by the foul air arising from a ship's hold, owing to the decomposition of vegetable substances in a hot climate, or to an accumulation of filth, without ventilation, when crowded with passengers. The malignant, pestilential disease, caused by inhaling this noxious atmosphere, often sweeps off portions of the crew and passengers; and those who visit a ship under such circumstances, and breathe the poisonous gases, even in a northern latitude, are liable to be attacked by this fatal disease. But the ordinary quarantine regulations will afford no protection in such a case. A few weeks' delay in quarantine after the crew have become acclimated, and fumigations, and sprinklings with acids in the cabin, until all hands are pickled or smoke-dried, will not purify the ship's hold, prevent the exhalation of pestilential gases, and arrest the progress of infection.

Then may we not hope that the expensive quarantine establishments, with sweeping, indiscriminating regulations, founded on prejudice, and continued through fear and ignorance, a disgrace to this enlightened age, and a dead weight on commercial enterprise, will soon be abolished? In their stead let a board of health be instituted, with an office where business can be transacted at all hours. Let the master of every vessel which arrives in port, and on board of which deaths have occurred during the passage, report the same at the health office, that judicious measures, such as are adapted to the particular case, may be resorted to, in order to protect the community or individuals from inconvenience or danger when INFECTIOUS diseases exist.

Time passes slowly in quarantine. The officers of a ship are generally taciturn, surly, and exacting; and the crew are unhappy, discontented, disposed to grumble, and ready to quarrel and fight on the most trivial occasions, and often without any occasion whatever. At the expiration of ten protracted days after we let go our anchor in the outer harbor of Gottenburg, we were again honored with a visit from the health officer. The crew manifested their vigorous physical condition by another clamber up the rigging. The officer came on board, shook hands with the captain, and congratulated him on being released from quarantine. The pilot took charge of the vessel, the men were ordered to man the windlass, which order was obeyed with alacrity. Faces diminished in longitude, and were lighted up with smiles. The anchor song of "Yeo, Heave O, " never sounded more musical or inspiring than on that occasion. Sail was made on the brig with magical dexterity, and the crew were in fine spirits, jocund, and happy, as we thridded the channel extending some ten miles to the city, looked with surprise upon the innumerable barren rocks and islets scattered around, and entering the strait, surveyed with increasing interest and pleasure cultivated fields, and neat-looking dwelling houses, and men, women, and children, busily engaged in their customary occupations. We felt that we were in the world once more.

Gottenburg is a large and populous city, situated on a plain near the extremity of the fiord, about thirteen miles from the Cattegat, but almost encircled by steep and craggy rocks, hills, and a bold and picturesque scenery, with a fine harbor, the entrance to which is easily defended; it is conveniently located for the foreign trade of Sweden, and next to Stockholm, has the most extensive commerce of any port in the kingdom. Its exports consist chiefly of iron and steel, brought from rich mines nearly two hundred miles in the interior, by a well-perfected system of inland navigation. We lay some weeks at anchor in the upper harbor, and I had abundant opportunities to visit the city, mark its peculiarities and note the character of its inhabitants, who, in Gottenburg and vicinity, as in other parts of the kingdom, are simple and industrious in their habits, and civil and hospitable to strangers.

After our cargo was discharged and a sufficient quantity of iron taken on board for ballast, the American consul informed Captain Allen that he had a prisoner under his charge, accused of a capital crime, whom it was necessary to send to the United States for trial, and that the brig Joseph had been selected for the honor of conveying the criminal across the ocean. The captain did not appear flattered by this mark of confidence on the part of the consul; he ventured a weak remonstrance, but finally submitted with a good grace. Preparations were accordingly made for the reception of the prisoner, who had made one of the crew of the large clipper schooner Plattsburg, on board which vessel mutiny, piracy, and murder had been committed.

The Plattsburg sailed from Baltimore about the 1st of July, 1816, bound on a voyage to Smyrna, in the Mediterranean, with a cargo of coffee, and $42,000 in specie. The schooner was commanded by William Hackett; the name of the chief mate was Frederick Yeizer, the second mate was Stephen B. Onion, and Thomas Baynard was the supercargo. The crew consisted of six persons, all of whom were foreigners, and among them were some desperate, hardened ruffians, who had learned lessons in villany on board Patriot privateers, some of which, under no legal restraint, and responsible to no government, were little better than pirates. The names of these men were John Williams a Canadian, Peter Rog a Dane, Francis Frederick a Spaniard, Miles Petersen a Swede, William Stromer a Prussian, and Nathaniel White an Englishman.

Before the Plattsburg had passed Cape Henry symptoms of insubordination appeared among the crew. One of the men, named John Williams, was particularly insolent and troublesome, and was chastised by the captain, after which the voyage was quietly pursued, and the crew were obedient and apparently contented. But beneath this apparent calm a terrible storm was brewing. A fiendish plan was devised by Williams and Stromer, and agreed to by the rest, to murder the officers and get possession of the money, which they knew was on board. They first determined to poison the captain, supercargo, and mates, but owing to some failure in their calculations, this plan was abandoned. When off the Western Islands, it was determined, after some discussion to seize on the officers while they were taking an observation of the sun at meridian, and, following the example of the mutineers of the Bounty, compel them to embark in the long-boat, and run their chance of reaching the shore. Williams and Stromer provided themselves with cords in order to bind the captain, and also with weapons to knock him on the head if he should resist; but when the time for action arrived, the hearts of their associates failed them, and the project was abandoned.

Williams reproached his shipmates for their cowardice. They were not lacking in rascality, but they wanted nerve to carry into effect the desperate design of taking possession of the schooner. Another consultation was held, and it was concluded that the SAFEST proceeding would be to massacre the officers before they could have an opportunity to make resistance. This plan was resolved upon, and all the details were carefully arranged, and every man had his part assigned him in the fearful tragedy which was about to be enacted.

Accordingly about midnight, on the 24th of July, being then but little more than a hundred miles to the westward of the Straits of Gibraltar, a loud cry was heard from the forecastle, of "Sail, ho! Right ahead! "

Mr. Yeizer, the mate, rushed forward to obtain a view of the vessel, and on stepping forward of the windlass, was felled to the deck by a murderous blow from a handspike in the hands of one of the mutineers. His body was instantly seized upon and thrown overboard. The second mate, who had just been called, hearing the cry of "a sail, " hastened on deck and was going forward, when he was struck a violent blow, and grappled by Williams, who exclaimed, "Here is one of the rascals! Overboard with him! " But the captain, alarmed by the cries and trampling on deck, now made his appearance, and Williams released his grasp on Onion and attacked the captain, who, unsuspicious of any mutinous intentions, was unarmed. He was summarily disposed of, being brained by a handspike or heaver, and thrown into the sea. Onion, greatly terrified, escaped down the companion-way, and concealed himself in the bread locker.

The mutineers now called upon Mr. Baynard, the supercargo, to show himself on deck. He hesitated, but on being assured that no harm was intended, and threatened with instant death if he did not make his appearance at once, he passed up the companion-way, and while conversing with Williams, was mercilessly murdered by Stromer and Rog.

Three of the pirates now entered the cabin in search of the second mate, and the question was raised whether his life should be spared. After some debate it was determined that he should not be killed, provided he would take an oath to be faithful to their interests and aid them in their future proceedings. Onion, on hearing the decision, came out of his hiding-place, took the prescribed oath of fidelity, and was admitted a member of the fraternity. As some proper organization for the management of the vessel was considered necessary, Stromer was chosen captain, Williams's chief mate, and Onion retained his position as second mate.

On the morning succeeding this terrible crime, the specie was taken from "the run" beneath the cabin and brought on deck. Each man including Onion and Samberson, the cook, who took no part in the outrage received a share of the money, which was measured out in hats and tin pots, a single share amounting to about five thousand dollars.

And now the important question arose to what part of the world should they direct their course, in order to sell the vessel and cargo and make their escape with their ill-gotten booty; for they knew the deed would soon be known and the avengers of blood be upon their heels. They, finally, concluded to shape their course to the northward, and enter some obscure port in Norway, where no very strict inquisition would probably be made into the character of the vessel of their intentions, and from which place they could easily find means of proceeding to other parts of Europe. Onion, who was a skilful penman, was directed to manufacture some new invoices of cargo and alter other papers in such a manner as to deceive, for a time at least, the revenue authorities of such port as they might enter; and Williams altered the ship's log-book to correspond with the story they had agreed upon.

They arrived at Cleveland, a small port in Norway, about the middle of August, and conducted their affairs in such a way as to give no cause for supposing anything was wrong, But when Stromer expressed a desire to sell the vessel and cargo, without being particular in regard to the price, suspicions were excited that all was not right; and those suspicions were strengthened by some careless remarks of Frederick and Rog after they had been drinking freely. The schooner was accordingly seized and taken possession of by the proper authorities, and brought round to another wharf, where an investigation took place. This of course alarmed the guilty crew, and before their iniquity was discovered, each man took his share of money so dearly earned, and in all haste left the shores of Norway.

Williams, Onion, Rog, Frederick, and Samberson embarked in a sloop for Copenhagen, where they landed in fine spirits; and under the direction of Frederick, who was a native of that city, undertook to open a store, and with this object purchased a variety of goods. But it was not long before some circumstances drew upon them the attention of the police. They were arrested, and Samberson exposed the whole horrible transaction. These men were thrown into prison, and intelligence of their arrest was sent to the American government; but more than two years expired before they were brought to this country in the United States ship Hornet.

Stromer and White went off together; and Stromer probably proceeded to Prussia with his share of the money. He was never discovered by the satellites of justice; but White was subsequently arrested and brought to trial. Petersen, who was a native of Gottenberg, returned directly to his home. He had parents in that city of respectable standing, besides brothers and sisters. He told his relatives an ingenious tale to account for his prosperous condition, but he was speedily tracked by the officers of justice, and one day while enjoying himself with his friends, and lavishly spending his money, he was arrested for the dreadful crimes of piracy and murder, and thrown into a dungeon, where he remained heavily ironed for nearly twelve months, when he was transferred to the brig Joseph for conveyance to the United States.

Chapter XXXVII RETURN OF THE WANDERER

We sailed from Gottenburg one morning about the first of September, 1817, bound to Boston. Having been long absent from my home without intercourse of any description with my friends and relations, and having seen during that period striking exemplifications of the caprices of fortune, having experienced "many ups and downs, " the downs, however, being decidedly in the majority, I felt a strong desire, a yearning, to return once more to my friends in New England. I was convinced there were worse places in the world than my own dear native land, and far worse people than those among whom my lot had been cast in childhood.

It was on a Saturday we sailed from Gottenburg. It had been Captain Allen's intention to sail on the previous Thursday, but he was unexpectedly detained. On Friday morning all the arrangements were completed; the brig was ready for sea, the wind was fresh and fair, but not a step was taken towards getting under weigh. Indeed our worthy captain plumply told Mr. Bowen that NO CONSIDERATION COULD INDUCE HIM TO GO TO SEA ON A FRIDAY! The crew, one and all, as well as the mate, were amused at this exhibition of weakness, which did not increase the respect for his character; for ALL sailors are not superstitious, although they are proverbially regarded as such.

Petersen, the prisoner, who was brought on board in irons, bore no resemblance in personal appearance to the ferocious, ill-looking, big-whiskered ruffian, whose image is conjured up by the mention of the word "pirate. " On the contrary he was a gentle-looking youth, only nineteen years of age, of a slight figure, pale complexion, and a pleasant, prepossessing countenance. He spoke English fluently, and by his conduct, intelligence, and plausible representations, soon won the favor of every man on board. He declared that he did not participate in the mutiny; that it was planned without his knowledge; that when the murders were committed he was asleep in the forecastle, and fear for his own life induced him to accept a share of the money and endeavor to conceal the crime.

His story was believed by Captain Allen and others, and he was relieved from his handcuffs every morning, and allowed to leave his quarters in the half-deck and range the vessel, mix with the sailors and assist in the performance of the various duties; and he showed himself an active, obedient, and intelligent seaman. He often expressed a wish that his trial should take place; he was confident of an acquittal, and longed to be once more at liberty.

I may as well state here that the trial of the mutineers of the Plattsburg, viz., Williams, Rog, Frederick, Petersen, and White took place on the 28th of December, 1818, before the U. S. Circuit Court, in session at Boston, Justice Story presiding. They were defended by able counsel, but convicted on circumstantial evidence, corroborated by the direct testimony of Samberson and Onion. It appeared on the trial that the mild and amiable-looking Petersen was one of the most forward and active of the mutineers. It was he who gave the signal for action by crying "Sail, ho! " and he subsequently assisted in throwing overboard the mate and murdering the captain.

The execution of these pirates was appointed for the 21st of January, 1819, but on the ground that the time between the sentence and execution, twenty-four days, was too short to allow the criminals to make their peace with God, a respite was granted until the 18th of February. On that day they were placed in a wagon, and a procession was formed of an imposing character, which, after passing through Court Street, State Street, India Street, and Milk Street to the Main street, now Washington street, proceeded to "the town land on boston Neck, " where the execution took place in presence of twenty thousand people.

These men died a terrible death, in a strange land, far from their homes and kindred. Although such number witnessed the execution, few sympathized with them in their sufferings, for all acknowledged that their sentence was just. Their execution, doubtless, acted as an impressive warning to others, and restrained desperate ruffians from the commission of desperate deeds.

In all ages, crimes of a dark dye when committed on the ocean, have been regarded as exhibiting a more depraved character in the criminal than crimes of a similar description committed on the land. At sea there are no constables or police officers, no magistrates or good citizens ready and willing to aid in preserving the peace of society, protecting life and property when endangered, and in arresting a rogue or murderer. For this reason laws relating to mutiny, piracy, and murder on the seas are punishable with death. In many atrocious cases it is difficult, perhaps impossible, to obtain proof sufficient to convict the offender; but whenever a violator of those laws, whether a principal or accessory, is arrested, tried, and convicted, THE PUNISHMENT SHOULD BE SURE TO FOLLOW. The certainty of punishment is a mighty preventive to crime. The impulses of that false philanthropy which seems to flourish in the present age, can never be more injuriously indulged than by persevering and unscrupulous efforts to influence the press and rouse public opinion in favor of setting aside the verdict of a jury, and snatching a red-handed murderer on the high seas from the gallows.

Nothing particularly remarkable occurred during our passage home. It was in the season of the year when severe gales are met with on the Atlantic, but the brig Joseph proved a good sea boat, tight as a drum, and could lie to or scud without danger of being overwhelmed by the combing waves. On this passage a little incident occurred off the Orkney Islands, that will convey some idea of the dangers to which those are subjected whose home is on the ocean.

We were lying to in a gale. The wind blew fiercely in flaws, and there was a high and turbulent sea running. The brig was at times uneasy, and in the pauses of the gale rolled heavily to windward as well as to leeward. Orders were given to send down the fore- top-gallant mast. I hastened with alacrity aloft for that purpose, and had reached the cross-trees, when in a lull of the tempest, the brig, lying in the trough of the sea, lurched fearfully to windward. I grasped firmly one of the top-gallant shrouds above the cross-trees, but the rope being old and decayed, parted in the horn of the cross-trees BENEATH MY HANDS.

I clung, with a desperate grasp, to the rope, but was thrown out with a jerk in an angle of forty-five degrees with the horizon, and when the brig suddenly righted I attained for a few seconds a horizontal position, and to an observer on deck must have looked not unlike a spread eagle burgee at half-mast. If I had relinquished my grasp at that moment I should have been thrown into the sea some thirty feet from the vessel's side, and a full period would have been put to the adventures of Hawser Martingale. But, notwithstanding the muscles of my arms were severely wrenched, I was fortunately able to retain my grasp. The next moment the action of gravitation, together with the roll to leeward, threw me back with terrific force against the topmast rigging, which I eagerly seized, and then rejoicing at my lucky escape from a great danger, and regardless of the bruises I had received, I went on with my work.

On the passage homeward I often indulged in reflections in regard to my future position in life; and while walking the deck at night loved to let my fancy roam and picture castles in the air, which, I fondly hoped, might at some future day be actually constructed. My highest ambition was to gain, as rapidly as possible, a thorough knowledge of my business, procure the command of a good ship, and by my own labors, acquire a competence before age should weaken the faculties or diminish a relish for society; and then, residing in my own house with a small piece of land attached which I could cultivate with my own hands, and within a few miles of the metropolis of New England, surrounded by a pleasant neighborhood, and enjoying domestic happiness in all its purity, gently sail down the stream of life.

This was not an extravagant dream. Yet the chances were at times terribly against its fulfilment. But I never despaired, and fully believed that if Providence should grant me life and continued health, THE CASTLE WOULD BE BUILT. In the darkest hours I kept a bright lookout ahead, far ahead for the cheerful and safe harbor which imagination had so often portrayed. And the dream has been realized almost precisely as it appeared to me in my youthful days; and I have enjoyed for many years, in the retirement which my fancy painted, as much happiness as usually falls to the lot of man in this checkered life, with a strong hope,

> "When the brief voyage in safety is o'er,
> To meet with loved friends on the far distant shore."

About forty days after leaving Gottenburg we reached the Grand Bank of Newfoundland, and crossed it in latitude of forty-four degrees. We fell in with many fishing vessels riding at anchor in thirty fathoms of water, the hardy crews of which, rigged out in their "boots and barvels, " were busily engaged in their useful but arduous occupation. When on the centre of the bank, the fog which had previously obscured objects at a distance, was suddenly swept away, and we counted from the deck seventy-four schooners at anchor, besides several which were under sail.

The Bank of Newfoundland is of enormous extent, reaching some two hundred and fifty miles into the Atlantic, from the southern part of Newfoundland and islands in that vicinity. Its southern extremity is in about forty-two degrees of latitude, and fifty degrees west longitude from Greenwich. The depth of water varies from twenty-five to fifty fathoms. The Bank is in the direct track of vessels bound to and from Europe, and many sad disasters have occurred to the fishermen, while lying at anchor in rough weather in a dense fog. In some instances they have been run down, crushed to fragments, by large ships under full sail, and every one of the crew has perished.

The fish on this Bank are chiefly cod, and have been taken in incredible numbers by the crews of vessels built and fitted out for this purpose, for more than two hundred years; and in times past this fishery has proved a certain source of income, and sometimes of wealth, to bold and enterprising men. But for a number of years this business has not been so profitable as formerly, and not so many vessels have been employed. It has been intimated by evil-disposed persons that the capital stock of the Bank is getting reduced, and that it will ere long fail to make discounts or pay dividends. But such rumors are the offspring of calumny; the Bank is undoubtedly sound, has a solid bottom, and its treasures and resources are inexhaustible.

The fishermen of the Grand Bank, in "days lang syne, " belonged chiefly to Marblehead and Cape Ann. They were a bold, hardy, sinewy set of men, inured to fatigue and reckless of danger, cheerful in their dispositions, impatient under restraint, fond of what they considered good living, ready with a joke or yarn on all occasions, and not a little inclined to superstition. Indeed the fishing vessels on the Bank, if we are to credit the tales told years ago, were often favored by the presence of death warnings, mysterious noises, ghosts, and apparitions. Sounds were heard and sights seen on board fishing vessels on the Bank, which filled the stoutest hearts with fear and wonder, and would even astonish the most inveterate spiritualist of the present day.

On shore the fishermen were a jolly set of fellows, social in their dispositions, not given to vicious indulgences, but somewhat careless of their earnings, regarding their resources as inexhaustible as "the fish in the sea. " They married early, made kind and affectionate husbands, and were, in almost every case, blessed with a numerous offspring; indeed, Marblehead fishermen of sixty years of age would remind a person of the Bible patriarchs for the number of their descendants. Their wives, fresh, blooming, spirited, and good-humored, were grandmothers at six and thirty, great grandmothers at fifty-four, and great great grandmothers at the age of seventy-four!

The fishermen were patriotic, too. They were dear lovers of their country and its institutions, and prided themselves on their attachment to democracy. In the war of the revolution the citizens of Marblehead and Gloucester, and Cape Cod, no longer able to pursue their accustomed vocations, joined the armies which fought for freedom, and rendered important services on the land as well as on the ocean. In the latest, and, we trust, THE LAST, war with Great Britain, they came forward almost to a man, to assist in manning our frigates and privateers; and no class of men rendered better services, or could be more confidently relied on when deeds of daring were to be performed, than the whole-hearted and hard-handed fishermen of Massachusetts Bay.

As a nursery for seamen for our merchant ships in time of peace, the fishing business has proved of immense advantage to the country, and that policy may justly be regarded as suicidal on the part of the national government which would throw barriers in the way of its success.

To those who are familiar with the extent and geographical position of the Grand Bank of Newfoundland, it may seem surprising, perhaps incredible, that fishing vessels have been known to seek for it, day after day, in vain. Yet that such occurrences have taken place in "olden times" is an established fact. But to the honor of our fishermen it may be said that such blunders in plain navigation have been exceedingly rare, and as much owing to a free circulation of the fiery liquid, which addles men's brains, as to sheer ignorance.

Many years ago a schooner sailed from Gloucester bound to the Grand Bank, in charge of a thick dunderhead of a skipper, and a crew of about equal mental calibre. In putting up the stores the grog was not forgotten. Indeed it was regarded as a necessary on shipboard, as a shrewd counsellor in difficulty and danger, a friendly consoler when borne down by misfortune, and a cheerful companion in prosperity, which could not be too often embraced.

The schooner met with head winds before she reached the meridian of Cape Sable, and was beating about for several days between Cape Sable and St. George's Bank. At length the wind hauled to the southward, and the skipper put the schooner's head to the north-east, and let her run, making a fair wind of it. On the following day, towards night, he got soundings in twenty fathoms. "Hallo! " shouted the skipper, "what a lucky fellow I am; I have hit the broadest and shoalest part of the Bank the first time of trying! I verily believe I could hit a nun buoy if it was anchored in any part of the ocean. But never mind, boys, let us freshen the nip; we'll stand well on to the Bank, then let go the kellock, and haul up the cod! "

He stood on for a couple of hours, when greatly to his mortification and amazement, he found his schooner floundering and thumping on a sand bank. She soon knocked a hole in her bottom, and the crew with great difficulty made their escape to land, which was not far off. Even then the skipper was disposed to believe ha had found an island on the Bank which had never before been discovered; and it was hard work to convince him that he was cast away on the Isle of Sable!

Another case is said to have occurred of clumsy navigation on the part of one of our Marblehead skippers. The tale is traditionary, but no less authentic on that account.

The fishing schooner Codhook was ready for a trip to the Grand Bank for a cargo of the deposits, when the skipper, a faithful, skilful, hardy old fisherman, as is the case with most of this valuable class of men, was taken sick, and compelled reluctantly to relinquish the voyage. It became necessary to find a skipper, and as it was a busy season, it was not an easy matter to procure the right kind of a man. After a time, however, it was concluded that nothing better could be done than to appoint old Jonas Hardhead skipper for this single trip.

Jonas, or "Uncle Jonas, " as he was familiarly called, had been to sea during the greater part of his life, but for the last few years had been engaged occasionally in the fishing business; and when he could be kept sober he was a valuable fisherman, for few could endure more hardship, or haul up the cod faster than Uncle Jonas. He also boasted of his skill in navigation, and according to his own story could handle a quadrant or even a sextant as adroitly as a marlinspike. It was finally settled that he should act as skipper on this voyage, provided he would promise to keep sober. Jonas gave the pledge with alacrity, although his feelings seemed hurt that his sobriety was doubted; he even declared that he was never otherwise than sober in his life; and was forthwith inducted into office.

In order to aid him in keeping his promise to the owners, Uncle Jonas took with him on board some ten or a dozen bottles of "old Jamaica, " a beverage which he dearly loved; and although he seldom got absolutely drunk when on shore, it was rarely the case that he went to bed sober. He had no doubt of his qualifications to perform well his duty as skipper, and was determined to have a jovial time at all events.

He had a quadrant and a Bowditch's Navigator, as well as a chart of the Atlantic Ocean and of the American coast. But all this machinery was of little use to Uncle Jonas. Indeed he secretly despised book-learning, regarding it as a humbug, and relied upon his experience and judgment in navigating his vessel. He was aware that by steering a course east, or east half south, and running in that direction for several days, he would strike the broadside of the Grand Bank, which he expected to know by the color of the water, the soundings, the many birds, and the fishing vessels at anchor. He also supposed that when he returned with a glorious fare, a westerly course would fetch some part of the coast, when he should certainly fall in with vessels, and easily ascertain the where-away of Boston Bay, with all of which coast he was familiar.

The schooner Codhook left the wharf with a roaring north-wester, and in order to secure a lucky cruise Uncle Jonas treated himself and his companions, a jolly set of fellows also, with a stiff glass of grog. He afterwards drank to a fair wind, to a continuance of the breeze, and repeated this operation so often, that what little knowledge and judgment he could boast of when he left the wharf, insensibly oozed away; and for nearly a week his mental faculties were a great deal below par. In the meantime the wind blew a fresh breeze from the westward without intermission, and the old schooner rolled and wallowed along with nearly all sail set, at a tremendous rate, and actually crossed the Bank on the fifth day after leaving port. But the weather was foggy, and the eyes of the skipper were dim. No change was observed in the water, no birds or fishing vessels were seen.

Onward the schooner went, with all sail spread to the wind, like a new Flying Dutchman, until the seventh day after leaving port, when the wind began to abate a little and haul to the southward. The horizon was now clear, and Uncle Jonas began to look out for vessels, and expressed a decided opinion that he was nearly up with the Bank. The sun went down and no fishing vessels were seen under sail or at anchor. He was confident they would be visible on the following day, and in order that his vision might be clearer, he swallowed a strong potation before he turned in.

On the next morning not a vessel of any description was in sight, and the skipper, confident that the Bank could not be far off, concluded to sound. The deep-sea lead was thrown, but he got no bottom with ninety fathoms of line. "Wheugh! " exclaimed Uncle Jonas, "what has become of the Bank? "

The wind now blew merrily from the south-west, and merrily sailed the schooner; Uncle Jonas keeping a sharp look-out for fishing vessels, and sounding every six hours. Ten days passed away, and he began to be alarmed, and expressed fears that the Bank had failed, refused payments, sunk, or cleared out! He continued, however, to consult his Jamaica friend, and sought its advice and assistance in his perplexity. It is singular that in times of difficulty and danger, when a clear head is particularly necessary, men who have charge of property, and the lives of their fellow-men, are prone to consult the rum bottle, which always produces an effect precisely the reverse of what is desired.

At length, on the twelfth day of the passage, Uncle Jonas, whose patience was nearly exhausted, saw a large number of gannets and gulls; the water was remarkably chilly, and seemed to have a tinge of green. "Aha, " said the skipper, "I have got you at last. " But he could not see any fishing vessels, or obtain bottom with ninety fathoms of line.

On the following morning, however, much to his gratification, he obtained soundings in sixty fathoms of water. "There, " exclaimed the skipper triumphantly to his men, "you more than insinuated that I was no navigator, but I have carried the ship straight to the Grand Bank in fine style. We will stand on until we get thirty fathoms of water, and then go to work like men. "

His companions acknowledged their error, asked pardon for doubting his infallibility, and promised never again to question his ability to navigate a vessel to any part of the globe.

But, much to the surprise and disappointment of Uncle Jonas, the water did not shoal, but rather deepened as he kept along to the eastward. He again became bewildered, and could hardly help admitting that there might be some mistake in the matter, as he never found such deep water on the Bank before. He repeatedly swept the horizon with his glass, hoping to conjure up some vessel, and procure definite information in regard to his whereabouts. In the afternoon he saw a ship approaching from the eastward, and his heart was gladdened at the sight. He hauled the schooner on a wind, hoisted his colors, and prepared to speak the ship. She proved to be the packet ship James Monroe, Captain Wilkinson, bound from Liverpool to New York. Uncle Jonas eagerly inquired of the captain of the ship if he had fallen in with any fishing vessels on his passage.

"Ay, ay, " was the reply; "I saw a number of them in the Irish Channel. "

"Irish Channel! " echoed the skipper, with a howl of agony. "Why, where are we, my good fellow; do tell us where we are. "

"We are about thirty-five miles south-south-east of Cape Clear, and on the Nymph Bank! "

Uncle Jonas dashed his trumpet to the deck, and sprang perpendicularly four feet by actual measurement so true, it is, that astonishment prompts a man instinctively to extraordinary gymnastic exercises!

The skipper was in an awkward dilemma. He had gone across the Atlantic, with a fair and fresh breeze, safely and expeditiously enough; but he cherished strong doubts whether his skill in navigation would suffice to carry him back. He explained the case candidly to Captain Wilkinson, who, after a hearty laugh at the expense of Uncle Jonas, consented to furnish him with a navigator. He accordingly put a young man on board the schooner who was a proficient in the art of navigation an art with which the commander of a vessel on the ocean should be somewhat familiar.

As a preliminary step, the new captain caused the remainder of the "Jamaica" to be thrown overboard, and every thing else which was akin to it. Uncle Jonas begged hard to retain it as a solace under trouble; but he was overruled by the new navigator, and also the crew, all of whom felt mortified at the result of the trip thus far, and overboard it went. The head of the schooner was got round to the westward, her sails were trimmed to the breeze, and the schooner jogged along quietly in the wake of the ship until the latter was out of sight.

In due time, that is, in about thirty-five days after having spoken the ship James Monroe, for the wind was westerly nearly the whole time, the schooner Codhook reached the Grand Bank. Neither the navigator nor the crew would consent to remain there any great length of time indeed, for various reasons, all were anxious to return to Marblehead. In about a fortnight afterwards they reached the port from which they started, after an absence of about two months, having had a glorious cruise, but bringing home a slender fare.

Uncle Jonas was laughed at until the day of his death; but he always warded off the ridicule by declaring that no fishing schooner had ever before reached Cape Clear from Massachusetts Bay in fourteen days from leaving port!

We crossed the Grand Bank in the brig Joseph, and proceeded on our way towards Cape Cod. But meeting with south-west winds after passing the Isle of Sable, we were forced to the northward on the coast of Nova Scotia. Here we were enveloped in fogs of a density which seemed appalling. Unable to obtain a meridian observation of the sun, and swept about by unknown currents, we were uncertain of our latitude, and more than once came near wrecking the brig on that dangerous iron-bound shore.

After beating to windward a few days, the wind hauled us to the southward and eastward, the fog towards noon, to a very considerable extent, dispersed, and Captain Allen obtained a meridian altitude of the sun, the horizon being as he erroneously thought, well defined. Having thus determined the latitude to his satisfaction, he ordered the brig to be steered about west-south-west, which, he supposed, would carry us round Cape Sable, clear of all danger.

This cape is well known as the southern extremity of Nova Scotia, a dangerous point, on which, notwithstanding the lighthouse on its extremity, many vessels have been wrecked, and a countless number of lives have been lost. The fog again gathered around the brig soon after the sun had passed the meridian, and became so dense that for several hour it was impossible to perceive any object, even at the distance of twenty yards from the vessel. But Captain Allen, confident in the correctness of his latitude by observation, manifested no anxiety, and kept the brig on her course, without ordering any particular lookout, which, indeed, would hardly have been of use, or using the lead.

There was a steady breeze, and the brig was going through the water at the rate of six or seven knots, when, just as the shades of evening began to fall, the thick curtain, which had hitherto surrounded us on every side, was suddenly lifted. The fog vanished as if at the will of an enchanter; and, to the consternation of Captain Allen and every person on board, we discovered craggy ledges of rock rising out of the water directly ahead and on either side, and not a quarter of a mile off!

We were running directly on Cape Sable. It was a narrow escape. The brig was immediately put round on the other tack, and we clawed off from the land with all possible speed, shuddering at the idea of the dangers which in the fog-darkness had surrounded us, and truly grateful for our preservation.

The fogs on our coast are a great impediment in the way of navigation. They screen from view the lighthouses in the night, and the headlands in the daytime, and are often the cause of perplexity and dismay even to the most skilful navigator, and have led to the destruction of thousands of vessels. The philosopher, who, stimulated by the spirit which led Professor Espy to attempt to control the storms, change the density of the atmosphere, and produce rain in times of drought, should succeed in placing in the hands of the navigator the means of dispelling fogs at will when navigating a dangerous coast, would indeed be a benefactor to sailors, and deserve the richest tribute of gratitude.

As we approached the shores of Massachusetts, having been six weeks at sea, every person on board was anxious to obtain a sight of land once more, notwithstanding our vessel was stanch and strong and our provisions and water abundant. There is always a pleasant excitement among a ship's company at the prospect of soon terminating a voyage. We drew towards Cape Cod, and one night when the soundings indicated that we were not far from the shore, a good look-out was kept from the topsail yard for the light; but no light was visible through the night. Soon after daybreak, the LIGHTHOUSE, right ahead, was plainly seen from the deck with the naked eye, being not more than five or six miles off. Whether the light had been allowed to expire through inattention on the part of an unfaithful keeper, or a thick haze had collected over the land and veiled it from the view of vessels in the offing, as was suggested by some good-natured individuals, was never known.

All was now bustle and excitement. The land was in sight; the "highlands of Cape Cod" were plainly visible; the wind was north-east, and every thing indicated that we should be safely anchored in Boston harbor, or hauled snugly in, alongside the wharf, before another night.

It is pleasant to witness the exuberance of spirits on such an occasion. Orders were promptly obeyed; every man moved as if he had been suddenly endued with a double portion of strength and activity; smiles lighted up every countenance; the joke and the laugh went round, and even Cato, the philosophic African, as he stood near his camboose and gazed earnestly on the barren sands, clapped his hands with glee, exhibited a store of ivory which would have excited the admiration of an elephant. Even the old brig seemed to participate in the joyousness that pervaded the ship's company, and glided along smoothly and rapidly, gracefully and merrily, as if conscious that a quiet haven and a snug resting place were at hand.

Passing Race Point we soon came in sight of the "south shore" of Massachusetts By, the land hallowed by the trials and sufferings of the Pilgrims. We passed near Cohasset Rocks, dangers, which, it is well known, have caused the destruction of many a noble ship and in full view of Boston lighthouse we received a pilot on board.

Pilots should be a happy as well as a useful class of men. When a ship arrives at the entrance of a harbor, after a long passage, the sight of a pilot carries joy to every heart. He appears truly in the guise of "a guide, philosopher, and friend, " is warmly welcomed, and treated with kindness and hospitality. The news is eagerly demanded, friends are inquired for, and the words which fall from his lips are attentively listened to, carefully noted, and prized as highly as the sayings of the Delphic oracles.

The dome of the State House was soon distinctly seen; a conspicuous object, which seems to rest lightly upon the countless edifices, a mural crown upon a kingly city. We thridded the narrows, and off Long Island Head Captain Allen suddenly recollected he had a prisoner under his charge. Petersen had been released from durance in the morning as usual, and light-hearted and joyous, had toiled with the crew, apparently sympathizing in their feelings. Speaking English fluently, and well acquainted with the harbor, for he had sailed a voyage out of Boston, it would have been easy for him to slip quietly over the bow and swim to the shore, where, it is possible, he might have escaped the fearful punishment that awaited him for his crimes. But he made no effort to escape, and was now conducted below by the mate, handcuffed, and confined to his quarters in the half-deck.

We had no sooner anchored off Long Wharf than Captain Allen went ashore, and in about an hour the United States Marshal, accompanied by a posse with handcuffs and shackles, came on board and demanded the prisoner. Petersen was brought on deck and delivered into his hands. But his countenance had undergone an appalling change within a few hours. He seemed suddenly to have realized the horrors of his situation. His features were pale, and his eye seemed glazed with fear as he looked upon the officers of justice, and, trembling in every limb, was assisted into the boat. A sense of his guilt, and the terrible consequences, now seemed to weigh upon his spirits. The penalty exacted by the laws for the crimes of piracy and murder stared him in the face.

We arrived in Boston on the 24th of October, 1817, having been fifty-four days on our passage from Gottenburg. I had not accumulated treasures during my wanderings, but I had improved my constitution, acquired a habit of resignation and cheerfulness which bade defiance to the freaks of fortune, gained some knowledge of the world, and rejoiced in robust health, one of the greatest of earthly blessings, and which as often cheers and enlightens the condition of the poor man, as his more fortunate fellow-mortal rolling in riches.

When paid off, I found myself in possession of means to rig myself out in decent apparel, and provide myself with other exterior appurtenances of a gentleman; and also to defray my expenses on a visit to my relations in New Hampshire, from whom I had so long been separated, and whom I longed to convince by tangible proofs that I was still in the land of the living. And thus I returned from my wanderings after an absence of nearly seven years, during which I had witnessed many eventful scenes, and had studied the page of human nature in various climes.

Notwithstanding my occasional hard fortune at sea, a seafaring life still possessed many powerful attractions. I was bound to it by a charm which I did not attempt to break. Besides, I had put my hand to the plough and I would not look back. Although I had passed many happy hours in the forecastle, free from care and responsibility, and associating with men whose minds, if may be, were uncultivated, but whose heads were well furnished and whose hearts were in the right place, yet visions of an important station on "the quarter-deck, " at no distant period, were often conjured up by my imagination; and I resolved that many day should not pass before I would again brave the perils, share the strange excitement, and court the joys which accompany life on the sea.

Chapter XXXVIII THE SEA, AND SAILORS

When we embark on the ocean, we are astonished at its immensity, bounded only by the horizon, with not a speck of land, a solitary rock, or landmark of any description, to guide the adventurers cast adrift on its broad surface, with "water, water, every where; " and when we see its face agitated by storms, and listen to the thunder of its billows, and reflect on its uncertain and mysterious character, and on the dangers with which it has been associated in every age, we wonder at the courage and enterprise of those early navigators, strangers to science, who dared embark on the waste of waters in vessels of the frailest construction, to explore the expanse of ocean and make discovery of,

> "New lands,
> Rivers and mountains on the spotted globe."

Even familiarity with the sea, which has become the great highway of nations, does not diminish its sublimity, its wild beauties, its grandeur, and the terrible power of its wrath.

The immensity of the sea, notwithstanding its surface has been traversed and measured by thousands of voyagers for centuries, fills the contemplative mind with awe, as a wonderful creation of Almighty Power. One can hardly realize its vast extent from figures and calculations, without sailing over its surface and witnessing its immensity, as day after day passes away, the cry being still "onward, onward! " and the view bounded on every side by the distant horizon.

On gazing down into its depths, when not a breath of wind sweeps over its surface, when its face is like a polished mirror, we find the water almost as transparent as the air we breathe, yet the keenest optics can penetrate but a few fathoms below the surface. The movements, the operations instinct with life, that are constantly taking place in that body of water, and the mighty changes which are going on in the vast tract of earth on which it reposes, are invisible to mortal eye.

Within a few years, the progress of scientific knowledge has enabled man to measure the depths of the ocean, which were formerly believed to be as unfathomable as boundless in extent. From soundings which have been taken, it is ascertained that the configuration of the earth at the bottom of the sea, is similar to that portion which rises above the surface, undulating, and interspersed with hills, and valleys, and plains, and mountain ranges, and abrupt precipices. The greatest depth of water at which soundings have been obtained, being between five and six miles, is deeper than the altitude of the highest mountain of which we have knowledge; and there may be cavities of far greater depth. Geological researches prove that at an early period of the history of the earth its surface was vastly more irregular than at the present time. Not only the mountains on the earth were higher, but the deepest valleys of ocean were far deeper. Disintegrations caused by exposure to water or the atmosphere, and abrasions from causes with which we may not be familiar, have lowered the mountain tops, and created deposits which raise the plains and fill the deepest chasms. And here geologists find the origin of the earliest formation of stratified rocks.

Men have striven in vain to develop the secrets which lie hidden in the sea. Imagination has been at work for ages, and in some cases has pictured the bottom of ocean as a sort of marine paradise, a nautical Eden, with charming grottoes, spacious gardens, coral forests, ridges of golden sands, and heaps of precious gems; and abounding in inhabitants with fairy forms, angelic features, and other attributes corresponding with the favored region in which they flourish, who sometimes rise to the surface of ocean, and seated on the craggy rocks, sing sweet ballads to charm away the life of the unwary mariner. Leyden, a Scottish poet, imagines one of these charming denizens of the deep to describe, in the following poetic language, the attractions of this submarine world:

> "How sweet, when billows heave their head,
> And shake their arrowy crests on high,
> Serene, in Ocean's sapphire bed,
> Beneath the trembling surge to lie!
>
> "To trace with tranquil step the deep,
> Where pearly drops of frozen dew,
> In concave shells, unconscious sleep,
> Or shine with lustre, silvery blue.
>
> "Then shall the summer's sun from far
> Pour through the waves a softer ray,

While diamonds, in a bower of spar,
At eve shall shed a brighter day."

Others, however, with fancies equally vigorous, but less ornate or refined, give us different sketches of the doings in Neptune's dominions. They picture the bottom of ocean as un uninviting spot, replete with objects calculated to chill the blood and sadden the heart of man; inhabited by beings of a character rather repulsive than prepossessing, as salt-water satyrs, krakens, polypuses, and marine monsters of frightful aspects and hideous habits; glimpses of which are occasionally seen by favored inhabitants of these upper regions, sometimes in the shape of monstrous sea-serpents, with flowing manes and goggle eyes, lashing with their tails the astonished waters of Massachusetts Bay.

In "Clarence's Dream: we find Shakespeare's idea of the sights exhibited far down beneath the ocean waves:

"Methought I saw a thousand fearful wrecks;
A thousand men that fishes gnawed upon;
Wedges of gold, great anchors, heaps of pearl;
Inestimable stones, unvalued jewels;
All scattered in the bottom of the sea.
Some lay in dead men's skulls!"

Although man can fathom the depths of the sea, and may by scientific experiments, conducted with immense labor and expense, succeed in mapping out the great ocean basins, and obtaining an accurate idea of the configuration of that part of the earth which lies beneath the waters, yet the true character of the scenery, vegetation, and inhabitants of that region must remain unknown until some new philosophical and mechanical principles shall be discovered to pave the way to a system of submarine navigation, and the enterprise confided to some daring Yankee, with the promise of an exclusive patent right to its use for a century to come.

In the mean time we may rest assured that no valuable gems or lumps of gold have yet been brought up by the plummet. Indeed, so far as is shown by the soundings, the bottom of the ocean is covered with microscopic shells, so wonderfully minute that thousands may be counted on the surface of a single square inch. We know also that the bed of ocean, for at least four hundred years, has served as a repository, a burial-place, not only for earth's choicest productions and myriads of human beings, gone to the bottom in sunken ships, but for disappointed hopes, false calculations, and sanguine schemes for the realization of fortune and honor.

The immensity, the majesty, and the wonders of the sea are manifest, and acknowledged by all. But what can surpass its beauty when in repose! What scene can be more sublimely beautiful than the sea when gazed upon from the mast-head of a ship, gliding along as if impelled by the breath of a fairy! Every thing in the vicinity, as well as the vast expanse stretching out on every side, is calculated to inspire confidence, invite security, and give complete reliance on its gentle and pacific character. While enjoying the delightful scene, the passions are hushed. The sea seems the blest abode of tranquillity. We are alive only to its beauty, its grace, its magnitude, its power to interest and charm, to benefit mankind and beautify the world.

And how calmly beautiful is the close of day! What nameless charms cluster around a sunset at sea! The heavens and light clouds are not clad in purple and gold; but the western sky is attractive and lovely in the richness of its sober brilliancy. The sun, with undivided glory, goes down in the west, sinking gently and gradually beneath the well-defined horizon, like the spirit of a good man in the evening of life, departing for a better world.

Night drops her curtain only to change the scene and invest it with holier attributes. The moon sheds her light on the surface of the ocean. No sounds break the stillness of the hour as the ship, urged by the favored breeze, quietly, yet perseveringly, pursues her course, save the murmuring ripple of the waves, the measured tread of the officer of the watch as he walks the deck, the low, half-stifled creaking of a block as if impatient of inactivity, the occasional flap of a sail awakened out of its sleep, and the stroke of the bell every half hour to mark the lapse of time, sending its musical, ringing notes far over the water. What a time is this for study, for contemplation, for enjoyment! The poet Gilfillan, in describing a lovely night at sea, says, with true poetic warmth and energy,

"Night closed around the ship; no sound
Save of the splashing sea
Was heard. The waters all around
Murmured so pleasantly,
You would have thought the mermaids sung

Down in their coral caves,
So softly and so sweetly rang
The music of the waves!"

Were such scenes always met with at sea, was its surface always smooth, the winds favorable and the sky unclouded, little resolution or physical endurance would be required to navigate the ocean; the energies which call THE SAILOR into life would no longer be necessary; the sea would be covered with pleasure yachts of the most fanciful description, manned by exquisites in snow- white gloves, propelled with silken sails, and decked with streamers, perhaps with flowers, while their broad decks would be thronged with a gay and happy bevy, of both sexes and every age, bent on pleasure and eager to enjoy the beauties of the sea.

But this attractive spectacle is sometimes changed with magical rapidity! The scene shifts; and instead of gentle zephyrs and smooth seas, the elements pour forth all their pent-up wrath on the devoted ship, and events are conjured into being which rouse into action the noblest faculties of man. If the records of the sea were truly kept, they would tell of hurricanes, shipwrecks, sufferings, and perils too numerous and appalling to be imagined, to struggle successfully against which demands those manifestations of courage and energy, that, when witnessed on the land, elicit the admiration of mankind. These chronicles, if faithfully kept, would tell of desperate encounters, of piracies where whole crews were massacred, of dark deeds of cruelty and oppression, of pestilence on shipboard, without medical aid and with no Florence Nightingale to soothe the pains and whisper comfort and peace to the dying!

And what may be said of the mariners, the life-long actors on this strange, eventful theatre, the sea, who perform their unwritten and unrecorded parts, face danger and death in every shape, and are heard and seen no more? Is it remarkable that, estranged from the enjoyments which cluster around the most humble fireside, and familiar with scenes differing so widely from those met with on the land, they should acquire habits peculiar to themselves and form a character of their own?

The failings of this isolated class of men are well known; a catalogue of their imperfections is scattered abroad by every wind that blows; they are acknowledged, even by themselves, and enlarged upon and exaggerated by those who know them not. True are the words of the poet,

"Men's evil manners live in brass;
Their virtues we write in water."

Those who are familiar with a seafaring life, and have had opportunities for analyzing the character of the sailor, know that it possesses many brilliant spots as well as blemishes, and that it would be cruel and unjust on the part of those more favored with the smiles of fortune, to steel their hearts against sympathy for his sufferings, or respect for his intrinsic worth.

The sailor is said to be rough and unpolished, as well as addicted to vices. It is true he is seldom a proficient in classical studies, or versed in the logic of the schools. But he is conversant with men and manners in various parts of the globe, and his habits of life, and opportunities for observation, supply him with a fund of worldly wisdom and practical knowledge, which qualify him to render good service when strong hands and bold hearts are in demand on the land as well as on the sea. It should be remembered, also, that the sailor has few opportunities of receiving instruction in polite literature, of learning lessons of moral culture, and of sharing the pleasures and refinements of domestic life. The many temptations to which he is exposed should also be remembered, and it will be found that, with his generous heart and noble spirit, he is far more worthy of confidence and respect than the thousands we meet with in society, who, in spite of words of warning and the example of good men, with every inducement to pursue the path of rectitude, voluntarily embrace a life of dissipation, consume their substance in riotous living, and become slaves to habits of a degrading character.

The same records that tell of stormy passions, profligate habits, thrilling disasters, and violent deaths on the sea, also chronicle the manifold deeds of philanthropy, heroism, self-devotion, and patriotism of those,

"Whose march is on the mountain wave,
Whose home is on the deep!"

Of those who, however rough and unpolished, are ever ready to lend a protecting hand to the weak, to spend their last dollar in encouraging the unfortunate or relieving distress, and to risk their lives in defence of the honor of their country, and the flag which waves over their heads.

When we look at the hardships, sufferings, and perils of the sailor, with his few enjoyments and recreations, and consider the services he renders society, that by his courage and energy we enjoy the countless advantages of commerce, and that through his means are spread abroad the blessings of civilization and Christianity, while for HIM "no Sabbath bell awakes the Sabbath morn, " we ought to cherish a sense of gratitude and indulgence for that class of men "who go down to the sea in ships and do business on the great waters; " to that class of men to whom we intrust, with confidence, not only our golden treasures, but our wives and our children, all which are most dear to us.

So far from despising the character and calling of the sailor, and regarding him with an eye of distrust, let us throw a veil over his faults, appreciate his virtues, be ready at all times to give him words of good cheer, and encourage him to keep within his bosom a clear conscience and an honest heart. Let us not grudge our influence or mite in favor of measures to elevate his character and promote his comfort while sailing over the tempestuous sea of life; or in preparing for his reception, towards the close of the voyage, when broken down with toil and suffering, a quiet haven, a SNUG HARBOR, where, safely moored, secure from storms and troubles, he can calmly await the inevitable summons aloft.

———————

My task is finished. I have given, in the foregoing pages, a brief, but strictly truthful, summary of my adventures during a few years of my early life. It would have been comparatively easy to concoct a series of incidents far more wild, romantic, and improbable, and, therefore, more interesting, than any thing contained in this simple narrative. But I have preferred to give a faithful transcript of events which actually occurred.

If the tale of my trials, temptations, resources, and enjoyments will tend to brighten a passing hour of the indulgent reader, throw light on the character, habits of life, recreations, and perils of the common sailor; guard an unsuspecting young man against temptations to vice, and encourage him to exert all his energies, and boldly press forward in the channel which leads to usefulness and honor; my labors will not have been in vain, and I shall never regret having attempted to lift a corner of the curtain, which has for centuries screened from public view, JACK IN THE FORECASTLE.

The End